JAPAN'S
NEW GLOBAL ROLE

JAPAN'S
NEW GLOBAL ROLE

Edward J. Lincoln

The Brookings Institution
Washington, D.C.

Library of Congress Cataloging-in-Publication Data:

Lincoln, Edward J.
  Japan's new global role / Edward J. Lincoln.
    p.   cm.
  Includes bibliographical references and index.
  ISBN 0-8157-5258-X (alk. paper).
  1. Japan—Foreign economic relations.   I. Title.
HF1601.L55   1993
337.52—dc20   93-25951
                                                                     CIP

9 8 7 6 5 4 3 2 1

The paper used in this publication meets the minimum requirements of the
American National Standard for Information Sciences—Permanence of Paper for
Printed Library Materials, ANSI Z39.48-1984.

Foreword

WRITING about the contemporary world always carries the risk that sudden events will overtake the analysis. For observers of international affairs, this problem has been especially acute in the past several years. In Japan, important political changes occurred in the summer of 1993, just as this book was about to go to press. Emergence of a new coalition government that excludes the Liberal Democratic party, which had held power continuously since 1955, could be a harbinger of broader and deeper political, economic, and social reform. The possible extent and speed of change was not at all certain at the end of the summer, but whatever the eventual outcome, the process that was unfolding underscores the basic message of this study.

In this book, Edward J. Lincoln analyzes the major economic changes that occurred in Japan over the course of the 1980s, including macroeconomic shifts, financial deregulation, yen appreciation, rising labor costs brought by long-term demographic changes, and technological success. These changes combined to thrust the Japanese into the world in new ways. A surge in outward foreign investment, particularly direct investment, involved the nation more intimately with the outside world than in the past. As a result, Japan has had to cope with some difficult new questions: how to participate meaningfully in the work of the major multilateral economic institutions and the United Nations, how to expand or change the country's foreign aid program, how to take part in the international debate on environmental policy, and how deeply to become involved in solving the world's political problems.

Overcoming the strong insularity and passivism of the years since 1945 will not be easy. Lincoln proposes several specific policies that would lead Japan toward a more productive international engagement and suggests

vii

that these changes will also serve the objectives of American foreign policy. The 1993 elections and the new coalition government increase the possibility of domestic change in the direction advocated in this book. Whether the coalition remains in power or the Liberal Democratic party returns, the mood of the nation has shifted away from continued acceptance of the policies of the past. There is now a greater opportunity for the American government to engage in a productive dialogue that can encourage Japan toward a more open and active global role.

The author wishes to thank Robert Angel, Hugh Patrick, and Kozo Yamamura for their comments on the manuscript; Yuko Iida Frost for research assistance; and Belinda Russ for preparing the manuscript. Nancy Davidson edited the manuscript; Susan Sherwin verified its factual content; Susan Woollen prepared it for typesetting; and Max Franke prepared the index.

Brookings is grateful to the Rockefeller Brothers Fund, the Andrew W. Mellon Foundation, and the John D. and Catherine T. MacArthur Foundation for financial support for this project.

BRUCE K. MAC LAURY
President

September 1993
Washington, D.C.

Contents

Figures

CHAPTER ONE

A Historic Transformation

FOR THIRTY YEARS after the end of World War II, the Japanese worked hard, saved hard, studied hard, and stayed at home, shying away from active involvement in most of the complications and problems of the outside world. Devastated physically and psychologically by a war caused by an uncontrolled, aggressive military establishment, they were content to concentrate on building their domestic economy and reconstructing a more democratic and stable political system. Exports grew rapidly and provided the illusion of international engagement, but this was largely an arm's-length relationship with the world, and other dimensions of involvement—inward and outward investment, manufactured imports, and the international movement of people—were all quite limited. International economic events—the business cycle in major export markets, movements in world prices for raw materials, or the unilateral decision of the United States to end convertibility of the dollar into gold in 1971—all had a major impact on Japan but were regarded as uncontrollable outside factors.

By the early 1970s, the result of three decades of frugality and hard work was an advanced industrial economy with a high per capita income level. The Japanese had accomplished something of which they could be proud and which the rest of the world recognized as an astonishing and admirable development. With recognition as a major economy, Japan was in a position to become a more active participant in international economic affairs. Some change did occur: foreign aid spending rose, and Japan was included in the annual economic summit meeting of major industrial nations. But just as the nation might have been expected to

1

seek new roles and a more prominent involvement in world affairs, the oil price and supply disruptions of the 1970s acted to reinforce a domestic focus. The prime ministers attended the multilateral economic summit meetings, but initially remained at the periphery of the discussion. In the mind of the Japanese public, this was symbolized by the fact that their prime minister always seemed to end up at the edge of the group photograph commemorating the meetings.

Reluctant as the nation was to become more involved, economic shifts led to fundamental changes during the 1980s, both domestically and in the nation's orientation toward the outside world. The most visible aspect of these changes was the emergence of large trade and current account surpluses and a massive accumulation of foreign assets, mainly portfolio and direct investments by the private sector. Becoming a large owner of foreign assets represented an epochal change for the nation, engaging it far more intimately in the economic and political affairs of the outside world than at any point since the end of the war and arguably more than at any point in its previous history.

A Reluctant Arrival

Ironically, the nation that desired nothing more than for the rest of the world to leave it alone now has to deal with a host of complex international issues by virtue of its success in concentrating on domestic development. Japan has been thrust into a position of international prominence with little concept of what it desires to accomplish and with few people who are comfortable moving in an international environment. It is not surprising that Japan was unable to engage in a more active role as soon as foreigners perceived it to be a major economic power in the 1970s. But the dramatic changes during the 1980s in the country's international economic position made uninvolvement and insularity untenable; the Japanese had arrived on the world scene and could not depart easily. The economic developments that led to the outflow of capital from Japan to the rest of the world represented long-term shifts that will continue to characterize the nation for many years to come, for reasons considered in chapter 2.

The long-term nature of these shifts is especially important. The collapse of Tokyo stock market prices and real estate prices, followed by the economic recession in 1992, once again deflated expectations at home and abroad concerning the nation's international economic and policy role. Concern that the Japanese were "buying America" seemed to be replaced by concern that they would take their money back home and retreat from contributions, financial or otherwise, to resolution of world problems. The litany of woes faced by industry provided an image of weakness that contrasted sharply with the seemingly endless competitive successes in the late 1980s. But Japan cannot now easily withdraw from its new higher international profile, as it did in the 1970s. Its growth rate, like that of all mature industrial countries, may not be high in the future, and its firms may face a stiff global competitive environment, but the economic downturn in 1992 will not prevent a continued substantial flow of new capital to the outside world. New investment abroad diminished from the blistering pace of the late 1980s, but a sizable flow of new money—especially for direct investment—will continue at least for the rest of this decade and probably longer.

The economic problems facing Japan in 1992 and 1993 were relatively serious, and the recession was the first time the economy had actually contracted for two consecutive quarters since 1974. But the problems were largely cyclical in nature and will not prevent eventual return to a moderate economic growth path that should compare favorably with that of other industrial nations. Fallout from the collapse of the stock and real estate markets—a large accumulation of bad debts held by financial institutions—implied a period of restructuring that could delay economic recovery but certainly not block it. The abnormal and heady days of high economic growth and very low interest rates that characterized the "bubble economy" of the late 1980s were over, but even without those advantages Japan will be a major factor in future international economic developments.

Political issues in 1993 reinforced a sense of return to an inward focus. The series of financial scandals starting in the late 1980s finally brought a political realignment in summer 1993, when a coalition of opposition parties took office. While political change was under way, uncertainty over international policy could not be avoided.

However, even if the public or the government in Japan wanted to return to an inward, insular focus, expectations and pressures from abroad to be actively involved in international economic and political issues will continue. Japan is simply too large and too engaged internationally to sit on the sidelines of major world issues.

Participation, though, poses considerable dilemmas for Japan, and agonizing soul searching promises to continue for years. Should the nation end the strict constitutional prohibition on the unilateral projection of military forces beyond its shores? Should it press actively for a permanent seat on the United Nations Security Council? Should it apply conditionality to its foreign aid to influence political developments in developing countries? What political and economic developments should it favor in those countries? Should it break loose from the comfortable role of being a supporter of the United States and develop a more independent foreign policy? These and many other questions are being asked by Japanese as well as Americans. Relatively few new answers have emerged yet from the ongoing debate within the Japanese polity.

The Domestic Policy Environment

The political or policy environment in which debate proceeds is important for understanding the outcomes. This study does not delve into the nature of that process in any detail.[1] However, some important assumptions underlie the analysis that need to be made explicit. Economic policy decisions in Japan emerge in a setting dominated by the central government bureaucracy and private-sector firms. Depending on the issue, politicians may also play an important role, although they are not consistently involved in all economic issues. Consumers or households as a group in society have had relatively little influence or input, and government policy decisions have generally had a strong probusiness orientation. This characterization of the decisionmaking environment is a common one, and a similar environment marks the response of the nation to international economic issues.

The political turmoil of 1993 led some observers to predict an end to this model, with consumers exercising more voice and a political debate on policy issues replacing bureaucratic dominance. How political change would affect the policy process was uncertain in the summer of 1993; a diminution of the central role of the bureaucracy and the bureaucratic-corporate nexus appeared to be one of the goals of the new governing coalition. A strong elite bureaucracy interacting with the corporate sector has been part of Japan's entire modern history and is so tightly woven in the fabric of society, politics, and economics that a major shift toward a consumer-centered system will be difficult to bring about. I assume here that the past model of policy formation will not change significantly in the near future.

Observers have long argued over which groups—politicians, bureaucrats, or business—wield the greatest influence in shaping outcomes. Some attribute the leading role to the bureaucracy, while others point to the business sector or the politicians (none give much of a role to consumers). Domestic policies during the 1950s and 1960s were heavily skewed toward business interests, while some change occurred during the 1970s, when a number of policies emerged that had a broader social benefit (such as a reallocation of government infrastructure spending away from harbor facilities and toward housing and sewer systems). But in the 1980s the overall probusiness direction of policy continued. For the purposes of this study, the driving force in decisionmaking is less important than the broader generalization that the process continued to favor decisions that advantaged the interests of the corporate sector.

Groups that might challenge the narrowly probusiness policy direction of government policy have been quite weak. Except for a flurry of activism in the late 1960s and early 1970s concerning debilitating environmental degradation, consumer groups have achieved little real influence in the decisionmaking process and have been unable to redirect policy toward a broader set of goals. Women, consumer advocates, the disabled, minority ethnic groups, environmental groups, and others who have had considerable voice in shaping debate and decisions in the United States have had only a muted role in Japan. The political realignment under way in 1993 could increase the policy voice of some of these groups, but such a shift will be evolutionary at best, with little real impact over the next several years.

Neither the bureaucracy nor the corporate sector represents monolithic interests. Factionalism and disagreements over policy direction are often sharp and serious. Some factions in each of these two power centers espouse ideals closer to those that might come from the household sector. However sharp the disagreements within the bureaucracy might be, the final outcomes have generally favored a continuation—or only mild alteration—of a conservative probusiness approach. Change is made more difficult by the relatively closed nature of the process; few requirements for open hearings or equal access during debate exist in Japan. If a portion of the government bureaucracy chooses to interact primarily with the involved business interests on a particular policy, other affected or interested parties have little ability to participate.

This general characterization of the economic policy process applies to the international arena that is the subject of this study. As noted above, the new international involvement has raised a number of important policy questions for the nation. The same dominant actors—the bureaucracy and the private sector—are providing the answers. With the newness of the issues has come a plethora of opinions; voices from the liberal and conservative ends of the political spectrum are clamoring to be heard as the system grapples with the difficult and fundamental questions that will shape the nation's role in the world in the coming decades. Even within the bureaucracy, divisive struggles have occurred between or within ministries over issues such as foreign aid policy or environmental policy.

Out of the clamor of competing views must emerge policy decisions and business actions. Most of the decisions or actions in the international arena have continued the dominant probusiness orientation that has characterized domestic policy formation. Those who might be labeled liberals or internationalists in Japanese society have made relatively little headway in altering the conservative business-oriented approach to the world. The following chapters of this study provide strong evidence of this continuing business orientation on issues ranging from the global environment to foreign aid and post-Tiananmen policy toward China.

A Leadership Role?

Much of the recent discussion of Japanese leadership has been cast in terms of whether Japan can or will replace the United States as the preeminent power and leader of the world. That stark alternative is the wrong way to frame the question. Clearly Japan cannot replace the United States, because it currently lacks the requisite combination of economic and military power. But becoming "the" leader is neither the most important nor the most interesting question about Japan's changing role in the world. Japan has a much larger economic presence than in the past, its actions have acquired greater influence on world events, and dealing with Japan from a U.S. perspective may be more difficult or complex as a result. The focus of this book is an analysis of where Japan is going economically, what is propelling it in that direction, and how the nation is exercising its larger voice. In any scenario, American global political-economic policies must come to terms with Japan in ways that they did not in the past.

The prospect of a higher profile for Japan in world economic and political affairs has been profoundly troubling to some people. Because of the insularity and passivity of the past, the Japanese government has provided few signals as to how it will behave. Without those signals, one can judge only from past and current behavior. Since the dominant bureaucratic-corporate agenda of a narrow identification of national interests with corporate well-being has led to similarly narrow international behavior, the government has faced criticism from abroad. A basic cause of that criticism is that the close identification of national and corporate interests has led to an asymmetrical economic relationship with the world in which other countries have felt disadvantaged.

In the earlier postwar years, the government promoted exports and severely restricted imports, restrained most forms of investment abroad by Japanese firms, imposed strong controls on inward foreign investment, and promoted corporate acquisition of foreign technology as intertwined pieces of an aggressive, nationalistic industrial policy. A slow, piecemeal process of dismantling this wall of protectionist policies began in the 1960s and continues today. However, the legacy of these policies was a nation in the 1980s that was still less integrated economically into the outside world than other industrial nations. Manufactured imports were still much lower than in any other industrial nation as a share of total economic activity; the two-way flow of goods at an industry level, known as intra-industry trade, was very low; and the amount of foreign investments in the country relative to the size of the economy was extremely small.

Massive accumulation of trade surpluses and investments abroad in the 1980s made this imbalanced relationship with the rest of the world glaringly obvious. "Internationalization," a popular buzzword for much of the past decade, implied a greater Japanese presence in the outside world without a reciprocal increased penetration of the world into Japan. Success of Japanese products abroad was unmatched by a greater presence of foreign goods at home; measures of the degree of intra-industry trade in trade flows actually declined a bit from the mid-1970s to the mid-1980s; and the stunning rise in direct investment abroad contrasted sharply with the very modest rise in inward direct investment. The image grew of Japan as a nation motivated by a very narrow, insular, and nationalist sense of self-interest. Whether or not these asymmetries could be justified on economic grounds, their existence worked against international acceptance of Japan in a stronger leadership role. Continued lack of extensive opening of the economy and society to foreign goods, capital, and individuals implied that Japan could not easily escape its unfavorable reputation. The nature of Japan's economic interaction with the world, how it changed in the 1980s, and some of the problems engendered by the asymmetries are explored in chapter 3.

A number of important substantive changes since 1985 have increased the inflow of foreign manufactured goods, capital, and people. These changes began to ameliorate some of the reality and perception of the nation as having an insular and narrow self-interest. Indeed, Japanese government officials often argue that the strong asymmetries of the past are gone. But the analysis of this book indicates that, although improvement occurred, asymmetries remain and continue to feed a negative reaction to Japan.

A Higher Profile

Perceptions matter because Japan's much more visible presence in the world, brought about by investment and other features of the economic shifts of the 1980s, provides an incentive to be more involved in international affairs and an expectation by other nations that Japan should play a more active role. The government, for example, has expressed a desire to have a permanent seat on the United Nations Security Council, and the United States pressed Japan to contribute to the multilateral effort mounted against Iraq in 1990–91. These desires and expectations conflict with the difficulty in altering some of the basic economic and social behavior patterns that produced insularity. Resolving this conflict will be difficult at best and will take considerable time.

Despite these problems, Japan cannot be dismissed as a player. A large economic presence, combined with substantial financial resources available to back its positions, gives the government important levers of influence it did not possess in the past and with which it is now gingerly beginning to experiment. International pollution control—considered in chapter 4—represents one area in which Japan has already taken a leading role, buttressed by a strong domestic technology base and substantial amounts of foreign aid. Positions advocated are not necessarily similar to those of the United States; the comfortable past of Japanese adherence to American views of the world is over.

An obvious avenue for Japan to exercise a larger world role is through the existing multilateral institutions: the United Nations, the World Bank, the International Monetary Fund, the General Agreement on Tariffs and Trade, and the Organization for Economic Cooperation and Development. However, questions remain about participation in the principal international economic and political institutions, discussed in chapter 4. In the General Agreement on Tariffs and Trade, Japan has hardly been a leader in driving multilateral negotiations to a successful conclusion. In the World Bank and the International Monetary Fund, the government has focused on obtaining larger voting rights but has maintained only a small presence of Japanese nationals working in these organizations. At the UN, Japan has also maintained a very small personnel presence and has generally played a minimal role in policy issues. It has substantially increased financial contributions to all these organizations, but not the human presence that would signal a sense of stronger integration and commitment. Much of the real initiative in Japanese international involvement, therefore, is coming not at a multilateral level but rather at a unilateral level, which is less subject to oversight or influence by other major powers.

A principal area of the world in which Japan is already exercising far greater involvement and influence than in the past—and largely on a unilateral basis—is Asia. Chapter 5 considers how this relationship is evolving and how it differed from American involvement with the region in the late 1980s and early 1990s. In the case of China, especially, Japan pursued a very different agenda than the United States after the Tiananmen massacre in 1989. But Japan's swiftly changing relationship with Asia holds important lessons. Americans often take comfort in the notion that the legacy of colonialism and war, as well as perceptions of narrow self-interest, will cause Asian nations to be wary of becoming closely involved with Japan. However, Japan is rapidly developing stronger ties of trade, aid, and investment with other Asian countries. These nations' concerns about Japan have not stood in the way of accepting a far larger Japanese presence and influence in regional affairs. The U.S. government has not yet addressed sufficiently how this new presence and influence fits with American interests and policy toward Asia.

Whatever the problems that may confront the Japanese government in exercising a more prominent role in world economic affairs, at least its position is enhanced by the size of financial flows from Japan. On international political and security issues, though, the government has been in a much weaker position. Japanese foreign policy during the postwar period has consisted of identifying closely with the U.S. coalition against the Soviet Union and otherwise remaining as far removed as possible from direct involvement in international crises. But the rapid change in Japan's international economic position during the 1980s created the expectation or assumption that it ought to play a larger or more responsible role in noneconomic affairs in the world. President George Bush and Prime Minister Toshiki Kaifu ratified the symbolism of this new role by using the term *global partnership* at a bilateral summit meeting in 1990. Nevertheless, the ability of the Japanese government to play a more prominent political role in the world remains in doubt, as does the probable nature of that role.

A critical issue is whether the inability of Japan to play an effective or more prominent political role stems from inexperience, or whether it denotes a more structural difficulty in dealing with difficult international issues requiring prompt and decisive action. Opinion among American scholars remains divided on this issue. A central theme of this book is that in certain fields the Japanese are very capable of making a contribution and playing a leadership role. Cultural, political, or historical liabilities may limit the kinds of roles the Japanese undertake successfully, but this by no means implies that they cannot or should not participate more actively in other areas. Among the areas where Japan can make a useful contribution are global environmental policy and active humanitarian assistance to the developing world.

Military Involvement?

International political problems raise the divisive and difficult question of whether to take on a military role in international affairs and move away from the strict prohibitions embodied in the constitution. The multinational military confrontation with Iraq in 1990-91 brought the issue of Japan's military role into sharp focus. These developments are considered in chapter 6. At that time the Japanese government proved unable to reach any decisive conclusion on sending troops to the Gulf region and sought to placate its coalition partners through a large cash contribution of $13 billion. That sizable sum failed to earn Japan international respect, much to the chagrin of the government, and led to renewed debate over overseas projection of military force. In 1992 that debate resulted in new legal authorization for Self Defense Force soldiers to participate in a limited manner in United Nations peacekeeping operations, with dispatch of a small force to Cambodia taking place late in the year. The death of a civilian policeman attached to the Cambodian peacekeeping operation in spring 1993 brought a strong negative reaction back home, indicating the continued divisions in opinion concerning the human costs of involvement.

For the debate in Japan to focus on the military issue as a means of gaining international respect ignored other forms of involvement through which the government could have been involved during the Gulf crisis but was not. Diplomacy, humanitarian assistance, and active participation in multilateral policy formation were all avenues open to the government but left largely unexplored. One explanation for the focus on the military aspect of participation is the long-standing desire of some groups in Japanese society and politics to restore national prestige by ultimately abandoning the constitutional prohibition on military force projection (either through changing the constitution or by simply reinterpreting it). As a result, the debate in Japan represented less a consideration of how to contribute to solving the Gulf crisis than a catalyst to advance the aims of these groups.

The American Policy Agenda

The final chapter of this study explores how the United States should react to the reality of a Japan more involved in global economic and political developments. How Japan will deal with critical and divisive issues such as the future role of the Self Defense Forces remains unclear. Those decisions must—and will—be worked out in the Japanese political system in whatever manner the body politic finds most acceptable. The ability of Americans or others to influence these decisions will be relatively limited but far from nonexistent. What the world or the United States expects from Japan has been and will continue to be important features of the debate in Japan. American positions on issues such as the role of the Self Defense Forces, therefore, must be carefully considered because of the impact they will have on the domestic debate in Japan. The U.S. government can neither prevent Japan from exercising influence out of concern that its positions or goals are incompatible nor expect the nation to play roles that conflict with basic social, political, or economic patterns.

Since Japanese interactions with the rest of the world can follow a variety of paths, the U.S. government must clearly decide the direction it would like Japan to take and nudge it to move that way. Among the policies that the United States ought to pursue are to encourage Japan to continue expansion of manufactured imports and inward direct investment, enmesh Japan more fully in multilateral organizations, discourage military involvement, avoid a simplistic division in which lack of military involvement means concentration on foreign economic aid (which benefits the interests of Japanese firms), and press hard on Japan to play a larger real role in international humanitarian activities.

Pursuing this agenda accomplishes two U.S. goals and should be consistent with Japanese national interests. First, from an American perspective, more open markets and greater multilateral involvement reduce the image of Japan as an ungenerous nation—although expectations should remain modest for how open the markets for goods, capital, and technology will become. Such changes are important for maintaining an ongoing close economic and political relationship between the United States and Japan.

Second, clear signals from the United States would reduce the probability of further alteration of the status of the Self Defense Forces, leaving it firmly in a defensive posture. Participation in UN peacekeeping operations is acceptable as long as that role is supported broadly by the Japanese public, rather than just by right-wing politicians who are motivated less by a sense of international responsibility and more by the national prestige symbolized by the ability to project military power unilaterally. Some Americans have seen Japan's lack of international military involvement as an unfair avoidance of global responsibilities or burdens, but it is far more likely that military participation would significantly increase regional tensions and undermine the bilateral relationship.

American expectations must be realistic. Fundamental structural features of society suggest that the Japanese government will continue to have difficulty playing a strong role in international political crises. Reactions to unexpected events remain chaotic, and decisions are slow to materialize. Equally important, Japanese initiatives will not always be consistent with American ones; emerging policies on atmospheric warming or toward Asia at the beginning of the 1990s attest to that reality. American pressure may continue to bend or modify Japanese initiatives somewhat, but a more independent stance is emerging.

Security without Military Force

Japan's experience over the past several decades represents several favorable and important developments that also should be recognized. Principally, the government has learned immensely important lessons in the years since 1945 about how to deal with the outside world without a military option as part of its policy array. Raw material supply, access to export markets, and reduction of risks associated with foreign investment are all issues that Japan (and other nations) dealt with in the earlier twentieth century through military power. Japan has prospered to an extent that no one would have believed possible without any military clout. An array of policies (including stockpiling, diversification of suppliers, substitution of materials, the allocation of foreign aid, insurance, encouragement of private-sector foreign investment, and careful diplomacy) provided Japan with the means to reduce the perceived risks in foreign economic relations.

These lessons are powerful and innovative. Even though these non-military approaches to the world do not always work as well as intended, it is difficult to imagine any threat to Japanese national interests that would be furthered by adding the military option. The policy agenda outlined above builds on these lessons; for Japan to cast them aside now that it is reconsidering its role in the world would be a great tragedy. For the U.S. government to encourage a reversion to a military option would be equally tragic.

Other aspects of Japan's economic approach to the world, however, have created problems. Resentment and lack of trust have been caused by the exclusivity associated with Japan's overseas economic ties, the commercial interest that continues to pervade much of foreign policy, the low level of manufactured imports and inward direct investment, and continued stringent restrictions on foreign workers.

This book will argue that Japan is in need of a major rethinking of its foreign policy and the tools to carry it out, based on long-term national interest. That interest lies in reducing foreign anxieties that have their root in both the militarism of the 1930s and 1940s and the narrowly commercial orientation of postwar Japanese domestic and international policy. The nation needs goodwill and acceptance from the rest of the world in order to preserve access to markets for raw materials, for export of its manufactured goods, and for the location of Japanese investment. How can Japan create that goodwill? The answer lies in several responses: a demonstration of a more open home market (a willingness to take as well as give), greater real participation in multilateral institutions, a continued reassurance that Japan is not a military threat, and a large effort to participate in humanitarian activities around the world to demonstrate that Japan is a benevolent power.

The military question may be something of a red herring, and it attracts attention partly because of the hysterical reactions of the Japanese political left to any effort to bend the interpretation of the strict prohibitions in the constitution. The probability of Japan's returning to the militarism of the 1930s is small, and a step such as participating in UN peacekeeping operations does not necessarily lead to eventual alteration of the constitution. No matter how foolish or exaggerated some of the concerns expressed in the domestic debate may seem, though, there are reasons to be concerned about moves that lead ultimately toward the unilateral projection of military force overseas. The primary domestic problem lies in the lack of strong accountability within Japanese society and politics. Once given an enhanced role, the military would be in a position to push an agenda—whatever it might be—to which other interests might have to give way. As long as the Japanese public itself fears such a situation, it is best for others to respect that concern, no matter how remote military dominance in Japanese policymaking may seem.

Combining firm opposition to alteration of the military stance with strong encouragement to pursue a humanitarian agenda, American policy would also help open an avenue for obtaining the international visibility and respect that the Japanese conservatives see in military involvement. Financial, personnel, and management contributions for natural disaster relief, public health work in developing countries, refugee work, and food and medical assistance to the victims of conflict could all be a part of a humanitarian agenda. This form of alternative service would give Japan a respected status in the world and build a more positive reaction to Japan in the United States. None of these policy directions is incompatible with Japanese domestic pressures or social-political factors.

In these ways, the policy agenda outlined for the United States reinforces and builds upon Japanese national interests. The American stance would be compatible with an interaction between Japan and the world that reduces anxieties and tensions while allowing and recognizing a more prominent global position for Japan. If, on the other hand, Japan maintains an economic insularity from the world, pursues a unilateral agenda rather than becoming more intertwined in multilateral institutions, moves toward eventual unilateral deployment of military forces beyond its own shores, and fails to engage in a more visible humanitarian role, world security will become more difficult to manage.

Because Japan remains susceptible to outside opinion and pressure, the United States retains some ability to shape the direction of change in Japan, as long as the direction is consistent with Japanese perceptions of their own interest. The rest of the 1990s will be a critical time to supply those opinions and apply pressure as Japan struggles through the difficult domestic debate about which options the nation should pursue in involving itself in the world.

Political realignment, including the emergence of a new coalition government in summer 1993, suggests the evolution of a more receptive political climate for the policies advocated here. How far political change will proceed remains uncertain, but change does enhance the importance and probable fruitfulness of bilateral dialogue.

CHAPTER TWO

The Domestic Roots
of Change

JAPAN'S EMERGENCE on the world stage has been propelled by several major domestic economic changes of very recent origin. Although Americans may have viewed Japan as a major international economic power since the mid-1970s, it was not until the 1980s or later that economic forces began to affect the nation in these new ways. None of these developments are temporary: economic conditions in Japan will continue to push the nation into the world. The sharp economic recession of 1992 temporarily alleviated or masked some of these conditions but could not do so for long.

What are these changes? The most important are macroeconomic developments that led to a dramatic rise of current account surpluses, a prolonged and substantial process of financial deregulation, yen appreciation, demographic change, indigenous technological advances, and a general sense of economic self-confidence. Emphasis here is placed on discrete economic developments rather than cultural or political change. Considerable debate has taken place about whether Japanese society, institutions, or politics are changing (or capable of change). But no one can deny the economic shifts that have characterized the 1980s. Whether society, institutions, and politics can adjust adequately to the new economic realities remains a critical and difficult question that is explored later in this book.

Together, all of these long-term structural shifts amount to a truly epochal change for Japan. It has been thrust into an international economic environment to a degree that it has never experienced before in its 125 years of modernization and industrialization. The newness and radicalness of this situation means that predicting the future on the basis of past behavior is risky. Policy, institutions, and individual behavior must adapt, but they could do so in a wide variety of ways with differing implications for Japan's international economic and political role.

Current Account Surpluses

From the late 1940s until the early 1970s, Japan experienced an extraordinary average annual 10 percent real (adjusted for inflation) growth in gross national product (GNP). That prolonged surge of growth lifted the nation from its incomplete industrialization and the devastation of war to the ranks of the advanced industrial nations. Mature industrial nations at the technological frontier cannot grow at such high rates, so growth moderated in the 1970s. In the case of Japan, the transition to lower growth rates was all the more dramatic because it coincided with the 1973 war in the Middle East and the resulting leap in oil prices, an event that contributed to both high inflation and the first real recession (in 1974) experienced since the end of World War II. From 1974 to 1992, the average growth of the economy was approximately 4 percent, less than half its previous level.[1] Even this performance was stronger than that of other industrial countries, an important point considered further below. The shift to lower economic growth was accompanied by alteration of important macroeconomic flows (savings, investment, and the government's fiscal stance) that led to trade and current account surpluses. Those changes explain much of what has happened to alter the relationship of Japan with the rest of the world.

Economic growth takes place in part because societies invest in industrial plants, production equipment, and supporting infrastructure to produce more goods and services than in the past. Lower economic growth, therefore, implies that such investments must have expanded at a more moderate pace. In a capitalist economy such as Japan, that slowdown had to be motivated by a reduction in the profitability of investment.

Figure 2-1. *Private-Sector Investment in Japan, 1970–90*
Percent of GDP

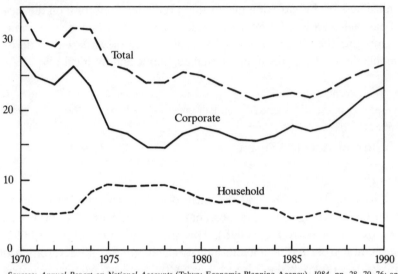

Sources: *Annual Report on National Accounts* (Tokyo: Economic Planning Agency), *1984*, pp. 28, 70–76; and *1992*, p. 82.

Changes in Private Investment and Savings Patterns

When the nation lagged behind the advanced industrial countries, the return on plant and equipment investment was high because of the incorporation of imported technologies yielding considerably higher productivity levels that were not matched by equally rapid gains in wages. As the technology gap between Japan and the industrialized nations diminished, though, new investment did not bring such dramatic productivity gains, and by the 1970s the abundant, flexible supply of labor that had moderated wage growth came to an end. As a result, the return on investment was lower, so less investment took place. Corporate investment in Japan dropped from a range of 23 to 28 percent of GNP during the final high-growth years from 1970 to 1974 to only 15 to 18 percent between 1975 and 1987, as shown in figure 2-1. In the household sector, investment (represented mainly by housing) also dropped as a share of GNP after 1978, so that total private-sector investment declined from over 30 percent of GNP in 1970 to less than 25 percent after the mid-1970s. In the late 1980s, corporate investment once again turned upward, reaching just over 23 percent of GNP by 1990, but this was a temporary development spurred by a very expansionary monetary policy and enhanced by the real estate and stock market bubbles (discussed later in this chapter). The recession of 1992 was a reaction to this unsustainable level of investment, and more moderate investment should prevail for the rest of the 1990s.

The money to finance real investment in an economy comes from savings, either generated domestically or borrowed from other countries. During the high-growth years, the Japanese economy generated sufficiently high domestic savings to meet the enormous private-sector demand for real investment. Rapid economic growth proceeded, therefore, without the nation's becoming dependent on financial borrowing from foreign countries—in great contrast to the pattern in developing countries that have experienced rapid economic growth more recently than Japan.

Once the economy shifted to a slower economic growth path in the mid-1970s, these macroeconomic features changed. During the high-growth years, households were large net savers and corporations large net investors. Household savings flowed to corporations (through the banking system), leaving the overall savings-investment position of the private sector in rough balance. After 1973, corporate investment declined while households continued to generate large net savings. The result was that the private sector moved from absorbing all of its own savings through investment to yielding a substantial surplus of savings over investment. This surplus amounted to 3 to 6 percent of GDP after 1975 (see figure 2-2). Only the temporary surge of economic growth in the late 1980s brought this surplus down (as corporate investment rose), but this trend did not continue in the 1990s.

Government Deficit Growth and Decline

For the economy to experience this large shift in private-sector savings-investment balances without going into recession implies that some other sector must have absorbed the net savings of the household sector that were no longer desired by the corporate sector. During the late 1970s and early 1980s, that absorption came from the government, which experienced rapidly rising fiscal deficits. These deficits were the result of slower growth in government tax revenues (the direct consequence of slower economic growth) coupled with continued rapid growth in expenditures caused by commitments made in the early 1970s to new or expanded social programs.

Figure 2-2. *Savings-Investment Balances in Japan, by Sector, 1970–90*
Percent of GDP

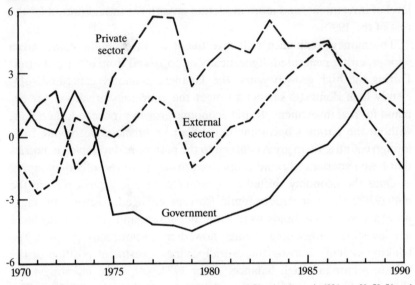

Sources: *Annual Report on National Accounts* (Tokyo: Economic Planning Agency), *1984*, pp. 28, 70–76; and *1992*, p. 82.

By the end of the 1970s, the central government—and the Ministry of Finance in particular—was very worried about the size of the deficits. At its peak in 1979, the deficit of the government sector (as measured in the national income accounts, which include central and local governments, plus the social security account) was 4.4 percent of GNP. Fearful that the deficit could place inflationary pressure on the economy, and that rising debt-servicing costs would occupy an ever-increasing share of government expenditures, the Ministry of Finance carried out a sustained reduction of government deficits in the 1980s.

Through a combination of tax increases (plus new taxes, such as the consumption tax imposed in the spring of 1989) and strong constraints on government spending, the deficit of the central government dropped throughout the 1980s. The size of the central government deficit fell almost continuously, plunging from ¥14.2 trillion in 1980 to only ¥6.6 trillion by 1989 and bringing down the share of government expenditures that were deficit-financed from 33 percent to 10 percent. In contrast, the size of local government deficits remained roughly constant during the 1980s, with a resulting moderate drop in the share of expenditures that were deficit-financed from 10.6 percent in 1980 to 7.5 percent in 1989.[2] Meanwhile, the surplus in the social security account ballooned because of demographic factors. On a national income basis, therefore, the overall government deficit of 4.4 percent of GNP in 1979 was reversed to a surplus of 3.6 percent by the end of the 1980s, a dramatic shift of 8 percentage points of GNP.

Throughout most of the 1980s, the sizable net surplus savings of the private sector continued, as shown in figure 2-2. Since the government deficit fell and then disappeared, some other sector must have absorbed the surplus savings being generated in the private sector. The balance, therefore, came from the external sector—the current account balance with the outside world—and that surplus rose in both dollar terms and as a share of GNP until late in the decade.

International Pressures

External events (mainly the rapid movement of the United States to large current account deficits) also contributed to Japan's current account surplus in the 1980s, and in that sense, the surplus was not created solely by the domestic imbalance between savings and investment. Had world conditions not been favorable for a Japanese current account surplus, other pressures—principally economic recession—would have acted to end the domestic surplus of savings over investment. On the other hand, international pressures would not have created such a large current account surplus without the existing tendency toward surplus domestic savings.

A weakening of the value of the yen against the dollar, induced by the sharp rise in oil prices in 1979, made Japanese exports more competitive on world markets (while foreign products became less competitive in Japan). Demand for Japanese exports was then sustained during the 1980s by developments in the United States, where strong economic growth and rising government deficits created a pull for goods and capital from the rest of the world, including Japan. The combination of a weak yen and strong demand from the United States pushed Japan to a large current account surplus. At its peak as a share of GNP in 1986, the surplus was over 4 percent of GNP. Although the current account surplus fell sharply in dollar as well as yen terms and as a share of GNP from 1988 through 1990, it remained positive and the long-term domestic forces pushing Japan toward some level of external surplus continued.

Table 2-1. *Components of Japan's Current Account, 1980–92*
Billions of U.S. dollars

Year	Merchandise trade	Services					Unilateral transfers	Total net current account
		Travel	Transportation	Investment income	Patent royalties	Total[a]		
1980	2.1	-3.9	-4.3	0.9	-1.0	-11.3	-1.5	-10.7
1981	20.0	-3.9	-3.2	-0.8	-1.2	-13.6	-1.6	4.8
1982	18.1	-3.4	-3.4	1.7	-1.2	-9.8	-1.4	6.9
1983	31.5	-3.6	-3.3	3.1	-1.4	-9.1	-1.5	20.8
1984	44.3	-3.6	-3.0	4.2	-1.6	-7.7	-1.5	35.0
1985	56.0	-3.7	-2.6	6.8	-1.6	-5.2	-1.7	49.2
1986	92.8	-5.8	-2.5	9.5	-2.3	-4.9	-2.1	85.8
1987	96.4	-8.6	-6.1	16.7	-2.5	-5.7	-3.7	87.0
1988	95.0	-15.8	-7.4	21.0	-3.4	-11.3	-4.1	79.6
1989	76.9	-19.3	-7.8	23.4	-3.3	-15.5	-4.2	57.2
1990	63.5	-21.4	-9.5	23.2	-3.6	-22.3	-5.5	35.8
1991	103.0	-20.5	-10.3	26.7	-3.2	-17.7	-12.5	72.6
1992	132.6	-23.3	-10.1	36.2	-4.1	-10.3	-4.7	117.6

Sources: Bank of Japan, *Balance of Payments Monthly* (April 1991), pp. 7–8, 29–30, 41–42; (August 1992), pp. 7–8, 29–30, 41–42, 47–48; and (December 1992), pp. 7–8.
a. Other components not shown separately are official transactions, management fees, and other fees.

Table 2-1 presents balance-of-payments data for Japan. From a deficit of $10.7 billion in 1980 (caused by the sharp rise of oil prices in 1979), the current account balance turned to surplus and expanded explosively, reaching a dollar-denominated peak of $87 billion in 1987. Responding to the sharp appreciation of the yen, the somewhat reduced pull for goods and capital from the United States, and more rapid growth at home, the current account then fell considerably to a temporary low of $35.8 billion in 1990 before rebounding to a new high of $118 billion in 1992.

Although the very high level of the surplus in 1992 has a cyclical component caused by the recession in Japan, which dampened demand for imports, it is indicative of the long-term macroeconomic forces that work toward continuation of sizable surpluses. The 5 percent annual economic growth (and high levels of private-sector investment that accompanied it) after 1987 could not be sustained, and at lower economic growth rates, the tendency for a desire to save more than the private sector wishes to invest reemerged when the economy slowed in 1991 and 1992.

Projections for the Future

What, then, will happen to the current account for the rest of this decade? Some analysts have argued that the era of Japan's current account surpluses will be short lived. For example, Bill Emmott, former Tokyo correspondent for the *Economist*, stated in 1989 that the current account surplus was destined to disappear in the near future as a result of rising consumption (and lower savings) by younger generations, the aging of the population (a trend discussed further later in this chapter), rising foreign travel, and a rising demand for imports as trade barriers continued to fall.[3] Some Japanese economists agreed. At the extreme, there are even predictions that Japan will become the world's largest net debtor by the turn of the century because of the rapid aging of the population.[4]

These projections rest largely on the assumptions that the elderly save less of their annual income than do working-age households and that members of the younger generation (those now in their twenties) save a smaller portion of their income than did their predecessors. These twin assumptions imply that overall household savings (as a share of GNP) will decline, reducing or eliminating the tendency toward surplus savings in the private sector. At the same time, the surplus in the government accounts will be reduced or eliminated because of rising social security costs (the surplus in the social security accounts will fall and then turn to deficit), as well as increased government investment associated with the needs of an older population (hospitals, nursing homes, and infrastructure for the physically disabled, such as escalators and elevators in train stations). With a smaller domestic savings pool and increased government demands on that pool, Japan would then have no surplus savings to spill over into the world in the form of a current account surplus.

Japan's population is aging rapidly, and savings rates for households have fallen over the past decade. Calculated on a national income accounting basis, the ratio of annual household savings to disposable income declined gradually but rather steadily from 18 percent in 1980 to 14 percent by 1990.[5] Further decline could take place, but predictions of future savings behavior are notoriously difficult.

The microeconomic side of balance-of-payments developments also suggests that sizable surpluses will continue during the rest of the 1990s. Much of the temporary drop in the current account surplus in 1987–90 came in services transactions. The merchandise trade surplus dropped by only about one-third from its peak in 1987 through 1990 (compared with the 60 percent drop in the current account balance), and in 1990 it was still higher than in 1985. The negative shift in the services accounts was driven principally by the enormous surge in expenditures related to personal travel as a wave of Japanese chose to travel abroad. The travel and transportation accounts combined went from a deficit of $6.3 billion to $30.9 billion between 1985 and 1990—a $24.6 billion deterioration. This negative impact was more than sufficient to outweigh the rapidly increasing net surplus in income earned on overseas investment (which grew by $16.4 billion from 1985 to 1990).

Likely trends in these components of the current account are the reason current account surpluses will probably continue in the rest of the 1990s. From 1990 to 1992, the combined travel and transportation deficit deteriorated by only $2.5 billion. As the growth rate of foreign travel expenditures diminishes, the inexorable rise in investment income resulting from cumulative past current account surpluses will act to reduce the services deficit in the current account. Over the same 1990–92 period, investment income jumped $13 billion. Furthermore, the surpluses in the merchandise trade component of the current account balance may remain high; it certainly bounced back, more than doubling from $63.5 billion in 1990 to $132.6 billion in 1992. This rise was partially due to the cyclical downturn in economic growth in Japan and the beginning of an upturn in the United States.

If domestic consumption patterns changed, with a fall in import barriers leading to increased purchases of imports, then perhaps the trade surplus would fall. Since the current account surplus is basically a reflection of the macroeconomic savings-investment balances, rising imports would reduce the trade surplus only if they led to a downward adjustment in surplus savings (if, for example, consumers purchased imports by lowering their savings rather than simply switching from domestic goods). Manufactured imports as a share of GDP rose after 1985 (from less than 3 percent of GDP to almost 4 percent) because of yen appreciation and some shift in attitudes and policies toward imports, as well as GDP growth.

Whether manufactured imports will rise further as a share of GDP in the 1990s remains unclear. The low levels of import penetration that prevailed in the past were the result of many factors, some of which may not be changing very rapidly (such as the willingness of the government to tolerate private-sector collusion, which results in restricted market access). On the other hand, long-run labor force pressures (considered later in this chapter) suggest increased incentives for Japanese firms to reallocate production of labor-intensive products abroad for the domestic market. At least in the short run, though, the wave of plant and equipment investment in the late 1980s brought installation of new equipment, allowing substantial cost reductions in manufacturing, which in turn helped to maintain international price competitiveness despite the strengthening of the yen.

Over time macroeconomic effects should bring the current account surplus down, but these factors may not play a major role until near the end of the 1990s. In the shorter run, pressures may keep the surplus high. The extraordinary increase in corporate investment during the late 1980s cannot be sustained. For several years, corporations faced extremely low interest rates because monetary policy was expansionary and because rising stock and real estate prices provided them with more collateral against which to borrow. Over the remainder of the 1990s, however, the ratio of corporate investment to GNP should subside to the lower levels that prevailed in the earlier 1980s. Unless the government chooses to return to higher levels of deficit spending, the reduction in corporate investment implies continuing pressure to pump surplus savings overseas in the form of a large current account surplus. That return to a higher level of external surplus certainly characterized 1991 and 1992.

Beyond the late 1990s, demographics should eventually bring a drop in the net savings of the household sector as well as a decline in the overall government surplus. Savings, however, are difficult to predict. The younger generation engages in more conspicuous consumption than its elders did at a similar age, but this trend does not seem to result in significantly lower savings rates: because of economic growth, these young people simply have much higher disposable incomes than their parents did when young. The current crop of young adults, therefore, can engage in conspicuous consumption by the previous standards of society and still save large shares of their income. Neither is it clear that elderly individuals engage in dissaving.[6]

Some of the conspicuous consumption in the 1980s (including foreign travel) was also prompted by perceptions of increased wealth, generated by the swift increase in real estate and stock market prices. Since prices in both of those markets dropped sharply in the early 1990s, savings could actually increase as households try to restore their ratio of wealth to income to a desired level.

Beyond the turn of the century, the picture of what will happen to savings is far more difficult to predict because the shifts in population age structure will be so significant (discussed further later in this chapter). Even if household savings remain stronger than anticipated, the government surplus should diminish when payments out of the social security account increase (and receipts diminish) as the proportion of elderly in the society grows, although the government could offset this change through a tighter fiscal policy (further reducing central and local general account budget deficits). Nevertheless, demographics should eventually produce strong downward pressure on the current account.

All these factors combined imply that Japan will continue to experience rather sizable current account surpluses for the rest of this decade. The ratio of these surpluses to GNP may be on the order of only 2 percent, but the dollar value will be substantial, running at or above $100 billion a year. Beyond the turn of the century, though, those who predict an end to the surpluses may well be correct. As the aging population comes to have a large impact on household savings and the government social security account, fewer funds will be available to sustain a current account surplus.

Financial Deregulation

The second major shift affecting Japan has been a sustained process of financial deregulation. Deregulation was a necessary outgrowth of the macroeconomic changes discussed above.[7] Changes in the net savings-investment balances within the economy caused a large shift in financial flows: first, an enormous rise in the role of government bonds in financial markets (to finance the large government deficits that emerged in the 1970s), and then a greatly increased net flow of capital overseas.

Such shifts in financial flows were impossible to fit into the highly regulated environment of Japanese financial markets, in which most major interest rates were strictly controlled by the government and financial institutions were restricted to finely segmented portions of the market. In the 1960s the Japanese financial system had virtually no truly market-determined interest rates (except for the short-term interbank lending market) and relatively few financial instruments. The primary purpose of the entire system was to collect savings deposits from households and lend the money to the corporate sector to finance plant and equipment investment. Government treasury bills, corporate bonds, commercial paper, bankers' acceptances, and other forms of finance in use in other countries were of minor importance or not in use at all.

Once the government became a major borrower by issuing large amounts of bonds in the 1970s to finance its growing fiscal deficit, this system of tight control began to unravel as some types of financial institutions found themselves disadvantaged by the shifts in financial flows. The resulting process of deregulation was cautious and piecemeal. Rather than making sweeping changes to strip away old restraints, the Ministry of Finance pursued an agenda of continuous tinkering with individual regulations, punctuated occasionally by legislation that primarily ratified the accumulated existing regulatory changes.[8]

A particularly important legislative element was the major reform in 1980 of the Foreign Exchange and Foreign Trade Control Law. In principle, this reform changed the earlier fundamental position that all international transactions would be prohibited unless specifically authorized by the government to one in which transactions would be free of control unless specifically targeted by the government. This reversal had no immediate sweeping impact but became an important endorsement of continued liberalization.

The government also made changes that would permit increased participation in international capital flows by allowing a growth in international presence by Japanese financial institutions. In 1975, when the new macroeconomic flows and the process of deregulation that they would spawn were just beginning, Japanese banks had 285 offices overseas. Half (143) were only representative offices, and only 42 were fully incorporated local subsidiary branch offices. By 1980 the overall number of overseas offices had increased to 452, and by 1989 it had more than doubled to 985, of which 269 were branches of incorporated local subsidiaries.[9] Securities companies underwent a similar explosion in their foreign presence, from 64 offices in 1975 to 101 in 1980 and then 222 by 1989. Foreign financial institutions were also permitted an increased presence within Japan. The number of foreign bank offices increased from 185 in 1985 to 261 by 1989 (of which 131 were full branches and 9 were locally incorporated subsidiaries), while the number of securities houses increased over the same period from 52 (of which only 2 were full branches) to 182 (with 55 full branches). Six foreign securities firms were even granted seats on the Tokyo Stock Exchange, beginning in 1986, and by 1992 this number had risen to twenty-two.[10]

These Japanese and foreign financial institutions operated in an environment that was gradually but continuously liberalizing. Beginning in the 1980s, Japanese insurance companies were allowed to hold a portion of their investment portfolio abroad, and that portion was increased in several steps, reaching 30 percent by the end of the decade.[11] The range of financial instruments in the domestic market that would interest foreign institutions and investors increased. Regulations permitting Japanese corporations to issue yen-denominated bonds abroad were eased in a series of steps, allowing a larger number of companies to issue such bonds. These and many other smaller regulatory changes facilitated a much larger flow of capital into and out of the country. The details of these flows are explored in chapter 3.

Financial deregulation, and even overall economic performance, was called into question by the speculative bubble that emerged in both the stock market and real estate markets in the second half of the 1980s. The Nikkei average of stock prices on the Tokyo Stock Exchange more than tripled from 11,500 in early 1985 to a high of 38,900 four years later. At the same time, real estate prices also rose dramatically. Official data on real estate are not entirely accurate, but they show a tripling of prices in the six major urban areas and a 50 percent increase in all urban areas. These twin financial bubbles were highly speculative; prices had moved far beyond underlying values on the belief that rising prices would continue. Like all speculative bubbles, these eventually came to an end. The government raised interest rates and used administrative guidance to get financial institutions to stop lending to individuals and corporations engaged in speculation. From its peak in 1989, the Nikkei average of stock prices was back down to 17,000 by 1992.[12] Real estate prices in major urban markets also began to decline, although estimates on the size of the drop varied widely.

Collapse of the twin financial bubbles left the financial sector saddled with bad debts. Furthermore, the collapse revealed a number of scandals, such as the compensation by brokerage houses for the stock market losses of some of their large clients. In some cases, scandals revealed unwise or illegal behavior (such as the enormous loans made to a restaurant owner in Osaka to speculate on the stock market).[13] The overhang of bad debt and the harmful effect of falling stock and real estate prices on wealth and consumption fed the 1992–93 recession. One possible outcome was a return to a more heavily regulated financial system to prevent a recurrence of speculative bubbles. However, the primary cause of the bubbles lay in excessive reliance on monetary ease to stimulate the economy when the yen rose in value against the dollar in 1985–88 (discussed below). Thus minor regulatory moves to deal with specific problems remain possible, but the basic deregulation that permitted the much larger net and gross flows of capital will not be reversed.

Yen Appreciation

From early 1985 to 1988, the yen underwent a large and sustained appreciation in value against the dollar and many other currencies, providing the third pillar underlying Japan's changed relationship with the world. Against the dollar, the yen rose from a low of ¥260 in February 1985 to a peak of ¥125 in spring 1988.[14] From 1988 through 1992 the path of the yen was mixed, with a gradual depreciation until 1990 and a return to the 1988 level by 1992 (followed by a renewed appreciation in

1993). In general terms, though, the yen roughly doubled in value against the dollar from 1985 to 1988—a major appreciation in value over a short period and one that proved to be a rather permanent shift.

Some of the shift reflects varying rates of inflation, which during the 1980s was higher in the United States than in Japan. Taking the GDP deflator as an indicator of the differences between the two countries, prices rose 38 percent more in the United States than in Japan between 1980 and 1988. The average nominal yen-dollar exchange rate in 1988 was 77 percent higher than it had been in 1980, so there was an almost 40 percent real increase after adjustment for the differential in inflation.[15]

Yen appreciation occurred for several reasons. Rapidly falling oil prices put upward pressure on the current account by lowering the dollar value of imports. Continuing long-term favorable trends in productivity relative to those in other countries meant that at any given exchange rate, the current account balance would rise over time because of the increasing price competitiveness of exports. Finally, the new cooperation or coordination among the major industrial nations on exchange rates, exemplified by the Plaza accord of August 1985, aimed at bringing the dollar down through both moral suasion and some adjustment of monetary policy.

Many in Japan feared that rapid appreciation of the yen would harm the economy. Rising exports had been an important source of growth in the early to mid-1980s, and the stronger yen would hurt exports (and increase import competition). By spring 1987, in fact, the negative effects of the exchange rate movement appeared to be driving the economy into recession. The government responded to this danger with economic stimulus, mainly through monetary policy and use of the government-controlled postal savings funds to encourage housing investment. Rather than going into a recession, economic growth rebounded on the basis of expanded domestic demand and brought important developments that encouraged Japan's changed position in the world. These included a real increase in manufactured imports, a jump in foreign travel by Japanese citizens, a surge in foreign investment (and especially direct investment in manufacturing), and an overall rise in national self-confidence because of the success in coping with yen appreciation.

Substantial growth in manufactured imports, foreign investment, and foreign travel all occurred in the second half of the 1980s because of favorable price effects. The investment impact is a bit of a puzzle: yen appreciation made foreign assets much less expensive from a Japanese

Figure 2-3. *Wholesale Price Indexes in Japan, 1980–92*
1985 = 100

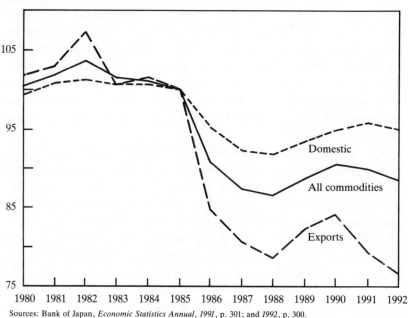

Sources: Bank of Japan, *Economic Statistics Annual, 1991*, p. 301; and *1992*, p. 300.

perspective, which encouraged investment. However, when yen appreciation began, it also caused large capital losses to all Japanese holders of foreign assets, which could have discouraged further investments. The large increase in gross capital outflow indicates that the perceived risk or discouragement effect did not materialize.

Confidence may be the more important long-term effect of yen appreciation. Once the driving force of the economy shifted from exports to domestic demand in 1987, the pessimism that accompanied the early phases of yen appreciation was replaced by a wave of optimism. The ability of the Japanese manufacturing sector to cut production costs and survive with lower export prices was a remarkable achievement. As shown in figure 2-3, the wholesale price index for export goods dropped by almost 21 percent from 1985 to 1988—a much larger drop than the 8 percent drop in wholesale prices of domestic goods. This disparity in the two series implies that manufacturers cut their export prices drastically in order to maintain market share in foreign markets. The size of the drop implies that manufacturers absorbed roughly one half of the total impact of the change in the yen-dollar exchange rate.[16]

Price cutting of this extent over such a short period should have severely damaged profits and led to a substantial slowdown of the economy. There was considerable concern in early 1987 that the economy would slip into a recession,[17] and the second quarter of that year actually showed a small contraction of the economy. But growth then accelerated rather than falling. The overall success of the economy in the face of the strong exchange rate shock did much to reinforce a sense of confidence in the manufacturing sector, and more broadly throughout Japanese society, concerning the ability of the economy to cope with fluctuating external conditions.

Why did the economy succeed? Expansionary monetary policy, increased public works spending, and the growth in wealth from rising real estate and stock market prices were all involved. In addition, manufacturing firms took an aggressive and flexible approach in dealing with the exchange rate movement through vigorous cost-cutting measures, including substantial investment in new capital equipment to reduce labor costs. Bank of Japan annual data on operating profits in the manufacturing sector (which exclude profits firms may have made by playing the stock or real estate markets) show that after a dip in 1986 operating profits had fully recovered by 1987 (and continued to grow in 1988 and 1989).[18]

Some of the confidence engendered by the successful response to yen appreciation should be tempered by the fact that success came at the cost of the serious speculative bubbles in real estate and the stock market. The government chose to respond to the deflationary impact of yen appreciation in 1987 through monetary policy rather than fiscal policy. Higher rates of monetary growth and extremely low interest rates did not cause overall inflation in the economy, but did lead to an enormous wave of investment in real estate and corporate equities. The subsequent crash of the real estate and stock markets at the beginning of the 1990s (combined with the recession of 1992-93) punctured much of the excessive enthusiasm and confidence of the late 1980s.

The collapse of the speculative bubbles imposed serious costs on the economy and provided a sobering message about the dangers of excessive monetary expansion. Nevertheless, the experience since 1985 does hold lessons that should restore a sense of confidence once the recession and restructuring from the bubbles comes to an end. Firms did respond well to the challenge of yen appreciation after 1985; they did become engaged in overseas production from which few will retreat; and overall economic

Figure 2-4. *Dollar-Yen Exchange Rate, 1973–74, 1978–79, 1990–91*

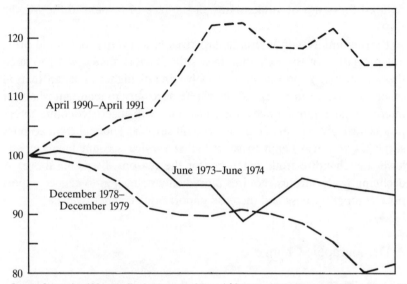

Sources: International Monetary Fund, *International Financial Statistics*, vol. 26 (December 1973), p. 211; vol. 27 (May 1974), p. 211; vol. 27 (November 1974), p. 211; vol. 32 (June 1979), p. 213; vol. 33 (January 1980), p. 225; vol. 33 (April 1980), p. 225; vol. 44 (January 1991), p. 309; and vol. 44 (June 1991), p. 311.

performance should be relatively high for a mature economy. The Japanese may have awakened from some of the excesses of the late 1980s with a painful hangover, but they should emerge from it with mature sobriety rather than retreating to a sense of vulnerability and weakness.

During the remainder of the 1990s the yen should remain strong against the dollar, despite the difficulties caused by collapse of the financial bubbles. This conclusion stems in part from the increased confidence and resilience to potential disruptions of the supply of imported raw materials (considered later in this chapter). Even the Gulf War failed to cause a decline in the yen, providing a fundamentally different response than the one provoked by the oil crises of the 1970s, as shown in figure 2-4. In the first two crises, the rise in oil prices and fears about oil availability resulted in substantial depreciation of the yen against the dollar (although to a greater extent in 1979 than in 1973). In sharp contrast, the yen actually appreciated substantially against the dollar in 1990, at least until November, and remained rather stable thereafter. The private sector was simply not worried this time that conflict in the Middle East would have a strong impact on oil prices or availability. As a large consumer of crude petroleum, Japan itself had some bargaining power, and an array of other policies to cope with imported oil dependency have reduced the sense of vulnerability in the face of turmoil in the Middle East.

Barring unforeseen international crises of a severity that could bring a depreciation of the exchange rate, other factors should work to keep the yen strong. If productivity growth remains higher in Japan than in other countries, yen appreciation will be necessary to maintain whatever international relative prices are consistent with macroeconomic forces producing a given level of current account surplus. Those current account surpluses will also begin to show higher service account balances and lower merchandise trade balances, for the reasons discussed above. A declining trade surplus requires a gradually rising yen to reduce export price competitiveness and increase import price competitiveness.

Demographic Change

A rapidly aging population, the result of very low birthrates and rising life expectancies, is beginning to produce a number of important long-term effects on the economy other than the savings effects considered earlier. Labor markets will begin to feel the impact of demographic change in the mid-1990s, providing another substantial source of sustained pressure for direct investment abroad.

Falling Birthrates

Official government figures on actual birthrates and estimated future population released in June 1991 showed that the 1990 birthrate hit a historic low, yielding a calculated rate of 1.53 children over a woman's childbearing age span. The rate had been sliding continuously over the previous several years; it had been 1.75 as recently as 1986—and even that was considered low at the time.[19] Since a constant population requires the average number of children born per adult woman to be slightly above 2, these rates imply a future decline in total population.

Stung by actual birthrates that were consistently below previous forecasts, officials making the new population estimates took into consideration these lower actual birthrates and assumed a relatively low rate into the future. The resulting population forecast shows a peak in 2010 at

129.4 million, falling thereafter to 100 million by 2068 and as low as 94 million by 2090 (the final year of the current forecast).[20] The previous official forecast, issued in 1986, predicted a peak of 136 million in 2013, so the revised estimate yields a smaller and earlier peak.[21]

The causes of this large and prolonged decline in birthrates are many. The increasing cost of raising children—including rapid increases in the cost of housing (conflicting with desires for larger amounts of living space per person), education, and weddings—probably played a major role. In addition, Japanese are marrying later in life, shortening the time span during which couples will produce children. In 1970, only 18 percent of women aged 25 to 29 were still unmarried, but this proportion then rose steadily, more than doubling to 40 percent by 1990.[22] Whether this trend toward later marriage reflected the rising financial cost of marriage (mainly the difficulty in obtaining housing, which may cause couples to postpone marriage) or a shift in social attitudes regarding the appropriate time for marriage, the trend has been steadily upward since at least 1970 and seems unlikely to be reversed in the near future.

These gradual and rather prolonged shifts in social behavior call into question even the 1991 population estimates. That estimate assumed that the number of children born over a woman's childbearing years would stop its decline at 1.48 in 1994 and then begin to climb steadily back to 1.85 by 2025 (a rate that would still yield a falling population).[23] If the birthrate fails to recover as predicted, then the total population will decline even earlier than currently predicted and the age composition of the population will be even more skewed toward the elderly. Criticism that the new estimate might be overly optimistic appeared in the press when the new estimates were released in 1991.[24] No one seems to think that the new estimate could be too pessimistic.

Even if the predictions of 1991 hold true, the proportion of the population in the labor force (those aged 15 to 64) will fall soon (figure 2-5). This age group was 69.76 percent of the total population in 1990, but the proportion will begin declining slowly but steadily after 1992, falling to 60 percent by 2014. The proportion of young children (ages 0 to 14) will also slide modestly—from 18.19 percent in 1990 to a temporary low of 15.18 percent by 2000. Offsetting these declines is a rapid rise in the proportion of those over age 65. From 12 percent in 1990, this segment of the population will more than double its share, reaching 20 percent by 2008 and 25 percent by 2019. These shifts in the balance among various

Figure 2-5. *Japanese Population, by Age Group, 1980–2025*

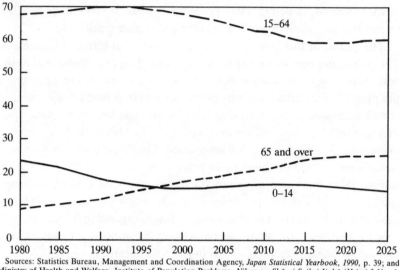

Sources: Statistics Bureau, Management and Coordination Agency, *Japan Statistical Yearbook, 1990*, p. 39; and Ministry of Health and Welfare, Institute of Population Problems, *Nihon no Shōrai Suikei Jinkō (Heisei 3-Nen 6-Gatsu Zantei Suikei)* [Japan's Future Estimated Population (Provisional Estimate, June 1991)] (Tokyo: Kōsei Tōkei Kyōkai, 1991). p. 10.

age groups will lead to a number of important changes in economic structure in the future, including lower savings, labor shortages, and a shift in economic activity toward services for the elderly.

Labor Force Impact

The key point from the perspective of labor markets is that not just the proportion but the absolute size of the population aged 15 to 64— the pool from which the labor force is largely drawn—will start falling in 1996, according to the new population projections. In sharp contrast, this segment of the population was still rising at 1 percent a year as of the mid-1980s. A sustained reduction in this growth rate did not set in until 1988, and now the growth will diminish rapidly each year until it reaches zero in 1995. Over the ten years to 2005, the average annual decline in this segment of the population is estimated to be 0.3 percent, then accelerating to 0.9 percent over the succeeding decade to 2015. Unlike population projections for the next century, this forecast is quite certain over the next fifteen years; all of the people who will be in this age segment up to 2007 have already been born.[25]

By itself, reduction in the age cohorts that constitute the labor force pool does not necessarily mean that the labor force or actual employment must contract equally, because the falling population pool could be offset by rising labor force participation rates. Virtually all men are already in the labor force in these age groups, but the percentage of women who participate could rise, although this is a trend that is notoriously difficult to predict and depends greatly on social norms.

More women have chosen to work in recent years, but the participation rates are already quite high and a substantial increase beyond current levels is difficult to imagine. In 1975, 45.7 percent of women aged 15 and above were in the labor force, reaching a level that had slid slowly downward as the population shifted away from agriculture toward urban employment. But after 1975 women's labor force participation rates drifted back upward, reaching 50.1 percent by 1990.[26] This upward drift reflected a number of trends, including expansion of temporary and part-time job opportunities that attracted more women to the labor market, as well as a growing dissatisfaction with traditional gender roles (especially among better educated women whose equal access to higher education dated only from 1945).

How much farther the shift might proceed is unclear. One forecast made in the late 1980s anticipated that the labor force participation rate for women would stabilize at close to 50 percent through the year 2000, and this may be a reasonable estimate.[27] Strong distinctions between gender roles remain in Japan, despite the changes that have taken place. Especially for college-educated white-collar families, women still carry virtually all of the responsibility for household management (including finances) and child rearing while men are expected to spend long hours (including after work at bars and restaurants) with their corporate colleagues. As long as these families place a high priority on their children's education, and the men continue to minimize their time at home, women will feel constrained from obtaining more than part-time positions.[28] However, the rapidly increasing pool of elderly in the future implies that more grandparents would be available to provide child care and domestic help. Three-generation households have not declined (as a share of total households with children), even though these involve complicated personal relationships which many in the younger (or elderly) generations would prefer to avoid.[29]

A Long-Term Labor Shortage

If the portion of women choosing to be in the labor force stabilizes, then the demographic trend does indeed imply that the labor force will be falling before the end of this decade. Official government forecasts announced in 1992 anticipated that the labor force would begin falling from the year 2000, with increased participation by women and the elderly postponing the impact of the 1996 decline in the relevant population pool by four years.[30] While the precise timing of a drop in the actual labor force involves large assumptions that are little more than speculation, it is interesting that both the Ministry of Labor and the Economic Planning Agency did not appear to be attempting to make optimistic assumptions; the message in these forecasts was that a long-term labor shortage was coming soon.

Two decades earlier had also been a time of tight labor markets, but the drop in long-run economic growth rates that began after 1973 produced considerable slack. For the rest of the 1970s and the first half of the 1980s, wage increases were very moderate, while unemployment and other indicators of job availability worsened. Only since the mid-1980s has the situation changed—and this time the changes were not a short-term phenomenon, even though the 1992 recession again alleviated tightness in labor markets.

The unemployment rate actually continued to rise, from 2.6 percent in 1985 to a peak of 2.8 percent by 1986 and 1987, and then began falling, reaching 2.1 percent by 1990, where it then stabilized even as the economy entered recession in 1992.[31] Unemployment data in Japan have never been comparable to those of the United States, and the unemployment levels prevailing in the mid-1980s had been widely perceived as being quite high. Another widely used measure of the job market is the ratio of job openings to job seekers registered at government-authorized employment agencies. By early 1991 that ratio was up to 1.47 (that is, 1.47 jobs available for every person registered as actively seeking employment), and even though it subsided back down to 0.92 by the end of 1992 because of the economic slowdown, these levels were still higher than those that had prevailed in the previous decade. In fact, this ratio had risen almost continuously from a low of 0.62 in the middle of 1986 after having previously peaked at 1.86 in late 1973.[32] By 1990 new graduates entering the labor force were reported to have an average of three job offers each.[33] A Bank of Japan index, based on survey data asking firms if they felt that they had too many or too few workers, moved to the "too few" side in late 1988 for the first time since 1974.[34] Ministry of Labor data, based on surveys asking firms how many unfilled positions they have, showed that unfilled positions were 6.1 percent of total employment at surveyed firms by 1991, the highest level since 1973 (when the ratio was 6.4 percent).[35] All of these indicators eased with the recession in 1992–93, but the emerging demographic trends implied that even moderate economic growth would bring a sense of labor shortage back into play fairly quickly after the recession ended.

Wages and Workweeks

Tighter labor markets ought to have produced an acceleration in wage settlements, but this impact was relatively mild through the early 1990s. All unionized workers in Japan work with one-year contracts that are renegotiated in the spring, during what is called the "spring wage offensive." Data on those settlements show that after an average increase of 5.03 percent in 1985, fears about the negative impact of yen appreciation led to a lower increase of only 3.56 percent in 1987. Since then, though, they have recovered: the 1992 level was 4.95 percent.[36]

The spring wage offensive covers only the unionized part of the work force. Nominal and real (adjusted for consumer price inflation) wage increases for all workers for 1980-91 are shown in figure 2-6. Nominal wages show some cyclical acceleration after 1987, and even the dip in 1991 left an increase higher than at any point since the early 1980s. But real wages have not been accelerating at all. The annual increases actually diminished after 1988, and the 1991 increase (less than 1 percent) was lower than at any point since 1985. How does the widespread perception of tighter labor markets fit with the reality of diminished real wage increases? Part of the answer could be what is known as wage illusion: workers experienced higher nominal wages but were unaware of how these increases translated into real equivalents.

Another explanation for the moderate wage response to tighter market conditions could be that workers are using their increased bargaining position to gain other benefits, such as shorter working hours, rather than focusing on wages. The data show a very gradual slide in annual working hours. From a plateau of 2,110 annual hours of work in 1984–88, the level had drifted down to 1,972 by 1992. Although this was only a 7.0 percent decline since 1988, the 1992 total represented a historic low and

Figure 2-6. *Wage Settlements in Japan, 1980–91*

Percent

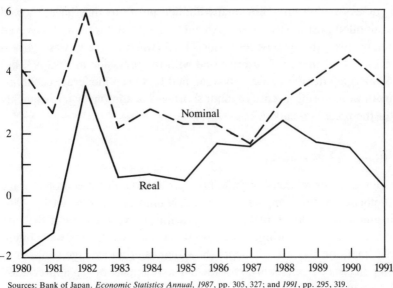

Sources: Bank of Japan. *Economic Statistics Annual, 1987*, pp. 305, 327; and *1991*, pp. 295, 319.

came when several years of rapid economic growth implied an increasing demand for labor that would logically have been reflected in more hours rather than fewer.[37]

Increasing social pressures for more leisure time would appear to have led to the observed decline in working hours, but the downward drift hardly amounts to a decisive shift in the pattern of work and leisure. A major reason for the gradual pace of change is the slow diffusion of a two-day weekend. Two thirds of all firms (67 percent in 1990) gave a two-day weekend at least once a month, up gradually but steadily from 48 percent in 1980. However, the percentage of firms providing a full two-day weekend every week was still low: only 11.5 percent of all firms in 1990, up from 5.4 percent in 1980.[38] But a trend toward a true five-day workweek should continue, even if slowly, during the 1990s.

Delaying the spread of a two-day weekend was the slowness of the government in altering the basic labor law that set the statutory workweek at forty-four hours, or five and a half days. In 1992 the Ministry of Labor finally proposed amending the law to make the workweek forty hours and to raise the overtime wage premium to be paid for work beyond forty hours. This bill became law in 1993 (to be enforced starting in April

1994) and should accelerate the movement toward a true five-day work-week (although small businesses will be granted a grace period through 1996 to comply).[39] The law applies only to hourly workers, but even white-collar workers could benefit if the legal change provides a general shift toward a five-day workweek.

Also hindering the movement toward a shorter workweek has been a five-and-a-half-day school week. With children in school for a half-day on Saturday, the incentive for workers to have the full day off was less-ened, since they would be unable to engage in day-long family activity. Minimal change in this situation finally came in 1992, when the Ministry of Education instituted a nationwide policy of eliminating school on one Saturday each month. Presumably this was to be the first of several steps toward eventual implementation of a standard five-day school week, but completion of that shift lies several years in the future, at best. Never-theless, the beginning of movement on the school week issue provides further impetus to move on the workweek issue as well. A continued slow drift toward a five-day workweek remains the most likely scenario.

Reactions to a Tight Labor Market

Recognition that labor markets were tight, and that the situation was more than a cyclical response to rapid growth in the late 1980s, was becoming widespread by the beginning of the 1990s. The government issued a variety of publications analyzing labor markets and worrying about how to deal with the problem in the future.[40] In early 1991 the Ministry of Labor began forming labor-management committees in seven industries to study the long-run labor shortage and policies to deal with it.[41] The Japan Development Bank—the government-owned financial in-stitution charged with making loans related to industrial policy—began a program in 1992 of low-cost loans for investment in labor-saving equip-ment to cope with coming labor shortages.[42] The Ministry of Labor also reacted to a recent rise in job changing with a threat of using adminis-trative guidance to control the fees and activity of consulting firms spe-cializing in headhunting.[43] This threat suggests conflict between economic reality (the increased willingness of people to change jobs and the will-ingness of firms to take them from other firms) and traditional norms of behavior. A leading business magazine began using the term *panic* in 1990 to describe attitudes about the coming drop in the labor supply.[44]

A sense of panic was also beginning to show up in books. One particularly inflammatory author claimed that long-term demographic changes would have a drastic impact on the economy, with both a labor shortage and insufficient domestic demand leading to falling investment and a stagnant economy. In his scenario, larger numbers of foreign workers would invade Japan (without Japanese-language ability), and undesirable foreign purchases of Japanese companies and real estate would climb as prices fell.[45] As exaggerated as this analysis may be, the fears seemed to strike a responsive chord in Japanese society.

Some of the concern over labor supply was simply a panic response to temporary cyclical tightness caused by unsustainable high economic growth from 1987 through 1991. When many of the indicators of labor supply and demand eased in 1992, a sense of relief began to appear in the press.[46] The situation bore some superficial resemblance to 1973, the previous peak in labor market tightness, which was followed by prolonged slack as recession and then more moderate growth dampened growth of labor demand. In the 1970s, however, the downward shift in economic growth was not fully matched by a decline in the growth of the population pool from which the labor force is drawn.[47] Now Japan is close to the absolute stagnation and decline in the labor force population discussed earlier. Even if average economic growth is lower than the 4 percent average of the past decade, pressure on labor markets should return rather quickly once the recession comes to an end.

Effects on Economic Activity

The long-term demographic change that is now beginning will be particularly severe and will have a major impact on many aspects of economic activity. These include a strengthened sense of economic confidence, accelerated economic structural adjustment at home, increased incentives to invest overseas, domestic pressures to import manufactured goods, and an inflow of foreign labor.

From the time of the first oil shock in 1973 to the mid-1980s, slack labor markets meant that adults in Japan had a sense of vulnerability (especially graduates just entering the labor market, who bear the brunt of labor adjustment). By the early 1990s a greater sense of personal confidence and self-worth was developing because of the emerging labor shortage. Temporarily quelled by the 1992–93 recession, this confidence should return once the recession comes to an end. Confidence about employment is an important underpinning to a larger international role for the nation: a government with a domestic labor force worried about jobs faces immediate pressures that work against a more open, involved relationship with the outside world.

Second, and closely related to the first point, the labor shortage became a signal to society that domestic economic structural change was acceptable and desirable. Structural changes—such as increasing openness to manufactured imports, ending the ban on rice imports, allowing more rapid expansion of large, labor-efficient retail stores, or changing land taxation—are essential ingredients to Japan's new position in the world. Tight labor conditions provide an environment in which those changes become more likely. Structural change involves moving workers out of low-productivity jobs in all sectors of the economy and relocating them to more productive employment. Relocation can take place only when jobs are available. The fear of not having alternative employment was a major stimulus for policies such as the Large Scale Retail Store Law, which preserved jobs for small, inefficient retail establishments after the 1973 oil crisis led to recession and ushered in lower economic growth. With renewed tightness after the temporary effects of the 1992 recession, however, the pace of structural change in the rest of the 1990s should continue or even accelerate.

Third, labor force pressures and domestic structural changes give firms strong incentives to relocate production facilities overseas. Labor-intensive industries or processes within industries will continue to become economically unviable at home. Firms wishing to remain competitive will continue to move these operations abroad to countries with lower labor costs (with a probable emphasis on southeast Asia, as discussed in chapters 3 and 5).

Fourth, manufactured imports should continue to increase as more labor-intensive products are sourced abroad—some from Japanese subsidiaries and others from independent foreign suppliers. The need to cut costs through overseas procurement should build a stronger domestic constituency for greater ease of access for imports to domestic markets.

Finally, the labor shortage is driving an inflow of foreign workers to Japan that should continue, although the numbers remain fairly small. This new trend challenges the exclusive nature of Japanese society. It is considered in detail in chapter 3, but it is worth noting here that official government publications give scant mention of accepting foreign workers in Japan as an appropriate solution to emerging labor shortages.[48]

This set of evolutionary changes motivated by the labor shortage is a central element in achieving a more active international role, moving Japan away from a stance that can be easily criticized by other countries as protectionist or structured to promote exports and inhibit imports.

Technology

An equally important factor involved in propelling Japan into the world has been its emergence as a world leader in industrial technology and the recognition of this fact by both the Japanese themselves and the rest of the world. During the postwar period, Japan did not simply catch up with the advanced nations of the world: important indigenous developments in manufacturing processes have propelled the nation into a position of international prominence.

Shortly after the Meiji Restoration of 1868 (which created the modern Japanese nation-state), the new government adopted a goal of making the nation a modern industrial economy based on Western technology. The initial motivation of that objective was to provide the wherewithal to withstand Western imperialism, but the institutional reforms of the late nineteenth century unleashed an entrepreneurial drive that led to a far broader economic advance.

After defeat in World War II, the government renewed efforts to encourage the private sector to borrow and adapt American and European industrial technology. The ability to carry out this goal was critical to the country's postwar economic success. The wave of aggressive corporate investment during the 1950s and 1960s incorporated those technologies and rapidly brought the nation closer to an advanced technological position in a number of industries by the 1970s.[49] In addition, however, the corporate sector pioneered new approaches to several critical aspects of the organization of manufacturing processes that gave it an advantage in some leading industries. These new approaches now form the basis of a very important technological influence on the rest of the world.

A Feeling of Superiority

Technological success led to an ability to face the outside world with a sense of self-respect that was lacking when the predominant domestic paradigm was one of borrowing or learning from a Western world that was presumed to be superior (at least in manufacturing expertise). Now Americans and others no longer saw the Japanese as merely imitators.

Exemplifying this new mood of self-confidence, Hiroaki Fujii, Japan's ambassador to the Organization for Economic Cooperation and Development, stated as a matter of fact in a 1991 article that Japan had the highest industrial productivity in the world, and that this situation would continue during the 1990s because of management "know-how," diligence, good labor relations, superior energy-saving technology, and strong investment in cost-cutting improvements.[50] A 1991 column in the leading Japanese business newspaper also touted Japanese technological superiority and went on to claim that the success of American weapons in the Gulf War was due to Japanese technology.[51] This kind of statement about technological superiority is now quite common and not just the province of nationalistic politicians such as Shintaro Ishihara.[52] After years of humble respect for the prowess of foreign technology—and a single-minded determination to obtain access to it for use and improvement at home—this new and strongly held assumption about the high level of domestic technology is a startling change.

The mirror image of self-respect is often contempt for others, especially the United States. Hajime Karatsu, a former engineer at Matsushita who was instrumental in the Japanese postwar technological revolution, has been a leading spokesman for this view. In a 1991 article he commented that "the U.S. is under the illusion that it is the only superpower today. This illusion will collapse by itself within 10 years if America does not wake up."[53] Americans may have been shocked by the similarly critical comments of Prime Minister Kiichi Miyazawa and Yoshio Sakurauchi, speaker of the Diet, in the winter of 1992 in the wake of President Bush's trip to Tokyo, but such sentiments have become quite common.

To the extent that such attitudes are an exaggeration of both the problems of the United States and the prowess of Japan, they contribute only to tension and antagonism rather than forming a basis for a useful expansion of Japan's role in the world. Coming after a century of regarding the West as technologically superior and lamenting the inferior status of their own nation, a reaction of hubris and contempt may be understandable and unavoidable, but it only reinforces unfavorable foreign views of Japan.

But respect for Japanese technology is not confined to the country's boosters. Over the past decade, Americans have come to recognize the

strength of Japanese manufacturing technology, as witnessed by the plethora of books available in the United States on Japanese management,
quality control, inventory control, and other aspects of manufacturing
technology.[54] This genre began with Japan-based business consultant
James Abegglen, who argued for recognition of Japanese corporate accomplishments for many years before the topic became popular, but
during the 1980s others took up this theme.[55] As one American author
looking specifically at the automobile industry puts it: "The Japanese are
changing the fundamental structure of the global automobile industry."[56]

The Elements of Japanese Technological Success

What is the nature of this new technological position in the world, and
why does the outside world now express interest in borrowing technology
from Japan? To some extent, success has come through the organization
of scientific and technical research to yield useful commercial results.
However, at the core of much of Japanese success in the 1980s was the
process of manufacturing, embodied in the organization of people and
machines and in the emphasis on continuous change or improvement in
their utilization. This success has been particularly pronounced in industries requiring complex assembly, preeminently automobiles.

Some of the individual dimensions of manufacturing technology are
briefly explored here, but the essence of Japanese success lies not so
much in any single one of these elements as in their totality and intimate
interconnectiveness. Together these elements appear to have given Japan
an advantage in a number of manufacturing industries through lower
costs of production, fewer defects in production, and shorter cycles for
bringing new products to the market.

These elements can all be loosely labeled "Japanese management,"
but considerable variation exists among companies, many of which conceptualize their own practices as unique to the firm (such as Kyocera's
"amoeba system" or Toyota's *kanban* system). Much of the variation,
however, concerns the practical details of implementing broad principles
that are relatively similar across corporations.

Perhaps the most prominent element of manufacturing success has
come from the approach to quality control. Quality control is difficult to
separate from other aspects of the Japanese revolution in manufacturing,
because quality itself is a broad, multidimensional concept. Nevertheless,
the bundle of activities involved in quality control represents an area of

great Japanese progress. Moreover, this success cannot be understood as simply a Japanese application of American principles.

The original work in modern quality control was done in the United States (by W. A. Shewart in the 1930s and others including Edward Deming, Joseph Juran, and Armand Feigenbaum). The term *total quality control* originates with Feigenbaum, and *zero defects* with Philip Crosby and others at the Martin Company (now Martin Marietta) in the early 1960s.[57] Even at the intellectual level (that is, the development of original concepts concerning quality control), however, the Japanese made some important contributions, including Genichi Taguchi's concept of a loss function, the just-in-time inventory system (begun by Toyota Motor Company in the 1960s), quality control circles (first proposed and implemented in 1962), companywide quality control (first introduced in 1968), and quality function deployment (first practiced in 1972 by Mitsubishi Heavy Industries). American quality control specialist David Garvin said: "Americans may have been the catalyst . . . but the Japanese ultimately developed a quality movement that was uniquely their own."[58]

One way to conceptualize the fundamental difference between Japanese and American approaches to quality control is that in the United States the notions of improvement in performance, features, and durability or reduction in the number of defects in the manufacturing process have generally been associated with higher material and manufacturing costs. In Japan, however, the dominant view perceives quality and cost as inversely related: specific activities related to quality control may impose additional direct costs on the firm, but these costs are lower than the resulting savings (such as less scrap, less reworking of defective products in the factory, and lower warranty expenses).

In one industry for which a careful bilateral study has been done—room air conditioners—Japanese firms in the early 1980s had far better quality control than American firms across the board, and the Japanese firm with the *poorest* record on quality of incoming parts, assembly defect rates, and service call rates exceeded the performance of the best American firm.[59] A more recent study found similar differences in American and Japanese auto parts industries. The average defect rate for finished products among a sample of U.S. auto parts manufacturers in the mid-1980s was 1.8 percent, while that for Japanese producers of similar auto parts was only 0.01 percent. Furthermore, the rate of reduction in the occurrence of defects was more rapid among the Japanese firms than the U.S. firms.[60]

A second element of Japanese manufacturing has been inventory control. The "just-in-time" inventory system is now a widely recognized part of Japanese manufacturing and has become almost a stereotype of Japanese success. The basic concepts and their original implementation, which came from the work of Taiichi Ohno, an engineer at Toyota Motor Company in the 1960s, constitute a major Japanese contribution to manufacturing technology.[61] By itself, inventory control reduces the costs of holding work in process, but an additional contribution is its effect on quality control. If parts must be supplied to feed directly into the assembly line, defective parts immediately and visibly disrupt the line, leading to rapid identification of problems as well as heavy pressure on suppliers to solve them. Therefore this system became a critically important ingredient in transforming relations between major assembly firms and their suppliers in a manner that significantly increased quality control and reduced production costs.

A third issue is close cooperation in the movement of new technologies and products from concept to production. All relevant parties in the firm—salespeople, engineers, financial officers, factory managers, and even some assembly workers—act together to reduce costs and improve ease of manufacturing and after-sales maintenance. This kind of cooperation is actually an integral part of quality control, since cooperation on design to yield a product that is easier to manufacture contributes to fewer defects in production. As simple and obvious as such principles sound, they have worked better or have been implemented more fully in Japan than in the United States. American firms have separated R&D functions from manufacturing, lowering the interaction or synergy that characterizes the process in Japan. Some analysts see significant differences between the two countries in the way innovations move from the laboratory or initial engineering stage to production.[62]

A fourth element in Japanese manufacturing technology success has been subcontractor relations. Japanese firms generally have longer-term and tighter relationships with their parts suppliers than do American firms.[63] Rather than seeing these tight relations between major manufacturers and their parts suppliers as confining, incestuous, or anticompetitive, a new view is emerging of these vertical *keiretsu* relationships as innovations in the management of manufacturing that have led to reduced costs and higher quality.[64] Reliance on subcontracting for major parts, according to this new view, appears to be a better approach to the organization of manufacturing of complex products than the internalization, or vertical integration, that has been the preferred choice in the United States. Long-term relationships enable the large assembly firms to entrust their suppliers with more proprietary information and to actively engage them in the design of new products (rather than simply putting out the parts specifications for bid once the product is designed). This process extends the cooperative design process beyond the final assembly firm, further enhancing the ability to reduce defects and manufacturing cost. The extent or tightness of ties between large and small firms should not be exaggerated (since many small firms have no close links to larger manufacturers), but something that went beyond the general approach of American firms in dealing with subcontractors clearly evolved in Japan.[65]

Subcontractor relations can also have less desirable aspects. Subcontactors' wages have been lower than those at large firms, job tenure far less secure, working hours longer, and working conditions more difficult. Unequal hierarchical relationships have placed subcontractors in a position of responding to demands for pricing, schedule changes, or emergency deliveries at which American firms would balk. Nevertheless, the principle of closer working relationships with subcontractors, stripped of its Japanese social characteristics, represents an important change in the organization of production that yields quality and cost improvements.

A fifth element of Japanese success has been an emphasis on continuous change. More than in American or European firms, successful Japanese firms seem to have a deeply embedded notion that product change and manufacturing process improvement must be a continuous, incremental process rather than one of major breakthroughs.[66] One Japanese author was so enamored of the principle of continuous change that he wrote an entire book on the subject, arguing that not a single day should pass without knowing that some improvement has been made in the company to reduce costs and improve quality.[67] While his evangelical approach to the subject may be somewhat overdone, his enthusiasm does seem to reflect the high priority placed on change in successful Japanese manufacturing firms.[68]

A sixth element of the differences leading to Japanese success has been in corporate control. The corporation is not viewed simply as a collection of assets owned by shareholders to buy, sell, or repackage as they desire. Many believe that the reduced role of shareholders provides Japanese firms with a longer planning horizon than that of American firms. At the root of this difference is the existence of a large portion of "stable" shareholders: other corporations that will not buy or sell shares without the approval of management. This is partially a *keiretsu* phenomenon, but not entirely, as the percentage of shares owned by other *keiretsu* members is generally far lower than the 60–70 percent of shares commonly viewed by Japanese firms as held by "stable" shareholders. Americans see such patterns of Japanese behavior as a problem, because, for example, they make purchase of existing firms very difficult for foreign buyers (considered in chapter 3), but the Japanese increasingly see them as a superior format for corporate organization.[69]

A seventh important accomplishment of Japanese firms has been to achieve a greater commitment from workers, a feature that is not confined to manufacturing alone. To some extent, success in building commitment may be a cultural phenomenon. That is, workers may be more committed merely because group activity is a central part of Japanese cultural norms. The Japanese themselves have long believed in this cultural uniqueness or superiority, a fact that contributed, in part, to their reluctance to invest in overseas production facilities. However, the rapid advance of Japanese firms overseas is now challenging these concepts. The commitment of Japanese manufacturing firms to running subsidiaries abroad suggests that much of what they can accomplish at home is transferable and therefore not tightly bound to Japanese culture. This conclusion is supported by recent research by sociologists that indicates that work organization in the United States and Europe is converging somewhat on Japanese patterns because of their superiority, but does not totally dismiss some deep cultural differences that prevent complete convergence.[70]

Much of the commitment of workers may come primarily from "empowerment," in which workers from the bottom of the organization are actively involved in many aspects of the company's activities. Involvement from top to bottom of the organization in the process of innovation and change is also part of this concept.[71] Such forms of worker involvement have little to do with unique Japanese cultural features.

A final related element of corporate behavior stems from a restructuring of vertical and horizontal human relationships within the firm, narrowing the number of ranks from top to bottom and forcing greater cooperative efforts across functional departments. Some Japanese authors place heavy emphasis on the stronger personal horizontal links in Japanese firms.[72]

Taken together, these eight aspects of the Japanese approach to corporate behavior, especially within the manufacturing sector, amount to highly significant technological innovations that simultaneously bring about substantial reduction of manufacturing costs and dramatic drops in defect rates. The extent of success should not be overdone; both the Japanese and Americans writing about Japanese management may exaggerate the superior nature of Japanese manufacturing technology. Not all Japanese firms put all of the above principles into practice to an equal degree or with the same diligence. But a strong case can be made that these elements add up to a revolutionary change in manufacturing processes and corporate organization.

Many Japanese certainly believed by the beginning of the 1990s that their nation possessed superior manufacturing technology. That belief, coupled with recognition that the rest of the world wanted their technology, gave them a strong sense of confidence about their position in the world that had been entirely lacking in the past. Although this confidence could be overdone and become the basis of an unhealthy contempt for the outside world, it was an essential ingredient for the nation's ability to play a larger role in the world. Both direct technology flows (considered in chapter 3), and an ability to participate with a sense of equality in international economic policy discussions stem from this important shift.

Overall Economic Confidence

I have already noted that one significant result of economic developments in the 1980s was an increased sense of confidence, stemming especially from the nation's ability to weather the strong yen appreciation of 1985-88 and from the recognition of its technological strength. For much of the postwar period, economic growth and prosperity seemed ephemeral, and much of domestic discussion emphasized the fragility of that performance. By the end of the 1980s, though, an awareness of economic size and strength finally began to penetrate the popular mind. Books describing the nation as large and prosperous and discussing how to maintain that vitality began to appear in the 1990s.[73]

Confidence and a sense of affluence provide a necessary underpinning for playing a more active international role, allowing government and public attention to broaden from a narrow past concentration on domestic growth. Not everyone in Japan agrees with the assessment that the nation is affluent, however. High per capita GNP has not provided as strong a sense of personal affluence as might be expected because of high prices, continued deficiencies in housing, long working hours, and a crowded transportation network. There is certainly some resentment that the nation has provided large amounts of foreign aid and other forms of international assistance while such serious problems remain at home.[74] But opposition to foreign aid does not appear to be widespread or forcefully articulated. Compared with opinion in some other countries, including the United States, agitation to spend government money at home rather than abroad actually seems quite limited.

The sense of economic confidence emerged from recognition that the nation performed well economically despite a number of serious shocks in the 1970s and 1980s. The 1992-93 recession deflated much of the confidence, causing some reversion to views that the optimism of the late 1980s was mistaken. But when the recession comes to an end, the domestic economy should continue to perform well during the 1990s for several reasons. The technology base will remain strong, and process technology that emphasizes constant change and improvement should underwrite a continuous growth in labor productivity. The work force is well educated, with a high average level of verbal and mathematical skills, which will be increasingly important as manufacturing technology becomes more complex and eliminates more manual jobs. Policies to cope with the uncertainties of imports of raw material supply will remain successful. Finally, society is relatively free of debilitating social conflicts that could shift the domestic policy focus from economic growth to division of the economic pie.

Economic forecasts for the rest of the 1990s lie in the range of 3 to 3.5 percent average annual real GNP growth.[75] Even if such forecasts prove to be overly optimistic, the array of favorable domestic factors pointed out above strongly implies that economic growth will remain at or near the top among the advanced industrialized nations.

A downward shift in the average growth level from 4 percent to 3 percent could cause some anxiety—as did the earlier shift from 10 percent growth to 4 percent in the 1970s. Nevertheless, the relative drop should be less than in the 1970s and the structural adjustments less serious. Shakeout of the distortions caused by the twin financial bubbles could take more time than anticipated by the government, but the 1992 recession and financial restructuring are, after all, temporary phenomena. The excessive exuberance of the late 1980s may not return, but emergence from the recession will renew confidence. Slowing population growth means that the lower average economic growth that should characterize the rest of the decade will not necessarily yield lower per capita income growth.

Beyond 2000, everything about the Japanese economy becomes much more difficult to predict because the demographic shift will become much stronger and the nature of technical progress less certain. Nevertheless, Japanese society has a record of flexibility in its response to new challenges, which at least suggests that the nation ought to weather the demographic change relatively well.

Another cause for confidence is the reduced sense of risk in the supply of imported raw materials. During the postwar era, Japan became highly dependent on imported raw materials and some basic foodstuffs; the most dramatic change was the shift away from domestic coal and charcoal to imported oil as an energy source in the 1950s and 1960s. Recognition of that dependency has always been strong, and anxiety about the implications of it was very high in 1973 in the wake of the short-term American soybean export embargo and the oil crisis (which temporarily disrupted oil supplies and led to major price increases).[76] A strong sense of vulnerability and anxiety did not provide a viable basis for a positive interaction with the world, and it reinforced a tendency to remain passive, hoping simply to avoid antagonism on the part of supplier nations. This heightened anxiety came precisely at a time when the completion of technological modernization and initial attainment of high per capita income levels should have led in the direction of greater involvement in the world. In fact, these trends were only beginning to emerge twenty years later, in the early 1990s.

Anxiety over imported raw materials finally diminished during the 1980s. This change in attitude came with the substantial drop in the price of oil and other raw materials during the decade. Confidence could diminish in the later 1990s if (or when) international material prices rise again. But other factors were involved as well. The government and the private sector reacted to dependency with a variety of policies, including long-term contracts, diversification of sources of supply, ownership of overseas extraction operations to reduce the risk of supply interruption, provision of foreign aid and other financial help to supplier nations to build goodwill, creation of stockpiles, substitution of materials, conservation, and technological change to reduce material inputs. These significant policy innovations brought an increased sense of economic security in an environment of substantial dependence on imports for many basic materials and foodstuffs.

The reduction in anxiety also came from recognition that the nation was a major player in international raw material markets and a major supplier of capital necessary for raw material extraction. This placed the nation in a strong position to influence market outcomes, ensure continuing supplies, and exercise counterbalancing power in bargaining over prices and production. It is always possible that raw material suppliers could conspire to restrict supply and raise prices, but the Japanese now recognize that they are not powerless in such struggles. This recognition represented an enormous change from the early 1970s, and it provided a stronger motivation for a more active and confident involvement by the government in international economic and political affairs.

The fact that this sense of greater security concerning the raw material supply came without any possible use of military force because of the prohibition built into the postwar constitution is also crucial to understanding the sort of role Japan can and should play in the world in the 1990s and beyond. This purely nonmilitary approach to economic security is a theme emphasized in chapter 7, where I argue that Japan should not unlearn these important lessons.

Conclusion

Combined, the developments identified in this chapter represent massive changes for Japan. One cannot overemphasize what a fundamental reorientation of the economy and society is under way, driven by the macroeconomic developments, financial deregulation, the rise of the yen, long-term demographic change that will cause the labor force to shrink, emergence of a strong technology base, and a self-perception of strength and security after more than a century of humility and humiliation. Never before in the nation's long history has it faced such a situation.

Unlike the brief burst of confidence twenty years ago just before the 1973 oil crisis, the changes rocking the economy in the 1990s will be long lasting. The 1992–93 recession blunted some of the changes temporarily, but it could not have prolonged effects like those of the 1973 oil shock; the long-term trends will soon reassert themselves. The macroeconomic conditions producing current account surpluses will eventually be moderated by an aging population, but not for at least several years. No pressures exist to reverse financial deregulation to any extent. Manufacturing firms will see an ever-increasing incentive to invest in overseas production because of tight labor supply. The yen will remain strong against the dollar because of favorable productivity trends and the changing structure of the elements of the current account. Confidence in economic performance and security of raw material supply will not be erased unless a serious global crisis ensues. Finally, the strong technology base should continue, given the ingrained emphasis on change in the corporate world.

All of the changes identified here are also of very recent origin. Hardly had Japan finished the process of catching up with the West when economic forces jolted the nation in fundamentally new directions. Japan's current political and economic leaders were raised in a militaristic semi-industrialized nation, lived through a devastating war, and experienced a prolonged period of poverty, insularity, and emphasis on domestic economic development during most of their careers. They have been practical and adaptive in the past, but little in their experience will make them comfortable with the far more international economic environment now facing them.

Eventually, a new generation of leaders raised in a more affluent, less insular environment will take the stage. That transition may have begun in the political shifts of 1993, but completion of this process will take a number of years.

CHAPTER THREE

The Economic Dimensions of International Outreach

THE POWERFUL and sustained economic developments considered in the previous chapter have propelled Japan into the world in a manner and to an extent beyond the historical experience of the nation. With bewildering speed, Japan became a major owner of foreign assets, moderately more open to products from other nations, more involved in technology transfer, and far more engaged in human interaction. The nation that had quietly stayed at home and concentrated on domestic economic performance was suddenly traveling, living, and investing abroad to such an extent that the comfortable postwar isolation came to a decisive end.

The key development in this process has been the enormous outpouring of capital from Japan to the rest of the world, making it a large net and gross creditor nation. As a creditor, the nation is engaged in a different and more intimate manner with the outside world than it was during the earlier postwar period when its primary contact was trade. Capital outflow has involved both portfolio and direct investment. Both of these have increased international engagement, but the large direct investment flows—involving operation and management abroad—have had a particularly strong role in this process. For an unusually inward-looking industrial state, these are largely welcome changes.

Nevertheless, many of the shifts of the 1980s and 1990s have brought new problems or dilemmas as well. Much of Japan's international perfor-

56

mance continues to be characterized by a heavy element of asymmetry. The past decade brought a huge increase in investment abroad but only a moderate increase in foreign investment in Japan—and, as a result, a new source of foreign criticism. On the trade front, the second half of the 1980s produced a modest improvement in the penetration of foreign products in the domestic economy, but still left a disparity in import behavior in comparison with that of other countries. The need to manage overseas assets brought a sharp climb in the number of Japanese traveling and living abroad but a less drastic change at home, where foreigners remained few in comparison with those in other countries. These asymmetrical patterns remain serious obstacles to the ability of the government to be accepted fully as a global leader or active participant because they reinforce the image of a narrowly self-interested nation that continues to set itself apart from the rest of the world.

Investment

Underlying the transformation of Japan's economic relationship with the world has been the nation's rapid rise as a major international investor over the 1980s. This physical presence abroad through investment provided a major source of the recognition both at home and abroad that the nation should play a more active role in world affairs. While the growth in investment may slow somewhat during the 1990s, for reasons considered in the previous chapter, sizable additions to the already large amounts of investment, especially direct investment, will continue. Driven by the close relationship with the rest of the world that investment implies, Japan will certainly play a larger role in international economics and politics over the rest of the decade. However, this expanded investment position poses a variety of problems that could seriously hinder a smooth integration of Japan into world affairs.

Why is investment so important? During the 1950s and 1960s, Japan's main economic interaction with the outside world was through merchandise trade. This dominant pattern was not seriously altered in the 1970s, even though investment abroad rose somewhat. Trade required relatively little real economic intimacy between the nation or the society and the outside world. A large share of imports was channeled through a limited number of large general trading companies; manufactured imports faced stiff quotas and other barriers; and foreign firms often settled for arm's-length technology licensing arrangements because direct investment was also difficult. Even exports relied heavily on a few large trading companies, and adapting exports for foreign markets required only a relatively shallow understanding of foreign economies, cultures, or political systems that could be relayed through a handful of people with foreign expertise at trading companies and a relatively small number of other corporate representative offices. International economic behavior was thus entirely consistent with the political and social aspects of Japan's extreme insularity from the outside world.

Investment, on the other hand, requires extensive understanding and interaction with the world.[1] Even portfolio investments in foreign stock and bond markets require extensive and continuous knowledge of local economic trends and corporate behavior to be financially successful. But the strongest impact comes with direct investment. To put the matter at an elemental level, managing workers in Tennessee requires far more interaction or meaningful understanding of economic, political, and social aspects of the United States than exporting cars from Japan. Successful direct investments require an understanding of foreign cultures, legal systems, idiosyncratic conditions in local financial and real estate markets, political systems, labor supply conditions, labor law or customary work conditions, and a tolerance and acceptance of diverse ethnic and racial groups. Because of the rise in both portfolio and direct investment, Japanese society now faces the necessity of developing this understanding.

Foreign investment also requires far more contribution of personnel by the Japanese themselves than did exporting. Although in this age of electronic communication international portfolio investment can be managed to some extent from home, Japanese financial institutions have opened new offices abroad to facilitate foreign portfolio investment. For direct investment, manufacturing firms needed their own managers overseas to oversee the start-up and continuing operation of their new factories. Investment, therefore, has led to a rapid growth in the number of Japanese managers and their families living abroad, a substantial change for the society (considered below).

A final reason investment is important comes from foreign perceptions of Japan. Americans viewed Japan as a more important nation in the early 1990s than they did in the early 1980s largely because of the visible presence of Japanese investment. These perceptions have led to increased expectations that Japan should or will play a more active role in international policymaking, both economic and political.

The Increase in Foreign Assets

The most commonly used statistic indicating Japan's creditor position has been net assets, shown in table 3-1. From a low of only $10.9 billion in 1981, net external assets rose to $383 billion by the end of 1991, making Japan the largest net creditor in the world (ahead of Germany) while the United States had become a large net debtor. This explosion in net assets came after a temporary rise from $9.6 billion in 1976 to $36.2 billion in 1978. Net external asset growth is the direct result of the current account surpluses of the 1980s explained in chapter 2, since capital outflow offsets those surpluses in the balance of payments.[2] Because the United States moved simultaneously to the position of the world's largest debtor, the net creditor position has been the source of considerable Japanese pride and sense of superiority toward the United States and the rest of the world.

All data on international asset and debit positions should be considered as only crude measures. Official data measure only the cumulative value of the original flows. An asset will always be valued at the price paid when originally purchased, even though the value of that asset may have changed substantially. American assets held abroad may be particularly undervalued in official statistics because they have appreciated in value over time. Since many American assets abroad have been held much longer than the recent debts, the official net debt position of the United States is overstated. Japanese data suffer somewhat less from this distortion since the bulk of the investment has come within such a short period.

A focus on net creditor status is somewhat misplaced for other reasons as well. The extensive process of financial deregulation to accommodate the shifts in financial flows associated with the swings in domestic saving-investment balances yielded an enormous increase in gross long-term capital outflows (the change in Japanese ownership of long-term capital assets abroad).[3] Table 3-2 shows the net and gross flow of long-term capital from Japan to the rest of the world. The net flow rose from an actual inflow of $2.3 billion in 1980 to a peak outflow of $136.5 billion in 1987, and then subsided to $43.6 billion by 1990, followed by an unusual

Table 3-1. Japan's External Assets and Liabilities, 1976–91
Billions of U.S. dollars

Year	Direct investment		Loans		Portfolio securities		Short-term private sector		Total[a]		Net assets
	Assets	Liabilities	Assets	Liabilities	Assets	Liabilities	Assets	Liabilities	Assets	Liabilities	
1976	10.3	2.2	5.4	2.1	4.2	11.2	14.5	38.3	68.0	58.4	9.6
1977	12.0	2.2	4.3	1.8	5.6	11.9	14.8	36.1	80.1	58.1	22.0
1978	14.3	2.8	8.8	1.9	12.2	18.0	22.0	48.1	118.7	82.5	36.2
1979	17.2	3.4	14.9	1.8	19.0	22.2	31.1	64.4	135.4	106.6	28.8
1980	19.6	3.3	14.8	1.6	21.4	30.2	46.0	94.0	159.6	148.0	11.5
1981	24.5	3.9	18.9	1.5	31.5	44.0	92.2	121.0	209.3	198.3	10.9
1982	29.0	4.0	23.2	1.3	40.1	47.1	88.2	118.8	227.7	203.0	24.7
1983	32.2	4.4	29.3	1.3	56.1	69.9	75.5	125.1	272.0	234.7	37.3
1984	37.9	4.5	40.6	1.3	87.6	77.1	84.8	145.9	341.2	266.9	74.3
1985	44.0	4.7	46.9	1.2	145.7	84.8	108.8	177.0	437.7	307.9	129.8
1986	58.1	6.5	69.2	1.2	257.9	143.6	207.9	341.8	727.3	547.0	180.4
1987	77.0	9.0	97.5	1.1	339.7	166.2	343.3	583.1	1,071.6	830.9	240.7
1988	110.8	10.4	123.7	1.1	427.2	254.9	538.8	851.0	1,469.3	1,177.6	291.7
1989	154.4	9.2	137.1	18.9	533.8	374.0	666.7	1,004.1	1,171.0	1,477.8	293.2
1990	201.4	9.9	130.1	58.0	563.8	334.5	682.1	1,028.8	1,857.9	1,529.8	328.1
1991	231.8	12.3	141.2	99.7	632.1	443.8	685.4	924.7	2,006.5	1,623.4	383.1

Sources: Bank of Japan, *Balance of Payments Monthly* (April 1981), pp. 69–70; (April 1984), pp. 73–74; (April 1991), pp. 83–84; and (April 1992), pp. 83–84.
a. Also includes trade credits, government sector and other short-term assets, not shown here.

Table 3-2. *Components of Japan's Balance of Payments: Capital Flows, 1980-92*
Billions of U.S. dollars

| | Long-term capital flow | | | | | | Short-term capital flow (net) | Errors and omissions | Balance of monetary movements | |
| | Change in assets | | | | | | | | | |
Year	Direct investment	Loans	Securities	Total[a]	Change in liabilities	Net			Official[b]	Other[c]
1980	2.4	2.6	3.8	10.8	13.1	2.3	3.1	-3.1	4.9	13.3
1981	4.9	5.1	8.8	22.8	13.1	-9.7	2.3	0.5	3.2	-5.3
1982	4.5	7.9	9.7	27.4	12.4	-15.0	-1.6	4.7	-5.1	0.2
1983	3.6	8.4	16.0	32.5	14.8	-17.7	0.0	2.1	1.2	3.9
1984	6.0	11.9	30.8	56.8	7.1	-49.7	-4.3	3.7	1.8	-17.0
1985	6.5	10.4	59.8	81.8	17.3	-64.5	-0.9	-4.0	0.2	-12.5
1986	14.5	9.3	102.0	132.1	0.6	-131.5	-1.6	2.5	15.7	-60.5
1987	19.5	16.2	87.8	132.8	-3.7	-136.5	23.9	3.9	39.2	-68.8
1988	34.2	15.2	86.9	149.9	18.9	-130.9	19.5	2.8	16.2	-45.2
1989	44.1	22.5	113.2	192.1	102.9	-89.2	20.8	-22.0	-12.8	-20.5
1990	48.0	22.2	39.7	120.8	77.2	-43.6	21.5	-20.9	-7.8	0.6
1991	30.7	13.1	74.3	121.4	158.5	37.1	-25.8	-7.8	-8.1	84.4
1992	17.2	7.6	34.4	57.8	29.7	-28.1	-8.3	-9.6	-0.3	71.9

Sources: Bank of Japan, *Balance of Payments Monthly* (May 1991), pp. 7–8, 59–60, 65; (August 1992), pp. 7–8, 59–60, 65; and (January 1993), pp. 7–8, 59–60, 65.
a. Includes trade credits extended and assets such as subscription to international institutions, not shown here.
b. Changes in the government's foreign exchange reserves.
c. Changes in private-sector holdings of foreign-currency bank accounts.

temporary net inflow in 1991 before reverting to a modest outflow in 1992. The gross outflow of long-term capital, on the other hand, rose from $11 billion in 1980 to $192 billion in 1989 and then fell to $121 billion in 1991 and to $58 billion in 1992. These most recent flows were lower than the peak but still substantial. While the net flow declined sharply with the temporary drop in current account surpluses at the end of the 1980s, the gross flow remained rather large. The smaller 1992 flow reflects the temporary effects of the decline in domestic stock and real estate markets (reducing collateral for financing overseas investment) as well as the overall economic recession at home (reducing interest in overseas direct investment).

These annual gross flows produced a dramatic increase in the cumulative ownership of foreign assets, as shown in table 3-1. In 1980 the cumulative value of all Japanese investments overseas was only $160 billion. By 1991 the total was $2.0 trillion, for an average annual 26 percent growth since 1980 (ignoring the valuation problem explained above). Total overseas assets in the 1970s were so low—and were deemed so irrelevant by the government—that the Bank of Japan did not even publish statistics on gross and net assets before 1976. But Ministry of Finance data put the 1970 value of overseas assets at only $3.6 billion, and in no year during that decade were additions to the total any larger than $5 billion even though financial liberalization was getting under way.[4] In the space of the ten years of the 1980s, therefore, Japan moved from being a relatively minor world investor to being one of the largest. Measurement error due to the appreciation of assets over time would lower the growth rate shown here somewhat, but assets held before 1980 were so small that the distortions in the nominal data could not be large enough to detract from the phenomenal increase during the decade.

Capital flow from Japan involves far more than the direct ownership of tangible assets such as buildings, golf courses, and corporations. Direct investment has been a relatively small portion of total acquisition of foreign assets in most years, with loans and portfolio investment in stocks and bonds accounting for the bulk of activity, as indicated by the cumulative investment figures in table 3-1 and the annual flows in table 3-2. When the acquisition of foreign assets reached a peak in 1989, direct investment accounted for only 23 percent of the total new flow of investment while purchases of stocks and bonds were 59 percent. Only in 1990 did the share of direct investment rise sharply to 40 percent of total investment activity as bond purchases dropped precipitously, and in 1992 it was back down to 30 percent.

International Financial Intermediation

Investment overseas also came to involve more than just the flow of money from Japan, bringing another important change in Japan's involvement with the world. Japan actually has had a net inflow of short-term private-sector flows in most years (the increase in liabilities exceeded the increase in assets, shown as a positive number in table 3-2), whereas long-term capital (foreign direct investment, loans, and portfolio investment) had a net outflow (the acquisition of assets abroad exceeded the increase in liabilities to foreigners). In 1990, for example, the net inflow of short-term capital was $21.5 billion while the net long-term outflow was $43.6 billion. These data imply that Japan was becoming an international financial intermediary, borrowing short term from the rest of the world and then reinvesting in the world long term. This phenomenon indicates the extent to which Japanese financial institutions or investors were drawn out into the world in a way that was largely nonexistent in the 1970s.

The temporary reversal of these trends in 1991 would seem to negate this movement, since long-term capital shifted from a net outflow to an unusual inflow and short-term capital registered a net outflow. The reversal of the net long-term capital flow might be seen as an indicator of the troubles facing the Japanese economy, especially banks and other financial institutions as the twin bubbles of real estate and the stock market burst. However, this reversal in the net flow had little to do with the behavior of Japanese financial institutions, since the major shift was an unusually large inflow of foreign money into Japanese securities (bonds and equity). Furthermore, long-term capital reverted to its usual net outflow in 1992 (although with lower gross flows both into and out of the country that did reflect the effects of recession and the decline in the stock and real estate markets).

The unusual 1991 reversal of short-term flows is more difficult to interpret (since the data are not separated into the changes in liabilities and assets), but it does seem to reflect the postbubble financial difficulties. Banks began unwinding some of their international intermediation in order to meet the end-of-March 1993 Bank for International Settlements (BIS) equity standards for international lending. Journalists reveled in the problems besetting Japanese financial institutions in 1990 and 1991 and argued that these problems would reduce the presence of Japanese capital and Japanese financial institutions in international markets.

The Japanese were shaken in their self-confidence in 1991-92 by the falling stock market, the falling real estate market, and a series of stock market–related scandals that emerged in the summer of 1991. The drop in the stock market and real estate market reduced the collateral that individuals and corporations could use to finance their investments overseas and also affected the ability of the large international Japanese banks to meet the new BIS capital adequacy standards, causing them to moderate their international lending.[5] One American column in 1990 stated definitively that Japan's days as a "financial superpower" were over.[6] Although such stories may be comforting to those concerned about Japanese investment, they contained a large element of wishful thinking. Balance-of-payments data for 1991 and 1992 indicate a continued increase in loans extended abroad by Japanese financial institutions ($13.1 billion and $7.6 billion, respectively), although at a much slower pace than in the preceding several years.

Japanese balance-of-payments data are not entirely consistent with BIS international data, which do show a real contraction in the stock of external assets of Japanese banks (from a peak of $951 billion at the end of 1990 to $942 billion at the end of 1991 and to $893 by the end of the first quarter of 1992).[7] These changes represented a slide in the share of Japanese banks in total international banking activity (that is, lending across national boundaries). Banks in Japan held 15 percent of the total stock of international banking assets in March 1992, down slightly from over 16 percent at a peak in 1988 and 1989.[8]

Whether one focuses on the slower (but still positive) lending flow in the balance-of-payments data or the drop in the BIS data, the outcome was that Japanese banks were able to meet the BIS equity standards by the time they went into effect on April 1, 1993. More moderate lending activity was combined with efforts to preserve the equity base against which assets would be measured. Under the BIS rules, the banks could count 45 percent of the current value of their stock portfolios, and the stock market crash brought some danger that banks would slip below the standard. Ministry of Finance intervention in 1992 and 1993 stabilized stock prices, however, so that all the major banks were comfortably above the required level when the new standard came into effect.[9] Having met the BIS standard, Japanese banks were in a position to resume at least a moderate expansion of international lending. With that probable expansion, Japanese financial institutions should continue their role as financial intermediaries, borrowing short on international markets and lending long to the rest of the world.

Influences on Foreign Direct Investment

What characterizes the cumulative value of investment as a whole also characterizes direct investment (table 3-1). From only $19.6 billion in 1980, the cumulative value of direct investment totaled $232 billion by 1991, generating a 25 percent average annual growth for the decade, roughly equal to the growth in total external assets.[10] The flow of new direct investment subsided in 1991 and 1992 under the impact of recession and the aftermath of the financial bubbles, but it was still well above the levels of the first half of the 1980s (table 3-2). Direct investment is both more visible than financial portfolio investments and, as noted earlier, requires more active management, making it a critically important component of overall asset ownership in terms of a broader effect on the Japanese economy and society.

Of the industries involved in foreign direct investment, manufacturing is by far the most important component from the standpoint of transferring technology to the rest of the world (considered below). Manufacturing has been the largest single component of direct investment, although it does represent less than half of cumulative investment. Just about 35 percent of cumulative Japanese direct investment abroad in 1980 was in manufacturing; trade-related and financial-sector investment had a substantial but smaller presence. By 1990 the share of cumulative investment represented by the manufacturing sector had fallen to only 26 percent, while trade, finance, and real estate all expanded their relative shares. By way of comparison, 43 percent of cumulative American direct investment abroad in 1990 was in manufacturing.[11] After 1985 the flow of new manufacturing investment abroad accelerated (figure 3-1), but so too did investment in the real estate sector and the financial sector, while trade-related investments expanded more modestly. The surge in these other sectors caused manufacturing to diminish as a share of the cumulative value of direct investment.

Figure 3-1. *Japanese Foreign Direct Investment, by Industry, Fiscal Years 1980–91*
Billions of dollars

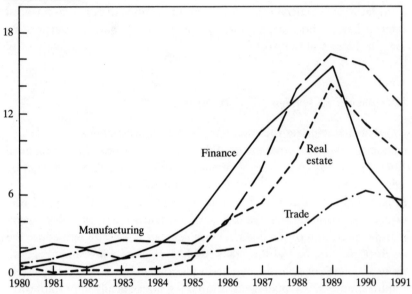

Sources: Ministry of Finance, *Okurashō Kokusai Kin'yūkyoku Nempō* [Annual Report of the International Finance Bureau] (Tokyo: Kin'yū Zaisei Jijō Kenkyūkai [Financial and Fiscal Research Group], 1991), pp. 462–63.

While yen appreciation provided strong incentive for the manufacturing sector to move labor-intensive operations abroad, other forms of investment faced even stronger incentives. Financial institutions, unleashed by continuing deregulation and a slower growth market at home, were eager to establish a foreign presence, and the extremely low interest rates at home gave them an important—if temporary—edge in competing for overseas business. Engagement in international financial markets, though, required a physical presence aboard. Real estate was also affected by low interest rates and yen appreciation, which made foreign real estate less expensive for Japanese investors, and by the domestic real estate bubble, which caused investors to look abroad for more reasonably priced assets and provided them with expanded collateral to finance loans for overseas purchases.

Part of the increase in foreign direct investment could be attributed to the simple effect of yen appreciation. Japanese investors work with yen-denominated financial resources and presumably make decisions about how a large a share of those resources to place in overseas assets.

Since each yen converted into more dollars as the exchange rate shifted rapidly from 1985 to 1988, a constant level of yen-denominated investment by Japanese firms and individuals became much larger levels of dollar-denominated assets abroad. However, the dramatic increases shown in figure 3-1 indicate that direct investment grew well beyond this exchange rate effect. From 1985 to the peak in 1989, the dollar amount of direct investment in manufacturing increased more than sixfold, to $16 billion, after having been rather stationary at close to $2 billion during the first half of the decade. The relative sizes of the increases in real estate, finance, and trade-related services were not quite so dramatic but similarly outpaced the shift in exchange rates.

Investment in real estate and the financial sector subsided in 1990, driven by higher interest rates at home and the ensuing collapse of the stock market and real estate bubbles. Falling stock and real estate prices at home provided investors with less collateral to finance their purchases abroad.[12] Manufacturing investment also dropped but remained the largest single component, a position it ought to retain for the rest of the 1990s. Correction of the distortions of the speculative bubbles will continue to slow financial and real estate investment, while demographic change will provide an ever-increasing incentive to move manufacturing operations offshore. Even overseas manufacturing investment was affected by the strong cyclical downturn of 1991–92, but this will be only a temporary drop.

The ratio of the value of manufacturing production abroad to production at home provides a very crude measure of the extent to which manufacturers have moved into the world. At the beginning of the 1990s Japan was still far below the United States and European countries in this ratio, although it was forecast to rise over the 1990s. In 1991 sales by Japanese manufacturing subsidiaries abroad were only 6.9 percent of the level of sales by the manufacturing sector at home, compared with 23.8 percent for the United States in 1989 and 17.3 percent for then-West Germany in 1986 (table 3-3). As is also clear from these data, though, the ratio for Japan, after hovering between 3 and 4 percent in the first half of the decade, began to climb fairly rapidly and steadily because of the jump in overseas manufacturing investment in the second half of the decade.

Because of labor scarcity and yen appreciation, MITI now boldly predicts the ratio of production overseas by Japanese subsidiaries relative to domestic manufacturing will reach as much as 15 percent by the turn

Table 3-3. *Offshore Manufacturing in Japan, the United States, and West Germany, 1980–91*[a]
Percent

Year	Japan	United States	West Germany
1980	2.9	19.5	14.7
1981	3.4	19.5	16.8
1982	3.2	21.1	17.0
1983	3.9	18.8	17.4
1984	4.3	18.1	19.3
1985	3.0	18.1	19.2
1986	3.2	21.0	17.3
1987	4.0	23.1	n.a.
1988	4.9	24.9	n.a.
1989	5.7	23.8	n.a.
1990	6.4	n.a.	n.a.
1991	6.9[b]	n.a.	n.a.

Sources: Ministry of International Trade and Industry, *Wagakuni Kigyō no Kaigai Jigyō Katsudō* [Survey of the Overseas Business Activities of Japanese Companies], no. 18–19 (1990), p. 15; and no. 21 (1992), p. 17.
n.a. Not available.
a. Sales in manufacturing by Japanese subsidiaries abroad as a percentage of total domestic sales in manufacturing.
b. Estimated.

of the century. A more cautious private-sector estimate sees manufacturing investment overseas in a range of 6.6 to 9.9 percent of GNP by 2000—not much different from the 1991 level.[13] Since the pressures to invest abroad for cost purposes will increase over the course of the decade, this estimate may be too cautious, and the reality should lie somewhere between it and the MITI estimate.

Is Japanese Manufacturing Technology Unique?

Foreign direct investment challenges deeply held Japanese notions of uniqueness. Through the 1970s and even the first half of the 1980s, Japanese firms strongly preferred to maintain manufacturing at home rather than engage in offshore production. Although not uncommon for a developing country with high rates of return on domestic investment, this preference was underwritten by an abiding sense of cultural uniqueness as it applied to success in manufacturing technology. Firms believed that replication of their success would not be possible in a foreign environment, since much of that success was assumed to be intricately intertwined with a unique Japanese culture. Corporate structure and management systems would be difficult or impossible to implement in a foreign setting where labor and local managers did not share a common linguistic or cultural background. Many of the aspects of manufacturing technology discussed in chapter 2 fit into this cultural image, including the ability to work in cross-functional groups, break down vertical barriers between management and workers, obtain close cooperation and coordination from parts suppliers, and force flexibility and cooperation among different professional specialties in product design. Japanese traits of group behavior, ethnic homogeneity, and hierarchy were assumed to be the cause of success in transforming manufacturing processes. By moving overseas, Japanese firms are now engaged in a large-scale experiment that tests whether these assumptions about uniqueness are true.

Academic opinion remains somewhat divided on the extent to which a distinctive Japanese culture matters in manufacturing productivity. One review of the automobile industry suggests that Japanese management and organization systems can adapt to a highly individualistic American society. Others are less certain of transferability because of the wide differences in culture and argue that Japanese firms do not actually practice "Japanese management" in their American operations.[14] Even as respected an economist as Ryutaro Komiya is pessimistic about the transferability of Japanese manufacturing technology abroad because of unique institutions such as company unions, lifetime employment, greater egalitarianism among workers, and close subcontracting relations. He believes that these features lead to great difficulty in establishing efficient operations outside Japan.[15]

However, pessimism over the transferability of Japanese manufacturing technology misses much of the point over what is happening. Total imitation abroad of what happens in factories in Japan is neither feasible nor necessary. Given cultural differences across national boundaries, many aspects of personal behavior will vary, but much of the variation may be irrelevant; American workers need not sing company songs or engage in group calisthenics in order to be productive. Other aspects of manufacturing technology are less embedded in culture, including the operational approach to solving quality control problems and the cooperative aspects of designing new products. Studies of the experience of Japanese firms operating in the United States are beginning to emerge that present a mixed but largely favorable picture of the transfer of manufacturing technology when defined in terms of cost and quality of production.[16]

Japanese auto assembly firms in the United States report defect rates that are close to those of plants at home.[17] The study of the automobile parts industry cited in chapter 2 found that the defect rate for Japanese auto parts transplants in the United States was approximately equal to the rate in Japan. Even more interesting is that the defect rate for U.S. firms supplying parts to Japanese auto assemblers in the United States was far lower than for American-owned firms supplying American-owned auto assemblers.[18] While not all Japanese transplants in the United States have been successful, these emerging studies suggest strongly that core elements of the bundle of changes that simultaneously lowered costs and defects in Japan can be transferred abroad.

Asymmetric Investment Flows

Technology transfer is an important benefit from investment that should be welcomed and encouraged, but investment has also raised a number of new problems for Japan and its relations with host nations. First among these is a rapidly growing asymmetry in investment levels. As shown in table 3-1, inward foreign direct investment failed to grow as much as outward investment during the 1980s, despite the overt liberalization of rules for inward investment that had taken place during the 1960s and 1970s. The cumulative value of Japanese direct investment abroad grew at a 25 percent annual rate from 1980 to 1991, but direct investment by foreigners in Japan grew at 13 percent. Indicative of this wide disparity is that even the reduced outflow of new direct investment in the recession year 1992 ($17.3 billion) was far larger than the inflow ($2.7 billion).[19] By the end of 1991 this wide disparity in the growth of outward and inward investment meant that the cumulative value of Japanese investment abroad was twenty-two times larger than that of foreign investment in Japan.

The Japanese government recognizes the existence of these wide disparities. The annual survey by the Ministry of International Trade and Industry (MITI) of foreign firms in Japan concluded that firms with 50 percent or more foreign ownership in 1991 accounted for only 1.2 percent of all domestic corporate sales and 0.5 percent of all corporate employment. And even in manufacturing, where foreign firms have had a large share in petroleum refining (through a series of joint ventures established in the 1950s), the sales ratio is only 2.6 percent. In contrast, Japanese affiliates in the United States produced 3.8 percent of all U.S. corporate sales and 0.3 percent of U.S. corporate employment. Overall, foreign-affiliated firms accounted for 4.8 percent of total employment in 1989 in the United States—almost ten times higher than the ratio in Japan.[20]

Why did this enormous disparity arise? Part of the answer lies in the timing of the removal of capital controls. As noted in chapter 2, Japan was a hostile environment for inward investment from the 1950s into the 1970s. Even when official impediments to investment began to ease in the 1970s, the government tolerated private-sector actions that often continued to deter inward investment. As a result, through the 1970s, less direct investment entered Japan than other major OECD nations, and the cumulative stock of that investment as a share of domestic capital stock remained far lower than in those other countries.[21]

The new foreign exchange control law of 1980 removed almost all remaining official barriers to inward direct investment so that foreign firms now had national treatment, but low levels of investment up to that point implied that new inflows would have to be very high to overcome the legacy of the past. New investment flows have increased rapidly, but not enough to substantially diminish the distinction between Japan and other industrial nations.

By the time inward investment was no longer officially obstructed, domestic firms in many markets had established strong positions and relationships that impeded successful entry by foreign firms. Labor costs were also high in Japan by the 1980s. Thus manufacturing operations in other Asian nations attracted investment that would have gone to Japan earlier. Furthermore, land acquisition became more expensive by the 1980s, although this is a common explanation offered by the Japanese government that may be of dubious importance. Finally, the appreciation of the yen after 1985 made all local prices less attractive to foreign investors for land, labor, and the corporate assets of firms that might be acquired.[22] Even with the overt elimination of official barriers to investment, a sense of Japan as a relatively difficult market to enter through investment seems to remain among many foreign businessmen.

Despite the problems of high cost and difficult market entry that may continue to discourage foreign investors, the value of inward direct investment flows did increase substantially during the 1980s. Annual flows measured in dollar terms rose from only $299 million in 1980 to $930 million in 1985 and to $4.3 billion by 1991.[23] The doubling in the value of the yen against the dollar after 1985 meant that the 360 percent increase in dollar value of direct investment flows from 1985 to 1991 worked out to a 181 percent rise in the amount of yen assets acquired. As encouraging as this upward trend is, it leaves inward investment far behind outward investment.

The Political Consequences of Investment Disparities

The wide asymmetry between inward and outward investment has had some consequences beyond the purely economic ones. Politically, one can think of direct investments as a form of hostage taking (or vested interest creation).[24] Foreign firms investing in a local economy develop local economic interests that would be harmed by import protectionism in their home countries or by other manifestations of deteriorating economic relations. Those firms thus act as a moderating influence on their own governments. The American Chamber of Commerce in Japan (ACCJ), for example, has long been regarded as a voice of moderation on American economic policy toward Japan. But Japan has had far too few such foreign vested interests that benefit from a presence in its economy and can speak up in their own countries to moderate anti-Japan sentiments. In particular, despite the behavior of the ACCJ, many American politicians have not operated with a strong perception of vital U.S. economic interests in Japan that would be jeopardized by worsening bilateral relations.

An example of the importance of direct investments in producing vested interests is the role subsidiaries play in generating business for American firms. A crude measure of that role is that local sales of foreign subsidiaries are often higher than direct foreign trade: sales by the foreign subsidiaries of American firms were three times larger than direct exports from the United States in the mid-1980s. But because of the limited amount of foreign direct investment in Japan, this ratio did not characterize American experience there, where local subsidiary sales were only roughly equal to American exports.[25]

Furthermore, U.S., Japanese, and European firms all prefer majority ownership of foreign subsidiaries. Worldwide, 75 percent of sales of subsidiaries of American firms in 1988 were from majority-owned operations. Japanese majority-owned operations abroad generate an even higher 86 percent of total sales. However, only 40 percent of American firms' sales in Japan are by majority-owned subsidiaries—another legacy of a past in which establishment of majority-owned subsidiaries was extremely difficult until at least the mid-1970s.[26]

If the world pattern for sales and ownership applied to the American presence in Japan, then American firms would be a greater voice of moderation in Washington policymaking. Until a major expansion of foreign investment materializes in Japan, the nation faces a problem. Japanese business and government appear to have understood only half of the equation involved. Faced with large trade surpluses and extensive foreign criticism of trade barriers in the 1980s, the government saw promotion of Japanese direct investment abroad as a means of appeasing that criticism. If Americans were concerned about imports of Japanese automobiles, then production of Japanese cars in the United States would solve the problem, in this view. As one recent government publication put it, "In reality, the expansion of Japanese direct investment in the advanced industrial nations during the 1980s helped to solve Japan's external imbalances."[27] Another publication, aimed at a Japanese policy audience, estimated how much local production would substitute for exports from Japan.[28]

This emphasis on foreign direct investment as a way to ameliorate trade surpluses and the friction they caused failed to recognize the importance of also promoting foreign investment in Japan (as well as a host of problems directly associated with investment abroad that are considered below). Foreign direct investment proved to be no panacea for improving the nation's external economic relations.

A Resistance to Foreign Takeovers

Even today, national treatment for foreign investment in Japan does not mean that investment is necessarily easy. A principal means for investing around the world has been the takeover of local firms, but Japan stands out as a nation where few foreign takeovers occur. The Japanese sometimes argue that mergers and acquisitions are alien to their culture and that national treatment implies foreign firms must adapt to these local conditions. Given the fact that mergers and acquisitions were quite common before World War II in Japan, this argument is of dubious merit. Whatever the explanation may be, the serious asymmetry in direct investment operates to the disadvantage of foreign firms.

Avoiding corporate acquisitions may be a postwar trait, but the overall level of domestic merger and acquisition activity does not appear to be substantially less than in the United States.[29] Furthermore, Japanese

Figure 3-2. *Japanese Mergers and Acquisitions, 1984–90*
Number of transactions

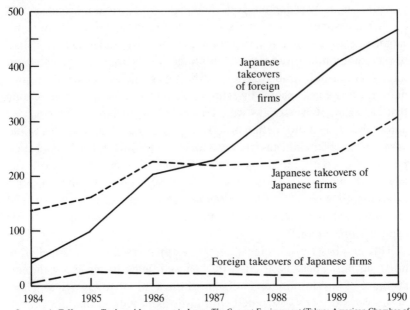

Sources: A. T. Kearney, *Trade and Investment in Japan: The Current Environment* (Tokyo: American Chamber of Commerce in Japan, 1991), p. 19; and Jon Choy, "Japan and Mergers: Oil and Water?" *JEI Report*, no. 14A, April 6, 1990, p. 9.

firms proved to be eager participants in the acquisition market abroad, as shown in figure 3-2. In 1990 Japanese firms acquired 464 firms abroad and 306 firms at home, while foreign acquisitions of firms in Japan totaled only 17. These figures represented a serious deterioration from 1985, when Japanese acquisitions abroad totaled a much smaller 100 and foreign acquisitions in Japan a somewhat larger 26. In contrast, foreigners purchased between 125 and 264 American firms each year from 1982 to 1987. The total value of this activity would provide a better indicator of the disparity, but only a portion of the firms involved revealed the value of the assets involved. For the portion that did, the average size of acquisitions abroad by Japanese firms during 1985–88 was ¥7.8 billion, somewhat larger than the ¥5.2 billion for foreign purchases in Japan over the same period.[30] If these data accurately reflect the average value of all acquisitions, then the total value of foreign acquisitions in Japan would look even smaller in comparison with Japanese activity abroad.

The problem is not the lack of hostile takeovers in Japan by foreign firms but the lack of friendly takeovers. Japanese firms do not actively seek foreign firms as potential purchasers. In the 1950s and 1960s government and business largely agreed that foreign corporate control was undesirable except when unavoidable because of foreign control of technology (as in the willingness to establish joint ventures in oil refining with the major international oil companies that dominated technology). The government gradually relaxed and then eliminated rules that legally restricted foreign acquisition of domestic firms, but the negative attitude of corporate managers to acquisition by foreign interests appears to have changed more slowly. To the extent that this attitude remains ingrained in the Japanese business mentality, rather than imposed by government, the prognosis for the future is not particularly bright. If Japanese firms intentionally avoid foreign buyouts, or do so even inadvertently through neglect, the result is an inward-focused behavior pattern not generally found in other advanced nations.

Government may not particularly favor acquisitions or direct investment in general, even though it has removed past restrictions. Government-business relations are close and complex, characterized by extensive contact and communication. Entry of new foreign firms complicates communications with the private sector, because the behavior of these firms is less predictable (since the Japanese government cannot rely on a previous history of interaction as a guide), and because they are assumed to be more resistant to pressure from the government. In other cases, feelings of nationalism still affect attitudes of some government officials toward particular foreign firms. While such nationalistic attitudes certainly affect attitudes and even policy in the United States (as with the blunt rejection of Matsushita as an owner of commercial concessions in Yosemite National Park in 1992), the quiet way obstacles can be raised by officials in Japan contributes to foreign firms' sense of uncertainty or unfairness.

One reason for the lopsided acquisition figures is the existence of stable shareholders. This system arose largely in the 1950s and 1960s, first as part of the attempt of Japanese corporations to regroup the firms that had belonged to the former *zaibatsu*, and then specifically to ward off the possibility of foreign takeovers when Japan began to liberalize its capital markets in the late 1960s.[31] Since mergers and acquisitions do take place in Japan, obviously these stable shareholders do not always seek to prevent them; but if those shareholders and corporate management are uninterested in (or biased against) foreign firms as possible suitors, then acquisitions by foreign firms will be more limited. This appears to be the case.

The government could use moral suasion or administrative guidance to boost the market for foreign takeovers and inward investment in general. By the end of 1990 the Japanese government was becoming aware that the extreme imbalance in direct investment created an unfavorable image.[32] But the extent to which the government can encourage takeovers by foreign firms if domestic firms are not interested or actively opposed remains unclear. Moving somewhat in the opposite direction, in fact, the Ministry of Finance (MOF) drafted a law in 1990 requiring extensive disclosure when a single investor acquires 5 percent or more of a company's shares, down from the existing disclosure level of 10 percent. Furthermore, in the same year, MITI recommended that firms be allowed to more easily increase share allotments to existing shareholders to help defend against takeover bids.[33] These policy initiatives may have been intended to discourage hostile takeovers but could also have a depressing effect on friendly or quasi-friendly activity by foreign firms.

At the same time, however, MITI officially has been attempting to promote a larger inward investment flow through administrative guidance, including formation of a committee of foreign firms in Japan to discuss the issue (Tainichi Tōshi Kaigi, or Committee on Investment in Japan).[34] Discussion of the issue will not necessarily result in any meaningful changes in behavior, but at least it represents a first step.

The Japan Development Bank (JDB), a government-affiliated lending institution, established a loan program for foreign firms desiring to establish plants in Japan as far back as 1985. In 1990 this loan program was expanded, and a similar program for foreign firms was established in the Hokkaido-Tohoku Development Finance Public Corporation.[35] Loans under the JDB programs to foreign-affiliated firms (defined as those with 50 percent or higher foreign ownership) totaled ¥45 billion (approximately $331 million) in fiscal 1990, of which ¥23 billion—or 51 percent—went to U.S.-affiliated firms.[36] Some ill-defined sense that loans from the JDB confer an informal stamp of government approval remains in Japan, which enhances the recipient firms. Whether the same is true for foreign-affiliated firms receiving JDB loans is unclear. However, a single small American firm, Applied Materials Japan, Inc., was one of the first to receive a loan and has now received eight separate loans from the JDB.[37]

This firm has been unusually successful for an American electronics equipment manufacturer that did not enter Japan until the 1980s, and its success may be partially related to its selection by the JDB.

The government moved somewhat further in 1992 to establish preferences for foreign investment. The Japan External Trade Organization (JETRO), a trade promotion and economic-political information-gathering subsidiary of MITI, was detailed to provide information abroad on investment opportunities in Japan. Other government measures included some preferential tax treatment for foreign-affiliated firms; accelerated depreciation for buildings and equipment in foreign-affiliated firms; exemption from special land-holding taxes; further expansion of the JDB and Hokkaido-Tohoku Development Finance Public Corporation loan programs for foreign firms; establishment of a government-owned corporation to provide support services to foreign affiliates (such as management and staff training, marketing services, interpreters, and translation services); extension of loan guarantees through the Facilitation Fund for Industrial Structural Adjustment to foreign affiliates; and special loan treatment for medium and small Japanese firms conducting business transactions with affiliates of foreign firms through the Small and Medium Enterprise Credit Insurance System.[38] These measures appeared to be a positive step in encouraging inward direct investment and certainly went well beyond the small tentative step taken when the JDB first offered loans to foreign firms in 1984.

Nevertheless, a missing element in any of the actions taken by the Japanese government to promote inward investment has been administrative guidance to encourage domestic firms to seek out foreign bidders for takeovers as a means of further promoting investment. As long as acquisitions remain very difficult for foreign firms, expansion of inward investment is likely to remain somewhat constrained.

Japanese Business Practices Abroad

Another set of problems surrounding direct investment comes from the behavior of Japanese firms that have investments abroad. These include accusations of poor records in hiring minorities and women in the United States, biased buying practices (favoring other Japanese firms), overly heavy representation of Japanese nationals in important managerial positions, an inability to mix culturally with local populations, and relatively low transfer of technology. These problems, and perceptions of problems, suggest that Japanese firms have taken abroad many business practices that are incompatible with behavioral norms in host nations. Such problems are not surprising, given the rather limited experience many firms had with overseas operations until the 1980s.

A study of the purchasing behavior of subsidiaries of foreign firms in Australia in the 1980s concluded that Japanese firms displayed a very distinctive pattern of national preference: they placed a strong emphasis in both their decisionmaking and purchasing behavior on dealing with other Japanese firms, whereas American and European firms demonstrated no measurable national bias.[39] One factor that could be involved in this bias is the relative newness of Japanese investments, since newcomers without local knowledge would be more inclined to stick to their traditional sources of material and equipment. However, the Japanese implicitly seem to accept the reality of a national bias in their behavior. Keizai Dōyūkai, a respected group of senior business leaders, issued a report in 1990 calling for more *genchika* (localization) through increased participation of local employees and increased local parts supply capability.[40]

A bias in business dealings would certainly be consistent with a variety of other information about the Japanese economy. Subcontractor ties are sufficiently strong (including bonds stemming from the presence of retired employees, capital provision, and marriage) that firms should experience some difficulty in distancing themselves from domestic suppliers as they relocate operations overseas. However, the walls are certainly far from impenetrable. In automobile parts, an industry that has generated considerable political reaction to the buying practices of Japanese transplant auto assembly firms, studies show that 45 percent of U.S. auto parts firms were supplying at least some parts to the transplants.[41]

Nevertheless, the perception and possible reality of bias have created both economic and political problems. Economically, the Japanese may actually be behaving inefficiently (ignoring efficient local producers in favor of preexisting ties to other Japanese firms). Politically, this behavior creates negative images of "invasion" or "colonization" because of the failure to incorporate enough existing local firms in their activities. Both these issues are raised by Japanese investment in the automobile industry in the United States, where some of the political reaction was quite extreme at the beginning of the 1990s.[42]

Creation of close subcontractor ties requires an investment of time and effort that Japanese firms may have been reluctant to repeat in the

United States, especially with a pool of unknown parts supply firms. But investment in building ties with local firms could yield quality and price outcomes similar to those in Japan—as seems to be the case for those American firms that have been accepted as suppliers in the auto industry. Furthermore, creation of a broader pool of domestic firms benefiting from sales to Japanese transplants would have strengthened the political acceptance of Japanese investment. While some of this has happened, the extent to which firms have engaged in ties with local firms—at least in the automobile industry—seems insufficient to build political support. Perhaps the problem originated in the length of time required to build close ties; most Japanese transplants in the auto sector are of such recent origin that relationships with local parts suppliers were still in the formative stage at the end of the 1980s. In addition, in the process of choosing suppliers, some firms will inevitably fail to fit successfully into the production system (and, as has happened in some cases, will make vocal complaints to the press and politicians). Nevertheless, a more determined effort to build ties with local firms rather than encouraging existing suppliers to relocate from Japan would have been a wise political decision.

An additional behavioral problem has been hiring and promotion practices. One publicized study in the late 1980s found that Japanese firms in the automobile assembly industry had a strong preference for locations in the United States with very low proportions of blacks and furthermore hired a disproportionately small number of blacks relative to their share in the local labor pool. Motivated by a rational desire to minimize labor problems Japanese businesses feel poorly equipped to handle (multiracial or multiethnic human settings), the Japanese were thereby engaging in behavior that created a negative image in the United States.[43]

Another group that poses a problem for Japanese firms is women. In Japan, women continue to face heavy discrimination in hiring and promotion for managerial posts, and Japanese managers appear to have carried those behavior patterns abroad. In the United States, where rules regarding such sexual discrimination have changed a great deal over the past several decades, this has caused a new source of tension.

Those local employees who are selected for managerial posts face additional barriers. Japanese firms have become known for reserving an usually high number of managerial positions for Japanese expatriates rather than delegating managerial responsibility to local staff. This phenomenon is the consequence of a managerial style emphasizing extensive interpersonal contact and discussion, facilitated by common cultural assumptions and language. Such a style would quite naturally lead many firms to believe that they must keep local non-Japanese managerial employees on the periphery of significant decisions.[44] There are no comparative data on the use of expatriates, but the Japanese government began collecting survey data on its own firms once criticism began on this issue. A 1991 government survey indicated that Japanese expatriates represented 2.3 percent of all employment at overseas subsidiaries, a total of 35,744 people.[45] These numbers sound small, but considering that few expatriates are needed for oversight and communication once foreign subsidiaries are operational, they appear to be quite high in comparison with the experience of some American firms.[46]

Again, this problem could be related to the relative newness of much of Japanese investment. However, a 1990 survey of Japanese firms in Southeast Asia found little shift away from expatriates in subsidiaries as operations became more mature. Of 299 firms surveyed, 43 percent reserved *all* upper management slots for Japanese nationals, with new firms (those in existence less than four years) at 52 percent and old firms (established before 1970) at 38 percent, not a large variation. Furthermore, the percentage of firms responding that Japanese expatriates occupied over 50 percent of upper management slots showed no variation by longevity of the investment.[47] Even in those firms where Japanese expatriates are not present in unusual numbers, complaints persist that local managers are not fully incorporated in decisionmaking and that the Japanese managers act only on the basis of consultation with the headquarters in Japan.[48]

Discrimination against hiring or providing significant responsibilities for local managers creates an unfavorable image for Japanese firms operating overseas. But ultimately such behavior should harm the productivity or profitability of foreign subsidiaries where expatriates maintain a high degree of control since the work environment may discourage the most competent local managers from seeking employment at these operations. In such an eventuality, the economic incentive to incorporate local talent more fully should bring about changes in corporate practices. However, this is likely to occur slowly, so employment practices will remain a dilemma for Japanese firms overseas for some time.

Another behavioral problem has been relatively limited mixing of expatriates with the local community. This is a complex issue involving both Japanese companies and individuals who have been thrust into unfamiliar foreign cultural settings and American communities with little or no previous experience with foreign investment and, in some cases, lingering racial or historical animosity because of the war.[49] Surveys of Japanese investment in North Carolina and Oregon, for example, noted that "the Japanese generally remain inwardly focused, and, as a rule, do not mix well in the community," and "there is not enough interaction between the Japanese . . . with the local community."[50] Broader surveys indicate wide variance in the efforts of Japanese firms to engage in "corporate citizenship" and in their opinions concerning local reception of their presence. A 1990 American survey found roughly one-half of Japanese subsidiaries largely uninvolved in local citizenship activities and only 19 percent very actively engaged.[51] It is an interesting commentary on American society that this lack of interaction is perceived as a problem; Americans care about social integration, whereas expatriate managers (or foreigners in general) in Japan are not generally expected to become involved in local society.

Responses to Local Antagonisms

These problems associated with Japanese investment abroad are now garnering recognition and a response from Japanese business and government. Concern over foreign opinions about Japanese investment has spawned a number of polls attempting to gauge foreign attitudes. A Foreign Ministry poll in spring 1989 found that 65 percent of Americans thought that Japanese investment was beneficial, while 24 percent said it was not—a very sizable minority, considering that the sample for the poll was restricted to "intellectuals." A MITI poll, not restricted to intellectuals, found a majority (53 percent) of respondents saying that establishment of Japanese plants and branch offices in the United States was undesirable and an even larger 75 percent opposed to Japanese real estate investment.[52]

Awareness of a problem led to a variety of responses, although conspicuous investment behavior continued through the late 1980s (exemplified by the purchase of the Pebble Beach Golf Course in the midst of the Gulf crisis in the fall of 1990, or the announcement of intent to acquire a majority ownership of the Seattle Mariners baseball team in the midst of a spate of antagonism toward Japan in the wake of President Bush's trip to Tokyo in January 1992). The response has been for the government to use administrative guidance to influence behavior while running public relations campaigns to deflect criticism.

The Japan External Trade Organization, for example, has been advocating a higher percentage of parts purchased locally, more localization of personnel, and more charitable contributions to alleviate criticism.[53] To encourage philanthropic activity by Japanese corporations, MITI successfully pressed for introduction of a tax exemption program for charitable donations made overseas. However, eligible donations are those for a "regional activity or project supported financially by MITI's Overseas Project-related Activity Council, an authorized overseas development corporation," which introduces a strong measure of central government influence or control over corporate philanthropic behavior.[54]

The message from MITI has been rather explicit: charitable contributions soothe local feelings about the presence of Japanese firms. MITI even began collecting data in its periodic survey of subsidiaries abroad on how many firms contributed to particular charities.[55] The data are even bluntly labeled *yūwa kōken* (soothing contributions)—financial contributions to smooth over or soften perceptions of local antagonism. MITI announced its intent to collect these data to the press, calling them part of a policy to reduce investment friction—both through publicizing how many firms do contribute locally and to provide an example to others.[56] The motivation in MITI policy was a simple and narrow focus on reducing the perceived negative response to Japanese investment abroad (principally in the United States).

In an additional move to promote charitable donations, the Ministry of Posts and Telecommunications (MPT) began a new form of postal savings account in which the holders could designate 20 percent of the interest income to be turned over for international charitable purposes. Proceeds are sent to MPT-selected nongovernmental development organizations engaged in improving the welfare of people in developing countries.[57] While different from corporate philanthropy overseas, this move also aimed at building goodwill in developing countries, which would indirectly create a better atmosphere for Japanese corporations operating there.

The private sector has also been organizing to deal with the response of foreign communities to Japanese corporate investment. Keidanren formed a committee in 1989 to promote better "corporate citizenship" by Japanese firms abroad—the Kaigai Jigyō Katsudō Kanren Kyōgikai (officially labeled in English the Council for Better Corporate Citizenship, CBCC)—as a broadening of a similar committee established the previous year aimed at investment in the United States (Taibei Tōshi

Kanren Kyōgikai—Council for Better Investment in the United States).[58] Chairmanship of the committee was awarded to Akira Morita, chairman of Sony Corporation, who took on the informal role of lecturing the Japanese how they should behave abroad, based on his years of service to Sony in the United States. This type of response is quite typical of Japanese behavior: reacting to a perceived problem through collective action to promote a change in corporate behavior or public relations activity.

Making local financial contributions and having employees engage in community voluntary work beyond the direct framework of the company are alien concepts for the Japanese. Indeed, volunteer work and charitable donations may be more developed in the United States than in most other countries. Justification for being better corporate citizens, therefore, has been rooted not in concepts such as civic responsibility but rather in a straightforward attempt to lessen local criticism. Japanese firms understand that if they meet local expectations of corporate philanthropy, then the community and their own local employees will be more accepting of the firm or feel greater loyalty toward it, thereby directly benefiting the company. As stated in one recent guidebook on how to engage in charitable activity prepared for the CBCC, "put in other words, corporate 'volunteerism' is a well-advised corporate policy." This same report also argues for high-level personal participation: "In order to get community recognition, it is necessary to have a company's top executives actively participate in a visible manner."[59]

Selfish corporate reasons undoubtedly motivate the charitable activities of many American-owned corporations as well, although American charitable and volunteer activity has deep roots in society that genuinely motivate individual and corporate participation. Should Americans care what the motivation of Japanese firms is so long as the activity takes place? If Japanese firms donate money and Japanese expatriate managers actually participate in volunteer organizations, some of them will develop a genuine interest and belief in the inherent value of those activities. Nevertheless, Japanese firms face two dilemmas regarding community participation. If they do not behave in a charitable fashion, they will be singled out for criticism (even though many American firms may be similarly uncharitable). If they try to repair their image problem, they face continuing criticism if the motivation is too blatantly self-interested.

The combination of a widening imbalance in inward and outward investment levels and the various criticisms directed against Japanese investment abroad create difficulties for the Japanese government and the nation as a whole. The nation faces a real need to gain foreign acceptance of a continuing flow of new investment abroad, especially in the manufacturing sector, for the reasons explored in chapter 2. A negative image based on the behavior of existing foreign operations may ultimately hinder that acceptance. At a broader level, the negative image created by these behavior patterns hinders the government's ability to be accepted as a leader or active participant in global economic and political matters.

Merchandise Trade

Japanese trade behavior in the 1950s and 1960s was the epitome of insularity. Severe import barriers obstructed entry of manufactured goods from abroad; a high share of both imports and exports was funneled through a small number of general trading companies; relatively few Japanese nationals needed to be abroad to manage trade (mostly in the trading companies); and firms regarded the outside world economy as exogenous, something that their own behavior would not affect. Government response to outside pressures to liberalize access to the domestic market was slow, grudging, and determinedly defensive.

Many elements of this trade behavior remained during the 1980s, posing a problem. How could Japan play a larger role in world affairs if other nations perceived its trade policies and behavior as unusually protectionist? As of the mid-1980s, considerable evidence indicated that Japan continued to absorb fewer manufactured imports relative to the size of its economy and to engage in far less intra-industry trade than did other major industrial nations.[60]

Debate has raged among economists over whether these features of Japanese trade are due to economic factors (the lack of raw materials and the relative endowment of land, labor, and capital) or to formal and informal protectionism. Many official trade barriers (tariffs and quotas) were gone by the 1980s, but complaints continued of myriad subtle, informal practices by both government and industry that restricted access for foreign products. Even if the low level of imports and intra-industry trade was due mainly to economic factors, such statistics conveyed a negative image to foreign governments and firms that exacerbated existing tension over trade issues.

Import Penetration

The ratio of manufactured imports to gross domestic product (GDP) provides at least a crude measure of the absorption of foreign products by a nation. That ratio obviously varies considerably with a variety of real economic factors (such as capital-labor ratios, resource endowment, or population size), but a wide variety of econometric studies have identified Japan as an outlier, with unusually low manufactured imports even when these factors are included. Not only was the ratio low, but it failed to rise over time despite the extensive lowering of official trade barriers (and in contrast to the pattern over time of other industrial nations).

From 1985 through 1988, yen appreciation against the dollar and other currencies triggered a number of moderately liberal changes in trade behavior that began to raise some measures of import penetration. Manufactured imports grew at an average annual rate of 25 percent from 1985 to 1990. Within that expansion, there was an especially rapid increase in imports of American products in categories that had been subject to negotiations during the 1980s. A Congressional Research Service study in 1991 found that the average annual growth rate of American products in these particular categories was 30 percent during 1985–90 (compared with a 21 percent average annual growth for American exports to Japan as a whole).[61] These are encouraging trends.

Rapid import growth also brought a rise in the ratio of manufactured imports to GDP. From 2.6 percent in 1985, this ratio rose to 3.8 percent by 1990.[62] This change represented a substantial improvement for this ratio, but still left Japan at less than half the level of the United States (7.8 percent in 1990) and by far the lowest in the OECD, as shown in table 3-4. Even India, a large continental nation with heavy import barriers, continued to have a ratio for manufactured import penetration (5.2 percent) higher than that of Japan, as did neighboring South Korea (20.6 percent). A more rapid increase in this ratio over this short five-year period might not have been possible, but for the level of manufactured import penetration in Japan to converge more closely to that of other industrial nations will require a continuation of the recent trends.

Table 3-4. *Imports of Manufactured Goods, Selected Countries, 1988, 1990*
Billions of U.S. dollars unless otherwise indicated

Country	1988			1990		
	Manufactured imports	GDP	Manufactured imports as percent of GDP	Manufactured imports	GDP	Manufactured imports as percent of GDP
Australia	28.8	233.4	12.3	34.3	261.1	13.1
Austria	29.5	109.9	26.8	40.7	137.1	29.7
Belgium	65.9	138.2	47.7	88.8	174.7	50.8
Canada	90.8	433.4	20.9	96.4	500.8	19.2
Denmark	19.8	91.8	21.6	23.8	111.0	21.5
Finland	16.0	92.3	17.4	20.8	120.9	17.2
France	130.2	836.8	15.6	172.5	1,036.9	16.6
Germany	179.2	1,071.9	16.7	252.5	1,336.0	18.9
India	12.2	244.1	5.0	13.7	263.3	5.2
Italy	89.3	773.9	11.5	117.6	1,093.4	10.8
Japan	78.5	2,684.0	2.9	104.7	2,729.2	3.8
New Zealand	6.0	37.5	16.0	7.7	37.5	20.7
Netherlands	69.3	209.9	33.0	90.4	256.8	35.2
Norway	19.1	78.2	24.5	22.1	94.3	23.4
South Africa	16.0	78.4	20.4	15.8	91.1	17.3
South Korea	33.7	154.7	21.8	44.4	215.3	20.6
Spain	41.5	316.6	13.1	61.8	450.8	13.7
Sweden	36.5	159.3	22.9	43.3	199.1	21.8
Switzerland	47.4	173.3	27.4	58.3	214.4	27.2
Thailand	15.6	51.6	30.3	25.6	68.7	37.3
United Kingdom	146.9	716.3	20.5	172.5	856.4	20.1
United States	363.6	4,499.9	8.1	392.7	5,048.4	7.8

Source: World Bank, *World Tables 1993* (Johns Hopkins University Press, 1993).

An argument can be made that the nominal trade figures understate the real change in imports. Because the yen appreciated against the dollar, the same amount of foreign manufactured goods could be purchased with fewer yen. In the short run, this effect of yen appreciation actually caused the ratio of manufactured imports to GDP to drop from 1985 through 1987 even though the dollar value of manufactured imports was expanding. The fact that a real increase in import penetration may occur without a rise in the nominal ratio of manufactured imports to GNP should be recognized. Nevertheless, the nominal ratio is more important for evaluating Japanese import behavior because it indicates how the society is allocating its income between domestic products and imports; a yen appreciation that produced a rise in the volume of imports while the Japanese actually spent fewer yen buying them (causing the ratio of manufactured imports to GDP to fall) would imply that behavior had not really changed. Only a choice to allocate a larger share of nominal GDP to purchase of manufactured imports demonstrates a fundamental shift in behavior in a more open direction consistent with patterns in other nations.

Intra-Industry Trade

Intra-industry trade has been the other major distinctive feature of Japanese trade. The simple theory of comparative advantage explains why nations export some products and import others; it does not explain why a nation would both export and import similar products. A large portion of trade, especially among industrial nations, is in exports and imports of products falling within the same industry classification. The United States, for example, is the world's largest exporter and importer of office equipment. Economic explanations of why this trade takes place rest on a combination of product differentiation (office equipment includes a wide variety of individual products that are not entirely similar) and economies of scale (firms can lower their average cost per unit by increasing production to supply export markets as well as the domestic market).

All nations engage in intra-industry trade to some extent, but national experience varies widely. Economists have found that the extent of intra-industry trade tends to rise as trade barriers fall, as nations achieve higher levels of industrialization, as they simply become larger economically, and as they converge in income levels. From the 1960s to the 1980s, Japan moved upward in all of these measures, changing from an economically small developing country to a large, advanced industrial nation. Contrary to the observed results for other nations, however, the degree of intra-industry trade in Japan did not expand. The standard measure of intra-industry trade in manufactured products for Japan actually declined somewhat between 1970 and 1985. The 1985 level was less than half that of the United States and even farther below the European nations'.[63] Since the degree to which individual industries and entire economies engage in intra-industry trade can vary with economic factors, economists have argued over whether such factors can explain Japan's unusually low level and failure to rise over time. While the debate remains unsettled, recent econometric contributions do find Japan to be an outlier even after adjusting for factors such as the low level of natural resource endowment.[64]

Intra-industry trade has also grown somewhat since 1985. One factor complicating this measurement, though, is the switch of all major nations to a new standardized industrial classification for international trade in 1988, making a direct comparison back to 1985 difficult. However, detailed Japanese data denominated in yen and based on a consistent classification are now available from 1988 through 1992. Calculations based on these data (using a four-digit harmonized standard industry classification) show that from 1988 to 1992, the measure of intra-industry trade increased from 24.8 to 27.8, a 12 percent increase over the four years.[65] These numbers sustain a conclusion that the degree to which Japan engages in intra-industry trade has recently increased modestly. The increases are fairly broadly distributed. Of the 973 industries in the four-digit HS classification, 516 show an increase in the degree of intra-industry trade. Thus the overall rise has not been the result of just a small number of industries with large trade volumes.

An unusual feature of Japan's trade patterns has been that in those industries that generate large exports, the level of intra-industry trade has been unusually low (that is, imports have been very low), in contrast to much higher levels of intra-industry trade in the successful export industries of other countries. But from 1988 to 1992 intra-industry trade rose in nine out of the top dozen Japanese export products (at the four-digit level), and in some cases the increase was substantial (albeit, in other cases, declines were significant as well), as shown in table 3-5. In the largest export industry, passenger cars, the intra-industry trade index number rose from 14.4 to 18.6 over this four-year period. For some other

Table 3-5. *Japan's Intra-Industry Trade in Major Export Categories, 1988, 1992*

Industry	Harmonized standard classification[a]	ITT index number[b] 1988	1992
Passenger cars	8703	14.4	18.6
Computers	8471	30.5	33.8
Other motor vehicles	8704	1.5	0.8
Auto parts	8708	8.9	15.4
Integrated circuits	8542	38.0	44.0
Computer parts	8473	32.2	47.8
Ships	8901	6.4	0.7
Transmission devices	8525	2.3	4.4
Heterocyclic compounds	2934	84.6	15.0
Copiers	9009	2.3	4.9
TV, sound recorders	8521	2.2	3.2
Telephones, fax	8517	13.5	22.4

Sources: Ministry of Finance, *Japan Exports and Imports: Commodity by Country* (Tokyo: Japan Tariff Association, December 1988, December 1992).
a. Harmonized Commodity Description and Coding System, adopted by Japan in 1988.
b. See Edward J. Lincoln, *Japan's Unequal Trade* (Brookings, 1990), app. A, for an explanation of the intra-industry trade index.

products (such as motor vehicles other than passenger cars), though, the level remained very low and virtually unchanged. Nevertheless, the evidence through 1992 implies that some real change was occurring in Japanese trade patterns.

This point about the experience of the large export industries can be generalized. Figure 3-3 graphs the share of total manufactured exports falling in a set of narrow intra-industry trade index number intervals. From 1988 to 1992 a discernable shift took place, in which the bulk of exports shifted moderately toward higher intra-industry trade intervals (indicated by the general movement of the line in figure 3-3 to the right). However, the distinctive pattern for Japan remained basically unchanged: few exports came from industries with high intra-industry trade levels, in sharp contrast to the experience of other major industrial countries.

Data on increases in the level of manufactured imports and intra-industry trade for the second half of the 1980s should be regarded as moderately encouraging despite the continued wide differentials between Japan and other nations. These changes are substantial enough to suggest some alteration of real behavior in a direction that makes Japanese markets more open to foreign products. The critical question for the rest of the 1990s is whether these changes will continue. Since Japan was still

Figure 3-3. *Distribution of Japan's Manufactured Exports across Intra-Industry Trade Intervals, 1988, 1992*

Percent of exports in each IIT interval

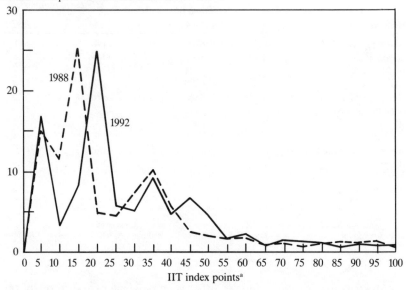

IIT index points[a]

Sources: Ministry of Finance, *Japan Exports and Imports: Commodity by Country* (Tokyo: Japan Tariff Association, December 1988, December 1992).
a. See Edward J. Lincoln, *Japan's Unequal Trade* (Brookings, 1990), app. A, for an explanation of the IIT index.

behind other major industrial nations in the early 1990s, further change will be necessary in order to demonstrate that Japan is not an outlier in the international system.

The answer to this question is not clear. For consumer luxury goods, the rapid increase in imports was related to the unusual financial developments of the late 1980s, when conspicuous consumption was enhanced by the bubbles in the stock market and real estate. Expensive German-made cars in particular led to a considerable increase in measured intra-industry trade in motor vehicles. But motor vehicle imports began declining when the financial bubbles collapsed: the dollar value of automobile imports in 1992 was down by 19 percent from its peak in 1990.[66] The trade data cited above suggest that the increases in manufactured good imports and intra-industry trade go beyond luxury consumer goods, however, and for other product areas, the trends that began in the late 1980s might be sustained into the 1990s.

Foreign direct investment also has an important bearing on these trends. The rapid rise in Japanese direct investment in manufacturing

Table 3-6. *Shipments from Japanese Subsidiaries Back to Japan, Selected Years, 1980–90*
Percent

Year	All Japanese manufacturing in the world	All Japanese manufacturing in Asia
1980	10.9	9.8
1983	11.6	10.8
1986	7.8	15.8
1987	9.1	16.7
1988	7.1	13.7
1989	7.9	15.8
1990	5.8	11.8

Sources: Ministry of International Trade and Industry, *Wagakuni Kigyō no Kaigai Jigyō Katsudō* [Survey of Overseas Activities of Japanese Companies], no. 18/19 (1990), p. 18; and no. 20 (1992), p. 18; and MITI Industrial Policy Bureau, International Business Affairs Division, *Kaigai Tōshi Tōkei Sōran* [General Statistics of Overseas Investment], no. 3 (Tokyo: Ministry of Finance Printing Office, 1991), p. 16.

abroad is bringing with it an increase in imports from overseas manufacturing subsidiaries. One of the factors involved in Japan's extremely low past level of manufactured imports was the paucity of intrafirm imports from overseas operations. Since the economic factors causing foreign direct investment will intensify during the 1990s, it is reasonable to assume that imports from those operations will continue to increase. This trend ought to cause a rise in intra-industry trade as well (with inward and outward exchanges of parts and finished products).

The rise in total intrafirm imports from overseas subsidiaries should not be confused with an increased propensity to engage in these imports. The share of output from overseas manufacturing subsidiaries (as measured by MITI surveys) going back to Japan actually fell during the 1980s, slipping from 11.6 percent in 1983 to only 5.8 percent in 1990 (see table 3-6). This drop came partly from the shift of investment away from Asia toward developed countries, where the motivation for investment was to circumvent local import protection rather than to produce for the Japanese market. But even in Asia, where firms have gone to seek lower wage costs, the share of output going back to Japan did not rise consistently. After gaining for several years, the 1990 level dropped back to what it had been in 1983. Even though the percentage of output going back to Japan fell, the rise in overall sales of Japanese subsidiaries abroad meant that the yen value of those shipments rose somewhat, from ¥4.9 trillion ($34 billion) in 1988 to ¥5.6 trillion ($37 billion) in 1990, representing 12 percent of total imports.[67]

Over the period from 1987 to 1990 the Japanese government appeared to be receptive toward the rapid increase in manufactured imports, representing a sharp contrast to attitudes throughout most of the postwar period. Government surveys concluding that retail prices were considerably higher in Japan than in other countries, white papers arguing that imports were beneficial to the nation, and a variety of programs to promote imports were evidence of the new attitudes.[68] After 1990, however, attitudes again appeared to be changing: the government argued that all necessary improvement in market access had occurred and that Japan was no longer different from other nations.

Representative of these hardening positions was a series of spirited attacks by Japanese government officials on the issue of low manufactured imports and intra-industry trade, explaining the differences through special economic circumstances.[69] All of these pieces argued that Japan may have been protectionist in the 1950s and 1960s, but that its import and intra-industry trade performance in the 1980s could be explained by the lack of raw materials. Since raw material imports were large, Japan had less "room" for manufactured imports and may have developed a stronger comparative advantage in manufactured exports, according to this argument.

Elements of this argument are economically sound. Resource endowment, in particular the limited domestic supply of raw materials and land, does explain part of the unusual trade patterns described above. However, although Japan does have relatively fewer domestic raw materials than many other nations, this difference does not fully account for the variation in trade performance.[70] Rather than continuing a progressive approach, therefore, the writings of Japanese government officials in 1990 and 1991 suggested a retreat to an earlier tendency to deny problems or differences (and, therefore, to deny the need for efforts to open markets or encourage imports to increase).

Complicating the situation was the 1992 recession, because the domestic structural change implied by rising manufactured imports is always more difficult politically when economic growth is sluggish. Since government is still important in signaling or guiding economic behavior, the shift to a less encouraging stance on manufactured imports could dampen further increases in imports as a share of economic activity, even after the recession comes to an end. This could cause problems if more advanced industrial products (such as those from the United States) still experience access barriers at the same time that labor shortages and a strong yen bring increased labor-intensive imports from Japanese subsidiaries in Southeast Asia. This will not erase images of Japan as an outlier.

Technology Flow

The trends in technology considered in chapter 2 imply that Japan should have moved toward becoming a net technology exporter. The long process of catching up through aggressive imports of superior foreign technology was over by the 1980s, and firms possessed their own technological base, which was of increased interest to the rest of the world.

Because Japan had lagged behind the industrial nations in the past, it had little technology to license to the outside world. This resulted in a lopsided imbalance in the balance-of-payments statistics on patent royalties, which are generally considered a proxy for technology flow. Rather than moving toward surplus in the 1980s, however, that deficit actually increased through the decade, reaching $4.1 billion in 1992 after declining slightly in 1991 (see figure 3-4). By way of contrast, the United States registered a $12.9 billion surplus on royalties and fees (on exports of $16.3 billion and imports of $3.4 billion).[71] This is a startling contrast for two countries both considered to be technologically advanced.

Part of the answer for Japan could come from its very recent move to international prominence in technology. Firms were only beginning to substitute serious internal development efforts for their previous pattern of modification and adaption of foreign technologies. The sharp rise in payments during the 1980s may reflect a rising price of technology to Japanese purchasers (due to the increased reluctance of foreign firms to sell technology to Japanese competitors), rather than any increased number of agreements. From 1985 to 1990, the average dollar value of technology-import licensing agreements almost doubled, from $160,000 to $311,000 (after having advanced at a slow pace in the first half of the decade, starting at $146,000 in 1980).[72]

On the export side of the ledger, the increase in receipts (technology exports) during the 1980s was actually quite steep, but the high growth rate came on such a small base that the dollar amount did not keep up with the movement in payments.[73] In twelve years, receipts went from a

Figure 3-4. *Japanese Royalties, 1979–92*

Billions of U.S. dollars

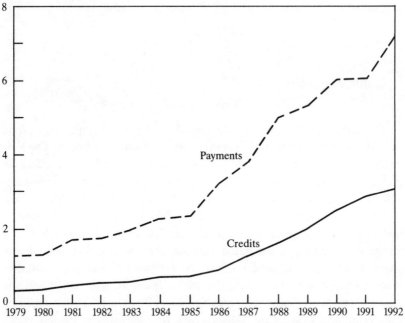

Sources: Bank of Japan, *Balance of Payments Monthly* (April 1984), pp. 35–36, 47–48; (April 1991), pp. 41–42, 53–54; and (December 1992), pp. 41–42, 53–54.

mere $321 million to $3.1 billion, a tenfold increase, but the amount was still less than half the size of payments for technology imports.

Balance-of-payments data may not capture true technology flow adequately, especially in the case of Japan. Since part of the Japanese technological success in the 1980s and 1990s was in the realm of manufacturing processes, transfer may not have involved royalties or licensing fees. There is no possible mechanism for measuring this sort of technology flow, except to note that the surge in Japanese direct investment in manufacturing in the second half of the 1980s should have enhanced the flow substantially. Increased publication of books and activity by consulting firms should also have enhanced transfer of this sort of technology. Anecdotal evidence from some American firms trying to overhaul production processes to meet competition from successful Japanese firms suggests that they achieved substantial reductions in production costs and simultaneous increases in quality through application of Japanese concepts. [74]

Technology transfer through direct investment has involved some criticism, though; developing country governments have complained that the transfer effect has been limited. This is a difficult issue to evaluate, since such allegations are largely anecdotal (and developing country governments have an incentive to exaggerate in order to pressure Japan). However, a study of U.S. and Japanese transfer of management technology in Southeast Asia during the mid-1980s noted that the U.S. affiliates had a lower number of expatriates and higher turnover rates than the Japanese affiliates. These results implied that local managers of U.S. firms were given more exposure to managerial and other skills.[75]

Aware of some of the problems of access, the Japanese government has made a few proposals. MITI suggested establishing joint Japan-U.S. high-technology research centers in both countries. Japanese researchers would be sent to centers in the United States, ostensibly to teach American researchers about Japanese approaches, thereby raising the level of effectiveness of U.S. research in high-technology industries.[76] Such concepts seemed naive; rather than eliminating "friction," they only served to raise suspicions that the real intent was to continue absorption of more U.S. technology.

In spring 1991 MITI also began studying a proposal to establish "centers of excellence" to engage in more basic research than in the past. The announced intent was to attract researchers from around the world. In 1990 BASF became the first foreign firm to participate in a MITI-funded research project. Although this represented a minor change from the past, it was also significant that MITI was interested only in American or European participants; no engineers from developing countries would be considered for MITI-sponsored research projects.[77] Such moves suggest either racial and ethnic prejudices that ill suit a leading industrial nation or a hope that invitations for foreign participation would lead to continued technology absorption.

Overall, the picture on technology is quite mixed. Although the outflow of technology, as represented by the rise in receipt of patent fees, indicates that some increase was taking place, the amounts remained relatively low, and other forms of technology flow or research and development behavior indicate continuation of a system designed primarily for absorption of technology from other advanced nations. Changing the system to enhance the outflow of technology through patent licensing or participation of foreigners in domestic research and development may be slow and difficult.

Foreign Workers

Tightening domestic labor markets have led to more than rising investment in overseas production: a new and visible inflow of foreign workers has appeared in Japan. Especially in service-sector industries such as construction, jobs cannot be moved offshore to compensate for labor shortages. Technical change can ameliorate only some of the excess demand for labor. Tighter labor markets have enabled Japanese workers to move away from undesirable, relatively unskilled jobs (the three k's in Japanese—*kitanai, kiken, kitsui*—or the three d's in English—dirty, dangerous, difficult). Foreigners from developing countries have now entered Japan to work in such positions.

This process of labor supply and demand drawing in workers from low-income countries may sound mundane to Americans, but it represented a startling change for Japan, where foreigners in general had been relatively few (considered below). The legacy of Japan as a relatively homogeneous ethnic group has such a long history and is so deeply ingrained in the national psyche that accepting this new but small wave of foreigners was quite difficult. Japan is one of the few nation-states that is also an ethnic group, and confusion of the two concepts abounds among Japanese.

Back in the late 1960s, when labor markets first began to tighten, the cabinet adopted an official policy of not permitting foreign workers in principle. Although this principle did not prevent foreigners from working in Japan, exceptions were limited enough that only 71,978 foreigners entered on work visas as recently as 1989.[78] However, these statistics seriously underestimate the number of foreigner workers truly resident in Japan, since the 1980s brought a large growth in illegal foreign workers. Many enter on tourist visas and are not registered as resident aliens, with rumored numbers as high as 300,000.[79]

One measure of the acceptability of illegal workers is the number of violations discovered by the police. The number of foreigners discovered to be working illegally increased from 2,339 in 1983 to 16,608 by 1989 and then almost doubled to 29,884 in 1990. This very rapid increase suggests that the willingness to tolerate illegal workers was decreasing.[80] On the other hand, the violations discovered were still only 10 percent or less of the total number of illegal workers supposedly present in the country, suggesting that the government was still not particularly serious about cracking down.

Recognizing the increased economic pressure to employ foreigners, a variety of government commissions began advising in the late 1980s that the rather strict limitations on foreign workers be eased, although the willingness to do so applied more to skilled workers than unskilled ones.[81] Keidanren, the organization representing the voice of big business in Japan, joined in the discussion but agreed with a cautious approach of relaxing limitations on visas for skilled workers (most in demand by Keidanren members), while remaining silent on the question of admitting unskilled workers.[82]

By 1991 the government was trying to regain some control over this inflow in a different but typical manner; it established a new organization, the Kokusai Kenshū Kyōryoku Kikō (Japan International Trainee Co-operation Organization, or JITCO) to handle foreign workers coming to Japan for "training." Under this plan, up to 100,000 workers would remain for one to two years. Any Japanese firm wanting low-cost, relatively unskilled workers from developing countries was then required to work through this organization and would be responsible for proving that the workers would receive some real training.[83] Trainees were supposed to spend one-third of their time in classes and the rest in "practical training." But JITCO was given a staff of only twenty-eight, implying that the monitoring of compliance would be virtually impossible.[84] Despite the fine rhetoric concerning training, therefore, the real goal of this move was rather obviously to regulate the numbers of unskilled foreigners entering Japan for work by creating a government-controlled channel for their processing. While it seemed doubtful whether this move would prevent the large-scale entry of illegal workers, at least larger firms (which could be more easily monitored) would be dissuaded from the illegal market.

As difficult as it may be for Japanese society to accept this new rise in unskilled foreign workers, their presence may be more tolerable than that of skilled workers. Official policy has been exactly the opposite: prohibition of unskilled labor until recently and acceptance of skilled workers when those skills were in need. However, at the skilled level a strong sense of nationalism remains virtually unchanged.

Once reliant upon foreigners to teach skills, Japanese society has generally been eager to eject those foreigners once the skills have been learned. Foreign lawyers, for example, were effectively banned in the mid-1950s, with only a modest reopening in the late 1980s after prolonged negotiations pressed by the U.S. government. In the medical profession, one Ministry of Health and Welfare official was quoted in 1991 saying "foreign doctors are no longer needed." The critical word in this quotation is "needed," a recurring concept, familiar to those involved with trade disputes, in which a product or service available from domestic sources suggests to the government (and affected industries or professions) that the foreign version should be excluded as unnecessary. Similar problems were emerging for foreign nurses at the same time.[85] Other professions (such as accountants, journalists, and stockbrokers) do not seem to face any entry problems, but the overall picture is certainly a mixed one in which nationalist sentiments have affected the inflow in some professions. These continuing problems are at odds with the notion of greater internationalization of the economy but entirely consistent with continuing attitudes of ethnic homogeneity and economic nationalism.

During the 1990s the pressure to accept unskilled workers will intensify as the working-age population pool stabilizes and then begins declining. Pressure eased during the cyclical downturn in 1991-92, but this will be only temporary because of the emerging demographic changes portrayed in chapter 2. Competition for workers will widen opportunities for Japanese adults to find higher-paying jobs with better working conditions, leaving the unskilled job market to face the brunt of tightening conditions. Unskilled jobs must be either replaced by automation, moved abroad, or filled in Japan with foreigners. Manufacturing can easily move abroad, but construction and many service industries must be located domestically, and the trend for increased foreign employment in these industries will continue. The government will continue to face the question of how large an inflow this ethnically uniform society can tolerate.

At least some debate emerged on this issue in 1992, with the quasi-official Japan Productivity Center arguing that increased employment of unskilled foreign workers would be necessary to maintain economic growth.[86] Nonetheless, the most likely outcome for at least the rest of this decade is that the flow of foreign workers from developing countries into Japan will remain at a relatively low level because of social aversion to such flows and government attempts to control them. The number of foreign workers coming to Japan will be insufficient to relieve the excess demand for labor, so a strong incentive to invest overseas will remain.

Other Human Interaction

An abiding feature of Japanese insularity until the 1980s was the relative lack of international travel or living abroad by Japanese citizens, as well as a relative paucity of foreigners in Japan. These patterns were a direct consequence of both the relative poverty of the nation (people could not afford to travel abroad, nor could corporations station many employees overseas) and the structure of the economy. By concentrating on domestic investment and production while holding foreign firms at bay with extensive controls on inward investment, economic behavior patterns discouraged the development of extensive human contact. Lack of personal international experience and limited contact with foreigners at home reinforced self-images of cultural uniqueness or separateness from the rest of the world.

Describing a nation that has had extensive trade relations with the world as insulated from extensive human interaction may seem strange. But most of that trade was handled by a very small number of large general trading companies that acted as the gatekeepers for the nation. During the second half of the 1960s, for example, approximately 62 to 65 percent of imports and 50 percent of exports were handled by the top ten general trading companies.[87] Although these companies were large and maintained an extensive network of offices overseas, they represented a remarkably large amount of trade handled by a relatively small number of individuals, especially those stationed overseas. As of the mid-1970s, these ten companies had a total of 5,894 Japanese employees stationed overseas, and the number in the 1950s and 1960s must have been even lower.[88] A very small number of people provided the nation's primary human interface with the world, and at that time many companies, pleading corporate poverty, stationed employees abroad without their families.

Japanese as Foreign Workers, Students, and Travelers

During the 1980s this situation changed rather rapidly. The number of Japanese living abroad has expanded throughout the postwar period, but it climbed rather slowly during the 1950s and 1960s. More rapid expansion began in the 1970s and continued during the 1980s (see table 3-7). In 1980, 445,372 Japanese nationals resided abroad, of whom 251,552 were considered permanent expatriates (emigrants to foreign countries who retained their Japanese citizenship, including an especially large number in Brazil), implying that 193,820 expected to return to Japan at some point in the future. All of the growth in the 1980s came in this latter

Table 3-7. *Japanese Living and Traveling Abroad, Selected Years,
1970–91*

| Year | Japanese living abroad | | Japanese exiting Japan |
	Total	Permanent expatriates	
1970	267,246	n.a.	936,205
1975	396,617	253,387[a]	2,466,326
1980	445,372	251,552	3,909,333
1981	450,873	n.a.	4,006,388
1982	463,680	n.a.	4,086,138
1983	471,873	248,272	4,232,246
1984	478,168	n.a.	4,658,833
1985	480,739	243,251	4,948,366
1986	498,196	n.a.	5,516,193
1987	518,318	247,927	6,829,338
1988	548,404	245,894	8,426,867
1989	586,972	246,043	9,662,752
1990	620,174	246,130	10,997,431
1991	n.a.	n.a.	10,633,777

Sources: Statistics Bureau, Management and Coordination Agency, *Japan Statistical Yearbook 1974*, p. 47; *1982*, pp. 36, 57; *1984*, p. 60; *1985*, pp. 46, 60; *1987*, pp. 46, 60; *1989*, pp. 46, 60; *1990*, pp. 46, 60; *1991*, p. 46; *1992*, pp. 46, 60; "Shyutsu Nyūkoku tomo Kako Saikō" [The Record High in Both Leaving and Entering the Country], *Nihon Keizai Shimbun*, May 4, 1991, p. 30; and "Ajia Kara Nyūkoku 14% Zou" [A 14% Increase in the Immigration from Asia], *Nihon Kezai Shimbun*, May 17, 1992, p. 34.
n.a. Not available.
a. 1974.

group. By 1989, 586,972 people were living abroad: 246,043 on a permanent basis and 340,929 temporarily. Thus the number of temporary residents abroad grew at a 6.7 percent annual rate: a low 4.1 percent in 1980-85 and then a higher 9.4 percent in the next four years.

Those working abroad were, in most cases, taking their families with them, in contrast to the pattern in the 1950s. This change in behavior meant that a small but significant number of children were now living and being educated abroad for several years at a time. In 1975, 16,316 school-age children were living abroad; that number increased to 27,465 by 1980 and then expanded significantly again to 49,336 by 1990.[89] These students were truly scattered across the world. In 1988, of a total of 44,123 students enrolled in schools abroad, 18,787 were in North America, 10,020 in Asia, 10,506 in Europe, 2,165 in Latin America, 1,489 in Oceania, 579 in Africa, and 577 in the Middle East. Of those in North America, about 18,000 attended American public schools.[90] Most of these children would return to Japan, bringing back with them ideas and behavior patterns shaped by their overseas experience.

Even though these numbers still represent only a tiny percentage of the population, they represent an elite group: managers (and families) in successful Japanese firms. They, and their children, are likely to have a disproportionate influence in future Japanese policymaking. On average, these people (especially the children) will develop more liberal and less ethnocentric views of the world than those who have not lived abroad.

Relative to American experience, though, the numbers remained small. In 1992, 6.3 million American citizens were recorded as resident abroad (excluding military personnel but including their dependents)— roughly five times more than the Japanese on a per capita basis.[91] Nevertheless, the sharp upward trend in Japanese living abroad appears significant enough to have a long-term influence on society as families rotate back to Japan. In the past the numbers were sufficiently small that those returning from prolonged stays abroad could either be shunted out of mainstream society or subjected to severe social pressure to shed their foreign or cosmopolitan attitudes and behavior patterns and reconform to the norms of domestic society. Although such pressures remain, the rapid rise in the numbers of returnees implies that society must bend somewhat to accommodate them.

Education abroad has also been increasing at the university level. A total of 121,645 citizens left Japan during 1990 for education or training, up more than five times from only 23,830 as recently as 1985. Other data indicate that in 1988 approximately 29,000 were enrolled as students in overseas institutions of higher learning.[92] By way of comparison, some 71,000 American students went abroad in academic year 1989-90 (a conservative estimate). Thus, on a per capita basis, Japanese students no longer lagged very far behind.[93]

American data provide a more complete picture of Japanese university students enrolled in the United States (where most Japanese students going abroad at this level are located). In the 1950s fewer than 2,000 Japanese students were enrolled in American institutions of higher learning. After twenty years of slow but steady growth, this number increased significantly to more than 12,000 by 1979–80. Although these numbers put Japan well within the top ten nations sending students to the United States, fewer students were present from Japan than from Taiwan or India in the 1960s. In 1964–65, for example, 3,386 Japanese students were enrolled in American universities, compared with 6,780 from Taiwan and 6,813 from India.[94] These figures underscore the relative lack of interest in education abroad, considering that at that time Japan had a higher per capita income level than these other two countries as well as a population much larger than Taiwan's.

During the 1980s the numbers of Japanese studying in the United States at the university level finally began to reach significant levels. Over the course of the decade the number of enrolled Japanese students tripled to over 36,000 by the 1990-91 academic year, with virtually all of the increase coming after 1985. This was an extraordinary jump.

Students from all parts of the world have come to the United States in increasing numbers, but even as a share of this rising total, the Japanese stand out after 1985. Japanese students represented 4.6 percent of all foreign students enrolled in American universities in the 1954–55 academic year, a share that diminished to 3.0 percent by 1985 and then tripled to 9.0 percent by the 1990–91 academic year.[95]

The rise in university education abroad represents a significant change. Earlier in the postwar period, most Japanese university students enrolled abroad were at the graduate level, sent abroad by their firm or government agency. Few young people opted on their own for education abroad, since foreign degrees had no value in the Japanese employment market and costs were beyond the reach of most families. By the early 1990s, though, it was no longer uncommon to find students and parents choosing undergraduate university education abroad—as the surge in enrollment in the United States indicates. Of the 36,610 Japanese students enrolled in American universities in the 1990–91 academic year, 69 percent (roughly 25,000) were in undergraduate programs.[96]

Furthermore, more Japanese were traveling abroad. Short-term travel (such as the popular short honeymoon stays in Hawaii or Australia at Japanese-owned hotels) may not provide much real exposure to the outside world, but any international travel remains a more broadening experience than staying at home. In 1970 Japanese nationals took only 0.9 million trips abroad (see table 3-7). This figure implies that fewer than 0.9 million individuals traveled abroad, since the statistics count the number of trips and not people. Trips abroad rose to 3.9 million by 1980 and then jumped to over 10 million by the end of the decade; even with the dampening influence of the Gulf War, there were 10.6 million in 1991. Most of the growth in the 1980s came in the second half of the decade: from 1980 to 1985 the number of trips expanded by about 1 million, but it rose by over 6 million from 1985 to 1990. More than twice as many trips were taken abroad in 1990 alone as in the entire decade of the 1960s, a fact that is eloquent commentary on the isolation of Japan in the earlier postwar years.

Foreigners Coming to Japan

The reverse flow—foreigners entering or living in Japan—also accelerated during the 1980s, although this is more evident for alien residents than travelers. In 1970, 775,061 foreigners entered the country (with multiple trips counted individually as with trips abroad); this number rose to 1.3 million in 1980 and 3.9 million in 1991 (table 3-8). The number of foreigners entering Japan, therefore, rose substantially but not as rapidly as trips taken abroad. The number of Japanese going abroad and foreigners entering Japan was near parity in 1970; by 1991 the ratio had reached almost three to one. Yen appreciation after 1985 made travel abroad cheaper for Japanese but travel to Japan more expensive, yielding this imbalance.

The number of foreigners living in Japan also increased. The total number of aliens rose very slowly from 708,000 in 1970 to 783,000 in 1980 and then more quickly to 941,000 in 1988. These numbers, however, involve significant problems because the data include Koreans and some Taiwanese who have lived in Japan for several generations without being granted citizenship, a result of the continuing insularity of Japanese society, which effectively denies citizenship to other ethnic groups permanently resident in Japan. An adjustment of the data to get a picture of the true inflow of foreigners living in Japan yields a 4.3 percent growth rate in the 1970s, followed by a very high 17.6 percent growth in the 1980s and an extraordinary 42 percent increase in 1991. By these calculations, only 65,478 foreigners other than long-term Korean and Chinese residents were living in Japan in 1980, a number that exploded to 469,790 by 1991. Resident aliens' share of the population, even if estimated illegals (staying and working on tourist visas) are included, comes to well under 1 percent, but since the base was so low before the 1980s their presence since then has become noticeable in larger cities.

Students provide another mixed picture. As of May 1990, 41,347 people were resident in Japan with student visas, compared with only about 6,600 as recently as 1980. A high 44 percent of these students were from

Table 3-8. *Foreigners Entering and Living in Japan, Selected Years, 1970–91*

Year	Registered aliens in Japan				Foreigners entering Japan	Total Japanese population
	Total	Koreans	Chinese[a]	Adjusted total[b]		
1970	708,458	614,202	51,481	42,775	775,061	103,720,000
1975	751,842	647,156	48,728	55,958	780,298	111,940,000
1980	782,910	664,536	52,896	65,478	1,295,866	117,060,000
1981	792,946	667,325	55,616	72,446	1,552,296	117,884,000
1982	802,477	669,854	59,122	79,167	1,708,306	118,693,000
1983	817,129	674,581	63,164	88,810	1,900,597	119,483,000
1984	841,831	680,706	69,608	107,103	2,036,488	120,305,000
1985	850,612	683,313	74,924	112,992	2,259,894	121,049,000
1986	867,237	677,959	84,397	134,684	2,021,450	121,672,000
1987	884,025	673,787	95,477	155,356	2,161,275	122,264,000
1988	941,005	677,140	129,269	208,693	2,414,447	122,783,000
1989	984,455	681,838	137,499	247,154	2,985,764	123,255,000
1990	1,075,317	687,940	150,339	331,621	3,504,470	123,612,000
1991	1,218,891	693,050	171,071	469,790	3,855,952	124,043,000

Sources: Statistics Bureau, Management and Coordination Agency. *Japan Statistical Yearbook 1984*, p. 45; *1987*, p. 45; *1989*, p. 45; and *1992*, pp. 24–25, 45.

a. Including Taiwanese.

b. The adjusted total compensates for those registered aliens assumed to be permanent immigrants. All Koreans are subtracted because the growth in the number of resident Korean aliens is less than the overall growth in the Japanese population (suggesting that the increase in the number of Koreans has come only from natural population growth—the children of aliens do not become Japanese citizens—rather than emigration from South Korea). The same is true of Chinese aliens during the 1970s, and their numbers are also subtracted to calculate the adjusted total. In the 1980s, however, the number of Chinese increased rapidly. Therefore, those who represent natural population growth are estimated by using the overall population growth rate and subtracted from the total to obtain the adjusted total.

China, and their number rose the most rapidly, up 66 percent just in 1990 (perhaps because of difficulty in getting permission from their government to go to the United States after the Tiananmen massacre).[97] As dramatic as this increase may seem, the number of foreign students is quite low compared with that in the United States (336,350 in 1988) or in western European nations.[98] Furthermore, because many on student visas, especially those from China and other nearby Asian nations, may be working illegally rather than studying, the rising number of students in the official statistics overstates the real change in Japan as an international center for education.

A final source of the inflow of foreigners has been refugees. Internal and regional conflicts in the 1970s and 1980s increased the flow of refugees on a global basis. Japan has been faced primarily with the question of Vietnamese and Chinese refugees. However, as might be expected of a homogeneous society, few refugees have been permitted to remain in Japan. From the end of the Vietnam War through 1990, only some 7,200 Indochinese refugees had been resettled permanently in Japan.[99] The annual number of refugees accepted for resettlement or asylum has been lower than in virtually any other industrial nation. While the United States is an outlier at one extreme (taking roughly half of all refugees granted resettlement in recent years), Japan is an outlier at the other end of the spectrum. In 1989 only 461 refugees were permanently accepted in Japan, with only tiny Finland, among the major resettlement countries, taking fewer.[100]

Problems of accepting students, refugees, and workers into Japanese society will intensify as Japan's economic success causes the demand for entry and domestic economic pressure to rise. Society will be confronted with the fact that it cannot continue as a largely isolated ethnic nation-state, but adjusting to the presence of visibly different people will be difficult, and discrimination will persist. The basic assumption that Japan is a homogeneous ethnic group has not changed, and that attitude provides a fundamental barrier to attitudes or policies that would facilitate a larger inflow of foreign workers and refugees. The most reasonable estimate for the rest of the decade is that the interplay of economic and political pressures will yield only a moderate expansion of foreigners in Japan. Perceptions abroad that Japan is not receptive to foreign workers or refugees reinforce the image of an ungenerous nation and hinder acquisition of a more active participatory role in global affairs.

Conclusion

Core elements of interaction between Japan and the world—investment, trade, technology flow, domestic labor force demand, and other human contact—all underwent important changes during the 1980s. Increasing international economic participation brings largely welcome developments to the nation. But the coupling of those developments with a continued sense of separateness and resistance to foreign penetration detracts from the accomplishment of internationalization.

The rise in investment outside Japan occurred with truly stunning speed. Even if the pace of increase moderates in the rest of the 1990s, investment has already thrust the nation into the world to an unprecedented extent. Learning how to manage assets abroad has to be a liberalizing experience for this previously isolated nation, and anything that acts to draw Japan out of isolation is a positive development.

But naive notions that investment would be a solution to trade problems proved wrong. The central feature of the problem has been the enormous asymmetries characterizing evolving international interactions during the 1980s and 1990s: Japan penetrated the outside world, but there was no reciprocal flow into the country. A depressing similarity runs through all the dimensions of international interaction explored in this chapter. Outward investment is larger than inward investment by an overwhelming amount; manufactured imports occupy a smaller share of economic activity in Japan than in any other industrial nation; measures of intra-industry trade are lower than for almost all other industrial nations; the deficit in technology flow continued to rise even though the nation became a technological leader; a surge of people traveled abroad while entry to Japan lagged behind; and businessmen flowed abroad to manage overseas assets while entry of foreigners to work in Japan was considered a national problem.

Government officials, academics, and businessmen could argue that special economic circumstances led to the observed wide imbalances. Whatever the explanations, these facts concerning Japan's interaction with the world at the beginning of the 1990s indicate a weak base on which to build a larger international policy role. Leadership or stronger participation in global affairs require an environment in which others accept that participation or leadership. Acceptance is enhanced by a sense of equal access to markets and social familiarity. The asymmetries in the case of Japan perpetuate a sense of unequal access, thereby impeding its acceptance in a stronger participatory or leadership role.

An optimistic explanation would say that the issues raised in this chapter represent a delayed response to the sudden appearance of new economic circumstances. Many of the factors propelling the nation into the world did not really begin to have an effect on international engagement until well into the 1980s. As the nation acquires more experience, some of the asymmetries might diminish. Pessimists, however, see the fact that disparities remain as indicative of fundamental insular tendencies in Japanese social and political behavior that will not change readily.

The data presented in this chapter demonstrated some moderate movement in a more open direction for all forms of interaction. That movement has been real; it cannot be entirely dismissed as simply public relations or cyclical changes. Manufactured imports rose strongly from 1985 to 1990, bringing up the ratio of manufactured imports to GDP; the indices of intra-industry trade rose moderately; the export of technology grew fairly strongly; direct exposure of Japanese nationals to the outside world through travel, work, living, and study abroad expanded sharply; and the number of foreigners studying and working in Japan has increased (even if it is still small).

These real changes suggest that extreme forms of the pessimistic view are unjustified. But they also imply that optimism must be guarded. Import penetration appeared to stall in the early 1990s; the investment imbalance was continuing to grow; and growth in technology exports remained far less than that of imports. Furthermore, government responses to a variety of problems—including how to deal with the influx of foreign workers, low levels of inward direct investment, or the need to demonstrate further openness of markets to imports—all suggest that progress in a more open direction has been limited.

The human dimension of the new interaction with the world may be the most important in the long run. Few nations can lay claim to the degree of ethnic homogeneity that characterizes Japan. The associated sense of cultural, linguistic, and social separateness or uniqueness pervading Japan has been a serious impediment in building a productive and closer relationship with the outside world. Separateness produced a paucity of citizens capable of acting comfortably in an international setting. If there is a ray of optimism in the data discussed here, it is that the current wave of travel and living abroad will eventually produce a much larger core of people who can fulfill these functions, especially as the children educated abroad mature and enter the work force. These people will be more cosmopolitan and should gradually drive the nation toward more effective participation in international affairs. But the operative word is *gradual*; these changes will take many years to emerge.

CHAPTER FOUR

Policy Dimensions of Outreach

AS A RELATIVELY small developing economy connected to the world through arm's-length trading relations and scarred deeply by the international policy disasters leading to World War II, Japan remained largely out of the international economic policy arena in the 1950s and 1960s. Japan could afford to treat the international economic and political environment as a given—something the government and business had to adapt to or comply with but could not influence or alter. The country did not begin a foreign aid program until the mid-1960s, which remained small until the late 1970s. Japan was accepted into the principal multilateral institutions but remained a minor and largely passive participant. Finally, the bilateral security pact with the United States allowed Japan to stay on the sidelines of international security issues, to the satisfaction of nations with bitter war experiences.

Although some of the demands of the outside world on Japan caused considerable angst (such as pressure to liberalize import and investment barriers), in many respects the early postwar environment was comfortable and simple. Rather than involving itself in difficult questions of policy formation, the government and private sector simply reacted to the rules imposed from the outside. As long as the rules and demands were generally rational and predictable, the economy could adapt and benefit through belonging to the international system. A concentration on domestic economic reactions allowed Japan to deal with even unexpected problems, including the oil crisis of 1973 or the unilateral American decision to end convertibility of the dollar into gold in 1971 (which brought an end to the fixed yen-dollar exchange rate that had prevailed

109

since 1949 and was regarded as one of the pillars of a stable economic environment).

The developments explored in the previous two chapters fundamentally altered this simple arrangement during the 1980s. The sheer size of the nation and its trade flows affected global trade policies; the highly visible current account surpluses created pressures from the international community to recycle some of the funds as foreign aid; financial deregulation and the resulting wave of overseas investment exposed financial institutions to the emerging debt problems of the developing countries; technological success created expectations in developing countries for technology transfer; and high wages motivated relocation of production abroad and attracted foreign workers. No longer could the government remain aloof from the economic issues and problems of the world.

Accustomed to its comfortable, insular existence, Japan was poorly equipped to forge active, progressive international policies on either economic or political issues. Few people with adequate foreign language training or international experience were needed or produced by a system that was focused almost exclusively on domestic development. Accustomed to staying out of multilateral policy debates and accepting the outcomes of those debates as a fact of life, the government faced the world of the 1990s with an international extension of its predominant domestic paradigm; it had few principles to motivate its policy positions other than a narrowly defined commercial interest. The pattern of close cooperation between the bureaucracy and the private sector to shape and promote the growth of Japanese firms for the overall benefit of the nation (as laid out in chapter 1) provided the principal mechanism for coping with the new international environment of the 1980s and early 1990s.

Scholars disagree about whether this response to the outside world stems from a simple lagged adjustment to the very rapid shift in the nation's international economic position or from more fundamental structural features of Japanese culture and politics. The conclusion that emerges from the following pages is mixed. On some fronts, progress is leading to a higher-profile policy role or even international leadership. One such area is international environmental policy. However, in many aspects of international policy a narrow definition of economic self-interest will continue to seriously impede movement toward a larger and more productive international role. Continued strong national commercial interest in foreign aid, a preference for working outside or on the fringe of major multilateral organizations, and a commercial motivation for much of international environmental policy all reflect continuation of close government-business relations in policymaking.

That Japan has become an important financial participant in many aspects of international economic policy is a fact from which there is no escape for either Japan or the rest of the world. The following pages consider some of the dimensions of that participation: foreign aid, participation in multilateral institutions, administrative guidance, and an emerging role in international environmental policy. If some of the aspects of that participation seem troubling, then the appropriate question for the United States is how to adapt or respond to what the Japanese are doing or how to nudge them along in a more open and liberal direction.

Foreign Aid

Japan's provision of foreign aid to developing countries originated in the 1960s, evolving out of postwar reparations payments to Asian nations occupied during the war. In the early years, the foreign aid program was small and, like that of many other nations, closely tied to purchases of goods from Japan, making foreign aid another form of export promotion. From that small base, the amounts rose quickly, making Japan a global leader in the dollar amount of its overseas development assistance (ODA) during the 1980s.

The terms *foreign aid* and *economic development* have a generous ring to them, but the details of Japan's foreign aid program in the 1980s and 1990s suggest continuation of a strongly commercial orientation. The financial amounts grew sharply, but the structure, motivation, and projects undertaken remained dominated by a desire to benefit domestic firms. Policies may not have been as singlemindedly commercial as in the late 1960s, but neither were they as liberal as the Japanese government wanted the world to believe; behind a facade of benign generosity lay a continuing strong economic self-interest.

The nature of the foreign aid program matters because the quantity of money involved increased rather dramatically. Japan's provision of foreign aid to the developing world experienced explosive growth in the 1980s, paralleling the country's growth in overseas investment. Thrust to the forefront of foreign aid donors, Japan became engaged with the

Table 4-1. Japan's Overseas Development Assistance, 1980–91

Year	Multilateral (billions of U.S. dollars)	Bilateral (billions of U.S. dollars)				Total ODA		
		Grants	Technical	Loans	Total	Billions of U.S. dollars	Billions of yen	Real value (yen)[a]
1980	1.3	0.4	0.3	1.3	2.0	3.3	749	734
1981	0.9	0.4	0.4	1.5	2.3	3.2	699	678
1982	0.7	0.4	0.4	1.6	2.4	3.0	753	702
1983	1.3	0.5	0.5	1.4	2.4	3.8	893	886
1984	1.9	0.6	0.5	1.4	2.4	4.3	1,026	1,011
1985	1.2	0.6	0.5	1.4	2.6	3.8	906	906
1986	1.8	1.1	0.6	2.1	3.8	5.6	949	1,118
1987	2.2	1.5	0.7	3.0	5.2	7.5	1,078	1,337
1988	2.7	1.8	1.1	3.5	6.4	9.1	1,175	1,491
1989	2.2	1.6	1.5	3.7	6.8	9.0	1,237	1,503
1990	2.3	1.4	1.6	3.9	6.9	9.2	1,335	1,590
1991	2.2	1.5	1.9	5.5	8.9	11.0	1,486	1,832

Sources: Ministry of Foreign Affairs, Japan's ODA Annual Report (1985), p. 10; (1988), p. 40; (1989), p. 4; (1992), p. 80; and Statistics Bureau, Management and Coordination Agency, Japan Statistical Yearbook 1984, p. 359; 1985, p. 359; 1990, p. 361; and 1992, p. 361.
a. Adjusted by wholesale price index for exports with 1985 as base year.

developing world to an extent that no one would have imagined in the 1970s.

The record of an expanding foreign aid program presents an important dilemma. Political support for the expansion certainly came from the business community, which stood to benefit, while the public expressed broad (but probably shallow) support for the basic notion of foreign aid. Had the program not had such a strong commercial orientation, the enormous expansion in the amount of ODA might not have taken place, given the importance of the corporate sector in shaping policy outcomes. Had the expansion not occurred, Japan would be criticized for a lack of foreign aid spending; now that it has taken place, Japan is criticized for the content of the program. The question is how or if the program can be changed without undermining the political support for it. A less commercial program would presumably receive less corporate support and would need a stronger commitment by the broader public. Given the traditionally weak voice of the public in policy formation, such a shift in foreign aid policy will be slow at best.

Trends in Aid Spending

The growth of Japan's total overseas development assistance in both dollar terms (a figure highly affected by exchange rate developments) and yen terms is shown in table 4-1. After stagnating in the first half of the 1980s because of yen depreciation, the amount shot up from $3.8 billion in 1985 to $9.1 billion in 1988. Relative stability in exchange rates after 1988 reduced the growth rate, but through 1991 some growth was continuing. The yen-denominated amounts in the table indicate the extent to which the perception of increasing foreign aid has been due to currency fluctuations. The upward movement in net disbursements began in 1983, and the 1991 level was double that of 1980—lower than the dollar-denominated rise but still substantial.

The real value of goods and services foreign aid can buy is affected by both currency fluctuations and inflation rates in the markets in which those goods and services are purchased. Under the simplifying assumption that overseas development assistance is used solely to buy goods from Japan, the fall in the wholesale price index for exports implies a stronger upward trend: the real yen value of ODA in 1991 was 2.5 times larger than in 1980.

Table 4-2. *General Account Budget for Overseas Development*
Assistance, Fiscal Years 1980–91
Hundred million yen unless otherwise indicated

Fiscal year	Final ODA budget	Increase from previous year (percent)	Total general account budget	Increase from previous year (percent)
1980	3,684	10.2	434,050	11.9
1981	3,929	6.6	469,212	8.1
1982	4,729	20.4	472,451	0.7
1983	4,780	1.1	506,353	7.2
1984	5,286	10.6	514,806	1.7
1985	5,715	8.1	530,045	3.0
1986	5,742	0.5	536,404	1.2
1987	6,529	13.7	577,311	7.6
1988	7,285	11.6	614,711	6.5
1989	7,622	4.6	658,589	7.1
1990[a]	8,020	5.2	696,512	5.8
1991[a]	8,459	5.5	703,474	1.0

Source: Ministry of Finance, *Zaisei Tōkei* [Fiscal Statistics] (Tokyo: MOF Shukeikyoku Chōsaka [Budget Bureau Research Division], 1991), pp. 240–49, 253.
a. Original budget.

A rising commitment for ODA is further confirmed by the general account budget (rather than the net disbursement data used in table 4-1). The yen-denominated budget for foreign aid rose steadily during the decade at a higher rate than the overall budget of the Japanese government, which was constrained by policies to reduce the government deficit (see table 4-2). Since some of the funds for foreign aid are raised through borrowing, the general account budget figures do not cover all of foreign aid spending, but they do provide a perspective on the government commitment to using tax revenues for foreign aid. While the overall general account expenditures grew at an average annual 4.5 percent rate over the course of the dozen years up to 1991, the foreign aid budget grew at 7.8 percent. This higher growth rate was true for most individual years during the decade, indicating the enduring importance of increasing foreign aid among competing government priorities.[1] At no point during the 1980s was any significant opposition raised against these increases; conflicts over aid versus domestic social spending were not a serious problem, as they were in the United States.

Because contributions to multilateral aid institutions did not keep pace with the overall amount, bilateral aid represented an ever-increasing share of the total. In 1980 the share of multilateral aid was 41 percent, and it reached a peak of 44 percent in 1984. From 1988 to 1991 the dollar amount of overall ODA was almost constant, but the amount disbursed through multilateral institutions dropped while bilateral aid increased. By 1991 multilateral aid was only one-fifth of the total and bilateral aid was four-fifths, so a substantial shift took place over the course of the decade. An international comparison shows that heavy reliance on bilateral aid is not at all unusual. In 1991 the United States disbursed only 17 percent of its ODA through multilaterals; France, 22 percent; and Germany, 34 percent.[2] Validating the decline in the multilateral share, the Foreign Ministry agreed that "in view of the importance of aid as a foreign policy tool for Japan, it is likely that bilateral aid will continue to account for the majority of Japan's aid activities."[3]

In 1991 Japan was the second largest net donor to the multilateral institutions (after Germany), so an even bigger increase might have swamped the delicate balance among donors to these institutions.[4] Nevertheless, the data indicate that rather than sticking with the multilateral aid institutions as a recipient, the Japanese government deliberately chose to move strongly in a unilateral direction. This choice is significant because in the early 1980s the government was urged to channel increased ODA spending through the multilaterals in order to allay concerns about the commercial orientation of aid and to deal with the shortage of trained specialists to administer an expanded (and less commercial) program.

The largest portion of bilateral aid has been in the form of soft loans. In 1980, 65 percent of bilateral ODA consisted of loans, and by 1991 that share contracted slightly to 62 percent ($5.5 billion), with the rest consisting of grants ($1.5 billion) and technical assistance ($1.9 billion). However, the increasing emphasis on bilateral ODA gave soft loans an expanding importance in total Japanese foreign aid. As a share of total ODA disbursements, bilateral loans went from 40 percent in 1980 to 50 percent by 1991. Loans, therefore, gained as the preferred vehicle for foreign aid. The choice is significant since loans are generally for large infrastructure projects with a stronger potential commercial effect than other forms of aid.

The Rationales for Aid

The Foreign Ministry has given five justifications for Japan's foreign aid: the nation's status as a superpower (imposing an obligation to follow the pattern of other superpowers); its position as a large creditor nation (with a need to recycle its surpluses); high dependence on natural resources (with aid as a means of promoting political and economic stability among the suppliers of these resources); Japan's position as a peaceful nation (limiting a military contribution to world stability); and the nation's status as a non-Western developed nation (giving it a special rapport with the developing world). There has also been an increased emphasis on a humanitarian rationale, but this has never been a primary motivation.[5]

Aid as an obligation of the nation is rightly at the top of this official list as a primary motivator of Japan's ODA program. In the late 1970s the government came under criticism for the small size of its foreign aid spending. At a time of rising current account surpluses and trade conflict with the United States, the modest aid program became another symbol of an ungenerous nation. To appease foreign critics and ameliorate concern over large current account surpluses, expanding foreign aid was a logical solution (along with increasing defense spending, another target of criticism in the late 1970s). Unfortunately, a consequence of this focus on appeasing critics was that larger sums of money became more important than the quality or integrity of the program.

Foreign aid as a means of responding to raw material dependency is also a significant motivator of policy. Faced with a need for imported raw materials and access to export markets, and with no recourse at all to military tools, Japan has openly used foreign aid to enhance security of supply. A number of raw material suppliers have been recipients of generous amounts of Japanese ODA. The flow of aid to developing countries is at least loosely related to the volume of import of raw materials from those countries, as shown in table 4-3. Virtually all the major recipients of foreign aid are major sources of raw material imports.[6] Security of raw material imports as a foreign aid motivation may seem crass, but protecting national economic security by reducing the threat of disruptions in the supply of raw materials was as important a national goal as fighting communism was for the United States during the cold war. Without the possibility of using military force as a backup for protecting economic security, foreign aid gained increased importance as an economic security policy, and (as argued in chapter 7) was reasonably effective.

The additional official motive for aid by Japan as a bridge between north and south is a commonly expressed theme. That is, because Japan was a non-Western latecomer to industrialization and only recently graduated from the status of a developing country itself, it has (in this view) a special rapport with of the needs of developing countries.[7] Of course,

Table 4-3. *Net Overseas Development Assistance from Japan and Raw Material Imports to Japan, 1990*
Millions of U.S. dollars

Recipient	ODA from Japan	Japan's import of raw materials from recipient countries
Bangladesh	373.6	39.7
Brazil	64.7	1,674.5
China	723.0	5,540.1
Egypt	98.9	61.9
Ethiopia	10.3	33.8
Ghana	71.9	64.1
Honduras	85.1	83.5
India	87.3	1,068.8
Indonesia	867.7	10,067.1
Kenya	93.2	16.3
Madagascar	14.0	30.0
Malawi	42.0	46.3
Mexico	24.1	1,471.5
Myanmar (Burma)	61.3	14.9
Nepal	55.2	1.7
Niger	36.9	0.0
Nigeria	78.7	13.4
Pakistan	193.6	60.4
Papua New Guinea	38.1	250.4
Paraguay	26.4	5.8
Philippines	647.5	1,357.0
Senegal	82.1	13.1
Sri Lanka	176.1	56.2
Sudan	38.9	9.3
Syria	5.5	4.0
Tanzania	40.7	15.7
Thailand	418.6	1,757.2
Tunisia	27.0	16.9
Turkey	324.2	123.7
Zambia	40.1	0.1

Sources: Organization for Economic Cooperation and Development, *Geographical Distribution of Financial Flows to Developing Countries 1987/1990* (Paris: OECD, 1992); and Ministry of Finance, *Japan Imports and Exports, Country by Commodity* (Tokyo: Japan Tariff Association, December 1990), pp. 19–773.

this attitude reinforces a desire to concentrate foreign aid to neighboring countries in Asia, where cultural and historical factors ought to make this understanding strongest.

The official motives seem quite sensible. However, the Foreign Ministry list leaves out an additional critical motivation of foreign aid. Aid must be rooted in some consideration of national interest other than simply as a necessary "cost" of being a member in good standing of the industrial nation club (although the Japanese government defines its national interest very much in terms of keeping the United States and other Western nations satisfied with its international performance). Securing raw material imports is a key portion of this national interest, but in a broader sense Japan's foreign aid reflects the fact that its national goals and policy have been oriented heavily toward benefit for domestic firms (and, by extension, the domestic economy). As noted in chapter 1, Japan stands out for the degree to which national economic well-being has been associated with the well-being of domestic firms (rather than consumer welfare).

The government vigorously denies that direct benefit for Japanese business is a motive for foreign aid, but the reality is that aid still appears to be justified largely by national commercial concerns. The overall increase in ODA during the 1980s may have been primarily to placate other industrial nations or reduce insecurity of raw material supplies, but the manner in which those monies have been spent indicates the strong influence of commercial interests. Japan's own commercial interests may not be entirely inconsistent with the needs of aid recipients, but at the very least this emphasis raises doubts about both the efficacy of the aid program and Japan's overall international leadership. The shift toward bilateral aid relative to multilateral aid during the 1980s, for example, is entirely consistent with a relatively narrow economic self-interest, since multilateral institutions cannot easily be influenced to dovetail with the interests of the Japanese private sector (except perhaps at the Asian Development Bank, considered later in this chapter).

With a primary emphasis on national commercial interest, broader strategic or political concerns have been relatively weak in the allocation of Japanese foreign aid (except at the request of the United States). However, a number of scholars have argued that the strict commercial orientation was modified during the 1980s as strategic and even some humanitarian concerns came into play.[8] Pakistan, for example, became a major aid recipient after the Soviet invasion of Afghanistan in 1980 (largely at the behest of the United States). Much of the discussion of the new role of strategic or humanitarian aid has concerned which countries were selected to receive money from Japan, rather than the specific nature of the aid programs put in place for those countries. Furthermore, even the country choices have not changed dramatically, with some recipients merely relabeled as strategically important to disguise the continued economic motive in giving them money.[9]

After the 1991 Gulf War, some further movement appeared to take place toward recognizing the desirability of using foreign aid for more overtly international political or strategic purposes. There was a new acknowledgement that foreign aid could contribute to global peace and stability. In April 1991 the government announced four new guiding principles for choosing countries to receive bilateral foreign aid. For the first time, these introduced the concept of conditionality into Japanese foreign aid. Aid was now to be made conditional on the recipient's record of military spending; its involvement in international arms trade (exports and imports); possession or development of nuclear, biological, or chemical weapons; and the degree of progress on democratization and market-oriented economic structures.[10]

The Administrative Reform Council (a private-sector advisory group that has influenced reform of government administration since 1980) endorsed conditionality in two reports issued in 1991.[11] Endorsement by this group provided a stamp of approval from the business community that has benefited from the commercial orientation of aid. Conditionality was attractive because it would provide an alternative to military involvement in political crises such as the 1991 Gulf War.[12] If Japan could claim that its foreign aid program had conditions attached to promote world peace, then the failure to participate in collective military operations would not convey so much of an image of Japanese aloofness from the tough problems of the world. Big business support for conditionality might seem surprising, but it should not. If conditionality reduced foreign criticism of the overall ODA program, then business could continue to benefit, albeit with a risk that some country favored by business might risk losing assistance.

However, what seemed to be a bold new initiative has yet to have much content. The general principles were not accompanied by any uniform standards to guide aid decisions; the government preferred to evaluate each individual case. The critical reason for the lack of real standards was a fear that China and India—both major aid recipients—would run afoul of the new standards. Government officials admitted that if the criteria were pursued strictly, only about four out of the top ten recipients of bilateral aid would meet all of them. One official stated publicly that "we certainly cannot say this [set of criteria] is realistic." Foreign Minister

Taro Nakayama even had to admit before the Diet that China would be officially exempted from application of the new principles.[13]

Given the lack of evidence that these guidelines were really intended to deny foreign aid to some of the more dangerous, ill-intentioned developing nations, the four principles appear to have been aimed at appeasing the United States and other industrial nations for Japan's failure to participate in the Gulf War except to provide money (discussed in chapter 6). As a means of helping to prevent future security crises, foreign aid conditionality was an appealing public relations solution, but it would need some real content and enforcement to be convincing. The first announced application of the guidelines came in fall 1991 with a severing of aid to Haiti (after a coup in September). This was a relatively easy decision to make; Haiti was geographically distant, was unimportant to Japan economically, and had received only small amounts of aid ($3 million to $15 million a year) from Japan in the previous several years. In addition, modest steps short of suspension were taken toward Kenya and Malawi out of concern over human rights violations.[14]

It is extremely difficult to imagine that Japan would seriously threaten one of its top bilateral aid recipients, such as China, with disruption of foreign aid flows because of insufficient progress on reducing international arms sales or improving its record on human rights. A 1992 military coup in Thailand that ousted an elected government brought nothing but assurances that aid would continue without interruption. Assumptions that conditionality would be nothing more than a public relations exercise may have been a factor in the business-sector support expressed through the Administrative Reform Council. One can only hope that the new initiative will gain greater operative content over time; at least a framework of principles now exists for the government to activate when or if it so chooses.

Domestic commentary on the new principles also illustrates some of the problems faced by any group trying to define a more active role in world affairs. Some academics actually criticized the guidelines because Japan, in their view, had no right to impose conditionality on any recipients; this reaction was typical of the postwar fear of exercising any international influence. Others complained that the principles represented a new form of strategic aid that would be subservient to U.S. interests and pressure in international affairs. As naive as some of these reactions may seem, they represented part of a real debate in Japan over the legitimacy of the nation's exercising any political influence in the outside world.[15]

Administering Aid to Benefit Business

Most donor nations have some commercial motives in the design of their foreign aid programs. In the past, tied aid—limited to the purchase of goods and services from the donor country—was the principal means by which donors accomplished this goal. Some aspects of commercialism, such as the extent of tied aid, have diminished in the case of Japan. However, a strong connection continues between the broad commercial interests of Japanese firms and foreign aid policy. This connection is not diminishing noticeably and remains far stronger than is the case in the United States.

Administration of the Japanese foreign aid program is split among three implementing agencies: the Japan International Cooperation Agency (JICA)—the grant agency, the Overseas Economic Cooperation Fund (OECF)—the soft loan agency, and the Export-Import Bank—a hard loan agency. Overseeing these agencies are the Foreign Ministry, the Finance Ministry, the Ministry of International Trade and Industry, and the Economic Planning Agency (EPA). Because there is no strong coordinating body, much is made of the administrative weakness of Japanese foreign aid and the struggles among the major ministries overseeing the operation of these agencies. Despite the struggles, however, some conclusions are possible concerning the overall thrust of foreign aid policy. The Foreign Ministry and JICA might prefer an increasing emphasis on humanitarian or strategic aid, but the locus of power in the allocation process continues to lie with the agencies interested in an emphasis on economic aid that provides a direct commercial benefit to Japan: the OECF and the Exim Bank and MITI, Finance, and the EPA among the oversight ministries. This orientation has not been seriously challenged.

The relative shares of aid disbursed by each agency are an indicator of their relative power in the process. The amount of the grant and technical aid budgets for JICA grew from ¥616 billion ($2.6 billion) in 1985 to ¥746 billion ($5.5 billion) by 1991, an average annual growth of only 3.2 percent in yen terms. At the same time, the total budget for the OECF expanded from ¥685 billion ($2.9 billion) to ¥909 ($6.7 billion), an annual growth of 4.8 percent.[16] JICA and its primary oversight agency, the Foreign Ministry, may have interjected a louder voice in a more liberal, less commercial direction than in the past, and JICA's budget has grown, but its relative financial position has diminished.

The Exim Bank has been the other main growing aid-related agency. Its primary function in the past was trade financing, and its loans have less of a grant element than those of the OECF.[17] Because of its trade-financing focus, only 3 percent of the bank's new lending commitments in fiscal 1984 were in the form of untied direct loans to foreign countries, but this percentage rose temporarily to a peak of 48 percent by 1989 before settling back to 21 percent in fiscal 1990. This represented an increase in loan value from ¥26 billion (approximately $109 million at 1984 exchange rates) to ¥329 billion ($2.3 billion at 1990 exchange rates), a thirteenfold increase in yen terms and an even larger increase in dollar terms because of yen appreciation.[18] This enormous increase in lending is entirely separate from the bank loans allocated for financial support of Japanese firms engaged in direct investment in developing countries; the untied loans are for governments and public corporations in these countries and are mainly for infrastructure projects. Little of this lending activity counts officially as foreign aid because of the limited concessional terms of the loans. Only ¥3 billion ($22 million) of Exim Bank loans to developing countries in 1991 were considered to be part of ODA.[19]

Even though little Exim Bank lending is counted as official foreign aid, this expanded activity must have increased the Exim Bank's relative voice in shaping foreign aid policy and overall economic policy toward developing countries. With an annual commitment of resources greater than $2 billion, the Exim Bank is a sizable new force in the collection of bureaucratic actors formulating those policies (although financially smaller than JICA or the OECF), and its voice clearly falls on the com-mercially oriented side of the equation.

The increasing importance of the OECF and Exim Bank in the foreign aid process implies that the emphasis on commercial benefit for the Jap-anese economy, and on loans as the primary mechanism for disbursing funds, has not been diminishing at all. This runs against the notion of an increasingly strategic-political-humanitarian orientation in Japan's for-eign aid programs. The use of loans in foreign aid also has continued to garner broad domestic support, even from liberals who might be assumed to have a less commercial view of foreign aid. Saburo Okita, the well-known international economist and former foreign minister, strongly endorsed the continued heavy reliance on loans rather than grants.[20] An advisory committee report to the Economic Planning Agency reinforced this point in very strong language, calling for a strengthened focus on "self-help" (the euphemism for loans) in the foreign aid program.[21]

This intellectual position in favor of loans is a central feature of what might be considered a Japanese approach to foreign aid. Charity based on immediate humanitarian concerns has played a far less important role in Japanese society in general than it has in the United States or some other Western nations. But programs to reduce the need for charity in the long run have been important, and the emphasis on repayment as a means of enforcing efficiency or encouraging successful completion of projects is consistent with economic rationality. Foreign aid loans, then, are a means of enforcing a discipline on developing nations consistent with this philosophy.[22] Such hard-nosed concepts give the Japanese government something to bring to the international discussion of the purposes and means of foreign aid. However, yen-denominated loans also provide a convenient way to keep aid money flowing into projects likely to benefit Japanese commercial interests.

The notion that foreign aid—grants or loans—should serve both government and private-sector interests is not controversial in Japan. A major explicit expression of the intention to maintain these purposes of foreign aid was contained in the 1987 New Asian Industries Development Plan (or New AID Plan) announced in Bangkok by then-MITI Minister Hajime Tamura. This plan evolved out of discussions among the OECF, MITI's subsidiary Institute of Developing Economies, and the Japan External Trade Organization (another subsidiary of MITI)—three major agencies with a commercial bent in their approach to foreign aid questions—and without any input from the Foreign Ministry. The plan stated clearly that Japanese bilateral foreign aid should encourage development through private-sector investment and that aid should be used to help individual countries develop appropriate industry choices. The plan called explicitly for Japanese financing (and technology) to develop industry, as well as promotion of Japanese direct investment in Asian countries.[23]

Although this plan was somewhat controversial, its essence appeared subsequently in a variety of forms. At a 1988 meeting between high-level Japanese and Asian government officials and academics, the Japanese presentation stated bluntly: "The public sector will provide loan grants for building up of infrastructure and the private sector will provide direct investment for building facilities." A commentary by a Japanese academic specialist on aid was even more explicit on the connection, arguing that the "easiest way to help other countries create export industries is for Japanese corporations to set up operations in them." The Ministry of Finance certainly concurred, as indicated by the 1991 statement of Tadao Chino, the administrative vice minister for international finance: by transforming foreign aid into "a magnet for private capital . . . Japan will increasingly use its aid . . . as seed money to attract Japanese manufacturers or other industrial concerns with an attractive investment environment." [24]

Even the Foreign Ministry—usually assumed to be at the liberal end of the foreign aid spectrum—espoused the same concept of relying on loans and government-business cooperation. One ministry spokesman has written that "deeply embedded in Japan's philosophy of development is the idea that the public and private sectors must work not as adversaries, but as partners in development." [25] The 1991 Foreign Ministry white paper on aid reinforced these positions, calling for reliance on Exim Bank financing of trade and foreign aid loans to "act as pump priming to ensure a smooth flow of private financing [to less developed countries]." [26] This steady drumbeat of public statements, especially those of the Foreign Ministry, implies in the strongest possible terms that both loans and government-business cooperation will remain at the core of Japanese foreign aid.

Although most of the focus of government-business cooperation involves loans, Japanese technical assistance is suffused with a similar cooperation. As of June 30, 1991, there were 1,540 experts (and 1,939 generalists) dispatched abroad in Japan's technical aid program. [27] In 1990, 235 of the technical experts were people on leave from corporations. "On leave" is the appropriate term; rather than simply being people from the private sector who chose to leave their jobs to become involved in foreign aid work, these people were lent by their corporations and returned to them afterwards. One Nippon Telegraph and Telephone (NTT) employee, for example, worked on communications systems in Kenya as part of a JICA project and then returned to NTT, where he became responsible for sales to developing countries. [28] The number of technicians on leave from corporations was a minority of the total dispatched abroad, but their presence was certainly a sizable one that helped maintain a commercial orientation in foreign aid programs.

The Nature of Commercial Benefit

The main mechanisms by which foreign aid has been connected to commercial interests have shifted over time. Earlier, much of ODA was tied explicitly to purchases of goods from Japan, as was true in other donor countries. After criticism that this approach was overly commercial, the portion of tied aid declined substantially in official statistics. Then criticism mounted that even though the aid was untied, Japanese firms still received an unusually high portion of the contracts or purchases. Such a result was only to be expected, since the initial development, feasibility, and engineering studies for untied projects are done by Japanese consulting firms, which allows them to provide specifications for Japanese equipment.[29]

Once again responding to criticism, the government compiled official statistics showing the share of procurement filled by Japanese products declined—although strong doubts remain as to whether the decline was real or illusory. Many projects that involve "indigenous" contractors are joint ventures effectively controlled by Japanese interests. These ventures' imports of equipment from Japan that are resold to the project count as local procurement.[30] Furthermore, a recent detailed analysis of firms granted procurement contracts under Japanese ODA loan projects shows far fewer foreign firms than indicated by official procurement statistics. In 1990, for example, only 6.5 percent of the value of current contracts went to foreign firms, yet official statistics show 73 percent foreign procurement.[31] Enthusiasm for quelling foreign critics seems to have overcome accuracy in data reporting, and the conclusion stands that project loans are still disbursed in a manner that primarily benefits Japanese firms.

However, the primary issue in the 1990s for the government-business connection was not one of tied aid or even the direct and indirect supply of equipment for the aid projects themselves. Direct investment in low-wage countries, initially motivated by the sharp yen appreciation after 1985 and set to continue as the domestic labor supply shrinks, now provides a strong incentive to use ODA funds. By making direct loans to investing firms and financing infrastructure projects, ODA is now facilitating these investments.

The concept of foreign aid as a catalyst to attract foreign direct investment has considerable appeal. If investment funds, technology, or entrepreneurial and managerial skills are lacking, developing countries should want to attract foreign direct investment as part of their development strategies. Infrastructure in energy, water supply, and transportation is a critical ingredient to attracting such investment, and often developing countries lack the financial or technical capabilities to provide a sufficient base to appeal to foreign corporations.

The Japanese government philosophy moves beyond this straightforward rationale for assisting developing countries to industrialize successfully, however. The key is who gets the contracts for the infrastructure projects and which foreign firms will be attracted to invest once the infrastructure is in place. The close relationship between government and business leads to a natural and strong focus on steering the benefits to Japanese firms. This may still serve the development aspirations of recipient countries, but, at the very least, conflicts of interest may arise between the optimal development strategy for a country and the interests of Japanese corporations.

Early examples of this use of ODA date to the 1970s, when there were concerns about securing raw material supplies and relocating energy-intensive industries. An aluminum plant in Brazil was established in a joint venture by thirty-three Japanese firms under the guidance of the OECF, with financing from twenty-three Japanese banks led by the Exim Bank. This helped to serve the goal of relocating aluminum production offshore under firm Japanese control when energy prices in the late 1970s made primary processing in Japan uneconomical. The OECF also supported, among other projects, a Japanese joint-venture steel plant in Brazil during the 1970s through soft loans of $100 million for related harbor improvements. A project in the early 1980s in Sarawak involved construction of a road ostensibly to benefit the local tribes but actually to serve the interests of a Japanese firm engaged in logging. Another case involved the construction of a large dam in Indonesia along with the largest aluminum smelting plant in Asia to serve as another captive source of aluminum ingots from abroad.[32] Officially, however, aid to Indonesia is considered to be strategic, since it is in proximity to an area of conflict (Indochina).

Such direct connections between foreign aid and firms investing in developing countries expanded in the late 1980s. In 1988 the Japanese government announced a $30 billion long-term recycling program for ASEAN countries. This large sum included private financing, but of the government portion $2 billion was to be in the form of foreign aid channeled through a newly created Japan-ASEAN Investment Company

(JAIC). This organization received funds directly from the OECF to be invested in new joint ventures between Japanese and ASEAN-based firms. In addition, the Exim Bank provided loans to these joint ventures.[33] The result was tight cooperation among the OECF, Exim Bank, and the private sector to promote Japanese direct investment in ASEAN countries.

Other connections are less direct, taking the form of aid-financed infrastructure investments to benefit Japanese manufacturers. Japanese firms wanting to move manufacturing operations abroad for lower labor costs faced inadequate roads, harbors, railroads, electricity supply, water supply, and sewage treatment in developing countries. These firms frequently complained about the poorly developed infrastructure to the host countries. For example, Japanese private-sector firms pressed the Indonesian government in the early 1990s to build more electric power plants and other basic industrial infrastructure.[34] The Japanese government has stepped in to use foreign aid to supply this infrastructure, but in a skewed manner to benefit Japanese firms. Infrastructure projects to enable or promote industrial investment are also a core feature of the lending programs of multilateral institutions and are certainly a necessary part of economic development. However, the Japanese bilateral lending program has a unusually strong emphasis on the benefit to Japanese firms investing in host countries.

An example of the way foreign aid money is used to further Japanese investment interests is the Siracha–Laem Chabang project in Thailand, located on the industrial eastern seaboard—a focal point of Japanese foreign aid to Thailand and an area that had been singled out in the Thai government's five-year economic development plan for the second half of the 1980s. The Japanese government extended loans over 1985–90 of ¥27.2 billion (about $180 million) for an industrial park and harbor facility at Siracha–Laem Chabang. The OECF provided 70 percent of the financing for the initial construction of the port (with the remainder of the money from local sources rather than aid from other countries). A World Bank report estimated that the total infrastructure costs in the region would come to $900 million, with an additional $315 million for industrial parks, housing, and urban services.[35] The money from the Japanese government, therefore, amounted to a significant portion of the investment costs anticipated for the development.

The Siracha–Laem Chabang project included harbor facilities (piers and loading equipment) that will eventually equal the capacity of those in Bangkok, an industrial park, an eleven-kilometer rail spur to serve both the harbor and the park, and new water supply and telecommunications facilities.[36] Not surprisingly, Marubeni Corporation (a large general trading company) and Kamigumi Corporation (the largest Japanese harbor transportation and facilities operator) jointly won the bidding for the lease to operate the initial container wharf in early 1991.[37] Once firms move into the new industrial park, it would be surprising if they were not predominantly Japanese subsidiaries and joint ventures.

A similar industrial park project is beginning in Dalian, China—the location of much Japanese industrial investment before the war, when it was the southern port terminal for the South Manchurian Railway. The initial Japanese expressions of interest concerning the project were made as early as November 1990 (while Japan was officially still refraining from new foreign aid projects as part of its reaction to the Tiananmen massacre). The initiative came from a group of commercial banks and general trading companies and was contingent on cofinancing with concessional loans from the Japanese government.[38] In September 1991 the OECF and twenty-five private-sector firms (trading companies and banks) announced formation of a joint venture with the Dalian city government, in which the Japanese ownership share was 80 percent. In addition to the OECF equity infusion, the project was also scheduled to receive ¥100 billion (approximately $800 million) to finance infrastructure for the park from the multiyear overall ODA loan package to China. As in other cases, location of firms in the industrial park would not be technically restricted to Japanese corporations, but the obvious intent is to build a Japanese-dominated operation—and one newspaper referred to the project as a "Japanese" industrial park.[39]

Private-Sector Initiatives

The Japan International Development Organization (JAIDO) is another recent example of the commonality of purpose and behavior between government and business. Created by Keidanren in the spring of 1989 to promote direct investment in developing countries, this organization was one-third funded by the government's Overseas Economic Cooperation Fund. The initial intent of this new organization was to promote direct investment in developing countries where Japanese private-sector firms were reluctant to invest because of political or economic risks. Subsidization by ODA funds would reduce those risks and thereby bring needed investment to these less successful developing countries, returning them to a path of growth and industrialization. Keidanren also established an internal group, the Committee on International Cooperation Projects, to oversee and approve JAIDO investments in accordance with the liberal-sounding objectives of the organization.[40]

By the end of its first year, JAIDO had approved twenty-nine investments, including creation of three computer software firms in China to develop Japanese-language software, a hotel in Cancun, an automobile assembly plant in Venezuela, and two industrial parks. Another was a Japanese trading company project to set up a pineapple canning factory in the Philippines, with the expectation that the output of canned fruit and juice would supply 10 percent of the Japanese market (as well as third markets).[41] Software in particular represented an extension of domestic industrial policy; long aware of a relative weakness in this industry, MITI had been encouraging the rapid development of a domestically owned software industry (to reduce dependence on American and other foreign software). The investments in China neatly fit this policy thrust.[42] How these investments fit with the announced purpose of JAIDO is difficult to understand. But as a subsidy to further the commercial interests of the private sector or the domestic industrial policy interests of MITI, they are quite easy to understand.

One observer called the creation of JAIDO "another fragmentation of Japanese economic cooperation policy,"[43] because it provided a means for Keidanren to enter explicitly into foreign aid politics. However, within this fragmentation, the significance of JAIDO is that it adds weight to the participants (such as the OECF, the Exim Bank, and the Ministry of Finance) sharing a basic common interest in using foreign aid to further Japanese private-sector commercial interests abroad. At least its role has remained small since its formation in 1989.

Despite the creation of JAIDO, Keidanren continued to press for an even greater consideration of private-sector interests in foreign aid policy. A 1990 position paper called for maintenance of the emphasis on loans, oversight of foreign aid by nongovernment "impartial parties" (a euphemism for business), greater coordination of aid projects for individual countries (such as integrating training programs with infrastructure projects), an end to nonproject aid (such as general balance-of-payments support), and promotion of other mechanisms for strengthening private-sector participation in foreign aid. The report's definition of participation included expanded private-sector access to information collected by aid agencies concerning local conditions and support for more education of private-sector specialists on developing countries. None of these proposals would move Japanese foreign aid in a less directly commercial direction. While the Keidanren report represented a strong business view that did not necessarily translate into actual foreign aid policy, the direction and strength of the pressure from Keidanren remains instructive.

The counterpart of Keidanren in the western part of Japan, known as Kankeiren, has made its own business-oriented proposal. In 1991 this organization issued a position paper calling for expanded use of ODA grant money to train people from developing countries in Japan at Japanese firms for periods up to three years.[44] Even in the United States, the argument is often made that using foreign aid money to educate foreigners in the United States creates a core of people in developing countries who are more likely to be sympathetic with American foreign policy goals or who will choose to work for American-affiliated firms. But these connections are at least indirect, whereas the Kankeiren proposal was an open, direct effort to expand the use of government aid money to subsidize the training costs for employees who will work in local subsidiaries once they return from Japan—or to provide firms with expanded and subsidized access to cheap foreign labor in Japan.

Personnel Issues

One of the laments often voiced in Japan by those reacting defensively to the pattern of commercial orientation described above is the small number of professional foreign aid personnel. In this view, the overall goals of foreign aid are not driven by a commercial intent, but very lean staffing opens the way for the private sector to skew projects in its own favor. In fact, the paucity of personnel is one reason the foreign aid agencies work officially on a request basis—evaluating project proposals from developing countries—rather than developing their own proposals. Japanese corporations often do the actual drafting of these proposals, opening an obvious window of opportunity to skew the program to their own benefit.

In 1990, there were only 1,490 foreign aid–related personnel in Japan, compared with 3,552 in the United States to handle an aid program of comparable size.[45] According to one estimate, the number of personnel in the various aid agencies expanded about 10 percent over the course of the 1980s while the dollar amount of ODA disbursed on an annual basis almost tripled. This estimate may be slightly exaggerated, since the number of personnel at JICA and the OECF, the two primary point agencies, grew from 820 in fiscal 1978 to 1,153 in fiscal 1988—a 41 percent increase.[46] But the point remains: staffing certainly did not keep up with the enormous increase in financial disbursements, and the disbursements per employee are very high.

The argument that foreign aid has been victimized by a lack of personnel is not entirely convincing. Even in the context of Japanese budget politics, which emphasizes maintaining a balance among ministries and agencies (presumably limiting the ability of aid agencies to add personnel if other government agencies cannot),[47] some flexibility was certainly possible. The fact that the bureaucratic process failed to yield a substantial increase in aid personnel as the amounts of ODA funding were growing rapidly implies that increased staffing did not have sufficient support among the concerned parties. This lack of support implies, in turn, that important bureaucratic actors were satisfied with the request-based system that lends itself to manipulation by the Japanese private-sector firms operating in recipient countries. While opposition to this system of dominance by corporate interests certainly exists, it remains weak, and the mainstream philosophy within the government supports the status quo.

This conclusion is reinforced by looking at how the government responded to calls for increased staffing by aid professionals. Rather than encouraging Japanese universities to expand their independent academic programs dealing with developing countries, policy was directed toward establishment of a centralized training center under MITI control. In 1989 MITI proposed establishing a graduate school program under the control of its subsidiary, the Ajia Keizai Kenkyūjo (the Asian Economic Research Institute, known in English as the Institute of Developing Economies, or IDE), to train specialists in developing economies.[48] The new school was the Ajia Keizai Kenkyūjo no Keizai Kaihatsu Sukūru (the IDE Advanced School, or IDEAS), established in 1990 to provide a one-year training program. The faculty for the school was drawn mainly from the government-affiliated IDE staff, with a sprinkling of professors from foreign universities and a prominent foreign academic in Japan, Gregory Clark, appointed as president. Enrollment was very small: approximately fifteen Japanese students and ten foreigners from developing countries.[49]

The Foreign Ministry also wanted to establish a program, and in 1985 called for a new specialized university on development issues. In 1989 the ministry offered a more detailed plan, and in 1990 it received a budget of ¥460 million ($3.2 million) for the Kokusai Kaihatsu Kōtō Kyōiku Kikō (the Foreign Affairs School for International Development, or FASID), which provided short one- to four-week training sessions. Some discussions then took place about combining and expanding the two ministries' programs, but nothing materialized.[50]

MITI's choice of IDE as the venue for specialized education reinforced a primary focus on Asia for Japanese foreign aid programs and created an educational program under direct control of the government. Both the Asia focus and the government control are consistent with previous patterns. Supporting a major expansion of university programs would leave MITI with far less influence on educational content. In particular, the IDEAS program became a mechanism for instilling the philosophy of government-business cooperation, despite the presence of several foreign faculty (who might have a different policy slant on economic development). The presence of Clark as president will not alter this orientation, as he has been a vocal supporter of the efficacy of Japanese industrial policy.

Summary

The forceful manner in which many Japanese government officials and academics have supported the notion of government-business coopera-tion and reliance on soft loans in foreign aid policy seems unlikely to change soon. That guiding principle, broadly defined, must also be rec-ognized as having some validity. If the long-term goal of foreign aid is to promote industrialization, so that recipient nations will not rely perma-nently on the financial generosity of the advanced nations, then a pro-gram designed to supply infrastructure and attract investment from de-veloped countries makes sense. Even an initiative on narcotics announced in 1990 emphasized use of bilateral ODA (rather than interdiction) to help change economic structures in producer nations.[51]

But while the basic philosophical principles have some merit, the ac-tual practice of Japan's foreign aid program detailed above indicates a pattern of active support of the overseas interests of Japanese corpora-tions. Although commercial interest is characteristic of the programs of other major aid donors, including the United States, the extent of the commercial interest in shaping Japan's aid program is pervasive, enduring, and generally nontransparent. Recipient countries certainly benefit from infrastructure development and the resulting inflow of direct investment from Japan, but the fact that bilateral aid subsidizes Japanese corporate competition remains troubling. Large-scale infrastructure programs would be better left to the more neutral multilateral lending institutions.

Participation in Multilateral Organizations

As Japan has become a larger economic presence in the world, one would have expected it to increase participation in the principal economic and political multilateral institutions. Such a trend would be especially natural given the renunciation of military force in the Japanese constitution; these institutions allow the government to become involved in the effort to build international economic and political cooperation and reduce the danger of armed conflict. Despite the seeming rationality of participation or even leadership in these institutions, Japan's record remains mixed. Financial support has increased, which suggests a rising commitment, as does pressure from the Japanese government for increased voting rights in these bodies. However, few Japanese are employed in the major institutions, and in some cases greater financial support has been skewed to maximize control over its use.

Voting Rights

The official voting rights assigned to members of the principal multilateral lending institutions are carefully crafted political compromises and are related to equity contributions. Considering the growing size of its economy and its rapidly rising levels of trade, foreign investment, and foreign aid, the Japanese government pressed for expanded voting rights in the International Monetary Fund (IMF) in the late 1980s and succeeded in obtaining the desired change.

At that time, Japan had a 4.47 percent share of voting rights at the IMF, placing it in fifth place behind the United States (18.9 percent), the United Kingdom (6.55 percent), Germany (5.72 percent), and France (4.75 percent). The change came in 1990, when a general capital increase produced a relative shift in national quotas and voting rights, elevating Japan to share second place with Germany, each having 5.65 percent.[52]

At the World Bank, voting rights have shifted marginally every year based on annual changes in capital subscriptions. During virtually all of the 1980s, Japan ranked number two in voting rights (with a share ranging from just under 6 percent to over 9 percent) behind the United States. But the decade did not bring any sustained increase in Japan's share of votes.[53]

One way to interpret the changes in voting rights at the IMF is that the Japanese government was more interested in playing an active leadership role. At the time of the change in IMF voting rights, one prominent Japanese economist wrote that the change would increase the nation's international political influence, but he also noted that the change "will enable Japan to compete more effectively with major developed nations for a higher status in the international organizations like the IMF."[54] This statement reveals a fundamental problem in the Japanese desire for greater participation in all of the multilateral organizations: status, rather than policy or real participation, has been the core issue. Few guiding principles concerning what policies these organizations ought to pursue lie behind the pressure; it is motivated instead by an abiding sense that national prestige will be enhanced, yielding some psychic value.

The only multilateral institution in which the Japanese government does have a leading role in voting rights has been the Asian Development Bank (ADB). The United States and Japan each have 14.975 percent of the equity shares and 12.388 percent of voting power in the bank.[55] Technically, this means that the two nations have an equal voice in shaping bank policy, but through a variety of financial means described below, Japan actually has the dominant voice at the bank, a situation that was widely recognized from the beginning.

Because the Japanese do not bring any well-defined sense of purpose to their higher financial and voting power in these organizations, a sense of unease persists over yielding them greater political representation. Nevertheless, certain features of a Japanese philosophy or approach to policy seem fairly clear from the bilateral aid programs discussed earlier. With a stronger policy presence, Japan is likely to press for a continued focus on large infrastructure projects and try to skew the behavior of the multilaterals to benefit Japanese corporations investing in developing countries. This is visible at the Asian Development Bank.

Although Japanese firms have not received a majority of ADB contracts, Japan clearly stands out relative to all other countries from which goods and services are procured for ADB projects. In 1990 the cumula-

Table 4-4. *Capital Share of Japan, the United States, and Germany in Multilateral Organizations, 1990*
Percent

Organization	Japan	United States	Germany
Multilateral Investment Guarantee Agency[a]	5.1	20.5	5.1
World Bank[b]	9.0	15.6	7.0
International Development Association[b]	19.2	27.0	11.6
International Finance Corporation[b]	7.4	21.6	6.8
Asian Development Bank[a]	15.0	15.0	4.8
Asian Development Fund[a]	37.0	18.4	6.6
Inter-American Development Bank[a]	1.1	34.7	1.0
African Development Bank[a]	4.9	5.9	3.6
African Development Fund[a]	14.2	13.3	9.1

Source: Ministry of Finance, *Okurashō Kokusai Kin'yūkyoku Nempō, 1991* [Annual Report of the International Finance Bureau] (Tokyo: Kin'yū Zaisei Jijō Kenkyūkai [Financial and Fiscal Research Group], 1992), pp. 490–504.
a. As of December.
b. As of June.

tive procurement from Japan amounted to 18.5 percent, with Indonesia the only other nation exceeding 10 percent and the United States reaching only 7.7 percent. This sort of direct benefit from bank participation has been diminishing, according to official statistics: in 1985 the cumulative share of contracts that went to the Japanese was 27.2 percent.[56] Even this downward trend, though, has been challenged as illusory by non-Japanese ADB staff members, who have contended that a variety of methods exist for Japanese firms to obtain contracts without being counted in the official data.[57] Whether or not these suspicions are correct, the important point is the strong image of a commercial agenda that the Japanese government and business have conveyed to outsiders through Japan's prominent participation in the ADB.

Financial Support

Japan's share in the capital subscriptions of the major multilaterals and some of their special funds is shown in table 4-4. In general, in the early 1990s Japan was in the second or third position as a provider of capital, roughly equivalent to the position of Germany. The United States still was the dominant financial supporter in most cases (except for the Asian Development Bank, as noted above). In many cases Japan had moved into the number two financial position in these organizations by the late 1980s. Because of the sensitive nature of these shares and the voting rights that go with them, it would have been difficult for the

Japanese government to have increased its position unilaterally, although it certainly pressed for the shift into the number two position.

A variety of special funds are also attached to the economic multilaterals, providing a mechanism for nations to contribute additional funds without raising difficult voting right issues. The World Bank has the International Development Association; the Asian Development Bank, the Asian Development Fund; and the African Development Bank, the African Development Fund. These funds are quite sizable; lending from the Asian Development Fund, for example, is as much as one-half the size of loans coming directly from Asian Development Bank accounts.[58] Japanese financial participation in these funds is quite high, since Japan was a new affluent donor in the 1980s, much as some of the Arab oil-producing nations became important donors following the increase in oil prices in 1973. Until the voting right issues could be settled, the special funds enabled Japan to respond to pressures to provide larger sums to the multilateral institutions.

The Asian Development Bank represents the clearest example of active Japanese involvement through special funds. The bank has three special funds: the Asian Development Fund, the Technical Assistance Special Fund, and the Japan Special Fund. By 1990 Japan had given the Asian Development Fund $6.1 billion (versus $1.7 billion from the United States), or 48 percent of the $12.7 billion total. Similarly, Japan provided $47.7 million to the Technical Assistance Special Fund (versus $1.5 million from the United States), or 27 percent of the $176.5 billion total, making it by far the largest single contributor. Finally, the Japan Special Fund was established in March 1988 for technical assistance and (occasionally) equity investments. By the end of 1990 Japan had contributed $156 million to this ongoing fund.[59]

Japan has also become a more important source of commercial borrowing by the multilaterals. As of 1990, 27 percent of outstanding bond issues of the Asian Development Bank were yen-denominated bonds issued in the Tokyo market.[60] Heavy participation in these special funds and in commercial fund-raising activities was related in part to financial recycling plans announced by the government when the nation's current account surplus was very high in the 1980s. For example, of a multiyear $10 billion recycling plan announced in 1986, $2 billion was earmarked for establishment of a Japan Special Fund in the World Bank. In 1987 the next $20 billion recycling plan led to formation of the Japan Special

Fund at the Asian Development Bank and another such fund at the Inter-American Development Bank, plus expansion of the scheme at the World Bank.[61]

When the European Bank for Reconstruction and Development (EBRD) was established in 1991, Minister of Finance Ryutaro Hashimoto announced formation of a Japan-European Cooperation Fund for loans to be awarded through consultation between the government of Japan and the EBRD. However, this fund was expected to provide only ¥850 million in lending for fiscal 1991 (approximately $6.25 million at 1991 exchange rates).[62]

The special funds are not the only mechanism through which Japan has been able to increase its financial participation. To stretch financial resources, the multilateral lending institutions engage in cofinancing, in which the institutions finance only a portion of a project and the rest is provided by other multilateral lending institutions, the bilateral aid programs of individual donor nations, and commercial banks. Cofinancing was quite important for the World Bank over the course of the 1980s: over 50 percent of all projects undertaken received some amount of cofinancing in recent years.[63]

The World Bank has not consistently published figures on the national sources of cofinancing, although in the late 1980s and early 1990s the annual amounts coming from Japan (from the OECF and Exim Bank) were in the range of $1.1 billion to $1.4 billion a year. Without being very specific, World Bank annual reports in recent years have indicated that Japan has been the largest single source of cofinancing.[64] One Japanese press report has put the cumulative share at 55 percent (totaling $10.6 billion) of the funds raised through cofinancing by the bank from 1987 through 1991. No other nation provided more than 6 percent of cofinancing (the United States gave only 5.4 percent).[65]

A similar reliance on Japan as a source of cofinancing funds has emerged at the Asian Development Bank, which has more detailed statistics available. Until the 1980s Japan was a relatively minor participant in this activity at the ADB. Between 1979 and 1981, Japan supplied an average of 21 percent of the ADB's cofinancing but dropped to only 8 percent in 1983–85 (see table 4-5). This ratio then soared to 48 percent over 1988–90. The principal agency for providing the money for Asian Development Bank cofinancing has been the OECF, and the rise came deliberately as a Japanese policy initiative. As put by one author, "Tokyo

Table 4-5. *ADB Cofinancing Provided by Outside Sources, 1979–90*
Millions of dollars unless otherwise indicated

Year	Total	Japan	Japan (percent of total)
1979	446.72	144.00	32
1980	390.83	40.60	10
1981	627.16	125.80	20
1982	n.a.	n.a.	...
1983	308.78	0.00	0
1984	1,162.99	49.30	4
1985	639.98	130.60	20
1986	492.32	23.21	5
1987	498.45	173.90	35
1988	774.18	572.70	74
1989	1,272.80	457.90	36
1990	1,256.55	427.50	34

Source: Asian Development Bank, *Annual Report 1979*, p. 24; *1980*, p. 26; *1981*, p. 27; *1983*, p. 30; *1984*, pp. 116–17; *1985*, p. 121; *1986*, p. 134; *1987*, pp. 142–43; *1988*, p. 158; *1989*, pp. 156–57; and *1990*, pp. 170–71.
n.a. Not available.

has repeatedly requested that the World Bank, ADB, AFDB, and IDB act as cofinancing, joint financing, or parallel financing institutions, together with Japan's public-and private-sector partners."[66]

The willingness or desire of the Japanese government to provide substantial funds through special funds and cofinancing arrangements can be interpreted in diametrically opposite ways. The Japanese government portrays this activity as a commitment to the goals of economic development and solution of the troubling third world debt problems of the 1980s. However, these same initiatives also represent a means to gain an increased voice in the lending agenda of multilateral institutions outside the carefully crafted voting rights structure. Cofinancing involves bilateral negotiation between the multilateral agency and the national donor, providing substantial opportunities to exercise influence in shaping the nature of the project involved. Motivation to provide the money would appear to be a mixture of these two elements: some genuine focus on world problems, and a strong interest in exercising some influence over the lending programs of the multilaterals for more traditional commercial purposes.

Personnel Involvement

Irrespective of voting rights, a permanent seat on the United Nations Security Council, or even financial contributions, involvement in the daily decisionmaking process in multilateral organizations requires a human presence. A large personnel presence would be a measure of both the Japanese desire to become involved in a multilateral approach to world problems and an ability to exercise real power or leadership in that process. The Japanese public certainly believes in the importance of organizations such as the United Nations; in a poll by the government in October 1990, 62 percent of respondents said that Japan should make its contribution to international peace and security through the United Nations.[67]

The actual level of Japanese involvement, however, is quite low. In the late 1980s, one author counted only 952 Japanese staff members at all multilateral institutions combined, representing only 1.2 percent of the total number of staff on their payrolls.[68] The World Bank does not officially report the nationality of its staff, but according to one Japanese newspaper the bank had only 86 Japanese nationals in 1991, or only 1.3 percent of the total staff of some 6,700. Other sources report that at the World Bank and International Development Association, Japanese employment was only 1.2 percent in the late 1980s, while at the IMF it was 1.3 percent (25 people) and at the International Finance Corporation, only 0.8 percent. Of the 27 IMF officers (managing directors, counsellors, and directors of the various departments), there was not a single Japanese name in 1990.[69]

The same picture applies to the United Nations. In 1990 Japan had fewer staff than most other major industrial nations and about half as many as the People's Republic of China, a nation that was excluded from the United Nations from 1949 until the 1970s (see table 4-6). Even tiny Switzerland had more than Japan, indicating the level of participation that is possible when a nation places the United Nations in the forefront of its foreign policy efforts. Among professionals, Japan still had only about one-half the number from China, and was well behind the United Kingdom, France, and West Germany. Japan did somewhat better in a comparison of the number of people at the director level.

The only organization with a strong Japanese personnel presence is the Asian Development Bank. Japan has had the presidency of the bank since its creation in 1966—in sharp contrast to the Inter-American Development Bank or the other regional banks, where the presidency rotates among developing country members. The presidency choice may have been made in compensation for the permanent American presidency at the World Bank and the European rotation for the presidency of the

Table 4-6. *Staffing at the United Nations, Selected Countries, 1990*

Country	Total	Under secretary general	Assistant secretary general	Director	Professional
China	267	1	0	10	171
France	852	1	1	19	235
Italy	177	0	1	9	55
Japan	131	1	1	15	96
Norway	44	0	1	1	18
Spain	174	0	0	7	65
Sweden	97	2	2	6	34
Switzerland	206	0	0	2	25
United Kingdom	540	2	0	19	166
United States	1,546	1	1	53	460
West Germany	175	1	0	9	122

Source: United Nations, *List of the Staff of the United Nations Secretariat: As of June 30, 1990, Report of the Secretary-General* (September 1990).

IMF. In 1990 ten out of eighty-eight top management slots (manager and above) were filled by Japanese nationals.[70] Higher personnel participation in the Asian Development Bank is consistent with the other aspects of this bank discussed earlier—the higher financial support and leading voting position, as well as a heavy presence in special funds and cofinancing.

Because of political sensitivities, all the multilateral organizations have at least informal quotas on how many nationals they will accept from any single country. But the Japanese are far from pressing against such constraints. In 1991 the Japanese press claimed that the ratio of actual employment of Japanese to the announced appropriate level at the United Nations was only 49 percent. This compared with 100 percent or above for the United States, the then Soviet Union, Great Britain, and France.[71] The World Bank director of personnel has given speeches in Tokyo pleading that more Japanese come to work at the bank, bringing with them their training and expertise. Another senior World Bank official has written: "Japan is one of the most effectively managed economies in the world. Its limited involvement in the staffing of the international institutions means that little of that experience influences their operation. This is difficult to understand in Japan and deprives developing countries of valid choices of strategies."[72]

If the problem is not quotas, why are so few Japanese in these organizations? The answer lies in the insular nature of postwar Japanese society, explored in the previous chapter. Since until recently few people traveled or lived abroad, the pool of people with international experience, interest, or strong language skills who might be naturally attracted to such employment on their own was extremely limited. For entrants to the labor force, there was almost no interest in a career in a foreign country at a multilateral organization; the isolated nature of society encouraged sticking to mainstream domestic alternatives. While these statements may be broadly true of all nations, a domestic orientation has been unusually powerful in Japan. For those few who did have international interests or strong foreign language skills, the Japanese private sector (principally the trading companies handling a large share of exports and imports) was the desirable career path. This suggests that the government perceived the actual allocation of these people as appropriate; the private-sector trading companies and major manufacturers represented the economically efficient location for this scarce human resource during the years of high economic growth and expanded international trade.

In lieu of a pool of individuals seeking employment at multilateral institutions on their own, Japanese personnel at these organizations are primarily government officials detailed from Tokyo for periods of several years. All governments engage in this practice, but it appears more prominent in the case of Japan. Those loaned to multilateral organizations have found themselves in a distant foreign setting that offered absolutely no career advantages. Government officials serve under lifetime employment arrangements. Continuing signals about career advancement are carefully watched—and a posting to the World Bank or some similar institution has not been a desirable move.[73] Therefore the government has even had difficulty designating its own officials to take such posts.

Because of yen appreciation after 1985, some argue that the problem is that Japanese officials are unwilling to accept the lower salaries at multilateral institutions.[74] But this complaint only underscores more fundamental underlying problems. If the government were truly concerned about participation, it could subsidize salaries or provide other compensation for those loaned to multilateral institutions. Nor does the salary question explain the limited number of new entrants to the labor force seeking permanent careers in such organizations, who presumably would be less moved by salary comparisons. The government also did little to encourage individuals to enter career positions in the multilateral institutions. Keeping personnel limited largely to loaned government officials is also consistent with the elitist nature of the Japanese government and its interaction with these international agencies: it gave the government a larger role in overseeing the behavior of Japanese working in these organizations. Even with the limited pool of people with international interests, experience, or skills in the past, it is difficult to believe that a larger personnel presence could not have emerged had the government desired and promoted such employment.

The recent changes detailed in previous chapters should have some favorable effects on the low level of personnel participation. Rapid increases in the numbers of children who have lived abroad should expand the pool of those seeking nontraditional international careers when they complete their education. Furthermore, the global reach of investment ought to increase the career value to government officials of a temporary posting at one of the multilaterals, although this may be true more at the small, elite IMF than at the far larger World Bank.

Women may provide a rich source of talent as these changes emerge. The major multilateral organizations are oriented toward nonmilitary, humanitarian interaction, values that may appeal to Japanese women for a career environment. Furthermore, women are more likely than men to become disenchanted with the employment opportunities and role models available to them within Japanese society after having spent time living or traveling abroad and thus more willing to enter nontraditional employment.[75] The precursor to such a trend may already be appearing. A 1989 survey of Japanese nongovernmental organizations (NGOs)— private organizations involved in international charity, health, and development—indicated that far more women than men worked in a sample of fifty-four organizations.[76]

As an example of the sort of role Japanese women could play in international organizations, Sadako Ogata, a professor at Jochi (Sophia) University, was appointed UN High Commissioner for Refugees (UNHCR) in 1990. Ogata is a highly qualified and well-respected academic and diplomat involved with international issues. An illustration of the liberalizing effects of foreign experience, she lived in both China and the United States before World War II (her father was a Foreign Ministry diplomat) and then received a graduate degree in the United States after the war. She had also held previous posts at the United Nations, including the first Japanese woman representative to the UN, the Japanese representative to the Human Rights Committee, and chair of the board of UNICEF.[77]

The fact that this remarkable woman received a great deal of attention and respect in her important and difficult position (dealing with refugee problems stemming from the 1991 Gulf War, the repatriation of Cambodian refugees in 1992, and the civil war in the former Yugoslavia) may provide a stronger role model for other Japanese women and encourage them to seek similar international careers. She certainly has sent a strong public message in that direction, saying that it "is my desire that the Japan of the future change from an economic superpower to a humanitarian superpower." Sadly, the agency over which Ogata presided had few Japanese staff members—fewer than 30 employees out of 2,000.[78]

A limited personnel presence does not necessarily imply an equally limited role in formulating the policies of organizations if those who are involved are in significant roles and exercise vigorous leadership. But this does not characterize many Japanese roles in multilateral organizations. The World Health Organization (WHO) is almost the only other international organization other than the UNHCR to be headed recently by a Japanese national (Hiroshi Nakajima). But his tenure has been controversial enough that his reelection in 1992 was actively (though unsuccessfully) opposed by the United States and some other major governments.[79] The only other post of significance filled by a Japanese national that stirred public interest was the appointment of Makoto Taniguchi as deputy secretary general at the OECD—the first Japanese to hold such a high post (made possible by expanding the number of deputy directors from two to three). Like Ogata, he came from a career of international posts (mainly through the UN) and appeared to be using his appointment as a platform to convey the message to the Japanese public that greater human participation in international organizations was desirable and necessary.[80]

A distinctive Japanese policy voice finally began to appear at the World Bank in 1992, arguing that the American insistence on free-market reforms in recipient countries was excessive and that the role of government in developing countries should be viewed more favorably.[81] This position was consistent with the nature of Japanese economic development and the philosophy of Japanese bilateral aid policy, but created some controversy among the staff and other donors to the bank. The result was to launch a major study of the development experience of high-growth East Asian nations, with Japanese government funding, to investigate whether the Japanese position on the role of government in successful industrialization could be validated. Whether or not such initiatives are uncomfortable for Americans and other nations, they do represent the beginnings of a more active voice that has been absent in the past.

At the United Nations, the Japanese government could have made an active commitment to play a stronger role many years ago, given the frequent statements about placing the UN at the core of Japanese foreign policy. Occasionally, but not frequently, it has actually played something akin to a leadership role. In 1985 Foreign Minister Shintaro Abe pressed for a UN reform commission that eventually led to structural changes that enabled the United States to moderate the hard-line opposition adopted by the Reagan administration and to resume payment of its financial obligations.[82] Selection of Yasushi Akashi to head the UN peacekeeping operation in Cambodia in 1992 provided another step toward greater involvement, and his choice fed into domestic political efforts that ultimately resulted in dispatch of Self Defense Force soldiers to participate in the nonmilitary aspects of that operation. Japan also demonstrated some movement toward formulating an independent foreign policy: its votes in the General Assembly diverged from those of the United States more frequently in the 1980s than earlier and more frequently than several of the European countries'.

Although there have been a few signs of more independent and active engagement in the United Nations, the conclusion must remain that Japan was less engaged in the 1980s and early 1990s than one would expect. The United Nations would be a natural forum in which to exercise a larger role. Rather than focusing on the real exercise of leadership or on increasing its personnel presence, the Japanese government chose to focus on the symbolic issue of a permanent seat on the Security Council. Aside from the fact that this desire was struck a serious blow by the government's behavior during the 1990–91 Gulf crisis (considered in chapter 6), opening the question of a permanent seat for Japan would involve an extremely complex set of issues, including revision of the UN charter and the possibility of permanent seats for other potential claimants (including Germany, India, and Brazil). If a larger and more effective role for the Japanese government were to be impeded by stubbornly pursuing this symbolic goal in the 1990s, the result would be an unfortunate loss of meaningful input.

The problem of lack of participation is also evident in less formal policy discussions. Japanese economists are now regularly involved in international discussions and conferences on international finance and other economic issues. However, other policy areas still seem underrepresented. For example, no Japanese participated in a 1992 international conference on humanitarian action that brought together individuals from major humanitarian organizations, academics, and government officials from a number of countries.[83]

The International Extension of Administrative Guidance

Government-business relations within Japan have been characterized by strong informal communications channels. Government can often influence private-sector actions through informal guidelines, advice, or threats that are not visible to the public or within the formal legal framework. *Administrative guidance* is the name given to this informal interaction with the private sector, although the relationships between government and business are often so subtle and private that it is unclear whether the government is guiding industry or industry is guiding government policy (to ratify business initiatives). Whatever the direction of influence, the overall framework of close relations between government and business is a central feature of the domestic political economy.

Faced with the rapidly expanding foreign investment presence of Japanese firms, the government—specifically MITI—moved to establish mechanisms for extending administrative guidance abroad in a wide variety of issue areas. Some of this was apparent in the discussion in the previous chapter concerning the reaction of the government to investment "friction" and resultant efforts to guide Japanese firms toward charitable efforts abroad to reduce such tensions. The overall picture emerging from some of the announcements in the early 1990s is that the nature of administrative guidance on foreign activities has not been not much different from what it was domestically. Rather than relying on individual corporate discretion, local governments, or international rules to guide overseas corporate behavior, the government has extended its policy reach toward the corporate sector into the international arena. Unlike the highly visible, legalistic approach the U.S. government has taken to accomplish the same goals—such as the Foreign Corrupt Practices Act—administrative guidance generally operates quietly and out of public view with little specific legal authorization.

Japanese government officials stationed at embassies and consular offices have always had as a major portion of their work interaction with the local subsidiaries of Japanese business. Officials attend meetings of the local Japanese commerce associations, and Foreign Ministry control over Japanese-language schools for expatriate children provides a mechanism for keeping in touch with the Japanese business presence. However, recently the mechanisms for interaction have taken a more formal turn.

MITI announced in fall 1990 that it would establish local organizations of Japanese firms in a number of Asian countries to meet periodically with MITI personnel stationed at the embassies and consular offices. The announcement was part of what MITI termed specifically "local guidance," a clear statement of intent to extend administrative guidance to an overseas setting. The first of these groups was formed in summer 1990 in Bangkok, followed by similar ones in other Asian countries in 1991.[84]

Late in 1990 MITI also announced formation of a new organization including government and private-sector firms and specifically aimed at resort-related firms. This new organization would issue guidelines to reduce "trouble" when Japanese firms develop resorts abroad (with Hawaii considered a principal target).[85] When this is added to the other signals discussed in chapter 3—such as promotion of corporate charity— the obvious conclusion is that MITI was unwilling to leave the behavior of Japanese firms abroad entirely to the private sector and saw an opportunity to extend or maintain its bureaucratic role.

Even the decision over where and how much to invest overseas was beginning to attract more attention by the government. In spring 1992 MITI announced formation of a study group with major consumer electronics firms to discuss guidelines concerning which products to shift to overseas production. In this case the motive was not to assist firms in cutting costs or dealing with host country problems, but to hold down the export from Japan of politically sensitive products to major markets (such as the United States) by relocating production outside of Japan.[86] As usual in such cases, the extent to which the government actually influences the overseas investment choices of these large firms will be unclear, but the format of industry and government engaging in discussion and sharing extensive information is a familiar one, and the outcomes will certainly be influenced in communal ways that are different from the individual choice model of American business.

One of the innovations in administrative guidance has been to provide advice or guidance to foreign countries themselves, principally in Asia. In 1990 MITI announced that it would give advice to Asian countries on how to set up "techno parks" (similar to the "technopolis" program in Japan) to act as centers for high-technology firms and industrial research activity. This advice, of course, would provide a more favorable setting for attracting Japanese private-sector firms.[87] MITI officials have also drawn up forecasts or plans for the regional distribution and development of manufacturing across Asia that sound similar in concept to the MITI "visions" at home.[88] Whether Asian countries would welcome such a role was another matter entirely, but the impulse to organize and plan on a regionwide basis was certainly present and likely to grow.

The government also announced in 1992 that it would establish an employment program to help place Asian students studying in Japan with Japanese corporations. One of the presumed foreign policy benefits from the education of foreigners is the creation of a pool of people who will be more favorably disposed toward the country in which they are educated; this belief was certainly an important cause of American enthusiasm and government programs for educating foreigners in the United States during the cold war. Some of those people educated in the United States who returned to their own countries undoubtedly found employment with local subsidiaries of American firms, but that process was left to the private market. The Japanese government was less inclined to leave such potential connections to the vagaries of the market and announced the formation of a government-private cooperative organization to place foreign students in Japan in touch with companies looking for employees for their overseas operations.[89]

Even the activities of nongovernmental organizations involved in international development or charity work became subject to the organizing impulse of the government. Private organizations involved in third world development work have been relatively small and few in number in Japan; even with a boom in the late 1980s, only about 200 small groups were in existence in 1991. But to promote their activities, and to provide a conduit through which to oversee or influence their activities, in 1987 the government established the NGO Katsudō Suishin Sentā (NGO Movement Promotion Center). Even the autonomy of the groups is questionable, since 37 percent of the total funds expended by NGOs in 1988 came as subsidies from the government, limiting their independence.[90] The motive involved—government promotion of NGOs in a society largely unfamiliar with them—was laudable, but the opportunity was there for manipulation or influence.

Running through all of these examples is an overriding principle: the international behavior of Japanese individuals and organizations should not be allowed to proceed in an independent environment. The government identifies for itself a legitimate role in guiding and organizing these activities. Sometimes the motives may be admirable, such as preventing excesses in environmental degradation. But just as often the result is to stifle independent voices, such as those that might criticize the continued commercial orientation of foreign policy or environmental policy (considered below).

At one time scholars argued that the wave of international investment by Japanese firms would weaken administrative guidance, because the firms operating overseas would be beyond the reach of the government. But this has not been the case, as the government has endeavored to transfer domestic modes of interaction to an international setting. Private-sector organizations do not have the degree of autonomy—for better or for worse—possessed by most American organizations. On some issues, and at some times, the government will significantly influence the overseas behavior of Japanese organizations, or at least create a communal setting in which the government will participate in a cooperative policy-setting process. Since administrative guidance and the other mechanisms to bring about cooperative or collective actions are so prominent in domestic government-business interaction, their international extension should be no surprise. This behavior, however, presents other nations with the disquieting image of the Japanese government interacting with its private sector within their own borders in quiet, informal ways. No matter how irreproachable the motives may be, the image is not one to engender receptivity toward a more active Japanese role in global affairs.

International Environmental Policy

The rapidly emerging international focus on environmental issues provided a new opportunity to the Japanese government to become actively engaged in a global setting. These issues presented the nation with a nonmilitary arena in which it could play a positive role and thereby enhance its international prestige, accomplish some needed changes in global affairs, and indirectly enhance its own economic security by building a better relationship with developing countries. For the first time, the government was actually moving forward to play a more active role in the late 1980s and early 1990s. But the picture remained somewhat mixed, and it is still unclear exactly how aggressive the government is capable of being in pressing international environmental issues.

Initially, interest in international environmental issues appeared to center in the Foreign Ministry, with its broader and somewhat less commercial view of international affairs, while MITI and the business community remained highly skeptical. By the early 1990s, though, MITI had not only joined the effort but appeared to have emerged as the leading bureaucratic actor in shaping the government's approach to these issues.[91]

Behind the Japanese confidence in playing an active international role was a belief that the nation managed its domestic environmental problems in an exemplary fashion in the 1970s, giving it a record of successful policy accomplishment that could be projected internationally. The domestic record does show considerable success in areas where an opportunity existed for industry to develop new products or processes to be sold (such as pollution control equipment or more energy-efficient consumer appliances). The record on conservation issues, however, has not been very good; society provided less support for attacking issues related to the preservation of nature, either for aesthetic reasons or for the saving of endangered species.[92] Indices on air pollution, though, show Japan in quite a favorable light, with emissions of carbon dioxide, nitrogen oxides, and sulfur oxides all much lower in Japan than in the United States when measured in terms of absolute tons of annual emissions, as a ratio to total economic activity (GDP), or per person.[93]

The record on pollution control should not be accepted uncritically, however. Business pressures in the 1980s were able to roll back some of the measures put in place during the environmentally active years of the early 1970s. In a law designating victims of pollution, corporate interests managed to force a change to prohibit any new additions to the list of recognized victims, arguing that the problems had been solved to an extent that people were no longer in danger of debilitating exposure to pollutants.[94] Indices of emissions for some pollutants also show that the considerable improvement in the 1970s was followed by stagnation or deterioration during the later 1980s; carbon dioxide and carbon monoxide emissions, for example, declined until 1985 but then began to climb slowly.[95] Continued economic growth, falling petroleum prices, larger cars, and perhaps lax enforcement began to overwhelm the gains of the 1970s and elicited no new wave of domestic policy change until the 1990 international agreement on carbon dioxide emissions.

The dynamics of domestic decisionmaking implied great difficulty in dealing with preservation issues because of the strong consideration given to interests of adversely affected groups (such as fishermen or the lumber industry). The Japanese government record on international conservation issues is not an admirable one. The government very reluctantly agreed in the mid-1980s to an international ban on whaling, but immediately announced a "research" program that involved catching minke and sperm whales (including, for the sake of "efficiency," sale of whale meat once the whales were "studied"). In 1988 the Fishery Agency of the Agriculture Ministry actually announced that its research effort was such a success that it would be expanded (to 875 whales). Even in 1992, "research" whaling continued, and when the French government proposed to the International Whaling Commission a permanent ban on whaling in the Antarctic region, the Japanese Minister of Agriculture and Fisheries provocatively and ostentatiously objected by attending a whale meat festival in Tokyo (along with other politicians and government officials) and eating whale meat from the "research" catch.[96]

Whatever the scientific merits of a ban on whaling might be, the way the government dealt with the emerging international majority position was unproductive. Rather than choosing either open rejection or compliance, it endeavored to appear compliant while continuing to violate the spirit of the agreements. The widespread visibility of whaling issues meant that the government damaged its international political reputation, perpetuating an image of supporting commercial interests damaging to the environment.

The government may have been correct in believing that conservation issues such as whaling were being pushed too far in the absence of clear scientific data. Government officials felt their nation was being singled out unfairly on these conservation issues, with one Foreign Ministry official saying cynically in 1991 that international environmental groups needed enemies (such as Japan) to attack in order to attract attention and money.[97] However, the same lack of overwhelming scientific evidence characterized the issue of global warming, which the Japanese government embraced rather quickly. The critical difference between whaling and global warming was the potential for commercial gain in the latter case (from export of new technologies and products), a distinction that supports the conclusion of policies driven to a large extent by underlying commercial interests.

Similar defensive and obstructive approaches characterized the Japanese government response to other conservation issues. In 1989 the government agreed to limit use of huge drift nets (which kill ocean life other than the fish that are the target) only under heavy pressure from other countries, and then in 1991 finally prohibited their use under continued pressure.[98] Efforts to improve the nation's image, such as a 1990 agreement by a Japanese trading company to replant parts of the rain forest in Sarawak, appeared to be more public relations than substantive change in policy. Nissho Iwai and Mitsubishi Corporation, two large trading companies, also agreed to engage in similar reforestation efforts for Brazilian rain forests.[99] These efforts cannot be entirely discounted, but their real contribution to dealing with deforestation issues will be limited, and the image remains strong of Japan as yielding on conservation issues only under heavy international criticism.

Government International Initiatives

Despite such blemishes, Japan's record on domestic air and water pollution control was strong enough in comparison with other countries to build a sense of confidence in taking a more active role in these particular aspects of international environmental policy. Efforts to define this role began around 1988, when a spokesman for the Environmental Agency advanced the notion that the government could play a role in assisting developing countries with their environmental problems and complained of the lack of any long-term strategy in the government to do so.[100] What he suggested came very close to what Japan was actually doing by 1991: inclusion of environmental concerns in foreign aid policy; guidelines for Japanese corporations operating abroad; and promotion of contacts between environmental specialists in Japan and developing countries.

The issue took a more formal turn when Prime Minister Noboru Takeshita pressed a "save the earth" slogan, reflecting Foreign Ministry efforts to define an international issue on which Japan could take a higher-profile position. As part of this initiative, the government hosted an international meeting in September 1989 on global environmental issues. Another meeting for legislators from foreign countries took place in Japan in 1989.[101] The meetings may not have been highly productive in yielding international agreements, but their main purpose was to identify Japan as an organizer with progressive ideas concerning environmental issues.

Foreign aid quickly became a central part of emerging environmental policy. The Overseas Economic Cooperation Fund announced as early as 1989 that it was adopting a set of guidelines for concessional lending that would help protect the environment in developing countries. The new rules affected lending in sixteen project categories such as railroads and port facilities.[102] The Japanese government then committed itself at the annual industrial-nation economic summit meeting in 1989 to a three-year, ¥300 billion ($2.2 billion) environmental foreign aid program (although the definition of what constituted environmental aid was stretched very far by the government).[103] At the same summit meeting the following year (the Houston summit), the government publicized its domestic record on the environment and announced $25 million in technical assistance to Eastern Europe for environmental purposes.[104] In the five years from 1985 through 1990, the amount of ODA declared to be allocated to environmental problems quintupled from ¥33 billion to ¥165 billion (over $1 billion), amounting to more than 10 percent of total ODA disbursements—although these figures should be viewed with considerable skepticism since they were compiled by zealous officials desiring to include any projects with even a faint connection to environmental purposes.[105]

In 1991 MITI began using administrative guidance to convince Japanese firms to abide by the same pollution control guidelines abroad that they would be required to follow at home, as a measure to forestall criticism that firms were moving to developing countries to circumvent domestic controls.[106] Business pressure, however, managed to defeat a MITI effort to back this informal guidance with legislative teeth.

Critical to success in taking a strong international position was an ability to build a broad consensus among different government agencies, as well as between government and the private sector. Initially, Japanese business and MITI had been skeptical of these efforts to place the nation in the forefront of global warming issues.[107] Given the common perception that environmental controls harm economic growth, such opposition was fairly natural and not any different from the conservative stance of the Bush administration in the United States.[108] However, this situation changed quickly; business began portraying itself as cooperating with international environmental initiatives, and the economic agencies in government began to formulate progressive international policies. The change for MITI was rather obviously related to the emerging perception that international proposals for combating atmospheric warming would involve heavy reliance on new technologies and capital equipment, opening major opportunities for Japanese firms to develop and export new products to the world. Furthermore, environmental controls applied globally would impose comparable production costs on developing countries that were rapidly becoming competitors for Japanese products in global markets. Acceding to developing countries' demands that the advanced industrial nations shoulder much of their financial burden for pollution control also fit long-standing policies of keeping these countries satisfied so as to ensure uninterrupted supplies of raw materials and a continued welcome for private-sector direct investment.

The fact that MITI quickly recognized the potential for a convenient conjunction of international environmental policy and more narrow national commercial interests is not surprising (and why the Bush administration was unable to reach some similar conclusions remains a puzzle). A number of interesting and significant technological advances had already been made in Japan or were under development at the beginning of the 1990s. These included internationally recognized progress on fuel cell technology, selective catalytic reduction for electric power plants, fluidized bed combustion, coal liquefaction, combined cycle power plants, nuclear power, automobile efficiency, and solar photovoltaic cells.[109] In many of these technologies, the Japanese government was actively involved with funds and administrative guidance, exercised mainly through a set of quasi-governmental organizations that originated in the 1970s, including the New Energy Development Organization and the Electric Power Development Corporation. It was not difficult to see the opportunity to promote rapid expansion of exports of manufactured products embodying these technologies in the event of international agreements on carbon dioxide and other air pollutants.

After its conversion to supporting policies to arrest global warming, MITI acted quickly to gain dominance of the intragovernmental policy discussion. By spring 1990 the ministry had written a one-hundred-year plan for reduction of global carbon dioxide emissions, in time for presentation at a White House conference on the global environment.[110] This plan was very short on specifics and relied rather heavily in the first thirty to forty years on increased use of nuclear power plants—hardly a noncontroversial approach, but at least an original offering. In fall 1990 the government signed an international agreement pledging to reduce the nation's own carbon dioxide emissions, and MITI moved to put some content into the commitment. Almost simultaneously, the electric power industry—which historically has been extremely close to government even though the power companies are private-sector firms—announced preliminary thoughts on how to meet the new commitments on carbon dioxide emissions.[111]

The Private Sector Joins In

On the business side, the same realization of positive benefit from pushing an active response to atmospheric warming came fairly quickly as well. Keidanren established several industry study groups in August

1989 (steel, chemicals, and automobiles) to explore ways to minimize the amount of added investment that would be necessary to meet new international commitments on carbon dioxide emissions, to transfer environmental technology to third world countries, and to lobby the government against imposing overly stringent regulations.[112] The third point might be the most important; recognizing that the government was determined to play a more active role in international policymaking on these issues, industry perceived that its own interests were best served by being both cooperative and engaged in the process to prevent outcomes that it would find onerous.

The private sector also made several public relations moves to build a positive environmental image. JUSCO (a large retail chain that was quite active in other Asian countries) and its related firms petitioned the Environmental Agency in 1990 to set up an environmental foundation to which they would donate 1 percent of their pretax profits. Companies also rushed to issue "environmental credit cards" with a portion of the profits donated to various environmental causes.[113] These and similar efforts by Japanese corporations certainly contained an element of real content, but their main purpose was public relations, and they parallel somewhat similar efforts by American firms to improve their environmental reputations.

Developing a leadership position also involved close interaction between the government and the private sector, as is typical in many successful domestic policy initiatives. The desire to develop consultative mechanisms emerged in the approach to the 1992 UN environmental summit meeting in Rio. A year earlier, in May 1991, an umbrella committee including Diet members, industry groups, environmental groups, and academics was inaugurated in Tokyo, called the Japan Committee for Global Environment (Chikyū Kankyō Nihon Iinkai). This group included environmentally active organizations such as the Japan chapter of the World Wildlife Fund, but because the appointed chairman was Gaishi Hiraiwa, chairman of Keidanren, it was quite clear that business would have the dominant voice.[114] By including environmental groups, this mechanism acted to diminish their role as critics of the government or industry and their ability to embarrass the government at the environmental summit meeting. In the end, this strategy did not work perfectly, since some independent environmental groups did get to the Rio meeting, and their criticisms of Japan's environmental policies surfaced in both the Japanese media and the Western press.[115]

As commercial and self-serving as the eventual proposals from such confining cooperative mechanisms might be, the Japanese government was able to put forth proposals that its private sector accepted. Some of the proposals—such as an environmental tax to be levied on carbon dioxide emissions—were fairly innovative.[116] Although this was unlikely to become reality in Japan, it received real consideration.

The U.S. government, in contrast, remained far behind at the time of the Rio summit, hung up on the empirical question of whether atmospheric warming existed and espousing the view that environmental protection would be harmful to economic growth. These positions were consistent with the generally conservative approach of the Bush administration on many economic issues, and the 1993 advent of the Clinton administration brought important policy changes on environmental problems. However, during the Bush years, the contrast was sharp. For Japan, determination to carve out a leadership role and to promote its national interests in the process resulted in very little interest in finding empirical proof of global warming. The result was an ironic role reversal: the Japanese government was able to take a visible position and exercise some international leadership on this issue, while the United States (at least temporarily) lagged behind and presented an obstructionist, selfish image.[117]

The Rio summit may have demonstrated a successful Japanese policy thrust, but it also indicated the inexperience of the Japanese government in international politics. This meeting was billed as a summit meeting, with the leaders of industrial nations giving highly visible speeches. Even President Bush—after opposing much of what the meeting was originally intended to accomplish—attended and gave a credible presentation defending his government's position. Of all the major leaders, the only one who failed to attend was Prime Minister Kiichi Miyazawa. He stayed at home to oversee final passage of the bill authorizing participation in UN peacekeeping operations (considered in chapter 6), even though the debate was over and only the final, mechanical votes remained in the Diet. At that point the outcome was certain, and his presence was no longer needed to further the process. The prime minister thereby missed an opportunity to speak out on a visible world stage and to place his nation clearly at the center of the action.

Regional Actions

Although the political leadership may have muffed a chance to create greater global visibility, real action was proceeding on a regional basis. By 1991 international proposals began to take definite shape and were the most definite for Asia. In July 1991 the Environmental Agency announced that it had developed a basic ten-year strategic framework to deal with Asian atmospheric warming. A month later, the same agency announced it would engage in a survey concerning transfer of pollution control technology to China and two other countries.[118] Because of China's heavy use of high-sulfur coal in electric power plants, scrubbers to remove sulfur dioxide emissions were a central part of the proposals. Malaysia and Thailand were picked soon after as the other two recipients, and a modest budget of ¥6.5 billion (approximately $48 million) was set for the initial year. Government officials from Asian countries were brought to Tokyo by the Environmental Agency for a meeting to discuss regional atmospheric warming and the proposed Japanese initiatives.[119] These were initiatives set to proceed regardless of what would happen through the broader context of the UN environmental summit in Rio in June 1992.

The nature of the Japanese approach to Asia seems quite clear. Foreign aid money will be used to provide pollution control equipment manufactured in Japan to these countries. In the longer run, containing atmospheric warming in Asia will generate considerable business for Japanese firms. Such a trend is consistent with the generally commercial bent of foreign aid policy discussed earlier. These initiatives would also provide Japan with a central policy role in the Asian region—an emerging reality explored further in the following chapter. Taking the lead on regional environmental issues was an easy opportunity for the Japanese government since there were no American or European regional plans to work specifically with Asian countries on pollution control at that time.

Ambiguous Implications

The Japanese government's international policy initiatives in global warming and other aspects of pollution control raise a fundamental ambiguity for foreign analysts—and particularly for Americans used to a more open airing of differing positions between commercial and environmental interests. Should Japanese initiatives be dismissed as a thinly disguised commercial policy, resulting from a decisionmaking process in which noncorporate voices favoring stronger environmental policies have been excluded or subdued? Or should these initiatives be lauded as a progressive move that includes a cooperative position by business, in stark contrast to the often unproductive, contentious debate in the United States? Since pollution issues are intertwined with corporate activity, solutions ultimately depend on acquiescence and support by the corporate sector. Achievement of that support by the Japanese government is an important accomplishment, and this example of cooperation should stand as at least a partial model for those involved in the U.S. debate on these issues.

The record of domestic achievement in the 1970s suggests that Japanese policy is more than just a public relations effort. At the same time, however, the Japanese version of government-business cooperation must be clearly recognized as having strong commercial motivations. Policy will certainly not be pushed as far by the Japanese government as many environmental groups would like; issues that do not provide a benefit for Japanese corporations (such as animal and plant conservation) will be largely ignored; and areas receiving the most active support will tie into a new range of export products. The challenge is not to oppose Japanese efforts, but to ensure that American private-sector firms are not disadvantaged by the support that their Japanese competitors will receive under the rubric of environmental policy. U.S. environmental policy, goaded by this de facto Japanese leadership, needs to ensure that American firms do not fall behind in development of new technologies and products related to pollution control. In essence, the commonality of government and business interests in environmental policy in Japan should drive American policy in a more cooperative direction. The extent and nature of the relationships in Japan may be distasteful from an American perspective, but a cooperative stance in the United States need not proceed as far.

Japanese positions and policies on international environmental issues may well continue to present a combination of progressivity and narrow commercial interests. The government will endorse broad progressive goals and then skew their implementation for Japanese corporate benefit, thereby gaining private-sector support. The government will play on a world stage, but not as effectively as it might, while pursuing a more detailed agenda in the Asian region that works to its national economic advantage. But these will be real initiatives, backed by sizable financial resources, so that Americans will have to react to the challenge they pose.

Conclusion

Whether or not the nation is comfortable with its new international position, Japan had certainly been thrust into the world of international policy by the early 1990s to an extent far beyond that of a decade earlier. Much of this chapter has concentrated on the problems involved in that new prominence: the continuing narrow commercial interests that play such an important role in foreign aid policy, the limited personnel presence in major international economic and political institutions, the international extension of cooperative Japanese government-business relations, and a commercial motivation in the approach to international environmental issues. These problems relate both to the government's failure to define a new, less commercial framework for greater participation in world affairs and multilateral institutions and to the difficulty of the rest of the world in accepting Japan as a major player.

That such problems arose during the 1980s should be unsurprising, since the swift economic changes meant that there had not been much time to rethink or reshape basic policy approaches. Foreign aid rose to high levels in the 1980s, aided by currency movements after 1985. The major international organizations had not been central to government thinking until the 1980s brought Japan an enlarged financial role in their operation, motivating the debate over voting rights and exposing the country's low level of personnel participation. The wave of foreign investment after 1985 stimulated the international extension of administrative guidance. Finally, world focus on a variety of environmental issues largely dates from the late 1980s (except for a handful of earlier conservation issues such as whaling). To these aspects of international engagement, the Japanese necessarily brought their existing patterns of close government-business interaction, which did not always mesh well with the expectations or desires of other countries.

In general, the predominance of commercial interests in adopted policies complicates the process of achieving a more prominent global leadership role. Foreign aid programs still seem geared more toward furthering the welfare of Japanese corporations than meeting the broader development aims of recipient countries. Participation in multilateral organizations has been weak and hampered by the relative lack of any strong noncommercial guiding principles. International extension of administrative guidance was a natural extension of domestic patterns but presented a negative image aboard of opaque collusion. Environmental policy gained support as an issue because of the potential for new markets for high-technology exports. These approaches all indicate a continued priority for the welfare of domestic corporations, carried out in a manner that often irritates governments and corporations in other nations.

But the survey of this chapter should not be considered entirely bleak. Environmental policy is one area where the Japanese approach of government-business cooperation is an useful element in achieving progress. While some of the actual policies certainly fit the same mold of fostering domestic commercial advantage, the general principle of cooperation enabled the government to move forward relatively rapidly and take a more positive leadership position than in most other policy areas.

Will Japan's international policy engagement move in a less commercial direction during the remainder of this decade? This is certainly possible, and the advent of the coalition government in 1993 bolstered expectations of a broader approach to international issues. Nevertheless, some of the features of government-business interaction are deeply rooted in domestic society and institutions, and they are unlikely to change rapidly. American policy (considered in chapter 7) can certainly work to facilitate or accelerate that change.

CHAPTER FIVE

A Focus on the
Asia-Pacific Region

AT THE SAME time that Japan's presence and participation in the major global multilateral institutions remained at a relatively low level, its economic and policy role in the Asia-Pacific region were changing swiftly. An informal economic regionalism is now emerging in the Asia-Pacific region. Although Japan is not the sole propelling force in this evolution, no other country has its breadth of economic reach or combination of forms of involvement. A regional focus in policy and behavior that was remarkably weak in earlier postwar years has now become quite important without inhibiting global participation.

Behind this important development lie the economic features considered in chapters 2 and 3. The shortage of domestic labor, combined with rapid appreciation of the yen after 1985, led manufacturers to seek lower-cost production bases. Neighboring Asian countries were the logical choice because they were geographically close and demonstrated a degree of political stability and economic progress (relative to that in Africa and Latin America) that attracted Japanese firms. Furthermore, some neighboring Asian countries have been growing rapidly themselves, and the circle of countries experiencing dynamic economic growth has been expanding. Rapid economic growth has naturally attracted more trade and investment from Japan and has led to a new awareness of the region's potential. The government has been highly supportive of firms' desire to invest in the region and has used foreign aid in the manner described in chapter 4 to assist Asian countries in providing the industrial infrastructure necessary to satisfy the needs of Japanese firms. The change in the Japanese presence across the region since the mid-1980s has been enormous, and it promises to continue during the rest of the 1990s.

Much of what is now happening between Japan and the rest of the Asia-Pacific region, or even among the other Asian nations themselves, is driven by ordinary economic market forces. Because of cold war tensions, lingering animosities toward Japan because of World War II, and even the residual effects of former colonial economic ties to European countries, the nations of the region had maintained an unnaturally low degree of economic interaction among themselves that is only now in the process of being reversed. Beyond economic forces, though, a discernibly greater emphasis on Asia-Pacific regionalism is appearing in government reports and newspaper articles. Whether benign or not, the evolution of a stronger Japanese regional focus must be taken into account in American policy toward Japan and the region.

The Past

Geographically, Japan is an Asia-Pacific country.[1] Culturally, it shares some features with its neighbors (although these are more tenuous than the cultural connections that characterize Europe). The geographical proximity and modest cultural connections make it natural for Japan to have a very strong trade and investment relationship with the rest of Asia. Ever since the Meiji Restoration of 1868, and the conscious decision shortly thereafter to bring Western industrialization to Japan as a matter of state policy, there has been a struggle between those Japanese who have viewed the nation as primarily Asian and those who have seen it as a member of the Western industrial nation club. Japanese imperialism in the early twentieth century—itself an emulation of European imperialism—focused on control of neighboring Asian nations. The increasingly extremist and militarist form that Japanese imperialism took in the 1930s involved a determined rejection of the West and an embrace of an Asia-centric definition of national orientation, in which Japan was portrayed by its military leaders as the savior of its Asian brethren from Western domination.

Trade with Asian nations increasingly dominated overall Japanese trade patterns. In the first two decades of this century the share of

Japanese exports destined to the United States approached 40 percent (even higher than the levels prevailing in 1980s), and those to Asia were only slightly higher. During the 1930s, though, the share to the United States dropped rapidly (to only 18 percent by 1939), while that to Asia (principally Manchuria and North China) rose to 65 percent.[2]

Once this strong Asia-centric view was discredited by the tragedy of World War II and further weakened by virtual closure of the Chinese market after 1949, Japan was rather forcefully torn away from many of these prewar economic ties. Emulation of the West, particularly the United States, dominated economics, politics, and culture once again. Interest in Asia was never absent, but Japan was not a major player there either economically or politically in the 1950s or the 1960s. Some of those who had been involved with Asian affairs before the war wanted a return to a stronger Asian orientation, but their voice was generally on the losing side of policy debates (for example, on the question of whether Japan should recognize China after the 1949 Communist victory, which Japan did not do in deference to the United States).[3]

The relative lack of a Japanese presence in Asia or the broader Asia-Pacific region does not mean that Asia did not figure in Japan's international economic relations at all. In 1960, 26.3 percent of Japan's exports went to other Asian countries. But this level was substantially less than before the war (especially since Taiwan and South Korea were not part of prewar international trade statistics).

In the late 1960s some changes led to a revival of a stronger policy focus on the Asia-Pacific region. Strict controls on outward foreign direct investment began to be loosened as the balance-of-payments problems that had inspired those controls eased. The growing need for raw materials led to new economic ties with Australia (principally for coal and iron ore), a development responsible for expanding the regional focus from Asia to the Asia-Pacific region. As total Japanese foreign direct investment rose rapidly in the late 1960s and early 1970s, so did the amounts destined to the region: the flow of new direct investment from Japan to Asia-Pacific countries expanded from $197 million in 1969 to $998 million by 1973. However, it is somewhat questionable to what extent this represented a sense of return to a deliberate regional orientation. Overall investment flows remained small, and one-third to one-half of the reported flows in each of these years was directed to Indonesia, largely for raw material development projects.[4]

When pollution controls began to come into place in Japan in the early 1970s, there was also much discussion of simply exporting pollution-intensive industries to elsewhere in Asia, although it is doubtful that much of Japanese regional investment was ever motivated by such a consideration. The one industry for which a new regional orientation did develop was textiles. Starting in the late 1960s, this industry increased regional investment so that by 1981, 18 percent of the Japanese manufacturing sector's cumulative direct investment in Asia was in textiles, representing 56 percent of Japanese global investment in this industry.[5] Japan's foreign aid policy also had a strong Asian orientation when it began in the late 1960s, with as much as 90 percent of the bilateral aid in this program going to Asian countries. This emphasis was a result of renaming war reparations obligations to create the initial foreign aid program.

In all these ways, activity directed toward the rest of Asia increased in the late 1960s and early 1970s. Although the quantities were very small relative to those that developed in the late 1980s, reaction against the sudden surge in the Japanese presence at that time led to public protests in a number of Asian countries, including demonstrations in Thailand and Indonesia during Prime Minister Kakuei Tanaka's visit in 1974.[6] Memories of the war were far from gone, and the new, visible influx of Japanese-made consumer goods was disturbing to some in these countries, which were still trying to define their own national identities.

The 1970s brought new economic problems for Japan, but these did not necessarily drive the nation closer to its Asia-Pacific neighbors. There was talk of moving away from the close economic ties with the United States, since the postwar trust in American reliability and benevolence had been severely shaken by the "Nixon shocks" (announcement of the intent to recognize China and the decision to cut convertability of the dollar into gold in the summer of 1971, plus the temporary embargo on the export of soybeans in 1973). Furthermore, the oil shock of 1973 and the ensuing general raw material price inflation led to much higher levels of anxiety over the security of imported raw material supplies.

In response to these problems, many geographical areas experienced bursts of new Japanese attention, but ultimately these new enthusiasms fizzled out. Economic ties with the Middle East—including trade, foreign aid, and direct investment—rose and then fell with the price of oil. At the peak (in 1977), the Middle East absorbed 25 percent of bilateral

Japanese overseas development assistance (ODA), but this then subsided to 8 to 10 percent by the late 1980s.[7] Development of Siberian raw materials was frustrated by inability to agree to suitable terms with the Soviet government and then by the demise of détente in the later 1970s. Brazil appeared to be a vast, untapped source of raw materials (including a replacement for American soybeans), but proved to be a quagmire as the Japanese discovered how little they understood about achieving results in an unfamiliar Latin American cultural setting. By the early 1980s, Brazilian debt problems led to a virtual collapse in Japanese interest in building closer economic ties.[8] The only Asian country to benefit substantially from the anxieties about raw materials during this period was Indonesia, which attracted large amounts of foreign aid and investment money for oil and natural gas development, as well as the aluminum-related hydroelectric project mentioned in the previous chapter. Other private-sector investment also came to Indonesia as part of the policy of buying goodwill with raw material suppliers.

In the early 1980s the burst of interest in countries possessing raw materials subsided, but other economic events conspired to further delay a return of regional interest in Asia. The macroeconomic developments that led to rising global trade surpluses for Japan and deficits in the United States sucked Japanese goods and capital into the U.S. market. The share of Japanese exports destined to the U.S. market rose from 24 percent in 1980 to a peak of 38 percent in 1986.[9] Those same macroeconomic developments led to a prolonged period of exchange rate weakness for the yen, so domestic manufacturing firms felt relatively little need to move their operations abroad to reduce costs.

Furthermore, attitudes toward Asia, or at least that region's newly industrialized economies (NIEs) seemed to be dominated by the "boomerang effect," in which Japanese businessmen worried that a transfer of technology or continued economic success of these countries would allow them to take away global markets from Japanese firms. While the Japanese government or industry could not entirely prevent the spread of technology, such negative imagery certainly acted as a deterrent to direct investment and explicit technology transfer. As a consequence, Japanese direct investment in Asia lagged badly. The annual dollar amount of new investment stagnated, and it declined rapidly as a share of total new Japanese foreign direct investment. From the levels of 30 to 36 percent of total foreign direct investment flows to Asia in the second half of the 1970s, the share sank in the first half of the 1980s to only 10 percent by 1986.[10]

Finally, the high debt levels of some Southeast Asian nations, including Indonesia, the Philippines, and Thailand, militated against higher investment. These countries seemed to be mired in the same combination of falling raw material prices, high debt, reliance on inefficient and bureaucratic state-owned enterprises, and heavy corruption that affected Latin America and other regions.[11] Differences in the level of economic development, continued political conflict, and economic problems in the region meant that even in the late 1980s the Japanese people maintained a relatively strong inclination to view their nation as Western rather than as Asian.[12]

The New Japanese Interest in Asia

Starting in the mid-1980s, significant changes began to reverse the stagnation or decline in Japanese interest and activity in Asia. The basic building blocks of trade, investment, and foreign aid were already present, but the relationship became much broader and deeper at a rapid pace that promises to continue and even accelerate during the rest of the 1990s. These changes are evident in the positive interest given to Asian countries in the media (including both official and private-sector publications) and in the formation of new institutions and policies.

The Japanese business media began an increased emphasis on the four Asian NIEs—South Korea, Taiwan, Hong Kong, and Singapore— around 1987 and the other Association of Southeast Asian Nations (ASEAN) countries in 1988. With an new upbeat economic assessment of the region, the media promoted the concept that these countries were now capable of producing goods of sufficient quality for the Japanese market, thereby endorsing the idea of direct investment in these countries by Japanese firms. This portrayal continued unabated in the early 1990s.[13]

The concern of earlier years that the Asian NIEs were economic competitors for the U.S. market was largely replaced by the new enthusiasm for greater economic interaction with these nations. Indeed, the Japanese now take great pride in the fact that as an Asian nation, they are part of the most rapidly growing region of the world, compared with Latin America, Africa, and the Middle East, which all face continuing problems. A popular, self-flattering notion in the early 1990s was that of the "flying geese" pattern, with Japan as the head goose. This imagery implied that Japan was the permanent Asian economic leader; that the success of the others flowed from Japan; and that their level of economic development will remain comfortably behind. In this view, it was Japanese foreign aid and direct investment that created high economic growth rates in these countries.[14]

The notion of regionalism that emerged in Japanese writing began to raise the possibility of a need for an economic bloc in the event of a failure in the Uruguay round of global trade negotiations in the framework of the General Agreement on Tariffs and Trade (GATT). The Japanese were certainly concerned about a possible failure of the GATT negotiations and about a global move toward bilateralism or regionalism should that happen. The economic unification of Europe in 1992, and its potentially protectionist policies, was a highly publicized theme at the beginning of the 1990s. So, too, was the U.S.-Canada Free Trade Area and its probable expansion into a North American Free Trade Area (NAFTA), as well as President Bush's plan to offer similar arrangements to other Latin American nations. Should these developments materialize during the 1990s, a defensive move to create a parallel formal trade arrangement in Asia is a possibility. Concern over the potential negative effects of NAFTA was widespread in the Japanese government and among businesses, with an undertone of turning to Asia. However, most of the discussion of Asia in the Japanese press and most of the other developments presented in this chapter were occurring without any relationship to the fortunes of GATT or NAFTA. Regionalism as a possible response to NAFTA was more of a bargaining position in the effort to ensure that the final rules would not be unduly prejudicial to Japanese interests.

Regional Business Strategies

As part of the emerging regional focus, an emphasis on the region as a whole, rather than solely on individual countries, has emerged. Although the terms *newly industrialized economy* or *newly industrialized country* and the Association for Southeast Asian Nations have been part of the Japanese vocabulary for many years, the expression of business strategies toward the entire Asian or Asia-Pacific region is relatively new. Press reports of Japanese corporate activity in Asian countries, for example, now routinely place these moves in the context of the firm's or industry's Asian strategy. This view appeared first for the large Japanese retailers, which have been building solid ties across the region, and more recently show up in descriptions of the activities of the financial sector and manufacturing as well.

The advance of the retailing sector across the Asia-Pacific region has been quite substantial, including both purchasing offices and local retail outlets on a large scale in major urban centers in Asia. As part of this trend, the Saison Group established a broad "Asian Retailing Affiliation Network" in 1990, which included cooperative ties between Saison and major retailers in Indonesia, Thailand, Taiwan, Hong Kong, and Malaysia. Takashimaya, another large Japanese retail chain, created local subsidiaries in Hong Kong, Taipei, Bangkok, and Sydney, with the intent of establishing what the company called a "trans-Asia-Pacific network."[15] Much of the initial interest of Japanese chain stores was to capture the market for Japanese tourists visiting other Asia-Pacific countries, including those on specialized "shopping" tours. But they have become more interested in serving the demand among the local population as well, and by 1991 Japanese firms had a total of seventy-three large retail outlets across Asia and the western Pacific.[16]

On the financial front, in 1990 the Fuji Bank, Mitsubishi Bank, and the Sanwa Bank announced establishment of subsidiaries in Asian countries; press reports placed the moves in the context of broad Asian strategies.[17] The financial sector, in fact, could easily become a focal point of Japanese regional strategies as the developing countries of the region gradually open their domestic financial markets to foreign participation. In Indonesia, Japanese banks, investment banks, and insurance companies flocked in as soon as foreign institutions were allowed to enter after 1988.[18] The four largest investment houses in Japan all created subsidiaries that became members of the Singapore stock exchange simultaneously in summer 1992.[19]

In manufacturing, the Japanese auto firms were motivated by a 1988 ASEAN policy decision to demand a regional allocation of production. Toyota had several small operations in the ASEAN region, and Mitsubishi Motors was also actively producing parts and completed cars in several ASEAN countries. Matsushita, the large manufacturer of consumer electronics, established an Asian subsidiary based in Singapore that was responsible for managing its broad and growing network of local subsidiaries (with as many as fifty separate manufacturing operations across the region).[20]

Overall, the statistical evidence on the regional behavior of Japanese firms is less clear. According to survey data, the subsidiaries of Japanese manufacturing firms operating in the Asia-Pacific region in 1990 sold close to 13 percent of their output to other regional countries (excluding Japan).[21] This share has risen somewhat over time (from 8.2 percent in 1983), while the share of output sold within the country of the investment declined modestly from 67 percent to 60 percent over the same eight-year period. The rise in the regional sales orientation of Japanese manufacturing operations located in the Asian-Pacific region through 1989 was still relatively small, but the strong evidence of emerging regional strategies implies that this ratio should rise further in the 1990s.

Expressions of Regionalism

Japanese government officials, businessmen, and academics talked openly in the early 1990s about emerging regionalism and Japan's leadership position in the process. Although this theme was never entirely absent from earlier Japanese academic writing, the sense of Japanese leadership in a real move toward regional economic integration became much stronger after the late 1980s than at any point in the earlier postwar period and was now articulated openly by many government officials.

Expressing the essence of these views, an opinion piece in a leading Japanese newspaper in 1990 argued that the end of the cold war opened the way for Japan to pursue an independent foreign policy (using foreign aid as a key element) focused primarily on Asia.[22] A former Ministry of Finance official wrote in an influential magazine in 1991 that regional blocs were a desirable direction for the world (based on the success of the EC) and advocated support for Malaysian Prime Minister Mahathir Bin Mohamad's proposed East Asian Economic Caucus—a regional trade group that would exclude the United States and Australia.[23] Makoto Kuroda, the former chief trade negotiator for MITI, stated in 1989 that Asia was heading toward a natural economic integration.[24] Kuroda's statement is especially interesting considering that much of his time in government was spent negotiating with the United States rather than focusing on Asia.

Similar views about Japanese leadership in the de facto regional economy have been expressed by such senior figures as Yukio Suzuki (the former head of research at the Bank of Japan) and Michihiko Kunihiro (Japan's ambassador to Indonesia and former economic minister in the embassy in Washington), who have been generally associated with a more global or U.S.-focused view of Japanese foreign policy. Suzuki reminded the Japanese that their primary focus should be on Asia (even as Japan takes on broader world responsibilities), and Kunihiro emphasized that Japan's role in Asia would continue to grow as the United States retreated (because of its economic problems at home).[25] Newspaper editorials and academics were also echoing these themes, emphasizing the economic integration taking place in Asia, Japan's rising role in the region, and the desirability of playing an even stronger role.[26]

The Economic Planning Agency (EPA), staffed by economists who also generally have a broad international view, joined the new focus on Asia. An advisory commission report to the EPA (which one can assume conforms rather closely to EPA views), distanced Japan from total commitment to a Western framework for Asia. The report states, "While Asian countries appreciate the role that the United States and the European nations have played in Asia, we fully recognize that U.S./European values have negative aspects, and that in parallel with this, we strongly desire a role based on Asian concepts. For Japan—a member of Asia—to forfeit an Asian viewpoint and behave in a manner based on a European/U.S.-centered world scenario and value system, causes uneasiness and a certain type of resentment from other Asian countries."[27] Despite the typically vague language (with terms such as an "Asian viewpoint" or "Asian concepts" never defined), this document is significant because it goes beyond simply seeing a role for Japan in Asia to claiming that Japan will have a distinct and superior approach to dealing with the region because of its Asian cultural identification. This is mildly reminiscent of the heavy Asian focus of the 1930s, and the report even uses the term *kyōchōteki han'ei kankei* (a cooperative prosperity relationship), a term not far removed from the "co-prosperity sphere" of prewar vocabulary.

By no means all writers adopt such a strong enthusiasm for regionalism, and some have spoken vigorously about the dangers that might be inherent in moving toward a regional economic bloc with other Asian nations.[28] However, relative to earlier postwar years, the level of enthusiasm and the volume of writing advocating some form of regionalism is very evident.

One of the stumbling blocks in the past to a stronger role for Japan in Asian or Asia-Pacific regionalism was opposition from other regional Asian countries themselves, driven partly by memories of Japanese behavior before and during World War II. Even this attitude appeared to be changing in the 1980s; or at least the Japanese believed that the rest of Asia was now broadly receptive to a larger Japanese leadership role. One poll conducted by a Japanese newspaper in 1992 found that 70 percent of those polled in Asian countries were in favor of a larger regional leadership role for Japan (China and South Korea were the only two countries in which this opinion was not in the majority). Foreign Ministry–sponsored polls found similarly favorable views toward Japan (with positive attitudes by 61 to 70 percent of pollees among individual ASEAN countries), and on the question of inward direct investment from Japan, favorable attitudes were even stronger (85 to 91 percent across ASEAN countries).[29] Expressions of concern across the region about both the economic and political dimensions of Japan's regional position remain commonplace, however, leaving some doubt concerning the real extent of receptivity.

Much of Japanese-language writing about Japan and the Asia-Pacific region does not include the United States. At the diplomatic level, substantial support remains behind the broader concept of the Pacific Basin (including the United States, Canada, Australia, and New Zealand), and Japan is a member of the panoply of Pacific Basin organizations (the Pacific Basin Economic Council, the Pacific Trade and Development Conference, the Pacific Economic Cooperation Council, and the Asia-Pacific Economic Cooperation Council). However, much of domestic writing focuses more narrowly on Japan and the NIEs plus ASEAN, with China included upon occasion. References to the United States are often only in terms of its declining power or presence in the region, fitting into the thesis of a regional integration centering upon Japan. The sense of Japan as an alternative or competitor to the United States is actually quite striking, although this does not always appear in official Japanese foreign policy documents.

New Institutions

In addition to the increased interest expressed in print, new institutions have sprung up in Japan to focus more attention on Asia. MITI has its subsidiary, the Institute of Developing Economies (IDE), which has always had a strong focus on Asia. Of 140 researchers in 1985, 96 specialized on Asia and the South Pacific, while 44 dealt with the rest of the developing world (with small groups working on Africa, Latin America, the Middle East, and the Soviet Union plus Eastern Europe). Similarly, the overwhelming majority of foreign researchers invited to spend time at the institute have been from other Asian countries.[30]

New institutions proliferated in the 1980s and 1990s that greatly broadened the institutional base for research and personal interaction between Japan and Asia, often independent of the broader Pacific Basin framework (that is, without the United States). The Foreign Ministry established a post of ambassador for Asia-Pacific cooperation.[31] In the private sector, the Matsushita Institute of Government and Management, a small but influential educational institution, began a program in 1989 to educate young employees at Japanese firms about particular Asian countries and launched a broader program of research and exchange programs on the region.[32] The National Institute for Research Advancement (NIRA), a government agency that funds social science research, began a number of research projects and conferences with Asian countries in the 1980s, including a series of conferences with China.[33] Another organization, the Tokyo Club Foundation for Global Studies, set up in 1987, began by building ties with research institutes in industrial countries, but established a separate network of relations across Asia in 1989.[34]

Finally, beyond the formation of new institutional arrangements, the Japanese government began to engage in leadership in a regional context. Then-Prime Minister Noboru Takeshita went to the 1988 industrial nation economic summit meeting in Toronto with the announced intention of raising the issues and concerns of the Asian NIEs, assuming a self-appointed mantle of regional representation that the Japanese government continued to claim at subsequent summit meetings.[35] Regional leadership was the clearest in the early 1990s on the issue of atmospheric warming, discussed in chapter 4. On those issues where the government was beginning to frame a global role, the specific action came first at a regional level on a unilateral basis.

Given the geographical, cultural, and historical ties between Japan and the rest of the Asia-Pacific region, the emergence of institutions, programs, and conferences dealing with the region is quite natural. The more interesting question is why so little activity concerning the rest of the region took place in Japan before the late 1980s. Among those causes lie the legacy of the war, the general postwar Japanese timidity in foreign policy, the overwhelming focus on domestic economic development, cold war divisions, and economic concerns about the "boomerang effect." Whatever the past obstacles, though, institutional activity certainly increased rapidly after the mid-1980s and formed a changed and expanded environment for Japanese thinking and behavior toward Asia and the broader Asia-Pacific region.

The statements by government officials, the articles in the press, and the increased institutional activity do not necessarily imply that a regional economic bloc exists or is being formed. Japan is most certainly not returning to the exclusive yen bloc it constructed in the late 1930s. But the developments outlined here do represent an important shift of thinking and behavior that is a necessary precondition for the evolution of regionalism. Asia received far more attention than in the past, the concept of regional economic integration (with Japan and without the United States) was expressed more often, and government officials and others advocated a more active role for Japan in bringing about this integration. Although these concepts were not universally subscribed to in Japan, they motivated much of the nation's real policy and business behavior toward other countries in the region.

Trade Ties

Given the rising focus on the Asia-Pacific region delineated above, one would expect substantial growth in the trade linkages between Japan and other Asia-Pacific nations. Some movement has taken place in that direction, but not as much as one might anticipate. Trade data provide a moderate view of movement in the direction of regionalization.

The percentages of Japanese and American exports destined to this region are shown in the top panel of figure 5-1. Both countries' share of exports going to the region has risen, and that share has always been higher for Japan (almost 37 percent in 1990) than for the United States (20 percent). Since 1985 the rise has been quite rapid for Japan, consistent with the increased attention given to the region discussed above, and by 1991 it was common to hear references to the fact that this share was larger than that going to the United States. Data on the share of imports by Japan and the United States from the region, not presented here, show essentially the same trend. Thus, from a Japanese perspective, the nation's merchandise trade was becoming more closely tied to the region.

A regional perspective, showing the share of the exports of Asia-Pacific countries (other than Japan) that goes to the United States, Japan, or the region, is shown in the second panel of figure 5-1. Strong appreciation of the yen and depreciation of the dollar after 1985 should have made the Japanese market a more profitable destination than the United States for those exports. However, the share of Asian exports destined

Figure 5-1. *Asia-Pacific Trade Patterns, 1960–90*[a]

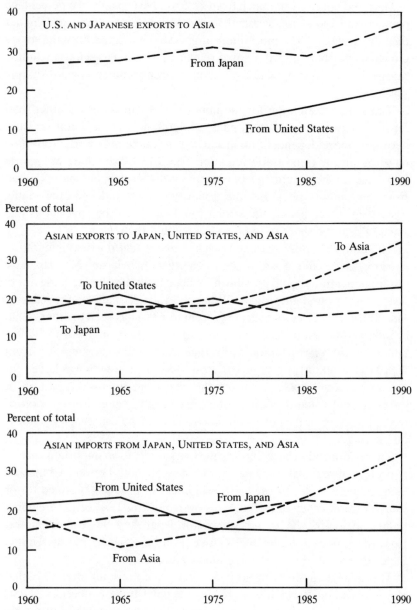

Percent of total

U.S. AND JAPANESE EXPORTS TO ASIA

From Japan

From United States

Percent of total

ASIAN EXPORTS TO JAPAN, UNITED STATES, AND ASIA

To Asia

To United States

To Japan

Percent of total

ASIAN IMPORTS FROM JAPAN, UNITED STATES, AND ASIA

From United States

From Japan

From Asia

Source: International Monetary Fund, *Direction of Trade Statistics Yearbook*, 1960–1964, 1962–1966, 1973–1979, 1983–1989, and 1984–1990.

a. The countries other than Japan included in the definition of the Asia-Pacific region here are China, South Korea, Taiwan, Singapore, the Philippines, Thailand, Indonesia, Malaysia, Australia, and New Zealand. A narrower focus excluding Australia and New Zealand alters the percentages only by a minor amount.

to Japan did not rise very much from 1985 to 1990 (up only two percentage points), and the share destined to the United States remained higher than that to Japan. The most interesting development has been the strong growth of the share of exports that remained within the region (excluding Japan). These intraregional exports have been trending upward sharply since 1975.

The same information for the imports of Asian countries other than Japan is shown in the bottom panel of figure 5-1. These countries were becoming more dependent upon Japan as a source of imports from 1960 onward, but the trend stabilized after 1985. In 1990 the share of imports into these countries coming from Japan was higher than the share sourced from the United States, but the disparity has not widened appreciably since 1975. Once again, the strong trend has been the continuous rise since 1975 in the share of imports from within the region.

The data shown in figure 5-1 suggest that a real regional integration is taking place among Asian countries other than Japan. Non-Japanese intraregional trade could possibly have been facilitated by Japanese direct investment around the region. But only a small share of the sales of Japanese subsidiaries in Asia (13 percent in 1990) has been to other Asian countries. The estimated total value of those sales in 1990 was ¥965 billion (roughly $6.7 billion at average 1990 exchange rates), up from ¥570 ($4.4 billion) two years earlier in 1988. This growth was large, but not large enough to have caused the change in the overall pattern of intra-regional trade.[36] Most of the increasingly regional orientation of trade, therefore, is part of a shift independent of the rising Japanese focus on the region.

These data and this conclusion must be subject to an important caveat. A portion of regional trade has been a flow of goods between China and Hong Kong, which represents transhipment of products destined to, or sourced from, other countries. This overstates the level of intraregional trade and lowers the shares shown for Japan and the United States. However, it does not alter the relative position of Japan and the United States to one another in this regional context.

Two important shifts in attitude took place in Japan after 1985 that played a role in the nation's growing regional trade connection. First, receptivity to manufactured goods from developing countries in the region increased, and these products made visible inroads in some markets in Japan (including bicycles, cotton underwear, and electric fans). The increase in imports from Asia after 1985 was not disproportionately large (since absorption of manufactured imports increased in general), but more receptive attitudes by business and consumers had to buttress the increase that took place.[37] Japan could well continue to experience an increase in imports from the region, although one should be cautious in predicting how far this trend might go. The fact that the manufactured products entering Japan from these countries are often from Japanese subsidiaries with Japanese brand labels (and generally with no country-of-origin label) should further ease receptivity.

Second, Japanese discussions of intra-industry trade have often been placed in a regional context. As an empirical phenomenon, intra-industry trade is more prevalent among industrial nations, rather than between industrial nations and developing countries. For Japan, statistical measures of intra-industry trade were unusually low in the past (as noted in chapter 3), but there is an emerging belief that trade with the developing countries of Asia (rather than with industrialized countries) could and should move in this direction.[38] This, too, was a new development in Japanese writing indicative of a changed and more receptive attitude toward Asian nations. This change also implied an explicit endorsement of regionalism by advocating a form of interaction with regional nations that more logically would have occurred between Japan and its major industrialized trading partners.

Whether these two developments will seriously alter trade patterns toward a stronger regional orientation during the rest of the 1990s remains to be seen. If one focuses on the past, the evidence is mixed: stronger regional ties from a Japanese perspective, but not so much from the perspective of the region. However, the apparent increased receptivity to manufactured imports from the region and the more positive discussion of intra-industry trade suggest the possibility of a further move toward greater regionalism in Japanese trade over the next decade.

Investment

Data on Japanese direct investment provide an ambiguous picture of relations with the region. While the amount of investment has risen sharply, the 1980s actually brought a relative shift in the location of investment away from Asia and toward the industrial nations, as shown in table 5-1. In the decade from 1980 to 1990, the cumulative value of Japanese foreign direct investment in the ASEAN countries plus the

Table 5-1. *New Direct Investment from Japan, by Geographical Region, 1980–90*
Amounts in millions of U.S. dollars

Year	ASEAN and Asian NIEs[a]		United States		European Community		Total
	Amount	Percent	Amount	Percent	Amount	Percent	Total
Through 1979	8,554	26.9	22,098	69.5	3,497	11.0	31,803
1980	1,164	24.8	1,484	31.6	544	11.6	4,693
1981	3,295	36.9	2,354	26.4	721	8.1	8,931
1982	1,359	17.6	2,738	35.5	790	10.3	7,703
1983	1,770	21.7	2,738	33.6	944	11.6	8,145
1984	1,495	14.7	3,359	33.1	1,691	16.7	10,155
1985	1,315	10.8	5,395	44.2	1,851	15.2	12,217
1986	2,085	9.3	10,165	45.5	3,324	14.9	22,320
1987	3,610	10.8	14,704	44.1	6,281	18.8	33,364
1988	5,230	11.1	21,701	46.2	8,329	17.7	47,022
1989	7,682	11.4	32,540	48.2	14,031	20.8	67,540
1990	6,597	11.6	26,128	45.9	13,305	23.4	56,911
Total (1980–90)	35,602	12.8	123,306	44.2	51,811	18.6	279,001
Cumulative total	44,156	14.2	145,404	46.8	55,308	17.8	310,804

Sources: Ministry of Finance, *Ōkurashō Kokusai Kin'yūkyoku Nempō* [Annual Report of the International Finance Bureau] (Tokyo: Kin'yū Zaisei Jijō Kenkyūkai [Financial and Fiscal Research Group]), *1987*, pp. 451–53; and *1991*, pp. 458–60.
a. Brunei, Hong Kong, Indonesia, Malaysia, Philippines, Singapore, South Korea, Taiwan, and Thailand. (Singapore is a member of both groups, but is included in the table only once.)

Asian NIEs increased almost fivefold (from $8.5 billion in 1980 to $44 billion in 1990), with the dollar value of new direct investment flows rising substantially after 1985. Nevertheless, an even greater acceleration of Japanese investment in the United States and Europe occurred at the same time. Japanese cumulative foreign direct investment in the United States roughly equaled that in Asia in 1980, but by 1990 cumulative investments in the United States had soared to $145 billion, almost four times those in the NIEs and ASEAN. For Europe, the stock of investment in 1980 and the flow of new investment in the early part of the 1980s was less than that going to Asia, but rapid acceleration after 1985 brought the cumulative total beyond the level of Asia by 1990.

The same picture emerges if the focus is restricted to investment in the manufacturing sector. From 1985 through 1990 the cumulative value of Japanese investment in manufacturing grew at an annual pace of 40 percent in North America, 45 percent in Europe, and only 20 percent in Asia. In 1985 total investment in manufacturing in Asia and North America was almost equal ($7.4 billion), while Europe was far behind ($1.9 billion). But with the differential rates of growth, the totals at the end of 1990 put North America far ahead ($40.3 billion), and Europe ($12.5 billion) not as far behind Asia ($18.5 billion) in relative terms as it had been.[39]

The surge of Japanese direct investment in the United States relative to that in Asia suggests that Japan has not had any rising regional focus. At the margin, firms chose activity outside of Asia in the second half of the 1980s, which perhaps is evidence of an increasing regional focus on the United States. But what is the appropriate frame of reference? If the question is the importance of the Japanese presence within Asian countries, then the focus should be Japan's investment position relative to other foreign investors in the region.

A broad picture of regional investment ties is difficult to develop, since nations have no uniform standard for collecting investment statistics. As of the early 1980s, though, a general conclusion from available data would be that Japan and the United States together appeared to be the dominant foreign investors throughout the region. In some countries the United States was the largest single source of inward direct investment by a modest margin, and in some cases Japan held this position. After the mid-1980s, however, the acceleration of Japanese investment moved Japan to a substantially larger absolute and relative presence in a number of Asian countries. The rough parity of the past was broken.

A 1989 Japanese study, assembling foreign direct investment data from several Asian countries, showed Japan to be the largest source of cumulative direct investment in Korea (51 percent of total), Thailand (24 percent), Malaysia (42 percent), and Indonesia (34 percent).[40] In Hong Kong, concerns about the future after reversion to Chinese ownership in 1997 were beginning to hinder foreign investment in the early 1990s, but even there Japanese investment was increasing.[41] As Japanese foreign direct investment in these countries and the rest of Asia continued to accelerate after 1987, Japan's relative share of total foreign investment in the region continued to rise.

In addition, even though the average increase in investment in Asia lagged somewhat behind the increase in Japanese investment in the United States, there were exceptions. In Thailand, Japanese new direct investment flows increased explosively from a low of $48 million in 1985 to $1.3 billion by 1989.[42] Thailand was perhaps the country toward which Japanese attitudes changed most radically, from being seen as a corrupt, overregulated economy mired in debt problems in the early 1980s to becoming a virtual magnet for Japanese investment late in the decade. Cumulative foreign direct investment data for Indonesia as of June 1990 also showed Japan to be the largest single investor by a sizable margin, and there was speculation in Japan that Indonesia could replace Thailand as the most attractive investment location over the 1990s.[43]

A form of implicit favoritism toward the Japanese also appeared to be creeping into investment relations. In 1990 the governments of Singapore and Indonesia jointly set up a government-sponsored venture to build an extensive industrial park on Batam Island (between Singapore and Indonesia). Mitsui and Company, one of the largest trading companies in Japan, was permitted to be the only private-sector equity participant in the venture. As of late 1990 almost one-third of the firms that had decided to build plants on the island were Japanese, and Kansai Electric Power received the contract to build the power station for the island. By 1991 the Japanese represented the majority of firms locating on the island.[44] These were not exclusive relationships, since other foreign firms were free to invest on the island, but there remains a strong sense that Japanese participation was being given preference, signaled by the equity position of Mitsui.

Much of the sense of major change and increase in Japanese activity comes from looking at the ASEAN countries, since Japan had moved closer to some of the Asian NIEs at an earlier stage, including a rush of

Figure 5-2. *Japanese Ties to the Auto Industries of South Korea and Taiwan*[a]

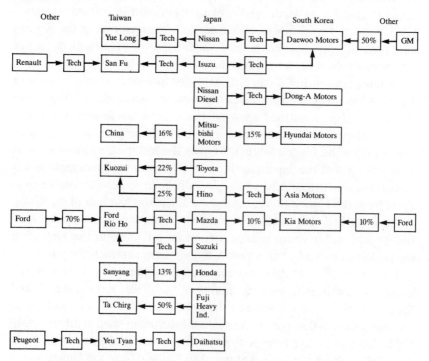

Source: Calculated from data in "The Automotive Industries of Asia NICS and Globalization of Japanese Auto and Auto Parts Manufacturers," *LTCB Research Economic Review*, no. 90 (May 1987), pp. 3–9.
a. Percentages represent equity ownership shares; "tech" indicates technical ties.

investment in South Korea after the two nations finally restored full diplomatic relations in 1965. As the closest of Japan's Asian neighbors, South Korea has had a strong trade and investment relationship with Japan since the 1960s, and that relationship therefore underwent less alteration after 1985.[45]

Animosity and competition are a continuing aspect of the relationship with South Korea, part of the overall historical difficulty Japanese and South Koreans have had dealing with one another.[46] However, it would be a mistake to confuse the animosity with a lack of close economic relations. Every Korean and Taiwanese automobile manufacturer has some relationship with a Japanese firm, and virtually every Japanese automaker has a tie with a firm in either South Korea or Taiwan (figure 5-2). These ties are more pervasive than those of American or European firms with Korean automakers. Mazda even used its tie with Kia Motors to create a joint venture to produce cars in the Philippines—an unprecedented example of Japanese-Korean cooperation in a third country.[47] Overall, some two-thirds of all the technical agreements of the Korean auto firms are with the Japanese, a rough indicator of the high degree of Japanese involvement with this industry.[48]

In Taiwan, the other Asian NIE with long historical economic ties with Japan, direct investment grew steadily over the course of the 1980s. From 1985 to 1991 Japan was the largest single source of new foreign investment inflows: 34 percent of new direct investment came from Japan (and 26 percent from the United States).[49] Given the historical economic ties, it is surprising that the Japanese share of foreign direct investment is not higher, but flows from Japan had generally been somewhat smaller than those from the United States during the 1970s and first half of the 1980s.

Australia had very weak investment links with Japan historically. Australian coal and iron ore became important for Japan in the 1960s, but the preferred pattern at that time was long-term contracts for purchases and loans to facilitate development of mining operations. Direct investment from Japan remained minimal until the 1980s. Earlier, the United States and the Britain had been the largest investors by far, and Japan was not even singled out in Australian investment data until the early 1970s. But cumulative foreign direct investment as of the end of 1990 was $46.4 billion from the United States, $46.1 billion from the United Kingdom, and $45.4 billion from Japan. Thus, even in Australia, with its strong historical links to the West, Japan had become an equal with the two previously largest investors. Unlike other parts of Asia, however, Australia had relatively little Japanese investment in the manufacturing sector.[50]

Should the differential trends in investment around the region continue, with Japan outpacing the United States, one might label Japan an "accidental" economic power in the region. Even though the shift in the relative allocation of resources by Japanese firms was actually away from Asia, the sheer size of Japan's total outflow of capital to the region caused the country to emerge as a much larger player in Asia.

The relative shift of Japanese investment away from Asia may well be reversed during the remainder of the 1990s. Some of the attractiveness of the United States as a location for investment (especially in real estate) diminished in the early 1990s, and defensive investment in the EC in anticipation of the European economic consolidation at the end of 1992 may have peaked. In contrast, forecasts for further rapid economic growth in Asia should continue to fuel a rising level of Japanese investment for the rest of the decade. The business press in Japan has begun to enthusiastically endorse an investment shift away from the United States back toward Asia.[51] Furthermore, lower wage costs as a motivation for foreign direct investment will become even more important as the decade progresses (as indicated in chapter 2). During the recession of 1992–93, direct investment flows diminished, but the combination of a reemerging need to move production to lower-wage countries and continued regional economic growth should result in a rebound in investment levels.

Foreign Aid

The foreign aid situation is dramatically different from either trade or investment. Japan now dominates overseas development assistance given to most of the developing countries in the region to an extraordinary degree, and its relative position has been gaining rapidly. This fact is especially important because Japanese bilateral foreign aid remains closely connected to other Japanese commercial interests, as discussed in the previous chapter. Foreign aid should be considered a principal means by which the Japanese government is exercising a new role of importance within the region.

Japan is the largest source of aid to the ASEAN countries by a wide margin (see figure 5-3). Overall, Japan provided 54 percent of the net receipts of ODA by ASEAN member nations in 1990 (excluding Singapore, which was no longer a net recipient of ODA from the world). Even this high share may be understated: in 1988 and 1989 the share was about 60 percent, and the dip in 1990 may reflect simply a temporary drop due to the timing of disbursements. As recently as 1980, Japan supplied a significantly smaller 39 percent of net receipts of aid by ASEAN countries, 15 percentage points less than in 1990. Even in 1984, the share was 44 percent, so the increase in Japan's role in regional foreign aid came in the second half of the 1980s (largely because of the strong appreciation of the yen).[52] Neither the United States nor the multilateral lending institutions are major sources of ODA for these nations: in 1990 the multilateral institutions supplied only 11 percent of ASEAN receipts and the United States an even smaller 7 percent.

Figure 5-3. *Net Receipts of Overseas Development Assistance,*
by Source, Selected ASEAN Countries, 1990
Percent of total net receipts

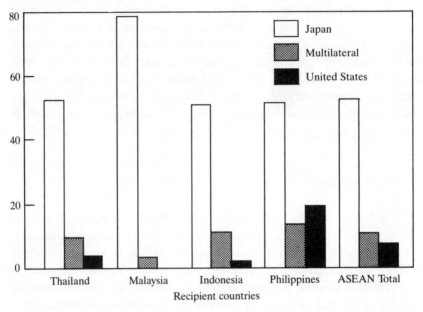

Recipient countries

Source: Organization for Economic Cooperation and Development, *Geographical Distribution of Financial Flows to Developing Countries, 1987/1990* (Paris: OECD, 1992).

For some other Asian countries, Japan is not quite as clearly the leading source of foreign aid. Japan provided 29 percent of net ODA received by China in 1991, less than the 37 percent from the multilateral institutions, but far higher than the small 6 percent of China's net ODA receipts Japan provided in 1980. Among the other socialist countries, Burma (Myanmar) received 48 percent of its ODA from Japan in 1991; Laos, only 14 percent.[53]

Despite Japan's rising share of the foreign aid market in Asia, the distribution of aid actually shifted somewhat away from Asia in relative terms. In 1991, 51.0 percent of Japan's bilateral aid went to Asian countries, down from 70.5 percent in 1980.[54] Nevertheless, the overall increase in disbursements of bilateral aid was so large that the absolute amount (and Japan's relative contribution compared with that from other donors) rose decisively. Further diminution of the percentage of Japanese aid going to Asia now seems fairly unlikely; government officials appear to support maintenance of the present proportional structure.

The nature of the Japanese aid program as portrayed in chapter 4—reliance on loans rather than grants and the preference for large infrastructure projects connected to the interests of Japanese firms—implies that heavy reliance on aid from Japan almost necessarily brings a much closer economic relationship. Japan has become the dominant source of aid to Asia to such an extent that these connections to the private sector become particularly important.

The Siracha–Laem Chabang industrial park and harbor facility in Thailand (discussed in chapter 4) represents the sort of strong impact Japanese foreign aid and its association with commercial interests can have on local economies. With this level of ODA support for building infrastructure useful to Japanese companies investing in Thailand, it is no great surprise that direct investment in Thailand by Japanese firms has risen so quickly. Nor is it any surprise that the new foreign aid principles, which included emphasis on movement toward democracy as a condition for providing ODA, were ignored in the wake of the 1992 Thai coup (in which a democratically elected prime minister was toppled by the military). Political stability was more important than democracy to Japanese business and government in order to promote a base for overseas investment by Japanese firms.

Heavy ODA support for projects like that at Siracha–Laem Chabang, which then attract direct investment by Japanese firms, encourages Thai development aspirations. However, the close common interests of the Japanese government and corporate sectors imply that support for industrialization comes with commercial strings. During the 1980s recipient nations obviously welcomed the aid and accepted the strings. But if this trend is pushed too far, firms in other industrial nations will feel disadvantaged, and recipient nations may become concerned about their increasing economic connections to Japan.

The Yen and Financial Regionalism

In the context of Asian regionalism, the issue of a yen currency bloc frequently emerges. In the past, the yen played little role as a global reserve currency or as a currency of choice for denominating international trade and financial transactions. Now, however, the yen could move into a more important role, at least in a regional context. However, there are three principal considerations working against a rapid evolution of the yen into a more important role.

First, consider the yen as the preferred currency for trade transactions. The yen has had a rather low role in Japanese global trade; as of 1989 only 35 percent of exports and 14 percent of imports were demoninated in yen.[55] To some extent, currency choice is a matter of negotiating power, with the stronger party preferring its own currency to eliminate exchange rate risk. Since Japan is a dominant economic power in the region, a rising share of Asian trade with Japan could lead to a larger regional role for the yen as Japanese traders insist on their own currency for the transactions. This could lead to a large difference between Japan's global behavior and its regional behavior. But the rising importance of Japan from an Asian perspective has been quite gradual on both the export and import side (as shown in figure 5-1). Furthermore, to the extent that Asian exports to Japan are raw materials, the products tend to have prices set by global markets where prices are denominated in dollars. Therefore any regional shift toward trade in yen will be gradual.

Second, the behavior of central banks around the region shows little movement toward pegging currencies to the yen. No nation in the Asia-Pacific region pegs its currency to the yen (while some have been pegged to the dollar). Most governments try to stabilize their currencies against a basket of currencies, the composition of which they do not reveal. Estimates of the implicit composition of those baskets reveal only a few temporary increases in the weight assigned to the yen during the 1980s. Overall, the dollar remained the dominant currency in these exchange-rate baskets during the decade; greater reliance on the yen was far from realization.[56]

Third, for a currency to be preferred either for transactions or as a reserve currency, a primary requirement is the existence of a large market for liquid, short-term financial instruments. Central banks and traders need to be able to acquire and liquidate their holdings of the currency quickly and easily. One of the principal reasons the yen has not become a more important reserve currency on a global basis has been the very slow speed at which such markets have developed in Japan. A major missing element has been a large, viable market in short-term government paper (treasury bills). Despite repeated promises and announcements about the development of such a market, it remained poorly developed as of the beginning of the 1990s. Failure to push financial change in this direction casts some doubt on the desire of the Japanese government to see its currency used more widely internationally. Officials have expressed concern that wider use implies loss of sovereignty or greater difficulty in managing domestic monetary policy.[57]

While most of the discussion of these issues has been framed in the context of global currency use, it applies regionally as well. The lack of any sustained rise in use of the yen in regional central banks' exchange-rate baskets should partly reflect this lack of deep short-term markets.

On the other hand, a new factor is now operative in the regional context that could increase use of the yen. This is the rapidly rising investment of Japanese firms in the region, coupled with the increase in foreign aid. Japanese foreign aid loans are denominated in yen, and commercial loans may be following a similar trend, although no public data exist on the currency denomination of Japanese commercial lending to Asia.

Borrowing, whether through foreign aid or commercial markets, imposes a need upon the borrowers to obtain yen to repay the loans.[58] For short-term transactions, this exchange risk can be hedged through forward markets, but this is not as easy with the long-term loans that characterize ODA and commercial lending for capital infrastructure. In this case, borrowers can either face a large exchange-rate risk by exchanging their own currency for yen for the continuing stream of interest payments and eventual principal repayment, or they can seek yen-denominated receipts, in the form of exports to Japan, to raise the necessary yen amounts. This strengthening financial connection, therefore, becomes a reason for Asian nations to actively encourage rising, yen-denominated exports to Japan. This point was strongly reinforced by the appreciation of the yen after 1985, which raised the repayment cost for countries that had what had been low-cost ODA loans from Japan.

This final point leads to a critical consideration. If the yen is to play a larger regional role, Japan must absorb more Asian exports as a means of providing those countries with the necessary yen-denominated receipts. This dilemma is similar to that faced by the United States in the 1950s, when the "dollar shortage" was a much-discussed problem. In the late 1980s Japan became more receptive to imports from Asian nations, a development considered above. Much, therefore, will depend on whether exports from Asian countries to Japan continue to expand in rest of the 1990s.

Investment and trade trends suggest a gradual increase in the role of the yen as both a reserve currency and a transaction currency within the Asian region over the 1990s. Very little, however, suggests that these trends are leading in the near future to a yen "bloc" in which nations would chose to tie their currencies closely to the yen. This is especially true since economic and productivity growth rates should continue to vary widely across the region, producing an environment in which the successful, rapidly growing developing nations will have currencies that appreciate relative to the yen over the next decade. Therefore, a strong variant of a yen currency bloc with currencies fixed or semifixed on the yen seems unlikely.

A Special Relationship with China

Much of the discussion above pertains primarily to the market economies of the Asia-Pacific region. One of the most rapidly changing arenas of Japanese economic activity, however, is with the Asian socialist economies, particularly China. On the diplomatic front, it is toward China that the postwar pattern of careful Japanese formal adherence to American foreign policy positions is breaking down the most rapidly, even though a certain amount of official deference to American positions remains.

Japan had an especially close relationship with China in the 1980s. Japan became China's largest overseas trading partner (other than Hong Kong, which is largely a port for transshipment), a major source of direct investment, and the largest single source of foreign aid money. Indeed, Japan was the first member of the OECD's Development Assistance Committee to provide bilateral aid to China.[59] A variety of factors explain why Japan chose to build this network of close ties with China, including historical relations, guilt over the devastation of World War II, geographical proximity, and cultural ties. The detailed nature of the ties between Japan and China also demonstrates a strong economic motivation. As a nearby economy with low wages, a large population, and rapid economic reform, China became more attractive as a market and location for investment (supplementing its value as a supplier of coal, oil, and other raw materials). And expanded economic ties became a mechanism for furthering other goals, such as maintaining China as a peaceful and relatively friendly neighbor. The overwhelming desire to maintain these relationships led to a sharp divergence between Japan and the United States in policy toward China in the wake of the Tiananmen massacre in June 1989.[60] After the incident, the Japanese government chafed at the boundaries of what it felt the U.S. government would tolerate and moved back toward a normal relationship as rapidly as possible.

The Japanese government officially joined the United States and other industrial nations in imposing some sanctions on China (including ceasing foreign aid and downgrading diplomatic contacts), but it never truly subscribed to the moral outrage that dominated American policy in the post-Tiananmen period. The government refrained from using the term *massacre* and instead stuck to less graphic terminology. Within three months of the massacre, the official magazine of the Foreign Ministry published a roundtable discussion that strongly criticized Western reactions, claiming that foreigners had no legitimate right to interfere with internal developments in China and that "human-rights diplomacy" was undesirable.[61] More important, the government never seriously scaled back its own or private-sector activity in China.[62] Foreign aid was temporarily disrupted, but disbursements under the final year of the existing multiyear loan program were resumed by fall 1989, and Japanese technical assistance personnel who had been withdrawn in June were back in China by the end of August.[63] With the quick resumption of foreign aid, net ODA disbursements to China for 1989 were actually considerably higher than in 1988—in sharp contrast to the stagnation of China's ODA receipts from all other sources.[64]

The basic decisions to move in this direction had been taken by the end of July, less than two months after the massacre.[65] Relatively high-level political contacts resumed by August, including a visit to Beijing by a Liberal Democratic party delegation of the Japan-China friendship committee, headed by former Foreign Minister Masayoshi Ito.[66] Missions of high-ranking businessmen resumed by fall 1989, and at the beginning of 1990 a new bilateral investment promotion organization was established.[67] Finally, the Japanese government did nothing to aid the plight of Chinese students who were in Japan at the time of the massacre and did not wish to return home when their visas expired.[68]

The government maintained it was abiding by international restraints on China as of late 1989 by refusing to reopen negotiations on the next multiyear loan package, which had been almost complete before the June massacre, and by eschewing any high-level official meetings with the Chinese. In theory, at least, the new loan package provided a point of political leverage for the Japanese government, enabling it to pressure the Chinese government on human rights or political reform in general as a condition for going forward with the new loans. But no serious pressure appears to have been exerted.[69] Very little remained to be negotiated on the loan package, and final meetings resumed as soon as the United States admitted that National Security Adviser Brent Scowcroft had traveled to China in December. By spring 1990, Japanese groups were in China doing assessment work on the first of proposed projects under the upcoming loan package. In addition to this governmental activity, commercial banks were also holding meetings in China concerning the resumption of long-term loans, paving the way for new lending in fall 1990.[70] All of these developments imply a tremendous eagerness to move forward with the package, rather than any serious effort to use the deal for leverage to obtain an easing of post-Tiananmen political repression.

By the time of the Houston economic summit meeting in July 1990, the ODA loan package was ready to be signed, and the Japanese government already had firm plans for the timing of the formalities even before it sought acceptance by the United States and other summit participants. Whether the government would have gone forward in the face of outright opposition from the United States is a moot point, since President Bush expressed what could be interpreted as at least weak acquiescence.[71] Possibly the administration was more supportive of the Japanese aid package in private, since its public voice was constrained by concern over negative reaction from Congress (which battled with the White House for a harsher policy toward China than that favored by the administration).[72] Furthermore, the Japanese were armed with a sensible rationale: those forces in favor of democracy would be helped by providing foreign aid and hurt by withholding it.[73]

Within two weeks of the Houston summit meeting, a flurry of visits to China began that skirted the earlier G-7 agreement on avoiding high-level meetings. Separate trips to China in summer 1990 to announce the upcoming ODA package, for example, involved Deputy Foreign Minister Hisashi Owada, Shin Kanemaru (a powerful figure in the ruling Liberal Democratic party, later ousted in a 1992 financial scandal), and Deputy Prime Minister Kiichi Miyazawa (the leading politician who became prime minister in 1991). Miyazawa's group met with Premier Li Peng to announce the intent to sign papers for the new loan package. Despite the obvious seniority of the people involved in these trips, the Japanese government was able to claim publicly that it maintained adherence to avoidance of "cabinet-level" meetings.[74] These meetings were only part of a highly visible flow of government and private-sector groups visiting China by early summer 1990.[75]

Still fearful of American criticism after the Houston summit meeting, the government officially termed the initial disbursements under the new ODA loan package to be for humanitarian purposes only, although this definition was extremely loose. The list of seven projects for initial funding included two hydroelectric power dams, a water supply system, a bridge, and three chemical fertilizer plants, hardly the sort of projects that would normally be considered humanitarian aid.[76] The government made a special point of noting that other nations were moving in the same direction of restoring economic relations, with the U.S. Exim Bank to resume trade financing and the West German government ready to make a small loan. But in reality, Japan had moved far beyond the U.S. position.[77]

Disbursements under the new five-year loan plan would amount to roughly $1 billion a year, which represented a substantial increase in Japan's ODA for China and would certainly raise Japan's share in the total provision of foreign aid to China. Thus the new aid package represented far more than simply a restoration of normal relations between Japan and China. It constituted a sizable upgrading of the aid relationship and also served as a positive signal to the private sector to move ahead. Once all the maneuvering was done, and the five-year ODA package was in place, the government then resisted other possible disruptions. As discussed in chapter 4, China was explicitly excluded from application of the new ODA principles announced in spring 1992. Evidence of rising military expenditures and missile exports during 1992 did nothing to alter this exemption.

As the Japanese government moved ahead quickly in late 1989 and 1990 to initiate its new ODA package for China, other moves also confirmed that a resumption and strengthening of economic ties was under way. At the time of the Houston summit, MITI announced a resumption of medium- and long-term trade insurance for China trade.[78] Private commercial banks were providing loans for new projects in China by early fall 1990; several significant new projects were announced almost simultaneously with the official signing of the new ODA package in early November.[79] Rumors actually suggested that commercial lending had resumed much earlier, by the fall of 1989, disguised through the Hong Kong subsidiaries of Japanese financial institutions.[80]

By early January 1991, Finance Minister Ryutaro Hashimoto announced (while in China) that China would once again be allowed to issue bonds in Japan (which had been prohibited after Tiananmen). Furthermore, the Ministry of Finance was prepared to permit new direct investment in China by Japanese firms, which supposedly had also stopped (although this statement was inconsistent with a plethora of announcements in the press through 1990 about new investments).[81] During the same trip, Hashimoto announced a ¥600 billion (approximately $4.6 billion) loan package from the Japan Exim Bank to China for resource development that was separate from Japan's multiyear foreign aid package.[82]

The final step in restoring normal relations, and defining a clear separation from American policy, came in summer 1991 when Prime Minister Toshiki Kaifu traveled to Beijing and thereby became the first leader of a major industrial nation to do so since 1989. During his visit, Kaifu announced the 1991 ODA disbursement at ¥130 billion ($965 million at 1991 exchange rates), with all pretense of sticking to humanitarian projects now gone.[83] As anticlimactic as this trip might seem, given the flood of other visits and announcements concerning loans and other economic ties that had taken place since early 1990, the Japanese press still waxed poetic about its importance, with one paper stating that Japanese direct investment in China would now "flow like water."[84] As though the Kaifu visit were not sufficient signal of a return to normal relations, Emperor Akihito visited China a year later, the first such visit since the end of the war. Despite objections by nationalistic groups in Japan, and cautious crafting of statements about the war, the imperial state visit provided the ultimate reassurance of a special bilateral relationship.

Developments in trade between China and Japan are a bit more ambiguous. Japan's exports to China peaked in 1985 ($12.5 billion), and after fluctuating between $8 billion and $10 billion through 1989, fell sharply to $6.1 billion in 1990. However, exports to China rebounded to $11.9 billion by 1992. These figures imply that the economic and political problems at the end of the 1980s did affect Japan's exports to China, but only temporarily. Exports from China to Japan, on the other hand, continued to expand strongly from 1988 to 1991. From $9.9 billion in 1988, imports from China rose each year to reach $17 billion in 1992.[85] Political considerations certainly did not impede this trade.

The history of Japan's moves toward China since June 1989 suggests little or nothing of the wariness of other industrial nations after the

Tiananmen massacre. While not openly or officially breaking with the United States (or other industrial countries), Japan pursued a very different agenda rather successfully. The net result was a strengthening—not just a restoration—of economic ties between China and Japan, in both absolute terms and relative to those of other industrial countries involved with China. Japan will become a more prominent supplier of foreign aid, and the private sector will become a relatively more important source of trade and foreign investment activity in China.

Even in the 1960s Japan had stayed close to the boundaries of U.S. policies toward China, adopting a de facto two-China policy that involved more extensive and regular contacts with Beijing than those of any other Western country.[86] Japan was then unable to take any leadership role in moving to restore diplomatic relations with China and had to wait until President Nixon's trip in 1972. By contrast, in the post-Tianamen environment Japan was truly a driving force in restoring and substantially strengthening economic and political relations, with few comparable moves by the United States.

Other Socialist Countries

What transpired between Japan and China, with Japan taking a leadership role among industrial nations in pursuing closer economic relations, also began to characterize Japanese relations with other socialist Asian countries, including Vietnam, Cambodia, North Korea, Mongolia, and eastern Siberia. The Japanese government refrained from improving official diplomatic or political relations faster than the United States. However, in anticipation that U.S. positions would soften, the Japanese government and business sectors were preparing at the beginning of the 1990s to become major economic participants in a number of areas.

Vietnam

In the case of Vietnam, Japan's interests appeared to be almost entirely economic, since the government did not play a very active role in pressing Vietnam on issues related to solution of the political problems in Cambodia. Despite its poor economic condition at the start of the 1990s, Vietnam held some potentially attractions, including a legacy of entrepreneurial activity in the south. Vietnam is also a potentially important source of raw materials, including oil, gas, and largely untapped timber resources. Japan's interest in timber was enhanced by controversy and restrictions that were beginning to afflict Japanese timber interests in other Southeast Asian nations. The first shipments of Vietnamese timber to Japan began in late 1990.[87]

The obstacle to a more active relationship with Vietnam has been the United States. Even though the Japanese government imposed no official sanctions on dealing with Vietnam (and allowed its businessmen to travel there), the government provided no bilateral aid, discouraged direct investment, and avoided trade financing through the Exim Bank. The only obstacle other than the United States was that Vietnam had ceased payment on earlier ODA loans, which needed to be settled before new aid could be extended. However, the amount in default was quite small and was not a major problem.[88] By the end of 1992 the Japanese government had made basic decisions to resume both ODA loans and grant aid and to assume responsibility (with France) for Vietnam's debts to the International Monetary Fund.[89] Resumption of bilateral ODA would become a strong signal to the private sector to move forward more rapidly with trade and investment projects. U.S. relations with Vietnam were also improving, but at the end of 1992 strict American economic sanctions remained in place.

Although bilateral aid from Japan did not resume until 1993, the Japanese private sector actually began building economic ties with Vietnam as soon as the Vietnamese army withdrew from Cambodia in 1989. Even in 1988, one-third of all foreign business people visiting Vietnam were Japanese, and the number grew rapidly in 1989. The MITI-affiliated Institute of Energy Economics formulated a master plan for developing Vietnam's electric power grid.[90] In 1990 Japanese trading companies and financial institutions, two important elements of trade and investment infrastructure, began opening offices in Vietnam in anticipation of a rapid expansion of business.[91] A key ingredient in producing the rapid upturn in activity in 1990 was the announcement by U.S. Secretary of State James Baker of his willingness to resume direct talks with the Vietnamese government.[92] Just as with policy toward China, small shifts or changes in nuance in U.S. policy became the trigger for quantum leaps in Japanese business activity, based on perceptions of what would be possible without provoking American anger.

In 1991 the rush of Japanese firms to become well positioned in Vietnam accelerated, propelled by the anticipation that the United States would ease its own sanctions on economic ties with Vietnam and that both the World Bank and Asian Development Bank would resume lending fairly soon. By summer 1991, all nine of the large general trading companies had established offices in Vietnam.[93] The Vietnamese government had pressed for Japan to take a leadership role in getting the IMF and the World Bank to extend financial aid, a request that the Japanese government responded to favorably.[94] Keidanren, recognizing the favorable trends, established an Indochina Relations Committee in 1991 and mounted its first trade mission to Vietnam that spring.[95] Japan Airlines Company established a joint venture with Air Vietnam to solidify ties (and engage in charter flights), anticipating an ability to establish regular flights within two to three years.[96]

Despite rising activity, the Japanese were not the largest investors in Vietnam. At the end of 1992 Japanese firms had $305 million invested in Vietnam, putting them in fourth place behind Taiwan ($789 million), Hong Kong ($522 million), and France ($306 million).[97] This implies that Japan was by no means the only country that distanced itself from the United States in terms of economic interaction, and what may characterize Japan is its caution in moving too far from perceptions of what the United States would find acceptable.

Nevertheless, the cumulative levels of direct investment in Vietnam through 1992 were quite low from all countries, and a burst of activity by Japanese firms could quickly propel them to a leading position at any time. The moves they had made from 1988 through 1992 left them well positioned to move ahead very rapidly as soon as they felt political conditions were favorable. An $800 million oil refinery was being negotiated in 1991 that could well mark the beginning of Japan's emergence as the leading foreign investor.[98] Furthermore, Japanese firms were using means other than direct investment, including contracts for technical assistance and equipment sales, to become closely involved in Vietnamese business activity.[99] The resumption of foreign aid was likely to provide the signal for a much higher level of economic interaction.

Japan's policy toward Vietnam could be viewed as an example of American leverage over Japanese foreign policy. At no point did Japan move openly away from American positions, despite the lack of legal constraints on business activity. Japanese caution was sufficiently strong that Vietnamese government officials spoke out on occasion, urging that Japan adopt policies more independent of the United States.[100] But behind the scenes, Japanese economic ties with Vietnam moved ahead quickly at each minor twitch in U.S. policy. The U.S. government perhaps was able to temporarily prevent Japan from forming closer political and economic ties with Vietnam, but it faced a long-term Japanese determination to become a major economic partner with Vietnam—and quite likely at the expense of American firms, which remained severely constrained by the U.S. embargo on commercial contact.

Cambodia

Relative to Vietnam, Japan's economic activity in Cambodia has been minimal, mainly because of the overwhelming nature of the country's political problems. On the political front, however, Cambodia became another opportunity for Japan to take a series of small steps toward greater international political participation. The Japanese government hosted one meeting during the extended negotiations to put together a peace agreement, but participation at that stage was minimal. The government was a member of the Paris Peace Conference, but more important is the fact that Japan became cochair (with Australia) of the Cambodia Reconstruction Committee, allowing it to be engaged in the economic side of Cambodian issues, which were more central to Japanese long-term interests.

In 1991 Japan did offer a "peace plan" that was a small step to clarify several points in the UN Security Council peace plan.[101] This plan represented a further small upturn in real participation. Larger steps came in 1992 with the choice of Yasushi Akashi, a Japanese permanent career official at the UN, to head the Cambodia peacekeeping operation. His choice was at least a symbolic move of some importance to Japanese self-esteem. Furthermore, the government passed legislation enabling Self Defense Force personnel to participate in the UN peacekeeping operation in Cambodia. Unarmed troops were dispatched to Cambodia in fall 1992, but their participation should not be construed as necessarily representing a real interest in Cambodia. The peacekeeping participation issue, considered more fully in the next chapter, was almost entirely one of domestic politics and the broad debate over the legitimate role of the military, and not one of deep concern specifically for Cambodia.

North Korea

Japan engaged in an unusual bit of independent diplomacy when Shin Kanemaru went to North Korea in September 1990 to meet with North

Korean leader Kim Il Sung, and the announcement was made at that time of an intent to initiate negotiations leading to diplomatic ties. North Korea, stung by Soviet recognition of South Korea, appeared eager to make these negotiations quick and successful.[102] The talks began in January 1991, but were quickly mired in two problems: a North Korean insistence for formal apologies for the period of colonization with payment of foreign aid as compensation, and the emergence of the question of North Korean nuclear weapons development. The nuclear issue became a binding constraint on the normalization talks in 1992–93, because of both U.S. and International Atomic Energy Agency concern and the Japanese government's own concern with the possibility of a nearby, unstable, nuclear-armed North Korea. But if the nuclear issue were to be resolved, then normalization talks would appear to be able to progress quite rapidly.

Since much of Japan's investment on the Korean peninsula during the colonial years was located in what is now North Korea (because of extensive mineral deposits), the private sector should be interested in trade and investment ties once the political relationship improves. High levels of literacy and other basic educational skills, combined with very low wages, provide a further economic incentive, and private-sector interests should help push bilateral political normalization once the nuclear issue is resolved.

Burma

Burma has been a recipient of Japanese foreign aid but is on the periphery of Japanese interest in Asia. Aid from Japan was suspended in fall 1988 along with that from other ODA donors (and Japanese businessmen were discouraged from visiting the country) because of severe human rights violations. However, just as in the case of China, the suspension was quite temporary; ODA disbursements were resumed in March 1989—although, as with China, the explanatory fig leaf was that only disbursements under the existing ODA plan were involved and that no discussions of a new multiyear plan would take place.[103] Apparently this decision came after considerable conflict within the Japanese government, in which the Ministry of Foreign Affairs (desiring to continue the suspension) was defeated by the more commercial interests of the Ministry of Finance and MITI.[104] In this case, the Foreign Ministry may have been able to use foreign aid to gain some leverage in pressing the Burmese government on human rights issues, but it did so very quietly behind the scenes.[105]

Japan Sea Region

The rigid cold war political divisions that marked the nations of northeast Asia after the end of World War II meant that little of the cross-border movement of goods and services that characterized other parts of the world was able to develop. Beginning in 1990, though, considerable discussion began in Japan and elsewhere about building stronger cooperative relationships in the Japan Sea region, which involved mainly Japan, Russia (then still the Soviet Union), China, South Korea, and North Korea. This is a region where geographic separation is measured in only hundreds of miles. Some proposals even called for formation of an "East China Sea economic bloc" with preferential tariff treatment.[106]

Most of the proposals related to the Japan Sea region were somewhat fanciful, including a United Nations Development Program proposal for creating extensive new port and transportation facilities in the area of the Tumen River (which runs along the border of China, Russia, and North Korea).[107] Proponents of large-scale programs to increase economic interaction within the region may discover that political divisions were not the only reason the affected regions of each country have been relatively undeveloped economically; climate (heavy snows), lack of year-round harbors, shallow water in rivers and harbors, and other natural factors are probably involved as well. Nevertheless, the very fact that Japanese scholars, businessmen, and some officials were participating in the discussion about possible initiatives to increase investment and trade among these geographically close areas was a change from the past.

Real progress on such subregional policy proposals, though, would require substantial change in relations with North Korea, which remained very uncertain in 1993. If relations with North Korea do change, then at least some movement toward expanded economic ties within this subregion is a possibility. Such ties would probably be buttressed by Japanese ODA for harbor facilities along the North Korean coast, as well as some Japanese private-sector direct investment in North Korea, Russia, and China.

Russia and Eastern Europe

To put this intensified interest and activity with Asian socialist countries into some perspective, it is worth noting that this interest and enthusiasm did not apply very much to the former Soviet Union or Eastern Europe. The exception is the coastal region of eastern Siberia (which is part of the Japan Sea regional interest). Japanese business had a long history of relations with Asian countries (including some firms that pursued ties with China and North Korea in the 1960s). The upturn in Japan's economic activity with the NIEs, ASEAN, and the Asian socialist countries came from carefully reached conclusions that these nations were sufficiently stable politically and ready economically for expanded Japanese involvement. Even though Japanese trading companies had been involved in the Soviet Union, the knowledge or understanding of either the former Soviet Union or Eastern Europe seemed much less substantial than that of Asia. Furthermore, it seems doubtful that Japanese firms would choose to engage in new and uncertain relationships in the former Soviet republics or Eastern Europe when the nations of Asia offer greater political stability and unrealized economic potential.

An illustration of that difference is that when Mikhail Gorbachev visited Tokyo in April 1991, not only did he achieve little on the so-called Northern Territories issue, but he received a rather cold reception in meetings with Japanese business leaders. Raw material prices were not sufficiently high to induce much Japanese interest in Siberian raw materials; the quality of Russian goods did not suggest much potential for substantial increases in their exports to pay for technology and goods from Japan; and Japanese businessmen were not particularly impressed with the profitability of investment opportunities in Soviet manufacturing.

These statements concerning the relative lack of interest expressed by Japanese firms should be tempered slightly. Recognizing that their country had to maintain an official stance of restraint because of failure to solve the difficult territorial issue of the four small islands off the coast of Hokkaido, Japanese firms began using other Asian countries as a base for trading with the Soviet Union. Mitsui and Company, Mitsubishi, and other trading companies, for example, were using subsidiaries in Thailand and elsewhere in Asia to engage in trade with Russia.[108] Nor should Gorbachev's trip to Tokyo in April 1991 be regarded as a total failure. Although the issue of the islands remained unsolved, the meeting produced a variety of modest agreements that would act to provide greater support for an upgraded economic relationship, including agreement on expanding flights between various Japanese cities and locations in both Siberia and the western regions of the Soviet Union.[109] Japanese firms might not show the same degree of interest in Siberia as in Southeast

Asia, but they certainly had no intention of ignoring the long-term possibility of engaging in business. As confirmation of this intention, a variety of business deals were also announced around the time of the Gorbachev visit.[110]

By fall 1991 the Japanese government felt enough pressure from the other major industrial nations to announce a $2.5 billion foreign aid package, but upon close inspection most of this package consisted of trade insurance ($1.8 billion, plus $200 million in Exim Bank credit guarantees) and Exim Bank loans for trade financing ($500 million).[111] These were relatively costless and cautious forms of aid that stand in great contrast to the large infrastructure projects that Japanese foreign aid was financing in Asia. In essence, the Japanese government offered to subsidize and reduce the risk for Japanese exports, eschewing (at least for the moment) efforts to build a deeper involvement in the Russian economy. American and European interest in expanding aid to Russia in 1992 and 1993 also left Japan in the position of agreeing reluctantly after some pressure. This reluctant provision of aid in cooperation with other industrial powers continued in 1993.

Eastern Europe presented an even less interesting prospect for Japanese business in the early 1990s. Some Japanese firms will certainly build economic ties, but one does not detect the sort of enthusiasm that characterized Japanese attitudes toward Asia. Prime Minister Kaifu announced a $2 billion foreign aid package (spread across several years) in early 1990 during a visit to the region. But this aid program was very much like the one announced for the Soviet Union in 1991; the bulk of the money was in the form of export insurance ($750 million) and Exim Bank trade financing ($1 billion).[112]

Because of the rather limited interest in Russia and Eastern Europe, Japan's interaction with socialist countries will definitely have a regional flavor. Continuing political problems in China, North Korea, and Vietnam could dampen Japan's ability to build closer ties with these nations, but the prospects were much better than with the former Soviet Union, and Japanese interest was much stronger. Japanese commercial interests were quite strong toward the Asian socialist countries. American policy constraints might affect the timing and style of Japanese contacts with these nations, but there was no doubt that the Japanese government and private sectors were moving rapidly toward a deepening political and economic relationship that went far beyond the cautious approach of the United States through the early 1990s.

Conclusion

Japan's relationship with the rest of the Asia-Pacific region was changing and deepening with stunning speed after 1985, and the pace promised to continue in the 1990s. After forty-five years of relative neglect, the rest of Asia, and the broader Asia-Pacific region, became a major preoccupation for many Japanese. The neglect came partly as result of the Chinese Communist revolution and the cold war, which served to separate Japan (with its tight security linkage to the United States) from much of the nearby Asian mainland. Other reasons included the legacy of hostility from war, Japanese embarrassment about that legacy, and the postwar occupation that pulled Japan into the U.S. orbit.

All of the forces that acted as a brake on Japan's regional role were gone or fading fast by the early 1990s. The decline or reform of Communist regimes raised new opportunities for broad regional trade and investment ties. China, Vietnam, and possibly Cambodia and North Korea could be drawn into a closer economic framework. Memories of the war were fading around the region, replaced by the reality of Japanese trade and investment presence. Finally, Asia's continuing rapid economic growth caused Japanese businesses to focus on the region more heavily, an interest fueled further by concern over a possible protectionist trend in the United States and Europe.

As a result of the surge in Japanese interest and activity in Asia, the rough equality in the economic presence there of Japan and the United States was shifting rapidly. In the earlier postwar period, Americans believed that the region's hostility toward the Japanese because of the war would prevent the emergence of a regionalism centered on Japan. But by the 1990s this no longer characterized these countries, and something that could be termed a "soft" economic regionalism centered on Japan was already materializing. In most parts of the region, emotional reactions toward Japan were tempered by pragmatic recognition of it as a useful source of direct investment, technology, commercial loans, and foreign aid and even as a role model for economic development. Only nearby South Korea, with its long-held animosity toward Japan, might be considered an exception, and even there economic connections were strong.

A more independent Japan is clearly evident in the wide variety of its dealings with this region considered above. Although a form of diplomatic deference to the United States remained, it is quite clear that Japan had its own agenda for the Asia-Pacific countries. Americans often miss the point by arguing that Japan has no unifying principles to sell to the world. For the developing countries in Asia, Japan has a very clear and strong principle: economic success is important, and it can be achieved through a modified capitalist framework that accepts a strong role for the government (and downplays emphasis on democracy or human rights). Nations in the region may be reluctant to see the soft regionalism solidify into something more substantial, given the disproportionate economic size of Japan. They may also look less than favorably upon the commercial strings attached to aid. But whatever their misgivings, nations throughout the broad Asia-Pacific have clearly accepted a much more involved and activist Japan.

CHAPTER SIX

The Limits of
Economic Power

MUCH OF JAPAN'S larger regional or global role has been economic. Atmospheric pollution control and foreign aid, in particular, are areas of increased involvement. However, not all of the world's problems are economic, and the nation still faces a major question: how to participate more fully in solving international political problems or crises. After almost half a century of not being involved in serious international political issues, Japan lacks clear notions about what it can, should, or will do to participate.

Because of the country's emphasis on economic issues and its history of providing financial support without real participation, some see the patterns of the past continuing in the future. Policies to promote economic development and reduce pollution certainly can indirectly lessen sharp political or military conflict, and this approach of seeking economic solutions to international problems has worked reasonably well in some cases. The record in Asia presented in the previous chapter, where international political or ideological divisions diminished and national economic performance became more important over the course of the 1980s, suggests that this approach may continue to work quite well for Japan. But not all international problems yield to the long-run economic strategies the government would prefer to pursue.

Japan is too large a member of the international community to be a completely disinterested bystander to international crises, as it was in the earlier postwar period. The Korean War, the Vietnam War, the Berlin Wall, the Cuban missile crisis, and the 1973 Mideast crisis all involved little or no active Japanese political involvement, other than tacit support for the position of the United States when necessary. But in the 1990–91 Persian Gulf crisis, the nation was profoundly shaken by a sense of international pressure to be more involved than in the past, and the domestic debate over what form that involvement should take proved to be difficult. Without any recent history of political involvement, the easiest route was to provide money—but this gift did not end foreign criticism that participation had been inadequate. Larger issues of appropriate participation remained for further domestic debate.

A critically important issue is whether the inability of the Japanese government to find new means of participating in the Gulf crisis was a result of inexperience or a reflection of deeper structural problems. By 1992 the government was able to pass a law allowing limited participation of military forces in UN peacekeeping operations, but this still left Japan very far from being a major participant in world affairs. Obviously participation has been hampered by the legacy of World War II and the prolonged postwar pattern of adopting a low profile in the shadow of the United States. However, the additional fact that Japan is a consensus society with a generally reactive posture toward the world (a feature of foreign policy even before the war) may prove to be a powerful force from which Japan cannot escape easily or at all. Much of the talk about participation in Japan deals with symbolic gestures; the desire to actually be involved in difficult international issues seems quite low because of these structural features of society and politics. This chapter explores the argument of whether issues of participation are transitory or structural, using the 1990–91 Gulf crisis and its aftermath as a central example.

Temporary Problems?

To some extent, difficulty in participating effectively in world political affairs may be a temporary legacy of past noninvolvement. The government and public have acted on a number of assumptions that were adequate in the past and have yet to develop new information, assumptions, and policies to meet the new circumstances. These inheritances have included a belief that a passive role in the world contributed sufficiently to global peace, a general lack of accurate knowledge of international affairs, and a failure to acknowledge responsibility for the devastation of World II in Asia. These beliefs or policies have impeded a more active global involvement, but they are not necessarily permanent features.

For many years, the dominant position of the Japanese public was that to be uninvolved in the world was a positive contribution to world peace because Japan had been such a disruptive force during the 1930s and 1940s. In this view, Japan's experience as the "victim" of the terrible and enormous destructive power of modern war—including the experience of being the only target of atomic weapons—would teach the world to be peaceful. To some extent, liberals and conservatives were able to share this view. Liberals opposed international involvement because they intensely feared a repetition of the slide into militarism and the abominations that a radical right-wing military government perpetrated on Asia and on Japan itself. Conservatives could agree because they believed the war was a failure and the nation would be better off to be closely allied with a powerful protector like the United States.

It is impossible to overemphasize the strength of this attitude and the deep isolationism of the Japanese public in the postwar period. As a result, Japan's postwar foreign policy was a simple one of following the lead of American policy when necessary and maintaining an extremely low profile whenever possible to avoid antagonizing foreign countries. This policy proved to be a highly successful strategy in the sense that the government did avoid involvement in difficult foreign issues and maintained a focus on domestic economic performance that brought the nation into the ranks of the advanced industrial nations by the 1970s. Political scientist Donald Hellmann has labeled this approach to the world "Japan in the American greenhouse," a particularly apt description.[1] When external events—such as the 1973 oil crisis—damaged the national economic interest, the response was to feel again that the nation was a victim of a harsh and antagonistic world.[2] Such views were easy to maintain when the government played no direct, active role in either the cause or the solution of international problems.

The Gulf crisis and war in 1990–91 provided a major jolt to the comfortable notion of passivity. Although other events (the Soviet invasion of Afghanistan in 1980 or the Iran-Iraq war in the 1980s) had brought somewhat greater awareness that passivity was inadequate, the Gulf crisis had a far more substantial impact. Since the recognition of international expectations that Japan should be more active is so recent, the failure to agree upon and articulate a new set of principles should not be surprising.

An important consequence of the past passive approach to international affairs was a naive and relatively uninformed view of the outside world. This meant that when the nation was faced with rethinking its global role at the beginning of the 1990s, it lacked an adequate foundation of information on which to base policy judgments. To the extent that this problem was due to past insularity, it could prove to be transitory.

Much of the attention given to international news in the Japanese newspapers in the past was devoted to the United States, and even that news often created unrealistic or skewed perceptions. The Japanese public was exposed to a barrage of news and analysis about the United States (especially concerning bilateral economic relations), but because most people had very limited personal international experience, they had little basis on which to put this analysis into perspective or judge its accuracy. Much of the coverage of the United States also emphasized negative or critical themes.

An example is the explanation given when the U.S. government reacted negatively to disclosure of a sale of sophisticated machine tools by Toshiba Machine Company to the Soviet Union in violation of Coordinating Committee on Export Controls (COCOM) rules in the mid-1980s. The head of U.S. operations for the respected government broadcasting network (NHK) explained American policy as entirely the result of then-Assistant Secretary of Defense Richard Perle's personal dislike for the parent company Toshiba because it went along with the Arab boycott of Israel in 1973. This trivialization and distortion of an important policy issue (in which Japan maintained its convenient position as a victim of external forces—in this case, capricious American policy) came from a man with a degree from Tokyo University, a long career of covering the United States for NHK, and four books to his name.[3]

Wildly idiosyncratic views certainly occupy a portion of the American media as well, but generally not from senior journalists affiliated with the largest mainstream news organizations. Anti-Semitic views and books, born largely out of ignorance and espousing positions such as denial of the Holocaust, continue to appear from mainstream publishers and gain some popularity in Japan.[4] These are part of the broader problem of accuracy of information about the United States and the rest of the world. The volume of news in the press concerning the United States has been large, but with distortions and inaccuracies that are not conducive to building a base of knowledge for informed decisionmaking on bilateral or international issues.

After having chosen to remain uninvolved in world affairs, Japan saddled itself with another dilemma in trying to forge a new involvement with the world. Because of the dynamics of domestic politics, the Japanese government—in the form of either the emperor or the prime minister—did not express full, formal, contrite apologies acknowledging responsibility for the tragedy of the war in Asia until the advent of the new coalition government in 1993. Failure to make these apologies has been a continuing source of Asian criticism of Japan; another is a number of recurring incidents in which the past has been deliberately ignored, covered up, or denied. Conservatives maintained pressure to diminish references in school textbooks to Japanese responsibility or guilt concerning the history of militarism and war.

Official efforts to downplay or deny aspects of the war experience continued into the 1990s. As recently as 1990, the Ministry of Education denied permission for a textbook to include references to the death toll in Asian countries during the war.[5] The government also tried to ignore a set of skulls uncovered in 1990 during a Tokyo construction project; they were suspected of being those of prisoners of war killed in a nefarious medical research lab in Shinjuku during the war. Efforts of private Japanese researchers to pursue the issue failed when government pressure allegedly caused a number of research labs to refuse to work on the remains.[6] In 1991 the government denied that large numbers of women (mainly from Korea and Taiwan) were forced to serve as prostitutes for Japanese military forces, only to be embarrassed when its position was refuted by discoveries by private researchers.[7] This particular episode was exposed just before a state visit by Prime Minister Kiichi Miyazawa to South Korea and led to contrite (but indirect) official apologies. But the initial denial of government involvement or responsibility in the face of reports of the large-scale wartime tragedy had done its damage.

Japan's international reputation was seriously harmed by the government's inability to deal openly and officially with a grim past in a manner that would reassure the outside world that the government and public truly repudiated what happened. The rationale that admission of official responsibility in such episodes would lead to heavy demands for monetary compensation from Asian countries is not convincing.

Since Japanese academics and journalists are often the leading actors in exposing these problems, it would be unfair to attribute to the broad public the unwillingness to admit guilt. The government's resistance continued a pattern of polarized politics, in which the bureaucracy and the very conservative political party that was in power continuously from 1955 to 1993 resisted the pressure of left-wing elements of society. But the left-right dichotomy of the 1960s seemed outdated by the 1990s, making the continued stiff resistance of the Liberal Democratic party to war guilt issues symbolic of its inability to disassociate itself from its right-wing supporters.

The idea of apologizing officially to Asian countries made some progress even before 1993, with the new emperor expressing resolve that Japan would "never repeat the horrors of that most unfortunate war" while visiting Thailand in 1991, a statement well short of formal apology or admission of responsibility.[8] When Prime Minister Toshiki Kaifu visited South Korea in May 1991, the wording of his statement of regret was the result of prolonged negotiations with the South Korean government, rather than coming as a spontaneous, unilateral action. At least when Kaifu went to Singapore later in 1991, he acknowledged "contrition at Japanese past actions that afflicted unbearable suffering," a statement more straightforward than most in the earlier postwar period.[9]

The issue of war guilt changed rather dramatically in 1993, demonstrating the possibly transitory nature of some of the obstacles to more effective international interaction. When the coalition of opposition parties formed a government in summer 1993, one of new Prime Minister Morihiro Hosokawa's first international policy acts was to make clear, explicit statements concerning the past.[10] His comments reflected the long-held position of some of the parties making up the coalition and indicated the sort of change made possible by the LDP's fall from power. If the LDP returns to power, it could possibly retract such language, but the apology and recognition of guilt, once made, will be difficult to repudiate.

In addition, the current emperor has the advantage of distance from the issues, putting him in a better position to issue sympathetic statements. Because his father was emperor during the war, left-wing groups and the media in Japan watched closely for statements that could be interpreted as an admission of personal guilt for what happened to the nation. Neither the Showa emperor nor his extremely conservative handlers in the imperial household wanted to allow any such possibility. Generational change, therefore, may make progress somewhat easier.

To the extent that the problems identified here have been the result of a lack of international experience, recent developments ought to move Japan in the direction of overcoming those problems. The surge in the number of Japanese traveling, studying, and temporarily living abroad, the increasing presence of foreigners in Japan, and the need for more accurate information to manage overseas direct investment and portfolio assets all help to bring a more informed knowledge about the outside world, as well as greater sensitivity to the views of foreigners on issues such as war guilt. But this prognosis is not particularly encouraging for the near future. The increase in foreign travel, education, and living experience is of such recent origin that the young people involved will not move into positions of importance in Japanese society for another fifteen to twenty years; they will not have much influence in dealing with immediate issues. Basic decisions on how the nation should interact with the world remain in the hands of a generation of political and bureaucratic leaders with little personal international experience. They will shape much of the continuing debate over the nation's international role during the 1990s. The 1993 ouster of the LDP by the opposition coalition certainly made a difference in official apologies for the war, but it did not alter the basic generational problem.

Structural Problems

Increased international experience may ease some impediments to political participation, but other problems may be more deeply rooted in social behavior patterns that do not change quickly. At the core of this issue are two questions: is the government able to act decisively in times of international crisis, and is it able to define a set of principles or goals to govern participation that go beyond the predominant emphasis on a narrowly defined national economic interest? These problems are related to political structure and more broadly to the nature of society.

Domestic decisionmaking has rested upon carefully crafted consensus solutions in which losing groups are generally compensated to win their acquiescence.[11] Two consequences follow from this process. First, successful solutions of difficult questions take considerable time as all parties concerned maneuver to determine winners and losers as well as the amount of compensation needed to generate agreement. Second, solutions are rarely decisive because winners need to temper the solutions greatly to satisfy losing groups so that they will not openly oppose the outcome.

The structure of government is consistent with these social dynamics. The prime minister's office, for example, has proven to be rather weak. The problem is not the constitutional authority of the prime minister but social expectations and the factionalized nature of party politics. Group dynamics in Japan rarely involve strong leadership and authority, and a strong, decisive prime minister would be inconsistent with expectations that political patterns should conform to general social patterns.

Furthermore, Japanese politics tend to be very factionalized. The LDP is divided into several competing factions built around personal and financial loyalties rather than ideological or policy differences. Struggle among these factions over the prime ministership or policy issues was often fierce, and solutions involved the same dynamics of consensus building and compensation. The coalitions among the various factions of the LDP are generally fragile enough that most prime ministers in recent decades were considered weak by the press because they could not push decisively or rapidly on difficult issues. The coalition of opposition parties forming the government in 1993 simply continued the tradition. Prime Minister Hosokawa could not proceed easily or quickly because of the fragile nature of the coalition, reinforcing the notion of weak leadership.

Lack of decisive leadership does not necessarily mean endless stalemate on purely domestic issues. In 1988 the Diet passed a law implementing a consumption tax, a relatively decisive step in tax reform. But the process of building sufficient political support to create the legislation and bring it to a successful vote took an entire decade, and attempts at leadership by individual prime ministers along the way did little to accelerate the process.

With weakness at the top, Japan's postwar history of dealing with international problems has not been one of decisive or forceful action. Global crises sometimes required the Japanese government to express support of the United States or engage in symbolic actions, such as boycotting the 1980 Moscow Olympics. Action in these cases involved clear, strong signals from the United States, so decisions were relatively easy to reach. Occasionally, however, small crises erupted that the government had to face on its own, such as those related to international terrorism carried out by tiny but extremely radical left-wing Japanese groups.

During the 1970s a small number of radical students joined the international terrorist network and made the Japanese government the main target of their activities. Starting with the hijacking of a Japan Airlines plane to North Korea in 1970, a series of incidents proceeded over the next two decades, including the massacre at the Tel Aviv Airport (1972), another hijacking in 1972, the bombing of oil storage facilities in Singapore in 1974, occupation of the U.S embassy in Kuala Lumpar (1975), another hijacking (1977), a mortar attack against the Japanese and American embassies in Jakarta (1986), the bombing of the USO club in Naples (1988), and possible participation in aborted actions intended to disrupt the Seoul Olympics (1988).

The actions involving hostages included demands on the Japanese government, which were generally met. Rather than standing firm, the government simply did whatever the terrorists wanted, a behavior pattern at odds with that of other national governments faced with terrorism and a product of weak domestic institutions to deal with crisis situations.[12] This historical record suggests that the Japanese government was poorly equipped to deal with larger international political problems that would require decisive, swift action. The record of government response to the Gulf crisis (considered later in this chapter) repeats this pattern: decisions generally lagged behind those of other involved powers.

Inability to find workable solutions to some domestic issues has proven to be so difficult that reliance has often been placed on *gaiatsu*, or outside pressure, to swing the balance. On issues ranging from import barriers to deregulation of financial markets and even taxation of real estate, domestic political forces have used or responded to foreign pressure— sometimes even inviting or encouraging it to help sway decisions in their direction. The U.S. government has been the principal source of the outside pressure, a role that has come about as a result of historical legacy (the war and occupation), a vague sense of international hierarchy (the Japanese still view the United States as more prestigious and powerful than their own country), an overwhelming focus on maintaining access to American markets for goods and investment (given the large shares of exports and investment destined to the United States), and a concern for maintaining the U.S.-Japan mutual security treaty as the cornerstone of Japanese foreign policy. This combination of factors has given political legitimacy in Japan to pressure from the United States as a motivation for domestic policy decisions.

Reliance on outside forces to obtain domestic change, and thus responding reactively to other governments' leadership, does not augur well for a more active role in world affairs. Even *gaiatsu* as a strategy presupposes a domestic group in favor of action, but it also represents a weak paradigm for handling difficult decisions because the responsibility or blame for the decisions is transferred to distant outside actors. As demonstrated later in this chapter, *gaiatsu* is a principal explanation for how the government dealt with the Gulf crisis. Policy responses came from perceptions of American pressure rather than from an independent assessment of the situation.

To some extent, structural problems in governance could be ameliorated by changes in organization. Some attempts were made to strengthen the office of the prime minister during the Nakasone administration in the 1980s. Two structural changes took place in the government then that could have enhanced the ability of the prime minister to exercise leadership. The first was the establishment of the Management and Coordination Agency in 1984, which brought more central control over a number of previously independent agencies (personnel management, administrative inspection, administrative structure oversight, and policy coordination). The second move was a general overhaul of the structure of the cabinet secretariat, including the establishment in 1986 of a Cabinet Security Council, complete with its own staff (made up of officials drawn from several ministries). The purpose of this exercise was to provide the prime minister's office (and the whole cabinet) with stronger institutional mechanisms for making decisions in the face of domestic or international crises.[13]

Unfortunately, the changes did not bring about the desired consolidation of power in the prime minister's office. Because of strong opposition from bureaucratic interests, the Finance Ministry, Foreign Ministry, and Defense Agency downgraded the level of their officials participating in the new security office from administrative vice-ministers (that is, the highest ranking career bureaucrats) to bureau directors. Furthermore, because staff people lent to the secretariat were reassigned to their respective ministries after their tour at the cabinet security office, their ministries retained a strong claim to their loyalty and actions while they were on loan.[14]   •

Yasuhiro Nakasone apparently used this new cabinet mechanism for formulating government policy, but it was not used effectively after his tenure during the Gulf crisis in 1990–91 or the Soviet coup attempt in August 1991. Atsuyuki Sasa, who had been head of the security office under Nakasone, criticized Prime Minister Kaifu for not making use of the new institution during the Gulf crisis and for allowing bureaucratic infighting to delay the government policy response.[15] During the August

1991 crisis in the Soviet Union, the Defense Agency possessed information relayed by the U.S. government about the lack of Soviet military troop movements, but did not pass this information on to either the security office or the Foreign Ministry (which, in the absence of this information, was leaning toward recognition of the coup leaders).[16]

Nakasone was an aggressive prime minister who created the new mechanism and chose to use it. Kaifu, on the other hand, was weaker politically and succumbed to more traditional decisionmaking patterns. Hosokawa came to office with a more assertive personal style, in the Nakasone tradition, but still remained dependent on a complex coalition. The Japanese political system produces more relatively weak, traditional prime ministers dependent on coalition politics than strong figures like Nakasone or Hosokawa. Thus the institutional changes in the 1980s were not likely to result in any meaningful change in decisionmaking patterns in government.

A strong theme in Sasa's complaint about crisis management during the Gulf War was the lack of any standardized policy "guidebook" for dealing with hostage crises (Japanese citizens were held along with other foreigners in Iraq and Kuwait after the invasion in August 1990). He accused government officials of harboring unrealistic, optimistic views rather than planning realistically or for worst-case scenarios.[17]

His criticism raised an important point. Certain aspects of international crises, such as how the government should respond when Japanese citizens are taken hostage abroad, could possibly be handled through routine practices worked out and accepted by the political system in advance. However, ultimately a "guidebook" would be far from sufficient. The essence of international political crises is their unpredictability and nonroutine nature, and what the government lacked was not a set of standardized policies but a means of forging political agreement to respond to nonstandard situations.

In an effort once again to move toward more decisive decisionmaking, the Administrative Reform Council, an advisory group to the prime minister that was instrumental in bringing about important structural changes in government organization in the 1980s, advocated in 1991 a new cabinet post of foreign policy minister (*taigai seisaku tantōshō*).[18] This proposal proved to be too controversial because it would have created a position separate from but overlapping with that of the foreign minister, and it was not included in the formal report of the council. Even if bureaucratic opposition had not killed this recommendation, though, it is unlikely that the creation of a new post would have solved the more fundamental problem of power and decisionmaking in the government.

One of the many justifications for electoral reforms being discussed in the 1990s was the creation of stronger political leadership. According to this argument, multimember districts for the lower house of the Diet led to factions in the LDP, as well as high campaign costs with attendant financial scandals. Single-member districts might reduce campaign costs and thereby lessen the role of factions as a mechanism for distributing political finances. But hopes that these changes would produce significantly stronger political leadership are unfounded. Weak or subtle leadership is such a deeply ingrained part of social dynamics that major change seems unlikely even with a shift to single-member election districts. The series of political scandals from 1980 to 1993 may have weakened leadership even further than usual, and reform that reduces the incidence of debilitating scandal is welcome, but expectations about the nature of ensuing government dynamics must be cautious.

These structural impediments in government decisionmaking are quite serious, and efforts to solve them by tinkering with government organization do not appear to have been very successful. A general social system of consensus building, powerful vested bureaucratic interests, and weak political leaders will change very slowly at best. Furthermore, the deeply ingrained pattern of legitimizing domestic decisions by pointing to foreign actions or pressures will not yield easily over time. A slow-moving, technical issue like international policy on atmospheric warming may allow a leadership role by a cautious, consensus-seeking government, but rapidly developing, unpredictable political crises will continue to show the Japanese government at its worst.

An Economic Definition of Participation

Not experienced or comfortable with the world's political issues and problems, Japan's political and bureaucratic leadership has focused largely on economic aspects of international involvement. Defining its world role in economic terms is consistent with the fact that Japanese self-esteem is centered in the success of the domestic economy. Japan's ambassador to the OECD in 1991, Hiroaki Fujii, expressed this role succinctly. Japan's international role in a post–cold war environment, he wrote, should center on economics because the nation is a supplier of capital (in a world where international capital may be more scarce in the future), has the "world's most efficient manufacturing sector," and is a world leader in research and development.[19] With this sort of supreme confidence in the capabilities of the economy, the nation sees its role as bringing its expertise to foster the growth and development of the rest of the world.

Others have been even more forceful, arguing that the economic contributions provide the real solutions to goals such as peace and democracy. Kanji Nishio, an academic, stated quite baldly that concepts such as democracy and peace are nothing but empty slogans, and what Japan has to offer is a far more concrete or realistic effort to push the world ahead economically.[20] A report from the Nomura Research Institute in 1988 argued that maintaining a healthy economy at home was the best contribution Japan could make toward the solution of world problems (along with steps to address the large imbalance in direct investment through policies to increase foreign investment in Japan).[21] And in response to the Gulf crisis in 1990, an editorial writer at *Nihon Keizai Shimbun* opined that dealing with the crisis by providing money was appropriate because such a response was a form of the use of economic power.[22]

In this economic view of Japan's world role, virtually all forms of monetary flow to the world are labeled as contributions to improving peace and stability. An interim report of the Industrial Structure Council (an important advisory committee to MITI) issued in 1990 defined a world role in terms of environmental initiatives, provision of technology and know-how, and human contact—all for the purpose of improving economic performance elsewhere in the world. Typical of this economic-centered view, the report argued that overseas development assistance by itself was a poor measure of the nation's global contribution, and that a more appropriate measure of what Japan was doing to promote global peace and development should include trade, foreign direct investment, commercial finance, and technical contracts.[23] By claiming that Japan's contribution should consist of encouraging all of these forms of international action, the report adopted an extremely narrow world view, in which actions undertaken to benefit Japanese firms should simply be relabeled as a global contribution to international peace and development.

Corporations are legitimately motivated by their own self-interest in market share and profits. They do not generally have much interest in broader economic or political issues that are not directly connected to these direct corporate goals, but a government policy that is little more than the summation of such individual corporate interests is inadequate. Because the commonality of interest between the government sector and business has been so strong in Japan, the government's international economic policies do not really meet the grandiose claims made about contributions to broad international goals of peace and development.

Exercising Economic Power?

Taken to its extreme, this narrow economic view of Japan's role has been profoundly disturbing to some, who see Japan using its financial leverage to pursue its own economic agenda rather than to further global peace and development. One American critic finds Japan's position as a global financial leader disturbing because Japan lacks "certain qualities necessary to be the kind of financial leader that can maintain stability and openness in the world's financial and trading system."[24] In such views, the Japanese role undermines the very international framework that provides a basis for peaceful economic interaction, and, although many of the concerns expressed by critics are exaggerated, the country's past record on trade and financial liberalization certainly does not conjure up images of international leadership.

Others see the newfound international economic presence of Japan leading to dominance or manipulation of other nations to fit a continued narrow economic agenda. Concern over such influence seems to be an underlying theme, though a poorly articulated one, in American public uneasiness over the wave of Japanese investment in the late 1980s. Bill Emmott espoused the view that capital was providing leverage for the Japanese abroad: "The more that Japan invests abroad, gives in development aid, or hands out as bank loans, the more the recipients become beholden to Japan and the more that Japan or Japanese institutions can demand in return."[25] Others argued that the Japanese government had already exercised this new power by threatening to keep Japanese institutions from buying U.S. Treasury bonds as a means of influencing trade disputes (and, in particular, to obtain elimination of punitive duties levied on Japanese exports to the United States in 1987 as part of a dispute over semiconductors).[26] Still others suggested that even if this particular unlikely threat did not occur, the Japanese government possessed an unprecedented ability to intervene in U.S. domestic financial markets, for whatever purpose.[27] All of these views contain a kernel of truth, though they are generally exaggerated.

All creditors possess some influence stemming from their ability to deny debtors further funds. This power has led the International Monetary Fund to impose conditionality on loans to high-debt developing countries, forcing them to make adjustments intended to alleviate their long-term debt problems. To the extent that the Japanese see themselves as possessing this power internationally, it is indicative of the strong asymmetry in Japanese investment; a nation can exercise its financial power to obtain policy changes in another only if there is a one-way flow of capital. Otherwise, power is reciprocal and represents something akin to the mutually assured destruction of nuclear strategy. The asymmetry discussed in chapter 3, with assets owned overseas by Japanese exceeding foreign ownership of assets in Japan, suggests partial fulfillment of conditions necessary to exercise influence. The largest imbalance, however, exists in direct investment, which is a less clear tool of power than loans because direct investments represent longer-term commitments: factories cannot be relocated quickly or easily in most cases (although presumably future flows of new direct investment could be affected).

While the imbalance in investment into and out of Japan might appear to confer some influence in world affairs, the reality may be quite the opposite. That the Japanese government tried to use the U.S. Treasury bond market to influence trade policy is doubtful at best, and in fact, during the 1980s the government generally encouraged financial institutions to buy U.S. Treasury bonds as a means of maintaining harmony in bilateral relations. Other examples suggest that the government continued to invest heavily in various international causes without gaining much influence. Chapter 4 considered Japan's rising contributions to multilateral financial institutions, which were eventually accompanied by a shift in voting rights but not by any strong sense of an effort to bend or shape the agendas of these organizations in new directions (at least until 1992, when Japan put pressure on the World Bank to reconsider the role of government in economic development). Huge financial contributions to the Gulf War in 1991 (discussed below), large contributions to the United Nations and its peacekeeping operations in Cambodia and Yugoslavia without strongly demanding a permanent seat on the Security Council, and other examples suggest that the Japanese government did very little to exercise any financial power in the late 1980s or early 1990s.

Nevertheless, some truth lies in the notion of Japanese economic power. By becoming major asset holders and substantial providers of new flows of international capital, the Japanese have gained a voice in world affairs that they did not have previously. The extreme version of this view—that Japan will dominate the United States or the world, or that some dark conspiracy exists in the Japanese government to accomplish this end—is fanciful. On the other hand, the discussion of developments in Asia in the previous chapter does imply a use of financial resources to shape developments in Asian countries to favor the interests of Japanese business. At a global level as well, the Japanese are an important part of discussions of financial issues simply because their share of financial flows has increased. Japanese financial institutions and government officials may not be leaders or even dominant voices in international policy discussions of financial issues, but they became participants in these multilateral forums by virtue of the large capital flows from Japan.

The Objectives of Influence

If Japan has achieved a presence and is in a position to exercise some influence in international economic affairs, what are the nation's objectives in exercising that influence? No clear statement of goals or objectives exists, other than the usual platitudes concerning maintenance of international financial stability and other aspects of the current international economic structure. Many say that Japan has no agenda, and many Japanese have difficulty articulating anything other than support for existing world institutions and policies. However, it is possible to identify some elements of a de facto Japanese set of policies or strategies toward the world. Vigorous arguments may continue in Japan from both the liberal and conservative direction, but the following are the most likely to represent the mainstream outcome.

First, the government is deeply committed to maintenance of some workable international framework in which it can interact economically with the rest of the world. Government, business, and the public are all aware that the nation depends on imported raw materials, exports to pay for these materials, and—more recently—overseas outlets for investment to maintain domestic economic prosperity. For the postwar period, that framework was provided primarily by the General Agreement on Tariffs and Trade, the International Monentary Fund, and the large U.S. market. While the thrust of policy may well be to maintain these institutions and access to the U.S. market, other configurations are possible, including a shift toward managed trade or a more Asian-centered regional focus, should perceptions change concerning the viability of the existing structures.

Commitment to particular institutions or markets has little to do with a broad ideological belief in principles and much to do with maintaining a system that provides the economic elements required for Japanese economic prosperity. For example, the Japanese government has readily acquiesced in voluntary export agreements, engaged in administrative guidance on investment, and even pursued diplomatic policies (as in the Gulf crisis) to satisfy the United States sufficiently to prevent more serious protectionist outcomes in the American market for exports and investment—the largest of all overseas markets for Japanese firms.

Second, Japan is increasingly interested in projecting onto developing countries its own economic institutional framework and development process, based on a growing belief that the Japanese version of capitalism is superior to that of the United States. This desire is visible in the emphasis on loans rather than grants in ODA, the effort to advise Asian countries on "techno parks," and the pressure on the World Bank to move away from the American obsession with deregulation and free markets within developing countries. The fact that the Japanese government chose to push the World Bank openly on this issue of development philosophy indicates its rising confidence in both the existence of a distinction between American capitalism and Japanese capitalism and the relevance of the Japanese version for developing countries.

Many who have doubted the ability of Japan to play a more active role in the world claim that it has provided no overarching ideas or ideology to which the rest of the world can relate. However, the Japanese version of capitalism is viewed by the Japanese—and by some developing countries—as an ideology or philosophy with as much moral validity as the American enthusiasm for democracy and human rights. Because the Japanese emphasis is on efficiency and pragmatism rather than political ideology, developing countries may be more comfortable relating to it and thereby attracted to closer relations with Japan.

Third, the Japanese outreach seeks to foster ties structured so as to strengthen the sense of national economic security. Preferences for controlled subsidiaries as a source of imports, for long-term financing plus long-term contracts for raw materials when equity ownership is not involved, and for dealings with other Japanese operating abroad are part of these patterns. To some extent these patterns represent an ethnic bias—a sense of unease in dealing with an outside world and a desire to reduce it by promoting transactions that replicate the familiar domestic context. Beyond that, they are a rational means of reducing economic uncertainty in an uncertain world over which business and government has had few other levers of influence. These patterns do not imply domination of the world—whatever that term could be construed to mean— but perhaps something akin to Japanese "ghettoes" scattered around the world. This tendency is exemplified by the coordinated action projected between ODA and Japanese private business-sector interests to create industrial parks dominated by Japanese firms (as in Dalian) or by heavy reliance on Japanese-owned subcontractors as suppliers to manufacturers overseas.

This agenda, then, represents a continued pursuit of a rather narrow economic self-interest, which some other nations (especially the United States) may find distasteful. But the sums of money involved in private-sector investments and foreign aid flows are large enough that other nations—especially developing countries in Asia—are willing to accept at least part of the Japanese agenda and find its pragmatic, nonideological basis attractive. Japan may not exercise as much influence in the United States or Europe, where its presence is small relative to the size of the economy (or because other diplomatic goals prevent heavy-handed use of such pressure). But Japan could have considerable influence among developing countries with which it has strong relations through ties of raw material sourcing, ODA, direct investment, and commercial loans.

The centrality of economics to the goals and international connections of the nation, though, implies that political issues—democracy, human rights, regional aggression—remain peripheral. The desire to maintain international ties for domestic economic benefit puts the nation in a weak position, since to challenge or pressure other nations on political issues often involves some risk to economic interests. As indicated in chapter 4, some change is taking place in foreign aid policy—with criteria related to democracy and military issues now officially included in foreign aid decisions—but vigorous application of these principles remains unlikely. The following discussion of the Gulf crisis indicates the continued dominance of this economic approach to the world: assessment of the economic impact on oil prices of Iraq's invasion of Kuwait took precedence over a focus on political or moral aspects of the crisis. Had the United States not pressured Japan to become an active participant in the coalition against Iraq, the Japanese government would have accepted the outcome of the invasion.

Are Japan's goals any different from those of the United States or other industrialized nations? The distinctions are not dramatic, but they do exist. The United States may be the outlier in terms of applying moral principles to international affairs, but Japan may be the outlier at the other end of the spectrum. Goals and policies can certainly change over time, and a commitment to broad principles such as democracy, human rights, or free trade is by no means absent in parts of Japanese society. However, as long as the government identifies the welfare of the nation primarily with the direct interests of the corporate sector, this predominance of commercial goals will continue.

The 1990–91 Gulf Crisis

The invasion of Kuwait by Iraq at the beginning of August 1990, the subsequent war against Iraq in 1991, and the aftermath of that war provide a poignant example of the difficulty the Japanese government has had in dealing with serious international political problems. Japan's official response to the events in the Middle East played out along very traditional lines, not reflecting any sense of the new, internationally influential Japan. The perceived need to maintain good U.S.-Japan relations dominated over defining a national interest directly related to the crisis. A focus on the United States led to a routine pattern of American actions, pressure on Japan to support those actions, and reluctant Japanese response to pressure. Furthermore, rather than dealing with the direct needs of the issue at hand, conservative politicians used this crisis to advance their long-held cause of altering the prohibition on the projection of military forces outside Japan.

An Oil-Centered Interest

To the extent that the Japanese government could define a national interest in the Middle East, it was the need to obtain supplies of crude oil. This reality drove Japanese foreign policy in the first oil crisis of 1973, when the government quickly distanced itself from Israel to placate its Arab oil suppliers. Japan's trade, foreign aid, and investment in the Middle East varied directly with the price of oil: when oil prices rose, foreign aid, investment, and exports to the region soared, but when prices fell in the 1980s, Japanese perception of the strategic importance of the region slumped.

Other than following economic policies intended to secure stable supplies of oil, Japan did not play any serious role in mediating in the tangled political affairs of the region. A brief attempt in the early 1980s to negotiate an end to the Iraq-Iran war, which achieved no discernible result, was the only exception. Therefore the outburst of a major crisis in which the government had little choice but to make a decision to favor one Middle East country against another posed an unwelcome and difficult dilemma to the Japanese government.

When viewed in traditional terms of oil supply and prices, the 1990 crisis was not significant to Japan. An ability to shift geographical sources of supply, longer-term efforts that had reduced the share of oil in total energy consumption, and anticipation that the acquisition of Kuwaiti oil supplies by Iraq would have a relatively limited effect on prices all contributed to a sense of confidence at the outset of this political crisis. Economic forecasts made after the onset of the crisis maintained an optimistic tone, in which the possible effect of the crisis on the Japanese economy was judged to be minimal.[28] Perhaps to reduce the public's sense of crisis, the government delayed action to permit oil companies to increase the domestic price of refined petroleum products. Not until mid-September were gasoline and other petroleum product prices allowed to rise, and then only after explicit government approval.[29]

When viewed from the economic focus of Japanese policy toward the Middle East, therefore, the invasion of Kuwait hardly seemed to require a strong response. Indeed, an antagonistic response that could have jeopardized acquisition of oil from Iraq could have had more serious economic consequences than simply remaining quiet. The government had learned in the years since 1973 that it possessed considerable bargaining leverage as a major purchaser of crude oil, so Iraq's increased control over oil supplies was not particularly troubling. The eventual responses of the government to the Gulf crisis demonstrate a number of failings, but at least the economic assessment of the crisis was far more rational and accurate than the hysteria that ensued back in 1973. Confidence concerning raw material supplies, discussed in chapter 2, was a major change for government, business, and society as a whole. The tendency to see the new crisis solely in economic terms seriously hindered the government's ability to forge a stronger participation in international responses, but at least the government was not held hostage to a dominant perception of a need to secure raw materials at any cost.

Disagreement over American Policy?

Official statements and the eventual policies adopted by the government give the impression of extensive support for the objectives of the sanctions, military buildup, and final military action taken against Iraq. However, behind the scenes disagreement with the fundamental premises of these actions was expressed—and not just by the usual opponents of military affairs in Japanese politics.

A senior government official said openly in the press in September 1990 that the United States had no need to send troops, adding that "the whole thing may be a ploy by the U.S. to sell arms to Saudi Arabia and Israel to bolster the sluggish U.S. defense industries."[30] Other commentators echoed the view that the nations responsible for the crisis were the United States and the Soviet Union (for having supplied arms) and that Japan had no responsibility to participate in any military solution (but, by virtue of its lack of responsibility, might be able to act as an "honest broker" in mediating a solution).[31] Even respected senior economist Ryutaro Komiya argued that while participation in economic sanctions was acceptable, Japan should make no military contribution (including money for others to use for military purposes), and that the nations that supplied weapons to Iraq should bear the financial burden of any solution. And even a senior Foreign Ministry official, Consul General to New York Masamichi Hanabusa, went on the record in a speech in the United States criticizing U.S. handling of the crisis, emphasizing the oil supply aspect and claiming that Japan had a superior (and nonbelligerent) approach to solving oil problems.[32]

This scattering of statements from mainstream participants in government policy formation implies at least strong disagreement within the government over the most appropriate policy. In fact, at the time, the view represented by these comments seemed widespread enough to be the majority opinion within the bureaucracy; the crisis did not require strong action, and certainly not a military response. American leadership to confront Iraq swiftly with military force (and then to actually carry through on military threats) was puzzling from this Japanese perspective. While concern over oil supply certainly was a factor in explaining why the U.S. government chose to make such a firm stand against Iraq,

Japanese criticism completely missed the overwhelming importance of moral principle (decrying Iraq's unprovoked military aggression) and concern over the delicate balance of power in the entire region.

As a major economic nation and one possessing visible investments around the world, however, Japan did not have the luxury of distancing itself from the crisis despite a preference to do so stemming from this economic-centered interpretation of events. For the first time since the end of World War II, the nation was expected to participate in some direct manner.[33] In previous international crises, Japan could sit on the side and either be passive or adopt inactive pro-U.S. positions with little real cost. It passively allowed U.S. bases in Japan to provide logistical support for both the Korean War and the Vietnam War and boycotted the Olympics in 1980 in response to the Soviet invasion of Afghanistan. But this time foreign expectations were that Japan should be involved directly in the decisions and actions related to the crisis.

The need to participate in a more active manner put foreign economic policy (which would have dictated a low profile) in conflict with the other major foreign policy objective, maintenance of good relations with the United States. As the following review of the events during the crisis indicates, concern over the U.S.-Japan relationship became the key objective in government behavior.

Initial Responses

Japan actually acted surprisingly quickly to follow the lead of the United States and the European countries. The invasion occurred early on Thursday morning, August 1, 1990. The Japanese government made a preliminary announcement on Friday, although this was primarily of a reactive nature, stating that it would abide by economic sanctions against Iraq if they were approved by the UN Security Council. With the European nations agreeing to sanctions by the beginning of the weekend, Japan fell in line on Sunday, a day ahead of the Security Council vote. The official announcement included condemnation of the invasion, an embargo of oil imports from Iraq and occupied Kuwait, an embargo of exports to both locations, suspension of investment and financial transactions, and a freeze on foreign aid to Iraq.[34] As usual, however, the government had not been willing to act until the European nations had made their decision, providing both a sense of greater pressure on Japan to stand united with other industrial nations and a sense of safety in numbers. The decision in favor of sanctions may have come quickly, but it still represented the pattern of followership and *gaiatsu* of the past, not a new sense of leadership.

Even this quick, relatively strong response was somewhat more muted when Japanese-language instructions were issued for the private sector a week later on August 14. Although the language of the announcement called for an actual embargo of imports (*yunyū kinshi*), the choice of words concerning exports to the two countries indicated that companies were to exercise restraint (*yushutsu no jishuku yōsei*), a far less forceful wording that technically left the way open for some exports to continue. A footnote to this official statement indicated that the government was considering use of the Foreign Exchange Control Law (which specifically grants the government the right to embargo or otherwise control exports in this sort of international political crisis) to enforce an export prohibition in the future, but for the moment was not doing so.[35] In actuality, the failure to use stronger language made little difference (since most firms would be unwilling to violate such strong guidance), but the fact that the government was unable to agree immediately to use the full force of the foreign exchange law to enforce an embargo on exports indicates the difficulty officials had in viewing the crisis seriously.

Having at least made an initial decision to support the American-inspired and UN-ratified sanctions against Iraq, the government was faced immediately with an opportunity to play a direct role in attempting to mediate or participate in policy formation concerning the crisis because Prime Minister Kaifu had a trip to the Middle East already scheduled for mid-August. But his trip was canceled just before it would have started, and Foreign Minister Taro Nakayama went instead (August 18–25).[36] The trip was canceled out of fear that the prime minister would appear to be seeking special favors in terms of oil supply to substitute for the embargoed supplies from Iraq. That fear in itself is eloquent testimony to the record of the past and Japanese recognition of the nation's reputation, as well as a commentary on its inability to escape from the confines of those images or behavior patterns.

The prime minister's trip could have been an opportunity to prove to the world that Japan was an important participant in world affairs. He could have gone as scheduled, conferred with regional leaders and consulted with President Bush and other industrial nations' leaders during and after the trip to demonstrate a Japanese presence in the discussion, and perhaps even have offered ideas for solutions.

A conservative Foreign Ministry and timid Liberal Democratic party squelched these possibilities by canceling the trip. They feared that the trip could be pointless because Japan had no "card" to play, ignoring the fact that even communication at this early stage would have given Japan visibility. The Foreign Ministry also expressed fear that a trip could jeopardize the safety of Japanese nationals in Iraq, although how the prime minister's visit would have imposed any danger, especially if he had added a stop in Iraq to talk with Saddam Hussein, is not at all clear.[37] The excuses provided by the Foreign Ministry reinforced notions of timidity and an inability to conceive of a role for the nation other than following in the wake of the United States.

Pressure for Involvement

Signals concerning what the United States might want beyond endorsement of sanctions were quick to appear. In mid-August, President Bush was reported to have made a personal call to Prime Minister Kaifu asking Japan to be more "forthright" in providing support to nonbelligerent Mideast countries adversely affected by the sanctions. At that time, the Foreign Ministry announced that the government would extend economic support (with the amount unspecified) to the nonbelligerent nations most affected by the sanctions, consider financial assistance for a multilateral military force, and study the possibility of dispatching nonmilitary personnel to the region.[38]

On August 29 these measures took clearer form, with the government announcing a $1 billion package of financial assistance. At the press conference where the measures were announced, Prime Minister Kaifu said very clearly that "these steps, including rendering cooperation in transportation, supplies, medical treatment and other areas, are the maximum Japan can take."[39] Given the subsequent behavior of the government, this seemingly firm statement became very embarrassing to Japanese government officials. Along with the money, the prime minister said that the government would dispatch about one hundred volunteer, nonmilitary medical experts to the region and would propose a UN "peace cooperation law" to allow official dispatch of personnel to participate in some form in the multilateral military force assembling in Saudi Arabia. He gave no details about what sort of personnel would be included in the force (although he specified clearly that he had no plan to send the Self Defense Forces abroad at that time).

These promises were apparently based on an evaluation of what the U.S. government wanted from Japan. At no point were official requests made by the U.S. government, but unofficial pressure was applied for not only a strong financial commitment but also a "physical presence" in the Gulf region.

September Concessions

The announcement by Kaifu was immediately considered inadequate in Washington, and in early September the government faced renewed U.S. pressure to supply financial aid to Mideast countries affected by the sanctions. In response, the government argued that the International Monetary Fund and World Bank were the appropriate vehicles for aid, claiming that a major increase in Japanese aid to these countries would upset the careful balance in Japan's aid program. The government went so far as to have Finance Minister Ryutaro Hashimoto visit European countries to present the concept of using the IMF and the World Bank to governments there just before a visit by Treasury Secretary Nicholas Brady to Japan.[40] Although the concept of minimizing large shifts in the relative amounts allocated to foreign aid recipients fits accepted notions of how Japanese policy operates, in this case the argument appeared to be an excuse to avoid a clearer financial role in the coalition. This position was also consistent with a hypothesis that the government was still trying to minimize its direct association with the U.S.-led coalition in the crisis. By distancing itself through the front of the IMF and the World Bank, the government could then more easily restore normal economic relations with Iraq as soon as the crisis was over.

This short initiative obtained no backers, and when Treasury Secretary Brady arrived in Japan in early September, he pushed officially for a greater Japanese financial contribution to the multinational military force, plus aid for nations in the region and for other developing countries damaged economically by rising oil prices.[41] Three days after Brady was in Japan, the Japanese government dropped the idea of using the IMF and the World Bank, an obvious and quick result of the Brady visit. On September 11, Kaifu announced the intention of supplying unspecified amounts of bilateral ODA to Jordan, Egypt, and Turkey.[42] American pressure had again shaped the Japanese government agenda.

As the government was about to make the administrative decisions on provision of aid, LDP Secretary General Ichiro Ozawa announced two important decisions that revealed the attitude toward the crisis: the start of the fall session of the Diet would not be advanced in order to debate policy on the crisis;[43] and Japan would participate in the fall 1990 Asian games even if Iraq participated.[44] Coming in the midst of the most important international crisis faced by the government in many years, this determination to proceed normally was a further indication of the sense of distance from the issue and the unwillingness to be too closely associated with the coalition.

By September 12 rumors were floated that the new aid package would include an additional $2 billion, offered mainly in the form of trade credits (the least costly and the most commercially beneficial form of aid from the standpoint of the Japanese government and business).[45] However, just as this amount was being discussed, the U.S. House of Representatives angrily passed an amendment to the defense appropriations bill by a vote of 370 to 53, requiring that Japan pay the full cost of maintaining U.S. troops in Japan (including salaries) or the United States would withdraw 5,000 troops a year.[46] This was a frivolous measure, which few expected to survive through the final passage of the appropriations bill, but it was intended to be a clear signal of congressional displeasure over the limited amount of Japanese support in the Gulf crisis. The immediate result of this action was an announcement on the following day, September 14, of an additional $3 billion in aid—$1 billion higher than had been rumored just two days earlier. As eventually disbursed, however, some of that aid was at best only tangentially related to the crisis—such as $600 million of soft loans for the Philippines.[47]

Taizo Watanabe, official spokesman for the Foreign Ministry, commented at a press conference in mid-September (when the $3 billion package was announced) that the United States should appreciate how much Japan was doing by announcing more financial support than any other nation up to that point. The Foreign Ministry also defended itself at home, claiming that all the policy actions taken since the beginning of August were done rapidly, were sufficient, and should be appreciated by the rest of the world as the maximum that the nation could provide.[48]

As a sidelight to the more pressing issues involved at that time, MITI managed to find a means to twist the crisis to promote domestic industrial policy goals. Expressing concern about the possibilities of oil supply restriction and price increases, MITI announced restrictions on importation of refined petroleum products (such as gasoline and kerosene) during the crisis. This initiative, justified officially as part of price stabilization policy, called for cutting back on (supposedly high-priced) imports of refined products while stimulating domestic production of these same products by Japanese refineries. The logic of this reasoning was fraudulent, since prices of imported refined products were based on the same global prices paid for crude oil in Japan, and prices for refined products have been higher in Japan than abroad because of the inefficiently small size of many Japanese refineries. Using the crisis as an excuse to manipulate import controls to support an inefficient domestic industry suggests again that officials experienced difficulty in moving away from old habits of defining international issues in commercial terms.[49]

Humanitarian Support

At a financial level, the Japanese responded to requests from humanitarian agencies. During the crisis the Japanese government provided $2 million to the International Red Cross and $58 million to the UN Disaster Relief Organization (UNDRO). Later the government gave UNDRO $100 million for assistance to the Kurds in the wake of the war—one-quarter of the overall amount requested of all UN member states.[50] Keidanren and the Japan Chamber of Commerce also provided ¥1 billion (approximately $7.4 million) for the UN High Commission on Refugees (UNHCR).[51] When the war began, the International Red Cross asked its members for additional contributions that were the equivalent of ¥15 billion; the Japanese Red Cross sent ¥50 million (in this case, only 0.3 percent of what the International Red Cross was trying to raise).[52] On the financial front, therefore, both the government and private sources appeared to have been reasonably forthcoming in responding to humanitarian efforts. But the truly disappointing response came on the question of real personnel participation in humanitarian efforts.

Another piece of the original announcement by Prime Minister Kaifu at the end of August had been that a volunteer group of medical personnel would be put together to send to the region. Response to this proposal was embarrassingly small. Only twenty-six people were sent in fall 1990, but they all returned in December, before the outbreak of hostilities. When they returned, the government said it would "study" the possibility of sending another volunteer group, but nothing was done.[53] There was little previous record of individual volunteer medical work abroad in difficult conditions, and the government did not exercise its coercive powers to generate larger numbers of volunteers from government organizations. Had the government felt a deeper commitment to this mission, it ought to have been able to construct a larger group.

In response to a later request by the International Red Cross in January 1991 for individual national chapters to provide personnel, the Japanese Red Cross sent nine people for a one-month tour of duty in Geneva to deal with Gulf War matters; they returned to Japan after a brief tour of the Middle East in March, after the end of the war.[54] In addition, a team of six Japanese Red Cross members visited refugee camps in Jordan and Iraq to arrange for shipments to Japanese refugees in late October 1990.[55] After the war ended, Japan was again asked to send personnel—this time by the UNHCR—to provide medical assistance for the Kurds, and only fourteen people were sent to run one small emergency medical center in northern Iran.[56] These small, brief excursions hardly add up to a picture of active involvement.

Debate about a Military Role

Doubt remains as to whether American officials specifically asked for *military* participation in the multinational force gathering in Saudia Arabia, a very sensitive issue for the Japanese government. American observers, however, have felt that at least some policymakers within the White House, Ambassador Michael Armacost, and officials in other departments were in favor of a Japanese military presence and made informal suggestions to this effect to the Japanese government.[57] If these suggestions were made, the process was informal and quiet; at no point did the U.S. government make open statements concerning the advisability of sending Japanese soldiers to the gulf.

The Japanese, on the other hand, were very open about announcing that the United States wanted dispatch of military forces. Katsura Kuno, head of Keidanren's Keizai Koho Center, wrote in summer 1991 that Ambassador Armacost "pushed rather too openly for the [LDP's peace cooperation] proposal, provoking the complaint that the government was again caving in to Washington's demands."[58] The notion that the U.S. government wanted Japan to send military forces became a strong argument on the part of those pressing for a law to allow such action. This gave greater legitimacy to the long-standing desire of conservatives to remove the constraints imposed by Article 9 of the Japanese constitution. The constitution had been interpreted earlier in the postwar period as allowing the maintenance of defensive military forces so long as they were not dispatched abroad. The prohibition on overseas dispatch included participation in UN or other multilateral military actions and even UN peacekeeping actions. Informal pressure to establish a physical presence and Prime Minister Kaifu's decision to introduce legislation represented unprecedented opportunities to move ahead with the conservative agenda.

As soon as the additional financial support was announced in mid-September, debate began over the legislation. Participation by members of the Self Defense Forces (SDF) was not necessary, since Japan's personnel would be strictly confined to noncombat roles. The issue, nevertheless, was immediately captured by conservative politicians desiring to restore the right to dispatch military forces overseas. In this sense, the issue had little to do with the appropriate response to the immediate crisis in the gulf; it was part of the long-standing and divisive issue of restoring the national right to international projection of military force. Since the dispatch of soldiers would be extremely controversial, the conservatives covered their position by claiming that the United States was pushing strongly in this direction, although, as noted above, this pressure was informal and may not have been specific enough to include a request for SDF inclusion.[59] As a result of the conservative insistence on including the SDF, the issue of sending nonmilitary groups to the region (doctors and other nonmilitary personnel to help refugees, for example) was sidetracked and ultimately defeated (other than the small group of volunteers dispatched in the fall).

To justify turning the discussion toward use of the SDF, conservatives argued that civilians could not serve in places of danger. Ambassador Hisahiko Okazaki, a respected intellectual in the Foreign Ministry, commented in fall 1990 that if Japan sent civilians to the Middle East, they would flee if conditions became dangerous, and that by so doing would cause the world to scorn Japan. Seizaburo Sato, a leading political scientist, concurred.[60] Proponents of SDF use ignored the possibility of creating a standing nonmilitary force of doctors and other civilians on order of the government (rather than a volunteer force), which would have the responsibility to remain in place regardless of personal danger.

By September 20 the LDP announced that SDF soldiers would participate in the UN peace cooperation force proposed by Prime Minister Kaifu and would do so without losing their status as SDF members.[61] Once actual debate began in the Diet over a bill to authorize formation and dispatch of a force to the gulf, many of the arguments seemed naive and little different from the polarized, unrealistic, ideological positions separating the political left and right in the 1950s. However, despite the determination of the opposition parties to prevent any alteration of the status quo or use of the SDF, some of the opposition groups were willing to permit a non-SDF group to be sent abroad.[62] Regardless of such overtures, the conservatives would not drop the SDF provision of the bill, although the permissible roles for SDF personnel were largely restricted to nonmilitary activities.

Argument then raged on whether SDF personnel would be permitted to carry sidearms and to use them, even in self-defense. From an American perspective, this debate may seem naive, but at stake was a fundamental alteration of the rules for engagement of the nation in the affairs of the world. Seemingly trivial details gained enormous symbolic importance, given the seriousness of the underlying issue.

Debate continued through October, and then the LDP abandoned the bill in early November. It was dropped largely because many LDP members were opposed to it, which would have been embarrassing if the bill had come to a vote. One newspaper poll at the end of October found that 56 percent of LDP members in the Diet opposed the bill, 60 percent opposed sending the SDF even in a noncombat role, and 73 opposed sending them in a combat role.[63] Opposition by LDP members reflected broader public attitudes. A high 78 percent of those polled by one newspaper in early November opposed overseas dispatch of the SDF in general, and 58 percent opposed the specific bill. It is worth noting that even 54 percent were opposed to an overseas force *without* the participation of the SDF (that is, opposed to sending any group of Japanese to an area of possible conflict), while only 30 percent supported such a concept.[64] Such attitudes suggested how deep-seated the public desire was to remain isolated from difficult and dangerous world events, going beyond an aversion to the use of military force by the government.

The bill was withdrawn from consideration on November 8, shortly after the latter poll was released. This decision was supposedly accompanied by agreement among members of the Diet from the LDP and two of the opposition parties to rewrite the legislation without SDF participation.[65] However, no new version of the bill appeared before the end of the Gulf War in 1991, suggesting again that the real agenda of the LDP (or at least its more conservative elements) was not participation in the Gulf crisis, but an overriding desire to have the SDF sent abroad. This impression is reinforced by the reintroduction of SDF participation in the 1992 legislation for participation in authorized UN peacekeeping operations.

Asian nations have consistently expressed concern over Japan's military policies, and the 1990 bill was no exception. The Foreign Ministry claimed that dispatch of the SDF would not offend neighboring countries because it would be limited to UN-sponsored activities. But opposition was voiced, and some of this was reported in the Japanese press.[66] Opposition from these countries was certainly not the determining factor in rejection of the bill, but concern over regional opinion may have been at least one element in shaping public opinion.

Reaction to Hostage Taking

As debate raged on the peacekeeping bill during fall 1990, the crisis created other dilemmas for society and the government: Japanese citizens were among the foreigners taken hostage by the Iraqi government after the invasion of Kuwait. Some 300 Japanese hostages were held, and they were subject to the same threats as those directed at other foreign hostages, of use as human shields to protect military targets. As noted above, the Japanese government had not established a strong record in dealing with hostages in the past, and it did little to alter this pattern in the Gulf crisis.

The first hostages returned in November, not long after the bill for SDF participation in the multilateral force was withdrawn from the Diet (a timing that may not have been accidental), as the direct result of a trip by former Prime Minister Nakasone to talk with Saddam Hussein. This trip once again thrust Japan into the position of being able to provide communication or mediation at the highest levels, but Nakasone used his trip only to obtain the release of Japanese hostages. This purpose was made all the more obvious by sending Nakasone ostentatiously on a Boeing 747 so that all the Japanese hostages could return with him. In response to his special plea, seventy-seven Japanese nationals were released.[67]

Nakasone partially achieved his objective, but the episode was another example of the government's inability to construct an international role beyond the very immediate and direct welfare of its citizens. Concern for the welfare of its own citizens was natural and laudable. But if the government desired to demonstrate to the other major powers that it had real involvement in the crisis, Nakasone could have bargained for all hostages, extended his mandate to the more fundamental issues in the crisis, or even filled the rest of the plane with Asian refugees displaced when Kuwait was invaded. He did none of these things, leaving an international image of a government devoid of a broader vision of its interest in the world.

A Loss of Interest

The rest of the hostages returned when Iraq released all Western hostages on December 6.[68] Once the bill to send SDF soldiers died in the Diet and the Japanese hostages returned from Iraq, the Japanese government and public lost almost all interest in the crisis. The government pursued no diplomatic initiatives in December or early January and made few statements on the situation. Return of the hostages eliminated the one link through which the nation could feel a sense of real involvement and left the government and public free to sit on the sidelines again and watch other nations deal with the problem.

Even as war became more likely in early January, the government remained largely silent, almost as though officials and politicians had forgotten the existence of the crisis and potential conflict. When U.S. Secretary of State Baker traveled to Geneva for his final tense meetings with Iraqi Foreign Minister Tariq Aziz on January 9, no Japanese government officials went to Geneva to keep the government close to the process. In commenting on the outcome of that meeting, the Tokyo press conference was held by the *jimujikan* of the Foreign Ministry (the administrative vice-minister, the highest career position, equivalent to an American undersecretary), not by a minister or the prime minister.[69] The top political leadership remained silent.

This single Foreign Ministry press conference constituted almost the only public statement by any government official during that momentous week. Almost all of the news reported in the newspapers about the Gulf crisis was from the Middle East or Washington, not Tokyo. Any Japanese reader would have received a continued, strong impression that the crisis was far away and no longer involved Japan in any real sense.

As if this impression were not already strong enough, the Foreign Ministry resisted canceling a previously scheduled state visit to the ASEAN countries that would have kept Prime Minister Kaifu out of the country on January 15, when the war began. The initial Foreign Ministry reaction in the wake of the Baker-Aziz meeting was that the trip did not need to be canceled, and it was not scuttled until January 11. Should war break out, the ministry said, the prime minister could always return home quickly.[70] That the war would actually begin while Kaifu would have been out of the country was obviously a development that could not be known in advance, but once the Baker-Aziz meeting failed, some form of military action was clearly about to happen and it would be a step of great importance for Japan and the rest of the world. That the Foreign Ministry would consider going forward with a courtesy visit to Asian countries at that point signifies how very far removed from the crisis the government felt.

Response to the War

Once the war broke out, the government again reacted to external events in a manner that conveyed little sense of a real interest at stake for the nation. The Diet was due to begin its regular session at the end of the month, and this date was not advanced in order to consider emergency measures related to the war (just as the opening of its fall session was not changed a few months earlier). When the session did open, normal procedure prevailed, with several days of broad policy speeches by leading LDP and opposition members, rather than moving to immediate consideration of war-related legislation. The choice to proceed entirely as normal reflects the lack of a sense of emergency or urgency.

Once again perceiving that Japan would be severely criticized by the United States if the nation did nothing, the Kaifu government quickly proposed an enormous additional $9 billion contribution. This time there were no hints of specific pressure from the United States; the proposal seemed to have been a unilateral decision to offset anticipated American outrage if Japan chose to sit on the sidelines while American soldiers died in battle. The large contribution was to be met through special three-year bonds that would be paid off by additional excise taxes on refined petroleum and other products (plus a proposal for increased corporate income taxes)—revenue measures that required Diet action. The LDP endorsed this proposal by January 24 and prepared to submit it to the Diet.[71]

Eager to play this development for immediate and maximum public relations value, the Japanese embassy in Washington made the potentially dangerous move of publicizing the new measure as a firm commitment of the government, even though there was still opposition in the Diet. The official English-language press release was titled "Japan Adds $9 Billion to Gulf Efforts, Will Transport More Refugees," when neither the money nor the refugee transport was fully settled.[72] Making firm promises of this sort held the potential of causing disappointment, anger, and frustration in the United States later.

Moving refugees out of Jordan by plane—another piece of this final effort—became yet another opportunity for the conservatives to press for bending the rules on use of the SDF. There was absolutely no need to use SDF personnel to provide passenger transportation for refugees, but the old arguments about only military personnel being able to enter a dangerous area were revived (even though Jordan was not directly involved in the war). The Kaifu government even tried to slip this action through without consultation with the Diet, claiming that it could authorize it through a section of the SDF law that dealt with transportation of guests of state. The government claimed it could move refugees on the basis of this provision by issuing a special order. This approach received cabinet approval on January 25.[73]

As debate over this new political maneuver unfolded, other decisions emerged that seem odd from an American perspective. The SDF announced that because of the potential danger of flying refugees it would not send eldest sons or only children as part of the anticipated 200-member team to run the operation (which would have involved five C-130 transport planes shuttling between Amman and Cairo).[74] The sense of fear over a potential loss of life from a nonmilitary action outside the area of direct conflict was extraordinary and indicative once again of the deeply ingrained isolationist attitudes. This move may also have been part of SDF attempts to exaggerate public perceptions of danger associated with this mission in order to justify the insistence on use of SDF personnel. Nevertheless, the exaggerated sense of danger conveyed by such announcements at a time when the coalition forces faced the real danger of military action portrayed Japan in a unfavorable light internationally.

Public opinion remained rather evenly divided on the issue of sending the SDF, even on this purely nonmilitary mission. A newspaper poll at the end of January found 43 percent favoring the refugee proposal and 48 percent opposed.[75] This was at least a bit of a shift from where public opinion had been the previous November: a higher percentage now accepted a nonmilitary function for the SDF abroad.

Eventually the use of SDF forces to move refugees was dropped as part of a political compromise with one of the opposition parties (Komeito) to win passage of the additional financial contribution. In addition, the Jordanian government (which apparently had not been consulted in advance), desiring to maintain its neutrality, expressed strong reservations about military aircraft entering its territory from a nation that it identified as part of the anti-Iraq coalition.[76]

After all the talk about the need for the SDF and the potential danger they would face, the irony is that the Japanese government actually did move refugees out of the region on chartered civilian planes (Japanese and foreign).[77] News of this humanitarian work, though, remained buried in the back pages of Japanese newspapers (on the pages reserved for human interest stories).[78] Private groups (including labor federations, local civic groups, and religious organizations), frightened by the implication of the SDF going to the region or embarrassed by the inability of the government to act, also financed flights for refugees.[79] These private actions, too, remained on the back pages of the newspapers. Just like the politicians, the press seemed obsessed with the military issue and therefore unable to give these other real humanitarian activities greater prominence in their coverage.

Once the proposal to send SDF planes to transport refugees was dropped, the LDP was able to assemble a coalition of opposition party support to pass the $9 billion contribution, which finally passed both houses of the Diet by March 6, well after the actual end of the fighting.[80] Even this rather dramatic amount of money was something of an international embarrassment for the government since the approval came after the war was completed.

Completion of the war opened yet another avenue for conservatives to press the SDF issue. A need existed to clear mines from the waters of the Persian Gulf, and the government offered use of SDF minesweepers. Since no hostilities were in progress, this decision was made without Diet approval and was formally announced on April 24, 1991. This move proceeded quietly and generated relatively little opposition.[81] After all the struggle and pressure to use the Gulf crisis to further the cause of dispatching military forces abroad, the conservatives finally won a victory. The role played by the vessels may have been small (most of the mines had already been removed by the time the ships arrived), but it served its proponents' larger purpose of establishing a precedent, which had been the objective all along.

Participants in UN Missions

A larger and more significant step in altering the roles for overseas military dispatch came in 1992 with a law to allow SDF participation in UN peacekeeping operations so long as the Japanese forces were restricted to nonmilitary activities.[82] This law was made possible by the divisive debate over the failed peace bill in fall 1990, even though it was passed more than a year later and emerged in direct response to the issue of participating in the proposed UN peacekeeping operations in Cambodia. This law was far more restrictive than the bill considered in fall 1990, since the Gulf operation was not a UN peacekeeping operation, but it did finally advance the cherished goal of its supporters: establishing legal authorization for dispatch of Japanese soldiers overseas.

This law permitted the government, without individual Diet authorization, to send a small force, including members of the SDF, abroad for nonmilitary functions in authorized UN peacekeeping missions, as well as for natural disaster relief (although this second function seems to be something of an afterthought). Participation in UN missions that might require small arms use requires specific Diet authorization. In Cambodia—the first mission under the new law—SDF soldiers provided road construction, bridge repair, and transportation services. In addition, civilians—policemen and others—provided election monitoring. These are the functions that would have been performed under the failed bill of 1990, with the difference being the restriction to UN peacekeeping operations rather than a UN-endorsed multilateral military action.

Two years of debate and modification of legislation produced an outcome that was supported by some of the opposition parties and the public. In this sense, the peacekeeping law was broadly consistent with public desires, rather than being just a manipulation of politics by the most conservative politicians. Even this limited acceptance by the public was tested quickly when one of the civilian policemen was killed by the Khmer Rouge in spring 1993. Despite some public sentiment to withdraw, however, the peacekeeping force remained in place through the elections.

A Reinforcement of Past Patterns

The record of events, debate, and policy response by the government during the Gulf crisis reinforces the conclusion that the political process in Japan does not deal quickly or well with nonroutine international crises. At least four major problems or dilemmas emerge from the discussion above.

First, the government had difficulty recognizing that a serious crisis existed and that Japan needed to be involved. The crisis was of sufficient proportions that its resolution required the collective involvement of all major nations. For several years the theme of international power and importance based on economic accomplishment had been popular in Japan. More important, the U.S. government recognized Japan as a major nation to a much greater extent than in earlier years. With an enhanced image as a major power, Japan could not avoid participation without incurring heavy criticism from the United States and European nations.

Despite the domestic talk of international power, however, the isolationist thinking of the previous forty years remained strong. Iraq and Kuwait were far away, the effect on oil markets was not strong, and once the Japanese hostages were home neither the government nor the public seemed to sense any direct connection to the events. Quick cancellation of the prime minister's trip to the region in August, hesitancy to cancel his trip to Asian countries as the war loomed, the lack of public comment by the government in early January, and self-serving statements about the "clean hands" of Japan all suggested an inability to recognize the seriousness of an international problem or a sense of involvement. Had the crisis occurred nearby in Asia, Japan's response might have been different, but in this case the country certainly lacked a consciousness of responsibility or involvement as a major economic power.

Second, interpretation of the meaning of the crisis ran along the narrow economic lines of the past. Political and bureaucratic leaders demonstrated difficulty in understanding or relating to the noneconomic aspects of the crisis. The invasion of Kuwait, the possibility of nuclear weapons in Iraq, or alteration of the delicate balance of power in the unstable Middle East were all issues remote to analysis in Japan, even though ritual references to such problems were often in official government statements. By contrast, the potential economic impact on oil markets caused by Iraq's acquisition of Kuwati oil fields did not frighten the government sufficiently to think that strong action was necessary. As an appraisal of the purely economic effects of the crisis, Japanese assessments were more realistic than much of what was being said in the United States as the crisis unfolded, but the government remained too timid to press its interpretation with the other allies.

Third, throughout the crisis, the main focus of both the government and the press was on the United States rather than on the Middle East. Japanese policy was determined by the fear of reaction from Washington rather than an independent assessment of what was happening in the region and what would be appropriate in response. Rokusaburo Ishikawa, a prominent businessman heading the Japan Chamber of Commerce, commented in late January 1991 that "we have no choice but to give [large amounts of financial support] when the decision comes from listening to and studying American requests."[83] By being so attentive to developments in Washington, the Japanese government managed to perpetuate the pattern of the earlier postwar period. The government projected an image of careful calibration of financial contributions to keep the Americans satisfied.

Some Japanese observers were distressed with this approach to foreign affairs. One newspaper lamented that the government was unable to come up with any policies on the Middle East in the absence of pressure from the United States. Another argued that failure to articulate any independent evaluation of the crisis meant that Japan would lose face in the world, which was an apt description of what happened.[84] The embarrassment was all the greater since Prime Minister Kaifu and President Bush had made a joint statement just a few months before the onset of the crisis calling for "global partnership" between Japan and the United States.

Fourth, when the government and society finally confronted the question of what to contribute other than money, the debate was unable to move beyond the divisive question of projecting the Self Defense Forces overseas. To the outside world, the government kept issuing reminders that action was constrained by the constitution. Internally, politicians manipulated informal American pressure to do more than provide money to justify their attempts to dispatch the SDF. Had the politicians been truly interested in contributing to a solution of the problem at hand, they could have devised a substantial nonmilitary group to provide medical and other humanitarian assistance for refugees, combatants, and other victims of the initial invasion and later war.

Conclusion

Japan has played only a peripheral role in world political affairs since the end of World War II, and it faces large difficulties in overcoming this legacy. Accumulation of large overseas economic assets propelled the nation into an environment of visibility and potential international influence so quickly that mechanisms or principles to guide international participation remained poorly developed in the early 1990s.

The simple notion that the government would manipulate economic variables to achieve foreign compliance with its policy objectives had some superficial appeal. It is certainly not beyond credulity that the government could obtain compliance from private-sector financial institutions or nonfinancial firms to pursue strategies to influence foreign behavior. Japanese firms clearly felt informal government pressure to restrain their investments in the former Soviet Union long as the Japanese government wanted to exert leverage to obtain return of the Northern Territories.

For some, this notion of international influence has been very troubling because of the self-interested economic objectives that often drive Japanese policy. The government does continue to view national interest and foreign policy in rather narrow economic terms. Security of raw material supplies and maintenance of secure markets for exports and investment are the highest priorities in policymaking. Provision of large amounts of foreign economic aid also gives the government influence in developing countries, but the degree of influence is often limited and the objectives are often unclear.

The very fact that Japan is widely recognized as a nation that pursues a narrow economic self-interest undermines the government's ability to wield influence. Nations resent any sense of Japanese dominance and react against it. Creditor-debtor relationships are complex; the creditor may have the power of the purse, but debtors may have the advantage that creditors need a profitable outlet for their investments, so the creditors are reluctant to pull away to punish behavior that they do not like. One could argue that the economic objectives that have dominated Japanese policy lead both business and government to avoid exercising much influence in the world because they do not want to jeopardize their continued access to international markets for goods and investment.

Real dilemmas occur when the country faces international political problems. An economic focus in policy led to the "omnidirectional" foreign policy touted as such a success in the past. Japan endeavored to avoid creating enemies (except for acceding to the East-West split imposed on it early in the postwar period by the United States, and even with that it played around the edges). But some contentious issues in the world require taking one side or the other and may require decisive action. The Gulf crisis illustrated the fact that the political and bureaucratic system was ill equipped to deal with such situations at the beginning of the 1990s.

Most of the domestic debate during that crisis centered on whether to provide military forces for the multilateral confrontation with Iraq. But the history of events sketched in this chapter makes clear that the problems were broader and deeper. The government was disinclined to participate in policy discussion or even communication among the major belligerent parties; it reacted defensively to pressure from the United States without defining any clear positions on the crisis; and it allowed response to an urgent international crisis to be distorted by a domestic conservative agenda of altering the status of military forces. This was a sobering experience for those who had begun to portray the nation as an increasingly influential international player.

Some of the failures may have been the result of inexperience, since the Gulf crisis represented the first time since the end of World War II that other nations expected Japan to be a major participant in the solution of a serious crisis. For example, it is not too surprising that without much global experience the Japanese saw the Gulf crisis as rather remote geographically and beyond their own interests. But to a large extent, the problems were more structural than temporary. A focus on economics as the driving force of foreign policy blinded the government to other, more complex, political and strategic dimensions of policy, and the ability of the government to alter its views and policy orientation may be poor at best. Domestic policy dynamics imply that the government has difficulty in choking off political debate and forcing decisive action. These problems are to some extent endemic to Japanese society in general and to some extent a legacy of the terrible experiences of the 1930s and 1940s when that society allowed government to move decisively and to play an international political and military role. The memory of those disasters may remain longer and more vividly in Japan itself than in the rest of the world, leaving the nation unable to play a much stronger international political role for many years to come.

CHAPTER SEVEN

Responses to a
Changing Japan

ALTHOUGH JAPAN'S position in the world has changed and expanded fundamentally, the relationship between Japan and the United States remains mired in an earlier postwar configuration. Prime Minister Kaifu and President Bush may have thought they were forging a new post–cold war relationship by coining the phrase "global partnership" in 1990, but little has happened since then to give this phrase any operational meaning. The alteration of Japan's economic relationship with the world, particularly the swift and enormous rise of foreign asset ownership, requires new roles for Japan in international affairs and makes the immobility of the bilateral relationship rather troubling. But the bilateral immobility reflects the difficult questions faced by Japan, the United States, and the rest of the world: What roles should or can Japan play? How should or can Japan and the rest of the world move toward accommodating those roles?

Choices made by the Japanese government concerning international involvement will necessarily be rooted in perceptions of national interest. Decisions about national interest and strategies to achieve those objectives belong to the Japanese government and to the society as a whole. Domestic discussion and debate (exemplified by the tortuous progress of the peacekeeping bill) will be lengthy and vigorous. Nevertheless, with an array of possibilities facing Japan, the United States and other nations have an opportunity to influence the direction taken. Some choices for

Japan lead in the direction of a more stable and prosperous international environment, while others might lead toward greater instability and tension. The interests of the United States lie in persuading Japan to move in the former direction.

American Goals

The purpose of this final chapter is to consider how the U.S. government can respond to a changing Japan in a manner that accomplishes this goal. A specific U.S. agenda for dealing with Japan over the rest of the decade should include the following seven key goals.

—Continue to push Japan aggressively, but carefully, toward making its markets for imported goods and inward investment more open. The gains of the 1980s must be reinforced and pressed forward. Chapter 3 noted that even after the progress of the 1980s, measures of the penetration of foreign products in the Japanese economy were still lower than in other industrial countries. Specific problems remain, and because many of them involve opaque informal practices, identification, negotiation, and successful removal can be difficult. But as long as Japan is characterized by import barriers that cause other nations to perceive it as more protectionist than other markets, developing a more active role in the world will be difficult.

—Vigorously resist any moves by Japan leading toward a regionalism that yields an Asian economic bloc excluding the United States. Resistance includes acting to maintain the centrality of the General Agreement on Tariffs and Trade as the primary international trade framework, actively engaging the Japanese government in efforts to strengthen or extend the GATT, ensuring that the North American Free Trade Agreement is not used in an exclusionary manner to discriminate against Japan or other Asian nations (thereby increasing the probability that they would seek an exclusionary grouping of their own), and more actively supporting the Asia-Pacific Economic Conference as the primary regional economic forum. A more protectionist regionalism in either the Americas or Asia would have negative economic and political consequences detrimental to the global interests of both the United States and Japan.

—Encourage Japan to become more fully engaged in the work of the major multilateral institutions, especially through a stronger personnel role. Enmeshing Japan more deeply in these organizations diminishes the share of policy and financial energy directed to purely unilateral actions and thereby reduces the strong commercial orientation of foreign aid and other foreign policy. This increased engagement will bring a Japanese policy input that will not always coincide with that of the United States, but this fact should not obstruct this movement. On the whole, the Japanese should be able to bring productive ideas and policies to these organizations.

—Keep Japan out of international military activity except within the strict confines of United Nations peacekeeping operations. To move Japan toward the potential use of military power on a unilateral basis would be dangerous because it plays to the desires of the nation's most conservative, nationalistic elements. Although a real revival of militarism has a low probability, there is no reason to promote a possible move in this direction. The greater probability is that a decisionmaking process that does not operate efficiently in crisis situations could lead to an incautious unilateral use of military power. Japan would gain nothing from moving in this direction because of the concerns it would raise among neighboring Asian nations and other industrial powers.

—Avoid a simplistic and unequal division of labor in world affairs in which the United States maintains global military security leadership and Japan emphasizes economic assistance to developing countries. The two functions are not comparable in cost or impact. Foreign aid should be a continuing important component of Japanese interaction with the world, but the division of labor advocated by some in the Japanese government has been primarily a ploy to continue commercially oriented policies without taking on new roles in world affairs.

—Push Japan aggressively to make a major contribution to humanitarian activities in the world as an alternative to a military role and an important supplement to economic aid. Pursuing this route would give Japan a greater sense of useful international involvement while avoiding fears about a revival of Japanese militarism. Humanitarian work has been a missing element in Japan's interaction with the world, and its absence has left other countries with no alternative to either a remembrance of the war years or an image of Japan as a commercially driven nation.

—Encourage Japanese efforts to seek a more active participatory role in international issues that are not at the crisis stage. These areas, requiring the slow building of international consensus, play to strengths in

Japanese government decisionmaking and provide a useful arena in which to build national self-respect and self-confidence through greater assertiveness.

This agenda follows from the analysis of the preceding chapters. Pressure on Japan in a direction that has no domestic support or that is inconsistent with national interest cannot succeed. None of the suggestions above is inconsistent with national interest, and they all build on directions that already have considerable support within portions of the Japanese polity. The probability that Japan will follow this path, however, will be greatly enhanced if the U.S. government were to encourage and cajole Tokyo.

Neither the Reagan nor Bush administrations recognized the importance of the changes occurring or considered how policy toward Japan should be restructured to promote movement in the most favorable direction. While the Bush administration pressed on the economic front, it did not conceptualize or pursue an agenda of moving Japan toward an active international pacifism. Indeed, the informal signals the Japanese perceived during the Gulf crisis were entirely in the opposite direction. The advent of new, less conservative administrations in both Washington and Tokyo during 1993 opened opportunities to reverse this recent legacy and move in new directions. The rest of the 1990s are critical years for the formation of the new basic Japanese orientation toward the outside world, as a half-century of insularity and passivity come to an end. The United States could have much to lose by making the wrong choices about which avenues of participation to encourage or discourage.

Japan's National Economic Interest

As an advanced industrial nation, Japan has basically the same economic needs as others: a reasonably secure supply of essential raw materials, continued access to markets in other countries for its exports, and a continued willingness by foreign markets to accept its capital investments. In all of these areas, the way the government chooses to achieve these interests is affected by the enormous changes in the nation's economic position in the world, as well as by the end of the cold war.

Dependency on raw materials has long been recognized as a critical Japanese security interest. Relative to the United States, Japan is more dependent on imported raw materials and food, although this distinction is often exaggerated. All the industrial nations are dependent on imported raw materials, and the degree of dependence for Japan is not all that much greater than for Germany and some other European nations.[1] Nevertheless, resource dependence is real, and the Japanese are well aware of both its existence and the potential vulnerability that it brings to the nation.

Access to foreign markets for Japanese exports is just as important as raw material dependence. As often expressed by the Japanese, the nation must export to pay for its raw materials and has nothing but manufactured goods to sell. Therefore an international system enabling Japan to export successfully is of critical importance. During the postwar period, the combination of the GATT and the International Monetary Fund has provided that framework, but the government has accepted it as given and immutable. Now Japan is such a large component of the world economic system that its own behavior and policies will shape the future direction of the international trade and investment framework.

The final interest—foreign direct investment—is new, and it represents an epochal change for Japan. From the end of World War II to the beginning of the 1980s, Japanese firms were only minor investors around the world. But in the course of the past decade, Japan exploded onto the scene of global investment, as detailed in chapter 3. Even though the flow of new direct investment to the rest of the world may slow somewhat from the feverish pace of the late 1980s, the cumulative total is very high, and some flow will continue as demographic change drives firms to seek labor abroad. National interest, therefore, lies in protecting the security of existing investments abroad and convincing the world to accept a continuing flow.

Some critics portray Japan's national interest as broader and far more sinister. International dominance or monopoly over major manufacturing industries is an implicit or explicit theme in some of the less flattering descriptions of Japan. Certainly domination yields some benefits (excess profits accruing to Japanese firms), but a willful attempt to control global production on a broad scale is far fetched. Japanese firms in some highly visible industries are very competitive, which has gained them higher global market shares, and certainly some firms engage in predatory competitive tactics to enlarge their market share. But in some respects, the Japanese have been reluctant participants in global investment. Sudden emergence on the international investment scene was dictated more by economic necessity than by desire.

An insular nation that was satisfied when others left it alone (and that erected trade and investment barriers to accomplish that goal in the earlier postwar period), Japan does not seem motivated by any strong desire to dominate internationally. Protectionism at home, coupled with competitive domestic industries, thrust some Japanese industries into leading global positions, and the new wave of investment has now given these industries an enhanced global reach. However, the inherent conflict between the outward thrust of Japanese business and continued insularity at home jeopardizes the long-run continuance of this success.

The problem for Japan at the end of the century is how to pursue its national economic interests in a manner that receives acceptance from the rest of the world. Fears and criticisms expressed abroad imply that satisfaction with Japan's past approach has lessened, necessitating some changes in future behavior. The central question is how to alter those policies, and the nation will continue struggling with this question for years to come.

Let the World In

The economic elements of change necessary to underwrite Japanese national interests are clear and straightforward. To build acceptance of a continued flow of goods and capital to the rest of the world, Japan needs continuation of a reasonably liberal international economic institutional framework.[2] The addition of large asset holdings to the past large trade dependency increases the importance of this need. This institutional framework—principally the GATT and the IMF—provided postwar Japan with enhanced access to global markets for the nation's exports, imports, and investment. Commitment of other nations to the GATT depends in part on the behavior of Japan itself because of the nation's large size. The most important action Japan can take to build confidence is to demonstrate that its own markets for goods and capital are not just open formally but are easily accessible to the rest of the world. As one recent article in Japan stated aptly, "The biggest international contribution [that Japan can make] comes from buying goods from foreign countries."[3]

At stake here is not just removing of official barriers at the border, but demonstrating to the outside world that the nation is a reasonable place in which to do business. The rest of the world did not see Japan as a reasonably open market for trade and investment in the past, but the changes that took place in Japan from 1985 through the early 1990s were in the right direction. Continued movement in this direction is important to build a stronger foreign recognition of openness in Japan. Defensive public relations efforts to prove that low levels of imports or inward investment are normal because of special circumstances simply will not be persuasive. If higher penetration of imports and investment is not normal, then the nation needs extraordinary programs to encourage higher levels. It is the real existence of threads of connection through trade and investment that will convince other nations that Japan is a full and supportive player in the international economic framework.

In the absence of such connections, the internationalization of Japan amounts to only a movement of the nation into the outside world without a reciprocal inward movement of the world. That sort of one-sided flow puts great strain on existing international liberal trade and investment regimes. Alteration of the current regimes in a less open direction would impose a great deal of stress on the entire international system. Therefore pressure on Japan to continue moving toward greater real openness must remain a central part of American policy.

Resist Regionalism

While the need for an open global trade and investment system is important for Japan, some scenarios see the government pursuing formation of a regional trading bloc with its Asian neighbors. The notion of a world moving toward three large competing economic blocs (Europe, the Americas, and Asia-Japan) has gained some popularity.[4] By moving ahead with the North American Free Trade Agreement, and by offering an extension of this arrangement to other Latin American countries through the "Enterprise for the Americas," the Bush administration sent the wrong signals to Japan and the rest of Asia. When the administration stated that as "we have begun to see in our trade with Canada and hope to see with Mexico, such agreements can offer significant and lasting benefits for both sides,"[5] how can increased Japanese talk of regionalism in Asia without American participation be any surprise?

The world could probably function in a system of large economic blocs, provided that the barriers among them are not unduly restrictive. Regionalism in Asia, however, is likely to be less open to penetration by American products than an American bloc would be for nonmember products. A Japan with a protectionist background itself, joining with other Asian nations that are only beginning to emerge from strongly protectionist development policies, would not bode well for creation of an open bloc.[6] Because of its global trade and investment ties, the Japanese government has avoided any endorsement of regional bloc proposals, but if it were to perceive that its real access to American or European markets were in jeopardy, then the government would consider a formal regional arrangement as being in its interest. As discussed in chapter 5, an informal regionalization is already taking place, with Japanese firms becoming more active participants in regional trade and investment. That development is acceptable as long as Asian markets remain generally open to other participants as well. A Japanese government motivated by genuine fear of declining access to American and European markets would work with neighboring Asian nations to acquire privileged access to their markets.

To forestall Japan-dominated Asian countries from drifting toward a protectionist economic regionalism, the United States should move cautiously on the Enterprise for the Americas, remain strongly involved in the Asia-Pacific Economic Conference (APEC), and discourage Japan from heading toward formation of (or participation in) an Asian regional bloc. Whatever happens in terms of regional agreements, the American side of the Pacific must remain as open as possible to Japan and others to diminish their interpretation of these moves as protectionist.

APEC, which includes the United States, represents the principal regional organization at the present time. The United States must remain engaged heavily with the region, and APEC provides the institutional means for doing so. It represents the best means of maintaining communication on issues of importance to all members of the Asia-Pacific community. Evolution of APEC into a bureaucratic structure similar to the Organization for Economic Cooperation and Development might not be useful, but, should such a move materialize, the U.S. government should endorse it as a means of strengthening APEC versus the alternatives. The Japanese government, desiring an institutional framework for its own rising interest in the Asia-Pacific region, has been very supportive of APEC. It is in Japan's own interest to deal with the region through

APEC to ease the concerns of its neighbors about Japanese dominance in bilateral relationships.

Participate in International Institutions

Beyond engagement in APEC, Japan needs to be more firmly enmeshed in the workings of the principal international institutions that shape the economic and political environment of the world. The General Agreement on Tariffs and Trade, the International Monetary Fund, the World Bank, and the United Nations are major institutions that need more Japanese input, as noted in chapter 4. Financing, voting rights and a permanent seat on the UN Security Council are among the issues here, as is greater participation of Japanese people at all levels of these organizations.

As imperfect as these institutions may be, they have provided a viable system for promoting peaceful international economic interaction. The longer the system exists, the larger the vested interests of participants in its continued existence and the less their interest in alternative economic behavior (increased protectionism or regional economic blocs) and the lesser the probability of military conflict to resolve political problems among member states. Building a stronger Japanese commitment to these organizations will be crucial to their future effectiveness because Japan is such a large member. Since the international economic system that these institutions have made possible is so important to Japan's national interest, greater participation in them is also in its national interest.

Financial burden sharing is one way of enmeshing Japan more fully in these organizations, and one that has already proceeded quite far, along with a concomitant increase in formal voting rights. Financing and votes are important, but as detailed in chapter 4, a sense of separateness remains, and overcoming it should be a goal of both the U.S. and Japanese governments.

As part of this effort, the U.S. government should continue to press the Japanese government to be more actively involved in defining the nature of the next round of global trade discussions after the Uruguay round comes to an end. Japan must be heavily engaged in that discussion, both because its size mandates participation and in order to lessen the attention given in Japan to moving in a more regional direction. The same is true at the World Bank, IMF, and other institutions where the

Japanese should be more involved in policy issues. The pressure mounted in 1992 to view Japan and East Asia as a development model at the World Bank may have roused resistance, but it brought closer Japanese involvement in the policy direction of the bank.

Equally important is that Japan provide a greater human participation in the daily work of all the principal institutions and not remain restricted to providing money or arguing about formal voting rights. The extremely low levels of personnel involvement in the major multilateral institutions, documented in chapter 4, leave the impression that commitment to the goals and work of these organizations is superficial. Any nation that wants to demonstrate to the world that its international engagement is entirely benign can do so by taking on a larger portion of the work of the major institutions that maintain the international framework that underwrites a peaceful, prosperous world. Although personnel involvement ultimately depends on the willingness of Japanese citizens to work in these organizations, the Japanese government can do a great deal to encourage such participation, and the U.S. government can strongly encourage the Japanese government to pursue such policies.

As long as the Japanese are willing to finance international activities without participating, perhaps Americans should not complain; indeed, getting the Japanese to finance a largely American agenda without interference would appear to be the best of all possible worlds, as was claimed by some during the Persian Gulf crisis. But there are three strong reasons to demand a stronger human dimension in Japanese involvement.

First, human participation becomes a means of enmeshing Japan in a set of international forums that help to shape or define the limits on Japan's unilateral activities. Simply supplying money to these organizations is insufficient because it does not build commitment or put constraints on Japan. As noted in chapter 4, even the large donations from Japan to the multilaterals represent a relatively small share of the nation's total foreign aid. Often the size of the multilateral donations is emphasized by Japanese officials as a sufficient indicator of commitment, but size alone is not convincing.

Second, human participation in these organizations creates a group of Japanese individuals who are imbued with the ideals these organizations represent. Policy experience provides these individuals with a more respectable platform from which to espouse those ideals within Japan. Even while they are working abroad, such people become a channel of communication back to Japan of the policies, concepts, and ideals of these organizations. Without this sort of personal representation, these institutions and their ideals remain a rather distant, academic presence for most Japanese. Active participation has been largely lacking except at the Asian Development Bank, where Japanese personnel have furthered the commercial interests of their own foreign aid program. That kind of commercialism is unhelpful, and the new crop of participants at the World Bank, IMF, and UN should come with fewer entanglements to the narrow national economic interests of the past.

Third, the presence of Japanese in these international settings provides an educational experience in the reverse direction as well. As greater numbers of Japanese are present, personnel from other countries will acquire more awareness and understanding of Japanese objectives and behavior. Suspicions and doubts about those intentions are easier to build when personal contact is lacking.

Not all Japanese personnel will be effective communicators, and complaints about the quality or behavior of some participants have surfaced, as in the case of Hiroshi Nakajima at the World Health Organization (discussed in chapter 4). But this is true of individuals from all societies and should not be an excuse to deny participation. However, the process of choosing individuals to be loaned from government agencies to the multilaterals has often involved political and social dynamics resulting in the dispatch of people not well suited to the international environment in which they must work. If the Japanese government is to make international service a higher priority, then it will also need to improve the selection processes. In addition, however, an increase in the number of people outside government who independently choose careers at the multilaterals would greatly broaden the pool of potentially effective participants.

Polls certainly demonstrate broad support among the Japanese public for acting through multilateral organizations. At the beginning of 1991 (just before the Gulf War), 62.4 percent of one poll's respondents said that the United Nations should be the center of Japan's international contribution.[7] At that time, the notion of contribution was framed entirely in the context of the looming military confrontation in the Middle East. There is not much broader recognition that the UN and other multilateral organizations need a stronger Japanese presence. The time has come for both the Japanese and U.S. governments to build on the recognition that does exist and increase human participation.

The justifications given in the past for low levels of personnel, especially the lack of suitably trained people, have lost any validity. Rapidly rising numbers of young people living and educated abroad provide an expanding pool of potential employees with fewer inhibitions about international interaction, far stronger language skills, and none of the inferiority complex of older generations. These well-trained, intelligent, and more cosmopolitan individuals would represent a great resource for all the multilateral institutions and provide international exposure for Japan. Women especially represent a skilled, underutilized group that may well see international service as an attractive career alternative to jobs in the domestic private sector. Increased participation is important at all levels, not just in high-prestige positions near or at the top of these organizations. The government has placed too much emphasis on obtaining these visible positions without concern for the overall level of real input from Japanese citizens. If the Japanese were to establish a firm track record of active, positive personnel participation, then objections by other governments to placing Japanese nationals in positions of high responsibility might be lessened.

These are moves that only the Japanese themselves can make, and the Japanese government can encourage participation through a variety of means. Possible steps to further the goal of increased international employment include government programs to promote education abroad (including more scholarships and junior year abroad programs), further promotion of more effective foreign language training in the educational system, active encouragement of recruitment of nongovernment personnel by multilateral institutions in Japan, and even subsidies or other compensation to government officials loaned to these institutions.

Given the overwhelming importance of an open trade and investment regime for Japan's national interest, the policy directions delineated above should have some resonance with the government and public. Actions to make domestic markets more accessible and more attractive for foreign goods and capital, maintenance of a focus on APEC as the appropriate regional economic forum, and greater engagement in the global institutions are all feasible, and all have proponents. Furthermore, recent economic developments—a growing secular shortage of labor, increased travel and educational experience abroad, and a strong currency—all move these policies forward. American encouragement of these policies would build upon these evolving domestic trends. However, the wrong signals, such as manipulation of NAFTA to seriously disadvantage Japanese competitors, would enhance the position of those in Japan who do not favor greater international outreach.

Military Security

Discussion of Japan's approach to achieving its national interests must include recognition of a crucially important fact: over the past forty-seven years, Japan has secured its national economic and political interests without projecting or using military force. This is a development of immense consequence for Japan and the rest of the world; in some respects, Japan represents the desirable nation-state of the future.

Armed invasion of Japan itself remains a remote possibility, but Article 9 of the constitution has been construed to permit a moderately sized, defensively postured military to deal with such direct danger. Expenditures for defense, even though limited to just over 1 percent of GNP, are large in international comparison because of the size of the economy. However, the critical development has been the strictly defensive posture of Japanese forces. Deployment of military force abroad has been denied by the prevailing interpretations of Article 9.

Before World War II, the emerging modern Japanese state adopted the approach of the Western powers to protect its interests: imperialism. Raw material supplies could be assured by owning the real estate on which they were located. Exports could be guaranteed by possessing colonies that must buy them. Investment could be protected by military forces. Japan took Taiwan from China as booty in the 1895 Sino-Japanese War; forcibly annexed Korea as another colony in 1911; took control of Manchuria militarily in 1931 and established it as a nominally independent puppet state; initiated a devastating war of conquest for the rest of China; and seized military control of areas possessing oil and other critical raw materials when it felt threatened by American sanctions in 1941. Even before takeover of Manchuria, troops were present to protect the Japanese-owned South Manchurian Railway. Although these actions were brutal and behavior toward local populations was egregious, the basic approach was little different from the pattern of imperialism followed by the Western powers from the sixteenth century through the first half of the twentieth century.

Since the end of the war, Japan has not had the use of any military tools to protect its international economic interests. Nevertheless, the nation has prospered beyond anyone's wildest dreams. This success points to Japan (and Germany, with its similar prohibition on military force) as a prototype of the future. Japan has not rescued hostages or otherwise dispatched troops to protect its citizens abroad, protected threatened assets owned by Japanese companies, fought against communist insurgents in developing countries, exported weapons to favored countries, or even protected its sea-lanes far from home. In all cases business and government learned to cope with uncertainty and risk through other means. Japan has negotiated its way out of most international problems and learned to live with (or financially insure against) international loss rather than use military force.

Dependency upon imported raw materials spawned a variety of government and business policy responses, including diversification of sources of foreign supply, long-term contracting, direct investment in supply sources, vigorous conservation policies, stockpiling of reserves, substitution of alternative materials, provision of generous levels of foreign aid to supplier nations, and a diplomatic posture designed to minimize antagonism on the part of suppliers. These policies have not worked perfectly. Providing aid and investment to Iraq, for example, did not prevent the Iraqis from bombing a large Japanese-owned petrochemical complex in Iran during the Iran-Iraq war in the early 1980s. But all policies have their failures, and overall the Japanese approach to raw material security has worked well. These lessons took some time to absorb; the reaction to the supply and price disruptions in the 1973 oil crisis was somewhat hysterical. But by the late 1980s, a much stronger sense of security and confidence in raw material supply characterized government, business, and the public.

The nonmilitary approach to achieving greater security of raw material supply also involved policies conceived to fulfill a very self-serving view of national interest. Large amounts of foreign aid seemed to be intended to impress the recipients with their size (and to benefit Japanese corporations) rather than designed to serve development needs. Efforts to remain neutral or disassociated from conflicts involving suppliers antagonized other industrial nations—especially the United States. However, the nonmilitary approach should not be discredited for its narrow conception of national interest; instead, the policies involved should be broadened so they are less exclusively self-interested. These failings seem no worse than those of U.S. policy in the postwar period, with its support of dictators in the name of democracy. The lessons gained from the postwar period remain of fundamental importance and should not be unlearned: security of raw material supply requires neither ownership of territory nor the potential use of armed force to deal with problems.

Achieving security for overseas investment also spawned nonmilitary approaches. All industrial nations have learned that international invest- ment risk can be reduced through insurance and avoidance of politically or economically unstable locations. Japanese businesses and government have found these approaches to investment risk adequate. Japanese firms have been very sensitive to local political and economic conditions; for example, they generally avoided Russia in the early 1990s and favored Southeast Asia over Latin America in the 1980s. In addition, the govern- ment has subsidized the insurance of foreign investments through the government-owned Export-Import Bank (which provided coverage for the ill-fated petrochemical plant in Iran). To a degree unknown in the United States, the Japanese government also works with industry to influence corporate behavior abroad so as to reduce political problems and minimize the danger of nationalization or restrictions on further investment. Extending this cooperative pattern from its previous domes- tic setting to an international one may be troubling to outside observers, but it has become well established and should generally operate to reduce tensions.

A common response to this recital of nonmilitary approaches to deal- ing with an uncertain world is that the ultimate guarantor of Japan's economic interests has been the U.S. military. By maintaining global peace, keeping troops in Japan to reduce regional anxieties about a revival of Japanese militarism, and guaranteeing the security of interna- tional sea-lanes, the United States has provided the implicit military backup for the success of Japanese nonmilitary policies. But that inter- pretation hardly seems relevant in the post–cold war world of the 1990s.

Internationally, the Japanese face three kinds of threats: hostility di- rected at local operations of Japanese firms and individuals (expropria- tion, punitive regulations, or physical violence), disruption of vital raw material deliveries by supplier nations, and interdiction of the sea-lanes on which Japanese imports and exports move. American military power has little influence on internal conflict or national policies that harm the interests of foreign investors. Association with the United States even complicated Japan's access to oil supplies in fall 1973. The nonmilitary policies discussed above provided more risk reduction than the American military umbrella.

Even security of sea-lanes for Japan does not depend on American military power. A worst-case scenario might be closure of the Molacca

Straits by the nations bordering it. Such a closure would certainly be inconvenient, affecting both the vital flow of oil from the Middle East and trade with Europe, but Japanese vessels could be rerouted readily— either farther south toward Australia or the other direction around the globe. Transportation costs would be higher, but not disastrously so, and the Japanese private sector would pay the cost. Meanwhile, the Japanese government has showered some of the countries in this strategic location with foreign aid, at least modestly reducing the danger of such a worst-case scenario from becoming reality.

Given the success of nonmilitary policies for dealing with international problems, moving ahead with the conservative agenda of restoring unilateral use of military force as a policy option would be a serious mistake. Participation in UN peacekeeping operations is not unilateral, and as long as the Japanese public is comfortable with dispatching Self Defense Forces (SDF) soldiers to participate in such multilateral operations, no great harm is done. Although the bill authorizing dispatch of SDF soldiers to the Gulf War was too controversial to pass the Diet, public opinion about participation of troops in authorized UN peacekeeping operations shifted and led to the cautious and very limited permission for SDF participation granted in the 1992 law. That bill's passage by a coalition of political parties reflected broad public support for this important change in the use of the SDF.

Given the manner in which the peacekeeping operations issue was handled by the conservative Liberal Democratic party, though, it is difficult to believe that UN peacekeeping participation was seen as an end to itself. Pressure to keep moving the boundary of the issue will continue whenever the conservatives are in power: to allow SDF forces to engage in military operations as part of UN peacekeeping operations, to join non-UN multilateral efforts such as that represented by the Gulf War, to unilaterally protect sea-lanes farther from Japan, and ultimately to alter Article 9 of the constitution. Each step along that route may seem minor or logical at the time the decisions are made, but the summation of the steps would be a fundamental alteration of the principles governing the existence and purpose of military forces in Japan. The more liberal opposition coalition that came into power in 1993 halted this agenda, at least temporarily.

What is wrong with allowing this agenda to go forward? The image of Americans dying in Kuwait while the Japanese stayed home provoked a sense of imbalance and unfairness among many Americans. Agreeing with the rhetoric of the conservatives in Japan, some Americans argued that the nation should take up its full responsibilities as a major power and bear the human burden of maintaining peace and security in the world.[8] The argument is an enticing one to some.

The principal part of the answer to this question lies in the lack of convincing controls in the machinery of Japanese politics and policymaking. The military ran amok in the 1930s because no other group in the prewar political system could stop them. Japan now operates under a quite different constitution, but the same inability to stop adverse behavior by determined actors remains a part of the domestic scene. Fifteen years after Narita International Airport opened outside Tokyo, it remained surrounded by barbed wire and patrolled by heavy security forces because of an unresolved conflict between a heavy-handed government and the local farmers (joined by radical students). Twenty years after decisions were made to move ahead with plutonium-using breeder reactors for electric power generation, a determined subset of the bureaucracy remained unchecked in its zeal to move ahead despite vehement international criticism and the strong security dangers posed by the policy. Once started, troubling policies can be extremely difficult to reverse.

Given the fact that the social status of the military has been immeasurably diminished since the prewar period, and given the clear civilian control over the apparatus of government embodied in the constitution, the dangers of an uncontrollable military emerging in the future are probably slight.[9] Indeed, military service is so unpopular that in 1991 ninety graduates of the Defense University, approximately 25 percent of the graduating class, opted not to pursue military careers.[10] But there still is some possibility of a shift in external circumstances and public opinion that would allow an aggressive use of military force by a determined military clique, and this possibility would be best left unexplored. The voting public in Japan has agreed with this general concern and, as naive as some of the public's concerns may be, it would be best to respect their continued skepticism over tampering with the military issue. Because of the very large size of Japan's economy, its high level of per capita income, its advanced technological base, and the existing large military budget, the potential for building a powerful military machine rather quickly is certainly present. This potential underlies much of the concern expressed in Japan and around the region.

There is strong evidence that abandoning its carefully defensive military posture would further none of Japan's national interests. In an Asian context, a shifting military stance in Japan would raise fears, provoke retaliatory spending programs, and induce shifts in force postures that would raise tensions and reverse some of the favorable trends of the 1980s. Concern over Japan's military posture would undermine the atmosphere of trust that is so important to the maintenance of the closer trade and investment relations that have evolved in the Asia-Pacific region. Economic relations with the United States could also be damaged, as American protectionist claims based on national security arguments would gain new salience. Rather than gaining a more secure international environment, Japan would face a less secure one. No legitimate reason exists for increasing military spending or being able to project force beyond the boundaries of the nation. The world may be a hostile place for individuals who might be taken as hostages, or for corporations that may face harm to their investments, but nonmilitary responses have worked for Japan and should continue to do so.

A Nonmilitary Alternative

A standard response to opposition to the use of military force is that there is a class of problems that does not involve direct threats to national interest but demands collective military action in the name of humanity. The problems in the former Yugoslavia, Somalia, and Cambodia are examples of situations in which there have been attempts to interject outside military force to keep warring factions apart or to take sides against a local aggressor. This is the class of international problems raised by those who argue that Japan has an obligation or legitimate right to alter its military posture. But alternatives often exist for dealing with such crises, so that even in the United States the use of military force is a heavily debated option in competition with reliance on economic sanctions and other possibilities. These crises do not provide a convincing argument for supporting a shift in Japan's overall defense posture.

Active Pacifism

Pacifism is not the same as passivity—and for the past forty-seven years Japan has been profoundly passive.[11] Advocating that Japan not alter its defense posture should not be taken as an endorsement for a continuation of all past behavior, however. It could follow a far more active pacifist mission in the world. This mission would involve direct participation in difficult international situations without a full-fledged military role.

An important first step toward building an active pacifism would be to follow through with the stronger personnel commitment to the major multilateral institutions advocated earlier. Peacekeeping operations by the UN represent only a fraction of the work involved, and employment of Japanese civilians at any of the multilateral organizations has never faced the same constitutional constraints as SDF participation. Why should the government have rushed ahead with the peacekeeping issue while ignoring the paucity of personnel in the broader work of the UN or other institutions? The imagery—of an unseemly eagerness to deploy soldiers abroad under any pretext—was the opposite of what should be in Japan's national interest.

An additional and critically important aspect of this activism should be involvement in humanitarian activities on both a multilateral and unilateral basis. One might think of this as similar to alternative service as it existed under the U.S. military draft. The granting of conscientious objector status carried an obligation to engage in some acceptable alternative national service. Pursued vigorously and visibly, this form of involvement on a national scale would provide respect and prestige and relieve some of the concerns within Asia and more broadly around the world concerning Japan's goals and economic involvement.

Humanitarian work does not carry the same degree of risk of death and destruction as military participation, but it can be dirty, difficult, and dangerous. Giving medical care and food to Kurds in Iraq or ministering to the victims of Mount Pinatubo in the Philippines are examples of such work. If the Japanese want to prove that they do not just sit at home reaping benefits while someone else does the difficult work of the world, then the government should get its citizens into the front lines of humanitarian work. The tiny private and government programs to engage in such work have been a start, but they have been very small for a nation that faces a need to define and demonstrate a positive international role.

In the past, the Japanese government proposed that foreign aid be considered as its alternative to a military role in the world, as noted in chapter 6. In this view, what matters is the financial burden placed on the nation; if Japan was constrained in its military spending, then it could remedy the imbalance through expanded spending on foreign aid. Since economic aid arguably enhances the economic success of recipient countries, it lessens the probability that recipients will resort to armed conflict (at least against the donor), thereby contributing to international peace and security. But as an adequate alternative contribution to global security this notion has several problems. Foreign aid, as analyzed in chapter 4, continues to provide strong direct or indirect benefits to Japanese firms, so that it is not a burden in the sense of military service. Furthermore, foreign aid, as practiced by Japan, has mainly involved the transfer of large sums of money, not a large, visible participation of human beings. Some form of international involvement that includes something other than money is still needed.

Financially, Japan has supported the work of multilateral humanitarian organizations attached to the UN, as noted in chapter 6. But these organizations, too, could use a much stronger personnel input. The appointment of Sadako Ogata to be UN high commissioner for refugees, as noted in chapter 4, represented a useful step toward a more positive personnel interaction. Ogata began using the Japanese press aggressively to push her agenda of humanitarian outreach to refugees and to educate the Japanese public on these problems.[12] She has provided an important positive role model of an active, involved person dealing with difficult world issues with which Japanese have been relatively uninvolved in the past.

The United Nations represents a forum in which Japan can pursue humanitarian activities in a multilateral setting. But these can be pursued on a unilateral basis as well. In 1991 one group proposed creation of an equivalent of the SS *Hope*, a medical ship flying the Japanese flag that could be dispatched worldwide to provide emergency medical aid and public health care. Commenting on this proposal, one leading editorial writer stated: "Elimination of poverty, protection of the environment and assistance in disaster relief constitute activities that will prevent disputes and ensure peace far more effectively than military battles."[13] This kind of attitude—if it results in real activity by the Japanese in addition to the provision of money to foreign or multilateral organizations—is precisely what needs to be encouraged in Japan.

The counterargument has been that humanitarian work of this sort is not compatible with Japanese social behavior; the society is not based on a Judeo-Christian ethic that includes charity toward strangers. As a group-oriented society, the Japanese are generous and humanitarian toward those who belong to their own reference groups (principally family and corporation), but not toward outsiders. Divergent social norms between Japan and the West are quite clear, but these need not inhibit the nation from pursuing an active international humanitarian agenda.

The Example of the Japanese Red Cross

The record of the Japanese Red Cross (JRC) suggests that a Judeo-Christian ethic is not a required element for actions that are broadly humanitarian. An organization similar in concept to the Red Cross was founded as early as 1877 at the time of the Satsuma rebellion, the last military challenge to the new revolutionary central government that came into power in the Meiji Restoration of 1868. This organization provided medical assistance to the wounded on both sides and was reorganized as an official Red Cross Society in 1887. Since very early in its existence, the Japanese Red Cross has benefited from official involvement of the imperial family, and since 1912 the imperial family has made financial contributions to the International Committee of the Red Cross as well (establishing the Empress Shoken Fund).[14] Imperial family involvement gave this new nontraditional form of activity an imprint of acceptability and official sanction.

Close association of the Japanese Red Cross with the government continues today, including the fact that the present version of the organization was established by law—the Japanese Red Cross Law of 1952. The empress is the honorary president, and other imperial family members serve as honorary vice presidents.[15] The government also contributes money to the Red Cross, especially for international disasters through the International Red Cross; in 1988, for example, government funding accounted for 54.2 percent of the JRC's international contributions. The government broadcasting system (NHK) has also been mobilized to run fundraising campaigns since 1983; funds from the NHK campaign provided 18.7 percent of total contributions received in 1988.[16]

The overall size of the Japanese Red Cross is impressive. By the end of 1989 it had 43,700 paid employees and 4.6 million unpaid volunteers. Paid employees were more numerous than those of the American Red Cross, partly because the JRC runs its own hospitals, but the number of volunteers is four times larger than the number in the United States.[17] One wonders why a society where volunteerism and charity are not supposed to be well established gets this high level of participation. Part of the answer may come from sexual role models in Japan. Although the statistics do not specify the gender of volunteers, it is quite likely that most are women, both because they have lower labor force participation rates than men (giving them more time for volunteer activities) and because humanitarian, charitable ideals are strongly identified with women in Japan.

Total voluntary contributions to the JRC came to ¥15.6 billion (approximately $113 million) by March 1989. These contributions were roughly one-third the size of those received by the American Red Cross ($333 million in 1989), making them only moderately lower on a per capita basis.[18] But there is an interesting difference between the two countries in the organization of contributions. Rather than relying as much on broad fundraising campaigns, the JRC has members who pay annual dues, including 325,111 corporate members (approximately one-quarter of all incorporated businesses).[19]

Given the corporate membership basis, and the operation of hospitals, the Japanese Red Cross is sufficiently different from that of the United States that direct comparisons are perhaps best avoided. Nevertheless, the overall operation of the JRC is large enough to imply that simplistic statements about the lack of volunteer or charitable activity in Japan are unwarranted. However, the hand of government has been important to the success of this humanitarian organization. Direct personal involvement of the imperial family, legal sanction by the government, use of the NHK for fundraising, and direct financial contributions from the government have all given this domestic organization a quasi-official standing that has undoubtedly enhanced its ability to gain corporate members and individual contributions. When a deeply ingrained religious or cultural motivation is not well developed, government and official promotion provide an important alternative mechanism for building successful institutional structures.

This model suggests the means by which similar activities might be promoted on an international level. The record of participation by the Japanese Red Cross during the Gulf crisis, as detailed in chapter 6, was minor: one small group briefly visited refugee camps and hostages in fall 1990, and another worked for a month in Geneva and then made a brief tour of the Middle East after the war was completed. The JRC provided funds for the International Red Cross, but human participation was insignificant. Response to the government's call for a volunteer medical group in September 1990 was also minimal.

A small private organization does exist in Japan to send doctors abroad. Called the Kokusai Kūkyū Iryō Chīmu (Japan Medical Team for

Disaster Relief—JMTDR), this organization claims to have 500 members. It came into existence in 1982, led by a retired professor from Fukushima Medical College. But it has sent only very small groups abroad and generally belatedly enough that little positive publicity has resulted.[20]

An International Humanitarian Corps

Instead of such unassisted volunteerism, the government could establish and command unilateral international humanitarian behavior. Imagine a standing corps of 10,000 uniformed people—doctors, nurses, nutritionists, drivers, and other assistants completely separate from the Self Defense Forces. Equip them with their own medical supplies, food, tents, planes, trucks, ambulances, and ships. Make them available for rapid deployment around the world to areas of natural disaster: volcanoes, earthquakes, floods, or typhoons. Extend that mandate to refugee and combatant assistance in times of conflict. Think of the government arguing with Iraq that these people must be unhindered in their access to Kurdish groups—as the French government did for Doctors without Walls in 1992. Make this force a standing body that could be dispatched at the discretion of the government without the delay of Diet debates. Simplify the political issues at home by excluding SDF personnel from the group.

Such an aggressive, human involvement in difficult conditions and in potentially dangerous locations would build quite a different image abroad for Japan than the current one of narrow economic self-interest laced with nebulous concern over future Japanese militarism. Japanese self-esteem and confidence would also benefit tremendously. The public continued to harbor strong concerns in the early 1990s about the role the SDF would perform in UN peacekeeping missions, even though those missions are far removed from what might be labeled real military activity. If there had been a solid record of international involvement in the humanitarian sphere, the public might have felt less uncomfortable about the UN peacekeeping role and might have reacted with fewer restrictions on the behavior allowed the SDF in this context.

Even though UN peacekeeping operations do represent an increase in involvement in world affairs, they are relatively small and infrequent, and Japanese forces may not be chosen each time for participation. Natural and man-made disasters, refugee problems, and public health problems, however, occur with distressing regularity around the world and provide an ongoing opportunity for participation, visibility, and even leadership.

Is such a scenario realistic? If playing an active humanitarian role were compatible with Japanese society or politics, would not Japan have already moved in this direction? The dominant conservative political forces in Japan led the battle for economic aid and military participation, virtually ignoring an active humanitarian policy as a desirable alternative. The natural advocates of such policies would have been the opposition parties, but far too often they did nothing more than oppose LDP proposals to alter the status of the military, leaving them mired in a naive and negative stance that went beyond pacifism to passivity. When these same opposition groups actually came into power as a coalition government in 1993, a new opportunity opened for defining innovative proposals for international engagement of this sort.

The public certainly endorses playing such a role in the world, although opinion polls provide little information on the extent of real action or involvement that people have in mind. In a poll by the newspaper *Nihon Keizai Shimbun* before the outbreak of hostilities in the Gulf War, 70 percent of the respondents advocated that Japan engage in international humanitarian work.[21] If at least the vague notion of playing a humanitarian role in the world has that degree of public support, then the Japanese government can and should press forward, and the U.S. government should feel comfortable that it is encouraging Japan to move in a direction compatible with public opinion.

Furthermore, the government has taken some small steps toward a larger humanitarian role, so a large shift to form a stronger program would build on this base. The Ministry of Foreign Affairs has an office for disaster relief (Kokusai Kinkyū Enjo Shitsu—the International Emergency Assistance Office), and an emergency team was being built within the Japan International Cooperation Agency (JICA). The government needed legislative authority to build this emergency team, which immediately led to the question of participation by the SDF. The Foreign Ministry worried that the presence of the SDF would give an inordinate voice in the running of the team. The Foreign Ministry did manage to use its office for disaster relief to send small teams in 1991 to assist with problems such as the Kurds in Iraq or the aftermath of devastating storms in Bangladesh. But the entire budget for international activity of this sort in 1993–94 was a mere ¥1.5 billion—about $14 million.[22]

Do the Self Defense Forces belong in an international humanitarian corps, as the conservatives insist? Public opinion was shifting toward acceptance of this position. A poll in late 1990 found 53 percent in favor of the use of SDF soldiers for nonmilitary international tasks (or at least stating that their use was inevitable). During the Gulf War, these opinions persisted: 54 percent supported SDF use in overseas disaster relief.[23] The Self Defense Forces themselves, eager to build some status and expand their area of operation, pressed for inclusion in international disaster relief efforts.[24] In addition, an advisory group to the government issued a report in spring 1991 calling for a standing group that could be dispatched abroad for disaster work. It explicitly included the SDF and placed its main emphasis on UN peacekeeping operations rather than on humanitarian work.[25]

The argument in favor of inclusion of the SDF stems mainly from efficiency. Since military units in Japan have faced no combat since the end of World War II, the only real activity for them—other than endless training for an imaginary war with the Soviet Union—has been to carry out domestic disaster relief in the wake of typhoons, earthquakes, and volcanic eruptions: precisely the sort of emergency role that Japan should fulfill internationally. On the basis of efficiency—preventing a duplication of personnel and equipment—or expertise in emergency rescue work, the argument is that the SDF should form the basis of an international disaster relief corps.

Although these arguments sound convincing, the SDF presence is not really necessary, could ultimately limit the size of the force (out of concern about too many Japanese soldiers in uniform appearing in foreign countries), raises concerns over the true objectives of the force, and could complicate its deployment (by requiring Diet authorization). The peacekeeping operations bill passed into law in spring 1992 allowed for SDF participants in groups dispatched to engage in international disaster relief as well as UN peacekeeping operations. But the organization envisioned by this law was too small and poorly funded to make any visible difference in international relief work. Rather than propelling Japan in a humanitarian direction, the peacekeeping law may have limited choices and choked off a more meaningful move.

These are questions on which the U.S. government could do much to shape the debate and outcomes in Japan. Strong signals welcoming a large, standing, nonmilitary disaster relief force would have a considerable impact on the debate in Japan. Instead, at the beginning of the

1990s, during the Gulf crisis, the Bush administration remained silent or sent implicit signals encouraging military participation. This was the wrong direction to take, and the Clinton administration has the opportunity to reverse direction.

Conclusion

The disastrous end of World War II had a devastating impact on Japanese self-confidence in an international setting. National goals were redefined to emphasize domestic objectives, and the result was a sustained burst of economic growth that brought the nation into the ranks of the advanced industrial nations by the 1970s. The economic changes explored in this volume moved Japan back into a closer engagement with the world as domestic economic success and the passage of time were yielding a renewed sense of confidence that led to serious thinking about the nation's global role.

The next fifty years will see a dramatically different orientation for Japan toward the world than the one that has prevailed during the past fifty years. The developments emphasized in this volume—the end of rapid economic growth as Japan reached the ranks of the advanced industrial nations and the macroeconomic changes associated with slower economic growth, financial deregulation, tighter labor markets, technological success and yen appreciation—intersected to make the Japanese large international creditors on both a net and gross basis over the course of the 1980s. The overall flow of investment from Japan included a particularly important rise in direct investment, making the Japanese large-scale owners of overseas manufacturing plants, financial institutions, and real estate. The trends causing overseas investment will continue once the economy recovers from recession and will be joined by long-term demographic shifts that will sustain direct investment by Japanese firms.

The real involvement in the outside world that necessarily accompanies the responsibilities of being an asset holder (and, in particular, an owner of direct investments) will continue to draw the nation out of its sheltered past. At one level, this internationalization of Japan requires individuals and corporations to learn how to manage their assets in foreign environments. At another level, it involves questions of how the government can or should participate in world affairs. Over the next decade the government and public will be engaged in a difficult continuing debate over how to participate.

From an American perspective, a changing Japan will require new policies on both sides of the Pacific. In devising these policies, firm rejection of two polar positions provides a useful starting point. Japan is neither so incompatible with the United States as to require exclusion from the international system nor does it share identical social values or international policy objectives with the United States. The emphasis on similarity was a fiction built largely out of the needs of the cold war, and the idea of total incompatibility represents an immediate counterreaction to those exaggerations. If the two economic and political systems are distinctly different, then the relevant issue is how to develop common grounds for accommodation and interaction.

With Japan taking on new, more assertive roles in world affairs, the search for acceptable patterns of interaction acquires new importance and urgency. The agenda of items laid out at the beginning of this chapter provides a basis on which to pursue that interaction over the coming decade. American policy should work to move Japan toward becoming more open economically to the rest of the world, more firmly enmeshed in a set of international organizations, and more actively pacifist through humanitarian work. Since these objectives are compatible with Japanese national interests, the U.S. government should be able to achieve considerable progress on this agenda.

Japan may not play a role that fits American concepts of a desirable leader. Nevertheless, the nation is in a position to participate in international issues to a greater degree than in the past, and its energies need to be channeled in a productive direction. Americans may continue to be disappointed in Japan's inability to participate fully in dramatic international political crises, but these arise infrequently. In other areas— including disaster relief, pollution control, and assistance to developing nations—Japan may have much to offer.

As Japan shakes off the passivity of the past fifty years, it could contribute greatly to enhance peaceful global development. The path to this constructive, nonmilitary engagement with the world is still far from certain. Alternatives—including less openness on trade and investment, a drift toward regionalism, or a stronger and more unilateral military stance—are far less desirable. The policy agenda advocated in this study would make these alternatives less likely and would promote constructive international engagement for Japan in the coming decade.

NOTES

Chapter One

1. Kenneth B. Pyle, *The Japanese Question: Power and Purpose in a New Era* (Washington: AEI Press, 1992), looks at the political and institutional side of the debate in Japan over an appropriate new international role, arguing that the nation continues to experience difficulty in moving beyond a response to foreign pressures and events.

Chapter Two

1. The macroeconomic developments of the 1970s and first half of the 1980s are the subject of Edward J. Lincoln, *Japan: Facing Economic Maturity* (Brookings, 1988), pp. 69–81, and are analyzed in much greater detail there.

2. Ministry of Finance, *Zaisei Tōkei; Heisei 3-Nendo* [Fiscal Statistics, Fiscal 1991] (Tokyo: Ministry of Finance Printing Office), pp. 63, 330–31; and Lincoln, *Japan*, p. 100.

3. Bill Emmott, *The Sun Also Sets: Why Japan Will Not Be Number One* (Simon and Schuster, 1989), especially pp. 221–41.

4. Shoji Yoneda, *Nihon Jinkō Bōkai: Shusseiritsu Ijō-Teika no Gen'in to Tai-saku* [Japan's Population Collapse: The Causes of and Policies toward the Abnormal Decline of the Birth Rate] (Tokyo: Koseido Shuppan, 1991), p. 15.

5. Economic Planning Agency, *Annual Report on National Accounts 1992* (Tokyo: Ministry of Finance Printing Office, 1992), pp. 90–91. These data differ slightly from those collected as part of the annual household income and expenditure data.

6. Fumio Hayashi, "Explaining Japan's Savings: A Review of Recent Literature," *Bank of Japan Monetary and Economic Studies*, vol. 10 (November 1992), pp. 63–78.

7. Financial deregulation from the 1970s through the mid-1980s, and the factors involved in driving the process, were discussed in detail in Lincoln, *Japan*, pp. 130–210. Also see Frances McCall Rosenbluth, *Financial Politics in Contemporary Japan* (Cornell University Press, 1989); Thomas F. Cargill and Shoichi Royama, *The Transition of Finance in Japan and the United States: A Comparative Perspective* (Stanford: Hoover Institution Press, 1988); and Robert Alan Feldman, *Japanese Financial Markets: Deficits, Dilemmas, and Deregulation* (MIT Press, 1986).

8. Rosenbluth, *Financial Politics in Contemporary Japan*, provides a series of case studies indicating the extremely convoluted nature of individual deregulation episodes.

9. Ministry of Finance, *Okurashō Kokuasi Kin'yūkyoku Nempō* [Annual Report of the International Finance Bureau] (Tokyo: Kin'yū Zaisei Jijō Kenkyūkai [Financial and Fiscal Research Group], 1990), p. 136. The three categories of foreign presence distinguished in the data are representative offices, full branches, and local subsidiaries.

10. Ministry of Finance, *Okurashō Kokusai Kin'yūkyoku Nempō*, 1992, p. 447; and C. Fred Bergsten and Marcus Noland, *Reconcilable Differences? United States-Japan Economic Conflict* (Washington: Institute for International Economics, 1993), p. 174.

11. Asahi Mutual Life Insurance Company, *Financial and Investment Business of the SEIHO* (*Life Insurance Companies in Japan*) (September 1991).

12. Bank of Japan, *Economic Statistics Annual 1991* (Tokyo: BOJ, 1992), p. 199; and *Economic Statistics Monthly*, no. 551 (February 1993), p. 133.

13. Such a view is expressed by Yoshio Suzuki, "Shōken Fushōji to Kanmin no Seido Kaikaku: Kisei Kyōka Ka Jiyūka Ka" [Stock Scandals and Bureaucratic Reform: Strengthening or Loosening Regulation?], *Toyo Keizai*, September 14, 1991, pp. 62–67. Suzuki, a leading economist in Japan, was director of research at the Bank of Japan in the 1980s.

14. International Monetary Fund, *International Financial Statistics*, vol. 38 (October 1985), p. 277, and vol. 41 (September 1988), p. 311. These exchange rates are monthly averages.

15. Calculated from GDP deflator data and exchange rate data for each country contained in International Monetary Fund, *International Financial Statistics Yearbook* (1990), pp. 444–45, 730–31.

16. Richard C. Marston, "Pricing to Market in Japanese Manufacturing," *Journal of International Economics*, vol. 29, no. 3–4 (1990), pp. 217–36, confirms this conclusion with a detailed investigation of what he terms "pricing to market" (that is, varying the yen-denominated export price to absorb a portion of exchange rate fluctuations) for seventeen product categories during the 1980s.

17. As reflected in Lincoln, *Japan*, which was completed in the summer of 1987 when available data showed the economy to be seriously slowing.

18. Statistics Bureau, Management and Coordination Agency, *Japan Statistical Yearbook 1987*, pp. 368–69; *1989*, pp. 368–69; and *1991*, pp. 370–71, show that manufacturing operating profits were ¥13.1 trillion in 1985 and were back up slightly to ¥13.5 trillion in 1987, followed by a jump to ¥19.4 trillion by 1989.

19. "Shusseiritsu 1.53 to Shijō Saitei" [Birth Rate of 1.53 Lowest in History], *Nihon Keizai Shimbun*, June 7, 1991, p. 1.

20. Ministry of Health and Welfare, Institute of Population Problems, *Nihon no Shōrai Suikei Jinkō (Heisei 3-Nem 6-Gatsu Zantei Suikei)* [Japan's Future Estimated Population (Provisional Estimate, June 1991)] (Tokyo: Kōsei Tōkei Kyōkai, 1991), pp. 6–11. This is the central estimate, with a high and low estimate also provided. Death rates, the other major element in forecasting population, are assumed to remain largely stable, with only a minor increase in the average age of death (rising from 1989 to 2025 from age 75.91 to 77.87 for men and from 81.77 to 83.85 for women).

21. "Shusseiritsu 1.53 to Shijō Saitei." This estimate is approximately equal to the high estimate provided in the June 1991 revision.

22. "Hirogaru 'Mikonka Genshō' " [The Spreading "Not-Yet-Married Phenomenon"], *Asahi Shimbun*, June 17, 1992, p. 4.

23. Ministry of Health and Welfare, *Nihon no Shōrai Suikei Jinkō*, p. 7.

24. "Shasetsu: Jinkō Suikei Wa Seimitsu ni Hayaku" [Editorial: Quickly, a Population Forecast with Precision], *Nihon Keizai Shimbun*, June 7, 1991, p. 2.

25. "Shasetsu: Jinkō Suikei Wa Seimitsu ni Hayaku." Data for the 1980s are from Bank of Japan, *Recent Changes in Japan's Labor Market and Their Impact—Synopsis*, Special Paper no. 202 (May 1991), p. 30.

26. Ministry of Labor, *Rōdō Hakusho* [Labor White Paper], 1991 ed. (Tokyo: Nihon Rōdō Kenkyū Kikō, 1991), p. 108.

27. Nomura Research Institute, *Kokusai Shakai no Naka no Nihon Keizai* [The Japanese Economy in the Context of International Society] (Tokyo: National Institute for Research Advancement, 1988), p. 89.

28. To an unknown extent, female labor force participation statistics are underestimated because much part-time work is unreported to the government to avoid income taxes. Tutoring, other teaching activity (flower arranging, tea ceremony, and others), translation work, and other jobs that can be managed from the home lend themselves to tax cheating.

29. Statistics Bureau, Management and Coordination Agency, *Japan Statistical Yearbook 1990*, p. 48. In 1975, 19.8 percent of all households with children were three-generation households, and that percentage was 20.4 percent ten years later.

30. "Rōdōryoku Jinkō: 2000-Nen Pīku ni Genshō" [Labor Force: Falling after a Peak in the Year 2000], *Nihon Keizai Shimbun*, March 24, 1992, p. 5.

31. Bank of Japan, *Economic Statistics Annual 1991* (Tokyo: BOJ, 1992), p. 291. These are average unemployment rates for the year. Monthly data for 1992 show the unemployment rate fluctuating in a range of 2.0 to 2.4 percent; Bank of Japan, *Economic Statistics Monthly*, no. 552 (March 1993), p. 11.

32. Ministry of Labor, *Rōdō Hakusho*, 1990 ed., supp. p. 19. Data for 1991 and 1992 are from Bank of Japan, *Economic Statistics Monthly*, no. 548 (November 1992), p. 11, and no. 552 (March 1993), p. 11.

33. "Gakusei wa Dono Naitei Gaisha o Erabu ka" [Which Offers Are the Students Going to Select?], *Toyo Keizai*, August 11, 1990, pp. 22–23. The article also makes a point of reporting survey results concluding that these graduates were more interested in personal goals than in helping their new corporate employers.

34. Ministry of Labor, *Rōdō Hakusho*, 1990 ed., pp. 35–37.
35. Ministry of Labor, *Rōdō Hakusho*, 1992 ed., supp. p. 58.
36. Ministry of Labor, *Rōdō Hakusho*, 1992 ed., supp. pp. 356–57.
37. Ministry of Labor, *Rōdō Hakusho*, 1992 ed., supp. p. 93; and Statistics Bureau, Management and Coordination Agency, *Monthly Statistics of Japan*, no. 384 (June 1993), p. 26. Before the first oil shock in 1973, annual hours had been 2,200 or higher; thereafter they ranged in an interval of 2,090 to 2,115 hours.
38. Ministry of Labor, *Rōdō Hakusho*, 1992 ed., p. 364. Other firms offering some version of a two-day weekend provide a number of different patterns: once a month (19 percent), twice a month (14 percent), once every other week (13 percent), or three times a month (9 percent).
39. "Rainen 4-Gatsu Kara Shū-40-Jikan Rōdō: Rōdōhō Kaiseian Seiritsu e" [A Forty-Hour Workweek from Next April: Passage of the Labor Law Revision Bill], *Nihon Keizai Shimbun*, June 2, 1993, p. 5.
40. Examples are Economic Planning Agency, *Rōdōryoku Fusoku Jidai: Genjō to Tenbō* [The Era of Labor Shortages: Current Conditions and Prospects] (Tokyo: Ministry of Finance Printing Office, 1990); Ministry of Labor, Employment Security Bureau, *Rōdōryoku Fusoku Jidai e no Taiō* [Response to the Labor Shortage Era] (Tokyo: Ministry of Finance Printing Office, 1991); and Ministry of Labor, Employment Policy Section, Employment Security Bureau, *Rōdōryoku Fusoku Jidai no Koyō Taisaku* [Employment Countermeasures for the Era of Labor Shortage] (Tokyo: Rōdō Kijun Chōsakai, 1992).
41. "Hitode Busoku Taisaku de Renrakukyō: Rōdōshō 7 Bun'ya de Setchi e" [Cooperative Communication on Labor Shortage: Ministry of Labor, Toward Establishing in 7 Areas], *Nihon Keizai Shimbun*, January 31, 1991, p. 7.
42. "Kaigin; Kigyō no Shōryokuka Tōshi Shien: Shinteiri Yūshisei o Sōsetsu" [Japan Development Bank; Supporting Corporate Labor-Saving Investment: Establishing a New Low Interest Rate System], *Nihon Keizai Shimbun*, March 15, 1992, p. 3.
43. "Rōdōshō ga Shidō Kyōka" [Ministry of Labor Strengthens Administrative Guidance], *Nihon Keizai Shimbun*, January 11, 1990, p. 5.
44. "Semarikuru '95 Hitode Busoku Panikku' " [The Pressing on of the "1995 Worker Shortage Panic"], *Toyo Keizai*, August 11, 1990, pp 16–20. The article cites a Ministry of Labor report which said that by 2010 a shortage of 1.9 million workers would exist, and then covers a variety of responses: more older workers, more women, and foreign workers (but with little emphasis on this final option).
45. Shōji Yoneda, *Nihon ga Abunai: Hōkai no Kiki ni Dō Taisho Suru* [Japan in Danger: How to Deal with the Crisis of Collapse] (Tokyo: Daiyamondo, 1989), pp. 19–21, 24–25; and Yoneda, *Nihon Jinkō Hōkai*. He argues in the latter (p. 25) that the purchase of Japanese companies by foreigners must be avoided at all costs.
46. "Hitode Busokukan ga Enwa" [An Easing in the Sense of Labor Shortage], *Nihon Keizai Shimbun*, March 10, 1992, p. 5, cites a Ministry of Labor study showing a drop in the proportion of firms responding that they had fewer

workers than desired. These results are also mentioned in Bill Clifford, "Slump Puts Labor Shortage in Lull," *Nikkei Weekly*, March 21, 1992, p. 4.

47. Because of the baby boom bubble, annual growth in this segment of the population averaged a high 1.6 percent during the 1960s and moderated to 1.0 percent in the 1970s. Thus population growth in this age segment moderated by less than one half, while economic growth moderated by more than one half, providing some explanation for the softness in labor markets in the 1970s and early 1980s. Growth rates calculated from data in Statistics Bureau, Management and Coordination Agency, *Japan Statistical Yearbook 1990*, p. 38.

48. For example, Ministry of Labor, Employment Security Section, *Rōdō-ryoku Fusoku Jidai e no Taiō*, pp. 94–95, gives one page for mention of foreign labor as one outcome of labor shortages, but clearly places its emphasis on a variety of other responses: increased employment of women and elderly, disabled, and young people, as well as investment overseas.

49. The history of technological borrowing in the postwar period up to the early 1970s is covered in Merton J. Peck and Shūji Tamura, "Technology," in Hugh Patrick and Henry Rosovsky, eds., *Asia's New Giant: How the Japanese Economy Works* (Brookings, 1976), pp. 525–85. Also see Terutomo Ozawa, *Japan's Technological Challenge to the West, 1950–1974: Motivation and Accomplishment* (MIT Press, 1974), especially pp. 67–70, 76–79.

50. Hiroaki Fujii, "90-Nendai no Kokusai Keizai to Nihon no Yakuwari" [The International Economy in the 1990s and Japan's Role], *Gaikō Fōramu*, no. 28 (January 1991), p. 51.

51. Hajime Karatsu, "Watashi no Kagaku Gijutsukan" [My View of Science and Technology], *Nihon Keizai Shimbun*, February 18, 1991, p. 17. Karatsu is a vocal critic of the performance of American manufacturing. Unlike Ishihara, though, he advocates that Japan play a more liberal role in transferring technology to the rest of the world.

52. Akio Morita and Shintaro Ishihara, *NO to Ieru Nihon: Shin Nichibei Kankei no Hōsaku* [The Japan that Can Say 'NO': A Card for a New U.S.-Japan Relationship] (Tokyo: Kobunsha, 1989), pp. 14–18.

53. Hajime Karatsu, "Time for U.S. to Wake Up," *Japan Times*, April 22, 1991, p. 22. Similar views are expressed in Hajime Karatsu, *Tough Words for American Industry* (Cambridge: Productivity Press, 1987), which had been originally published in Japanese with the more strongly worded title *Kūdōka Suru Amerika Sangyō e no Chokugen* [Straight Talk to American Industry That Is Being Hollowed Out].

54. Thomas S. Arrison and others, eds., *Japan's Growing Technological Capability: Implications for the U.S. Economy* (Washington: National Academy Press, 1992) provides a set of useful essays on various aspects of rising Japanese technological accomplishments.

55. These include James C. Abegglen, *The Japanese Factory: Aspects of Its Social Organization* (Free Press, 1958); Abegglen and George Stalk, Jr., *Kaisha: The Japanese Corporation* (Basic Books, 1985); and William G. Ouchi, *Theory Z: How American Business Can Meet the Japanese Challenge* (Addison-Wesley, 1981).

56. Robert R. Rehder, "Japanese Transplants: In Search of a Balanced and Broader Perspective," *Columbia Journal of World Business*, vol. 24 (Winter 1989), p. 26.

57. David A. Garvin, *Managing Quality: The Strategic and Competitive Edge* (Free Press—Macmillan, 1988), pp. 6-18, 180.

58. Garvin, *Managing Quality*, pp. 53-54, 184, 189-192, provides a table (p. 198) with dates for key Japanese contributions to the theory of quality control. He does not include just-in-time inventory control in this list, but it should be considered as another seminal contribution.

59. Garvin, *Managing Quality*, pp. 200-02.

60. Akira Takeishi, "Comparative Study on Japanese and U.S. Supplier Management," *Research Review*, vol. 6 (Autumn 1991), p. 3. This publication comes from Mitsubishi Research Institute (the research arm of one of the leading Japanese trading companies), and may present a biased analysis. Nevertheless, the article is based on an MBA thesis written by Takeishi at the Sloan School at the Massachusetts Institute of Technology.

61. Masaaki Imai, *Kaizen: The Key to Japan's Competitive Success* (McGraw-Hill, 1986), pp. 88-89.

62. Richard Florida and Martin Kenney, *The Breakthrough Illusion* (Basic Books, 1990), pp. 17-36, 141-64.

63. However, Garvin, *Managing Quality*, p. 210, found that in the room air conditioner industry, the average length of ties between the assemblers and their parts suppliers was roughly equal in Japan and the United States. This may be due simply to the relatively recent origin of the industry in Japan, or may suggest that the important issue is not longevity but the nature or content of the working relationships.

64. Michael J. Smitka, *Competitive Ties: Subcontracting in the Japanese Automotive Industry* (Columbia University Press, 1991), especially pp. 135-74, analyzes the cost advantages from the long-term subcontracting relationships that evolved in this industry after the 1950s. Similar views on economic efficiency are expressed by Masaru Yoshitomi in "Economic Functions of Keiretsu (Business Groups) in Japan," paper prepared for the U.S.-Japan Economic Policy (Core) Group Meeting, April 1991.

65. Taking the position that the linkages between large and small firms are often exaggerated is David Friedman, *The Misunderstood Miracle: Industrial Development and Political Change in Japan* (Cornell University Press, 1988), pp. 126-61.

66. Florida and Kenney, *The Breakthrough Illusion*, pp. 37-75, argue that the United States developed an unusual bias toward emphasis of breakthrough research since the 1950s, to the detriment of attention on continuous improvement.

67. Imai, *Kaizen*, p. 5.

68. This priority is high enough to impress foreigners who work in Japanese firms to see continuous change as being a distinctive approach. For example, John E. Rehfeld, "What Working for a Japanese Company Taught Me," *Harvard Business Review*, no. 6 (November-December 1990), pp. 167-76.

69. For example, Kunio Ito, "In Defense of Japanese Management Practices," *Economic Eye*, vol. 12 (Autumn 1991), pp. 19–22 [translated from the original in *Ekonomisuto*, June 25, 1990], takes a strong view on the superiority of Japanese corporate ownership patterns.

70. James R. Lincoln and Arne L. Kalleberg, *Culture, Control, and Commitment: A Study of Work Organization and Work Attitudes in the United States and Japan* (Cambridge University Press, 1990).

71. Imai, *Kaizen*, pp. 5–8.

72. Imai, *Kaizen*, pp. 125–42, emphasizes "cross-functional management" as key to quality control. He cites examples of Japanese firms in which the responsibility for cross-functional management has been assigned to members of the board of directors.

73. Among this genre were Michinobu Ozeki, *Keizai Taikoku Nihon* [Japan the Economic Power] (Tokyo: Sekai Nipposha, 1991); and Keiichi Imai, *Keizai Taikoku no Wasuremono—Bunka Akajikoku Nippon* [Forgotten Things of the Economic Power—Cultural Deficit Country Japan] (Tokyo: Nihon Keizai Shimbunsha, 1990).

74. Rin'ichi Kousaki, "Seikatsu Taikoku ka, Kokusai Kōken ka" [Lifestyle Superpower, or International Contributions?], *Bungei Shunju*, vol. 70 (August 1992), pp. 94–101.

75. Economic Planning Agency, *The Five-Year Economic Plan—Sharing a Better Quality of Life around the Globe* (press release, provisional translation), June 25, 1992, p. 71, estimates 3.5 percent growth for fiscal 1992–96. The government-run Japan Development Bank forecasted a somewhat lower 2.9 percent growth over 1992–2000 unless major policies were instituted to employ more women and elderly; "Seichōritsu 3% Ware mo; Rōdōryoku Fusoku de Kaihatsu Ginkō Bunseki" [Growth Rate Even Below 3 Percent; Because of Labor Shortage], *Nihon Keizai Shimbun*, February 8, 1992, p. 5. An earlier Nomura Research Institute forecast had been more optimistic: *Kokusai Shakai no Naka no Nihon Keizai*, p. 88, anticipated a 4 percent growth in full-employment GNP (with an estimate of actual growth at a slightly lower 3.7 percent) for 1985–2000.

76. Lincoln, *Japan*, pp. 26–37, discussed the anxiety of late 1973 and 1974, a time when some people believed that the economy would never grow again.

Chapter Three

1. Similar themes are emphasized by Kent E. Calder, "U.S.-Japan Cooperation and the Global Economy of the 1990s," *Washington Quarterly*, vol. 13 (Summer 1990), p. 99.

2. This is a straightforward accounting result. What enters the country must equal what leaves, just as in double-entry accounting. Put in the simplest terms, if a nation has a current account surplus, it has chosen not to buy as many goods and services from the rest of the world as it has sold, so it must have bought something else: assets. Even if one thinks of an extreme case, in which the surplus is held in the form of foreign currency (that is, the Japanese simply decide to

hold the dollars they receive for their exports and buy nothing with them at all), a capital transaction has taken place since currency represents non-interest-bearing debt instruments of governments. In reality, most of the surplus dollars or other foreign currencies resulting from the trade transactions are invested in real and financial assets (corporate equity, real estate, bonds, bank accounts, and other financial instruments) that yield a positive return.

3. Unlike U.S. balance-of-payments data, the Japanese separate flows into long term and short term, although the distinction between them is rather imprecise. Long-term transactions include direct investment, portfolio equity investment, and dealings in bonds or loans with a maturity of greater than one year. Short-term transactions represent dealings with a maturity of less than one year. Bank deposit transactions are not included in either category and are counted under the category of other monetary transactions.

4. Ministry of Finance, *Okurashō Kokusai Kin'yūkyoku Nempō* [Annual Report of the International Finance Bureau] (Tokyo: Kin'yū Zaisei Jijō Kenkyūkai [Financial and Fiscal Research Group], 1982), p. 350.

5. James Sterngold, "With Its Huge Banks Weakening, Japan Cuts Lending to the World," *New York Times*, September 24, 1990, pp. A1, D13. These points are emphasized in Michiyo Nakamoto and Robert Thomson, "Japan's Heavyweights Feel the Pinch," *Financial Times*, August 31, 1990, p. 19. This article also notes that Moody's Investors Service had downgraded Dai-Ichi Kangyo and Fuji Banks (from AAA to AA1). These themes are echoed in Marcus W. Brauchli, "Japan's Banks May Soon Resume Loans, But Go-Go Days Are Gone," *Wall Street Journal*, March 18, 1991, p. A9.

6. Roy C. Smith, "Japan, Land of the Setting Sun," *New York Times*, October 24, 1990, p. A25. Smith is a partner at Goldman, Sachs.

7. Bank for International Settlements, Monetary and Economics Department, *International Banking and Financial Market Developments* (Basel: August 1992), p. 2.

8. These ratios exclude assets held by local branches of the banks overseas; other data measuring assets held by international banks (cross-border lending plus loans held by local branches of foreign banks) indicate that Japanese banks held 31 percent of all international assets held by banks at the end of 1991, down from a peak of 38 percent in 1988. BIS, *International Banking and Financial Market Developments*, p. 67; and Hiroshi Toyofuku, "Banks' Standings Fall as Credit Ratings Slip," *Nikkei Weekly*, July 25, 1992, p. 25.

9. Hidetaka Tomomatsu, "Banks Eye Perpetual Bonds to Boost Capital," *Nikkei Weekly*, July 25, 1992, p. 25; and "9-Kō ga 9%-dai ni: Jiko Shihon Hiritsu" [Nine Banks at the Nine Percent Level: Own Capital Ratio], *Nihon Keizai Shimbun*, April 1, 1993, p. 1. The major banks included in this report were the eleven "city" banks, the Industrial Bank of Japan, the Long-Term Credit Bank of Japan, and the Nippon Credit Bank.

10. These statistics differ somewhat from the Ministry of Finance (MOF) series on foreign direct investment. Those figures showed a considerably larger $352 billion cumulative figure for Japanese direct investment in 1991. Ministry of Finance, *Okurashō Kokusai Kin'yūkyoku Nempō*, 1992, p. 479. The balance-of-

payments figures were used here for the sake of comparison with total investment. The MOF data yield a somewhat lower 24 percent average annual growth rate over the 1980–91 period.

11. U.S. data are from *Survey of Current Business*, vol. 71 (August 1991), p. 88; Japanese data are from Ministry of Finance, *Okurashō Kokusai Kin'yūkyoku Nempō*, 1991, pp. 462–63.

12. Neil Barsky, "Japanese Quietly Unload U.S. Real Estate; Move Comes as Property Values Fall, Japan Rates Rise," *Wall Street Journal*, October 5, 1990, p. A2. This story states that "conditions [are] ripe for a larger sell-off."

13. The bold MITI prediction is "2000-nen Nihon Keizai" [The Japanese Economy in the Year 2000], *Nihon Keizai Shimbun*, June 8, 1990, p. 3. This forecast appears to be a straight-line extrapolation of the 1985–90 trend in this ratio. The cautious estimate is Nomura Research Institute, *Kokusai Shakai no Naka no Nihon Keizai* [The Japanese Economy in the Context of International Society] (Tokyo: National Institute for Research Advancement, 1988), p. 150. But this is just a simple extrapolation of 1971–85 trends, and thereby does not take into account the acceleration in the post-1985 period.

14. The optimistic view is Robert R. Rehder, "Japanese Transplants: In Search of a Balanced and Broader Perspective," *Columbia Journal of World Business*, vol. 24 (Winter 1989), pp. 17–28. A more pessimistic view is Dennis Laurie, "Yankee Samurai and the Productivity of Japanese Firms in the United States," *National Productivity Review*, vol. 9 (Spring 1990), pp. 131–39. Gregory Clark, "A Doom-And-Gloom View of More Friction as Japan Continues Push into U.S., Europe," *Japan Economic Journal*, August 11, 1990, p. 8, is also pessimistic, especially on the ability of non-Japanese firms to understand and implement Japanese manufacturing-process technology.

15. Ryutaro Komiya, *The Japanese Economy: Trade, Industry, and Government* (Tokyo: University of Tokyo Press, 1990), pp. 142–44. These comments were originally written for a conference paper published in 1988.

16. Martin Kenney and Richard Florida, *Beyond Mass Production: The Japanese System and its Transfer to the U.S.* (New York: Oxford University Press, 1993), the most recent study, considers the record in automobile assembly, auto parts, steel, rubber and tires, and electronics. The authors find the most successful transfer of organizational technology in the automotive sector and a relatively limited transfer in electronics.

17. Kenney and Florida, *Beyond Mass Production*, p. 124.

18. Akira Takeishi, "Comparative Study on Japanese and U.S. Supplier Management," *Research Review*, vol. 6 (Autumn 1991), p. 3. These results are based on a relatively small sample of firms (twelve to twenty-five firms in each category), but this should not entirely negate the significance of the results.

19. Bank of Japan, *Balance of Payments Monthly* (February 1993), pp. 59, 65. These balance-of-payments figures actually show a contraction of cumulative foreign investments in Japan in 1989, followed by renewed growth. The MOF data show a higher 20.3 percent growth rate for inward direct investment for 1980–91 (*Okurashō Kokusai Kin'yūkyoku Nempō*, 1982, p. 364; 1992, p. 503). But an essentially similar asymmetry characterizes the new flow of investment in

this data series; the inflow for 1991 was $4.3 billion, compared with a $42 billion outflow.

20. Ministry of International Trade and Industry, Industrial Policy Bureau, International Business Affairs Division, *Dai-25-kai Gaishikei Kigyō no Dōkō* [The Twenty-Fifth: Trends in Foreign-Affiliated Firms] (Tokyo: Ministry of Finance Printing Office, 1992), pp. 1, 40 (survey results for March 31, 1991); and "MITI Surveys Businesses at Home and Abroad," *Jetro Monitor*, vol. 6 (May 1991), p. 1. U.S. data are from U.S. Department of Commerce, *Statistical Abstract of the United States 1992*, 112th ed. (Lanham, Md.: Bernan Press, 1992), p. 787.

21. Mark Mason, *American Multinationals and Japan: The Political Economy of Japanese Capital Controls 1899–1980* (Harvard University Press, 1992), especially pp. 2, 10–15, 199–252.

22. Dennis J. Encarnation, *Rivals beyond Trade: America versus Japan in Global Competition* (Cornell University Press, 1992), pp. 83–96, provides a nice summary of such market impediments to inward investment in the 1980s.

23. Ministry of Finance, *Okurashō Kokusai Kin'yūkyoku Nempō*, 1991, p. 481; 1992, p. 503.

24. Robert Z. Lawrence, "The Reluctant Giant: Will Japan Take Its Role on the World Stage?" *Brookings Review*, vol. 9 (Summer 1991), pp. 36–39.

25. Encarnation, *Rivals beyond Trade*, pp. 12, 14.

26. Encarnation, *Rivals beyond Trade*, p. 14. The ratio of sales by majority-owned foreign subsidiaries of Japanese firms was essentially unchanged at 85.7 percent by 1991; Ministry of International Trade and Industry, *Dai-21-Kai Waga Kuni Kigyō no Kaigai Jigyō Katsudō* [The 21st Survey of the Overseas Business Activities of Japanese Enterprises] (Tokyo: MITI, 1992), pp. 14, 159.

27. Japan External Trade Organization, *Sekai to Nihon no Kaigai Chokusetsu Tōshi; 1991 Jetoro Hakusho·Tōshihen* [Foreign Direct Investment of the World and Japan: JETRO White Paper on Investment, 1991 ed.] (Tokyo: JETRO, 1991), p. 68. Author's translation.

28. Economic Planning Agency, *Nihon to Sekai o Kaeru Kaigai Chokusetsu Tōshi* [Foreign Direct Investment That Will Change Japan and the World] (Tokyo: Ministry of Finance Printing Office, 1990), pp. 7–8.

29. Jon Choy, "Japan and Mergers: Oil and Water?" *JEI Report*, no. 14A, April 6, 1990, pp. 3, 9. Note that the statistics on the number of foreign acquisitions in both the United States and Japan do not measure the size of the corporations acquired. The asset value of firms would probably make the disparity even larger. For mergers and acquisitions as a whole, 2,032 transactions took place in the United States in 1987, compared with an even larger 2,364 in Japan, but the value of assets involved was $164 billion in the United States and $23 billion in Japan.

30. A. T. Kearney, Inc., *Trade and Investment in Japan: The Current Environment* (Tokyo: American Chamber of Commerce in Japan, 1991), p. 19; Masayuki Hara, "U.S. Direct Investment in Japan," *Journal of Japanese Trade and Industry* (November–December 1990), p. 17; and material from Yamaichi Securities, 1992.

31. Kokusaiteki Kigyō Baishū Mondai Kenkyūkai [The Corporate Acquisition Problem Study Group], *Kokusaiteki Kigyō Baishū no Tenkai to Nihon Shijō no Shōrai* [The Development of International Corporate Acquisitions and the Future of the Japanese Market], (Tokyo: Foundation for Advanced Information and Research, September 1990), p. 113.

32. "Tōshi Fukinkō Kukkiri" [A Clear Imbalance in Investment], *Nihon Keizai Shimbun*, January 30, 1991, p. 5.

33. Robert Tomkin, "Attitudes Change," *Financial Times*, October 18, 1990, p. 30.

34. "Tainichi Tōshi Kakudai e Senmon Kaigi Setchi" [Formation of Special Committee for Expanding Investment in Japan], *Nihon Keizai Shimbun*, April 23, 1991, p. 5.

35. Ministry of International Trade and Industry, *News from MITI: Measures for Promoting Foreign Direct Investment in Japan*, February 1992, NR-399 (92-7), p. 8.

36. Japan Development Bank, *Loan Programs of the Japan Development Bank for U.S. Companies*, August 1992, p. 6.

37. Japan Development Bank, *Loan Programs of the Japan Development Bank*, p. 5.

38. MITI, *News from MITI*, February 1992, pp. 19–24.

39. Mordechai E. Kreinin, "How Closed Is Japan's Market? Additional Evidence," *World Economy*, vol. 11 (December 1988), pp. 529–42.

40. "ASEAN Shinshutsu Jinzainan Nado Nayami" [Worries Such as Human Capital Difficulties in Advancing into ASEAN], *Nihon Keizai Shimbun*, November 28, 1990, p. 5.

41. Kenney and Florida, *Beyond Mass Production*, p. 149.

42. An example of this genre is Mid-America Project, Inc., *Keiretsu, USA: A Tale of Japanese Power*, July 1991, a report denigrating the exclusive behavior of Japanese auto assembly firms in the United States prepared by a group with Boone Pickens as cochair.

43. Robert E. Cole and Donald R. Deskins, Jr., "Racial Factors in Site Location and Employment Patterns of Japanese Auto Firms in America," *California Management Review*, vol. 31 (Fall 1988), pp. 9–22.

44. Christopher A. Bartlett and Hideki Yoshihara, "New Challenges for Japanese Multinationals: Is Organizational Adaption Their Achilles Heel?" in Vladimir Pucik, Noel M. Tichy, and Carole K. Barnett, eds., *Globalizing Management: Creating and Leading the Competitive Organization* (Wiley, 1992), pp. 281–86, discuss the problem of Japanese firms in accepting local employees in full managerial capacities and the problem this creates in retaining capable local managerial staff.

45. MITI, *Dai-21-Kai Waga Kuni Kigyō no Kaigai Jigyō Katsudō*, p. 30. Only surveyed firms are included, so that the total number of Japanese stationed abroad at subsidiaries is actually larger than this figure.

46. Bartlett and Yoshihara, "New Challenges for Japanese Multinationals," p. 282, cites the specific comparison of Matsushita, which has an expatriate ratio of 2 percent in its overseas operations, and 3M, which has 0.3 percent.

47. Keizai Doyukai, *1990-nendai ni Muketa Nihon·Asean Kyōryoku Sokushin no Tame no Ishiki Chōsa* [Awareness Survey on Promotion of Japan-ASEAN Cooperation in the 1990s] (Tokyo: Keizai Doyukai, October 1990), pp. 12, 30.

48. Catherine Macklon, "British Workers Sound Off," *Nikkei Weekly*, March 7, 1992, p. 11. Interviews with Japanese firms in Britain revealed a pattern of withholding information from local managers as well excluding them from decisionmaking.

49. David Gelsanliter, *Jump Start: Japan Comes to the Heartland* (New York: Kodansha America, 1992), especially pp. 120–21, 162–68, provides examples of negative local attitudes as Japanese auto firms arrived in the Midwest.

50. Kyoko Utsumi Mimura, Thomas W. Elkins, and John Sylvester, Jr., *Japanese Foreign Investment in North Carolina: A Case Study* (Commission on U.S.-Japan Relations for the Twenty First Century, June 1991), p. 13; and Wallace Bain, *Japanese Foreign Investment in Oregon: A Case Study* (Commission on U.S.-Japan Relations for the Twenty First Century, June 1991), p. 16.

51. Daniel E. Bob and SRI International, *Japanese Companies in American Communities: Cooperation, Conflict, and the Role of Corporate Citizenship* (New York: Japan Society, 1990), pp. 47–48.

52. Ministry of Foreign Affairs, *Beikoku ni Okeru Tainichi Seron (Yūshikisha no bu)* [American Opinion Toward Japan (Intellectuals)], April 1989, p. 7; and 1989 MITI opinion poll of U.S. citizens.

53. Japan External Trade Organization, *1990 JETRO White Paper on Foreign Direct Investment, Summary* (Tokyo: JETRO, 1990), especially pp. 20–21.

54. "A New Program Encourages Japanese Philanthropy," *JETRO Monitor*, vol. 5 (October 1990), p. 2.

55. MITI, *Dai-21-Kai Waga Kuni Kigyō no Kaigai Jigyō Katsudō*, pp. 30–31, 135–49.

56. "Kaigai Shinshutsu Dō Kōken" [How Does Overseas Advance Contribute?], *Nihon Keizai Shimbun*, March 9, 1990, p. 4.

57. From an advertisement titled "Kyō Kara" [From Today], *Nihon Keizai Shimbun*, January 4, 1991, p. 7. See also *Minna Chikyū Kokusai Borantia Chokin* [International Volunteer Savings for Everyone's Earth] (undated brochure issued by Postal Savings in spring 1991). Funds are distributed to a list of some 300 officially recognized NGOs in Japan.

58. Council for Better Corporate Citizenship, *Shadan Hōjin Kaigai Jigyō Katsudō Kanren Kyōgikai* [The Committee Concerning Overseas Corporate Activity], undated, unnumbered promotional brochure.

59. *Joining In! A Handbook for Better Corporate Citizenship in the United States* (New York: Japanese Chamber of Commerce and Industry of New York with the cooperation of Dentsu Burson-Marsteller, 1990), pp. 18–19, 28–29. The translation of the Japanese original differs from the official translation provided (printed on facing pages of this document), which reads "All of this comes down to the bottom line: community involvement and volunteer programs are ultimately good for business." "Top executives must take an active role in the program to create community recognition. Their participation creates visibility."

60. A detailed analysis of Japanese trade behavior through the late 1980s was the subject of my previous book, *Japan's Unequal Trade* (Brookings, 1990).

61. Peter L. Gold and Dick K. Nanto, *CRS Report for Congress; Japan-U.S. Trade: U.S. Exports of Negotiated Products, 1985–1990*, 91-891E, Congressional Research Service, November 26, 1991, p. 10. The report measures export growth, and not market share; there is no evidence as to whether these products grew faster because barriers were reduced or because the overall domestic markets for these products were growing unusually fast during this period. For growth in manufactured imports from 1985 to 1990 see World Bank, *World Tables 1993* (Johns Hopkins University Press, 1993), p. 351.

62. Data for 1985 are from Lincoln, *Japan's Unequal Trade*, p. 19.

63. Lincoln, *Japan's Unequal Trade*, p. 47. Intra-industry trade is usually measured statistically by a formula that produces a statistic varying over the interval [0,100], with the intuitive outcome that zero represents no intra-industry trade (either exports or imports are zero) and 100 represents perfect intra-industry trade (exports exactly equal imports). See Lincoln, *Japan's Unequal Trade*, app. A.

64. One recent Australian analysis argues that the biggest increases generally came in material- or labor-intensive products. That is, intra-industry trade appeared to be increasing to the greatest extent in those industries that were in decline in Japan (perhaps representing a transition toward a heavy dependence on imports), not those at the core of the manufacturing sector. John Ravenhill, "Managing Pacific Trade Relations: Economic Dynamism and Political Immobilism," paper prepared for the First Australian Fulbright Symposium, Australian National University, December 16–17, 1991. See also Philip William Lowe, "Resource Convergence and Intra-Industry Trade," Reserve Bank of Australia, July 1991, especially p. 25, which presents a model pooling cross-sectional and time series data on intra-industry trade for bilateral country pairs from 1965 to 1985. Although the model was intended as a general test of intra-industry trade behavior, without a specific focus on Japan, the results show Japanese intra-industry trade behavior to be significantly lower than predicted from the late 1970s to 1985.

65. Data are from Ministry of Finance, *Japan Exports and Imports: Commodity by Country* (Tokyo: Japan Tariff Association, December 1988, December 1992).

66. Bank of Japan, *Balance of Payments Monthly* (February 1993), p. 18.

67. Ministry of International Trade and Industry, *Wagakuni Kigyō no Kaigai Jigyō Katsudō* [Survey of Overseas Activities of Japanese Companies], no. 18/19 (1990), pp. 18, 74; and no. 20 (1992), pp. 18, 80; and MITI Industrial Policy Bureau, International Business Affairs Division, *Kaigai Tōshi Tōkei Sōran* [General Statistics of Overseas Investment], no. 3 (Tokyo: Ministry of Finance Printing Office, 1991), p. 16.

68. See Lincoln, *Japan's Unequal Trade*, pp. 114–20.

69. Among these were an article published in 1990 by an Economic Planning Agency economist, an article in the same year by economists Ryutaro Komiya and Kazutomo Iriye, and a 1992 article by a MITI official in a glossy MITI

English-language publication. Mitsuo Hosen, "Heisasei Hihan e no Hanron" [A Response to Criticism of Closedness], *Keizai Sentā Kaihō*, no. 619 (November 1990), pp. 15–20; Ryutaro Komiya and Kazutomi Irie, "The U.S.-Japan Trade Problem: An Economic Analysis from a Japanese Viewpoint," Discussion Paper Series no. 90 (Tokyo: Research Institute of International Trade and Industry, May 1990); and Satoshi Kuwahara, "The Fallacy of Trade Ratios," *Journal of Japanese Trade and Industry* (January–February 1992), pp. 44–46. Kuwahara's piece dwells on the ratio of manufactured imports to total imports (rather than to GNP), a ratio that does not have any particular meaning, and his discussion of intra-industry trade is seriously flawed.

70. Cross-sectional studies of both the ratio of manufactured imports to GDP and intra-industry trade find Japanese performance to be distinctively low even after factors such as raw materials or limited land are included, as noted above. See especially Lowe, "Resource Convergence and Intra-Industry Trade."

71. U.S. Department of Commerce, *Statistical Abstract of the United States, 1992*, p. 782.

72. Average dollar value per contract is calculated from data in Jon Choy, "Japanese Research and Development: An Era of 'Technoglobalism,' " *JEI Report*, no. 28A, July 24, 1992, p. 14. Because the yen appreciated against the dollar, the yen price facing Japanese firms importing technology rose only from ¥38.2 million per transaction in 1985 to ¥45.1 million in 1990.

73. Terutomo Ozawa, *Japan's Technological Challenge to the West, 1950–1974: Motivation and Accomplishment* (Massachusetts Institute of Technology, 1974), writing in the early 1970s, painted a very optimistic picture of Japanese technological exports (pp. 85–99), but the high growth rate that caused his enthusiasm resulted mainly from an extremely low starting base.

74. Robert Wrubel, "GM Finally Fights Back," *Financial World*, November 26, 1991, pp. 22–26, reports that the new H-car line introduced by General Motors in 1991 involved a large drop in total design time (thirty-four months, down from a previous average of fifty-five months), a 40 percent reduction in the number of parts, a 20 percent drop in assembly time, and a 75 percent decrease in defect rates compared with previous GM averages. See also Ronald Henkoff, "This Cat Is Acting Like a Tiger," *Fortune*, December 19, 1988, pp. 71–76.

75. Charles T. Stewart, Jr., "Comparing Japanese and U.S. Technology Transfer to Less Developed Countries," *Journal of Northeast Asian Studies*, vol. 4 (Spring 1985), pp. 3–19.

76. "Nichibei ni Haiteku Kyoten; Masatsu Kaishō e Shikin Kyoshutsu" [High-Tech Bases in U.S.-Japan; Appropriating Funds for Eliminating Friction], *Nihon Keizai Shimbun*, January 21, 1991, p. 17.

77. Nobuyuki Oishi, "MITI Planning Worldwide R&D Strategy," *Japan Economic Journal*, January 26, 1991, p. 13.

78. Ministry of Finance, Employment Stability Bureau, *Gaikokujin Rōdō Mondai Hikkei* [Handbook on the Foreign Worker Problem] (Tokyo: Rōmu Gyōsei Kenkyūjo, 1991), pp. 1, 14. The vast bulk of these (60,546) were in the entertainment industry (that is, mostly bar hostesses).

79. Nihon Seisansei Honbu [The Japan Productivity Center], *1992-Nenban Rōshi Kankei Hakusho: Rōdōryoku Fusoku Keizaika no Sangyō Shakai no Kadai* [1992 Labor-Management Relations White Paper: The Topic of Industrial Society in the Labor-Shortage Economy] (Tokyo: Japan Productivity Center, 1992), pp. 157, 187. The Japan Productivity Center estimated the total number of illegal workers in 1990 to be approximately 300,000, double the official estimate of the Ministry of Labor.

80. Ministry of Labor, *Rōdō Hakusho* [Labor White Paper], 1991 ed. (Tokyo: Nihon Rōdō Kenkyū Kikō, 1991), supp. p. 26.

81. Ministry of Labor, *Rōdō Hakusho*, 1991 ed., pp. 257–68.

82. "Toward Sustainable Growth and Adequate Labor Supply," *Keidanren Review on the Japanese Economy*, no. 135 (June 1992), pp. 8, 10. Keidanren also supported promotion of higher birthrates (p. 5) as a solution and opposed any across-the-board shortening of the workweek (p. 7).

83. "Ginō Kentei, Shūrō o Yōnin; Mijukuren no Gaikokujin Rōdōsha" [Approving Work by Licensed Skills; Unskilled Foreign Workers], *Nihon Keizai Shimbun*, June 27, 1991, p. 1. The organization began operation in October 1991; " 'Gaikokujin Shūrō' no Michi Hirogeru" [The Road for "Working Foreigners" Widens], *Nihon Keizai Shimbun*, September 27, 1991, p. 3.

84. "Japan to Help Industry Train 100,000 Foreigners," *Nikkei Weekly*, October 19, 1991, pp. 1, 3.

85. Kate Elwood, "Doctors from Abroad Need Not Call on Japan," and "For Nurses, Language Has Proved a Double Bind," *Japan Economic Journal*, January 19, 1991, p. 7.

86. Japan Productivity Center, *1992-Nenban Rōshi Kankei Hakusho*, p. 187.

87. There are now nine because of a merger. Lawrence B. Krause and Sueo Sekiguchi, "Japan and the World Economy," in Hugh Patrick and Henry Rosovsky, eds, *Asia's New Giant: How the Japanese Economy Works* (Brookings, 1976), p. 392.

88. Fumiko Mori, "Japan's Sogo Shosha," *Council Report*, no. 31, September 28, 1979, p. 12.

89. Statistics Bureau, Management and Coordination Agency, *Japan Statistical Yearbook 1991*, p. 671.

90. *Japan Times Weekly International Edition*, March 19–25, 1990, p. 12.

91. U.S. Department of Commerce, *Statistical Abstract of the United States 1992*, p. 9.

92. Statistics Bureau, Management and Coordination Agency, *Japan Statistical Yearbook 1991*, p. 61; and Ministry of Education, *Wagakuni no Bunkyō Shisaku: Heisei 3-Nendo* [Our Nation's Education Policy: Fiscal Year 1991], pp. 529–30. The enrollment data are not collected by the Japanese government (an indicator of the minor attention given in the past to education abroad) and are taken from UNESCO and U.S. government sources.

93. Institute of International Education, *Open Doors: 1990–91; Report on International Educational Exchange* (New York, 1991), pp. 84–85. The federal government does not collect data on the purposes of American travel abroad. The IIE data is based on surveys of American universities and colleges asking

how many of their students earned credit in the previous year at foreign institutions. This ignores those who have gone abroad on their own for education and those who fail to receive credit from their home institution.

94. Institute of International Education, *Open Doors: 1980–81* (New York, 1981), p. 11.

95. Institute of International Education, *Open Doors 1990–91*, p. 21.

96. Institute of International Education, *Open Doors 1990–91*, p. 74. This percentage is considerably higher than the 46.6 percent for all foreign students.

97. Only 1,810 students, by way of contrast, came from the United States. "Ryūgakusei, Saikō no 32% Zō" [Foreign Students, the Highest Rate of Increase at 32 Percent], *Nihon Keizai Shimbun*, February 7, 1991, p. 34; 1980 figure is from Ministry of Education, *Wagakuni no Bunkyō Shisaku: Heisei 3-Nendo*, p. 522.

98. Ministry of Education, *Wagakuni no Bunkyō Shisaku: Heisei 3-Nendo*, p. 524. For the late 1980s, this source reports 59,220 foreign students in England, 91,926 in then-West Germany, and 125,574 in France, all much higher than the number in Japan.

99. Margo Grimm, "Japan and the Global Refugee Problem," *JEI Report*, no. 26A, July 12, 1991, p. 6.

100. U.S. Department of State, Bureau for Refugee Programs, *World Refugee Report* (September 1991), pp. 38, 80, 117.

Chapter Four

1. The wide variation in growth of ODA expenditures from year to year is due partly to use of final settlement figures rather than budgeted amounts. Shifts in the timing of actual expenditures can yield a large variation between the expenditures and the budget in any single year.

2. Organization for Economic Cooperation and Development, *Development Cooperation, 1992 Report* (Paris: OECD, 1992), pp. A-72, A-73. The percentages for France and Germany include contributions made to multilaterals through the European Economic Community. OECD nations with ratios 30 percent or higher are Australia (31 percent), Belgium (40 percent), Canada (31 percent), Denmark (43 percent), Finland (37 percent), Ireland (60 percent), Italy (33 percent), the Netherlands (30 percent), Norway (38 percent), Spain (33 percent), Sweden (30 percent), and the United Kingdom (44 percent).

3. Ministry of Foreign Affairs, *Japan's Official Development Assistance: ODA 1989 Annual Report* (Tokyo: Association for Promotion of International Cooperation, 1990), p. 111.

4. OECD, *Development Cooperation, 1992 Report*, p. A-36. Net contributions include donations to all of the special funds attached to the various multilateral organizations. The top four donors are Germany ($2.32 billion), Japan ($2.09 billion), the United States ($1.88 billion), and France ($1.67 billion).

5. Ministry of Foreign Affairs, *Japan's Official Development Assistance: ODA 1989 Annual Report*, pp. 14–16. These principles closely parallel those originally announced in a 1980 Foreign Ministry policy statement on the philosophy of

foreign aid, cited in Dennis T. Yasutomo, *The Manner of Giving: Strategic Aid and Japanese Foreign Policy* (Lexington Books, 1986), pp. 30–38.

6. By the end of the 1980s, the major oil-producing nations of the Middle East were no longer among the major recipients of Japanese aid (partly because they no longer had income levels low enough to qualify). But during the 1970s, insecurity over oil supplies had temporarily made these nations major aid recipients; at the peak, in 1977, Middle East nations absorbed a quarter of all Japanese bilateral ODA disbursements (subsiding to under 10 percent by the end of the 1990s). Robert M. Orr, Jr., "Balancing Act: Japanese Foreign Aid Policy in the Middle East," in Edward J. Lincoln, ed., *Japan and the Middle East* (Washington: Middle East Institute, 1990), p. 35.

7. Robert M. Orr, Jr., *The Emergence of Japan's Foreign Aid Power* (Columbia University Press, 1990), pp. 57–58.

8. Yasutomo, *The Manner of Giving*, and Orr, *Emergence of Japan's Foreign Aid Power*, are the two foremost works on this subject.

9. Juichi Inada, "Japan's Aid Diplomacy: Economic, Political or Strategic," *Millennium*, vol. 18 (Winter 1989), pp. 399–414, admits that the recipients have not changed even though the espoused purpose of aid has.

10. "ODA Jisshi de 4-Shishin Gunji Hi·Buki Yushutsunyū· Kakuheiki·Minshuka" [Four Guiding Principles for ODA Operation: Military Spending, Weapons Export/Import, Nuclear Weapons, Democratization], *Nihon Keizai Shimbun*, March 29, 1991, p. 1.

11. "ODA Senryakuteki Katsuyō de Itchi; Dai-3-ji Gyōkakushin Sekai Bukai" [Applying ODA Strategically; The World Sub-Committee of the Third Administrative Reform Council], *Nihon Keizai Shimbun*, February 28, 1991, p. 2; and a later report detailed in "ODA: 'Senryakuteki Un'yō' Uchidasu" [ODA: Coming Up With a Strategic Operation], *Asahi Shimbun*, June 19, 1991, p. 3.

12. Akihiro Tamiya, "Issues and People: A New Era in Which There Is No Superpower; Former Defense Vice Minister Cites Aid as Means of Maintaining Security," *Japan Economic Journal*, March 23, 1991, p. 10.

13. "ODA Jisshi de 4-Shishin Gunji Hi"; "Teiryū: Jikkōsei Akumade Michisū" [Undercurrents: Enforcement Pushed to the Extreme Means an Unknown Number], *Nihon Keizai Shimbun*, March 30, 1991, p. 5; and Yuko Mizuno, "Humanitarism Redefined: Aid Plan under Fire," *Japan Economic Journal*, April 27, 1991, p. 3.

14. "ODA 4-Gensoku Hatsuekiyō; Seifu, Haichi e no Enjo Teishi" [First Application of the Four ODA Principles; The Government Stops Aid to Haiti], *Nihon Keizai Shimbun*, October 3, 1991, p. 7; Organization for Economic Cooperation and Development, *Geographical Distribution of Financial Flows to Developing Countries* (OECD, 1993), p. 144; and Ministry of Foreign Affairs, *Japan's Official Development Assistance: ODA 1992 Annual Report*, p. 29. Aid to Zaire was also suspended, but on the grounds that turmoil made disbursement impossible.

15. Mizuno, "Humanitarism Redefined," p. 3.

16. Ministry of Finance, *Okurashō Kokusai Kin'yūkyoku Nempō* [Annual Report of the International Finance Bureau] (Tokyo: Kin'yū Zaisei Jijō Kenkyūkai

[Financial and Fiscal Research Group], 1988), p. 537, and 1991, p. 487. These yen figures and their dollar equivalents may not match official dollar-denominated statistics for foreign aid. These figures represent yen-denominated budget authorizations; official aid statistics represent actual net disbursements.

17. As of March 31, 1990, the Exim Bank's total assets were ¥5.9 trillion (listed in report as $37.5 billion). Average interest earnings on the entire loan portfolio came to 5.3 percent. Export-Import Bank of Japan, *Annual Report 1991, Fiscal Year Ended March 31, 1991*, pp. 1, 25.

18. Export-Import Bank of Japan, *Annual Report 1989, Fiscal Year Ended March 31, 1989*, p. 26; *Annual Report 1991*, p. 23. The high peak in 1989 was due to a major Exim Bank commitment to Mexico as part of the new debt restructuring plan.

19. Ministry of Finance, *Ōkurashō Kokusai Kin'yūkyoku Nempō* (1991), p. 487.

20. Saburo Okita, "The Dazzle of the Asian Economies," *International Economy*, vol. 4 (August–September 1990), p. 70.

21. "Foreign Aid Should Promote Self-Help Efforts, Agency Says," *Japan Times*, September 12, 1991, p. 12. It emphasizes loans for infrastructure as having been important for efficient use of aid money, and argues that loans have promoted economic growth and development, especially in Asia (where it says Japanese-style aid has contributed to Asian dynamism).

22. Toru Yanagihara and Anne Emig, "An Overview of Japan's Foreign Aid," in Shafiqul Islam, ed., *Yen for Development: Japanese Foreign Aid and the Politics of Burden-Sharing* (New York: Council on Foreign Relations Press, 1991), p. 51.

23. Orr, *Emergence of Japan's Foreign Aid Power*, pp. 38, 77–78; and Ministry of International Trade and Industry, "Nihon no Sentaku: 'Nyūgurōbarizumu' e no Kōken to 'Shin·Sangyō Bunka Kokka' no Sentaku" [Japan's Choices: Contributing to the "New Globalism" and the New Corporate Culture] (Tokyo: Tsūshō Sangyō Chōsaka, June 1988), pp. 50–52.

24. Asian Forum Japan, "Material for Discussion: Japan's Economic Cooperation: Principles and Policy," *The Asian Era—Theme and Prospect: Asian Forum Japan Commemorative Symposium* (Tokyo, November 30–December 1, 1988), p. 24; Shin'ichi Kitaoka, "What Nonmilitary Assistance Can and Cannot Accomplish," *Economic Eye*, vol. 12 (Summer 1991), p. 21; and James Sterngold, "Japan's New Finance Official Plots an Independent Course," *New York Times*, August 6, 1991, p. D1.

25. Masamichi Hanabusa, "A Japanese Perspective on Aid and Development," in Islam, ed., *Yen for Development*, pp. 90–91. He admits that this philosophy leads foreigners to be suspicious of Japanese commercial motives in foreign aid, but cites the relatively low ratios for tied aid to say that this is a "misunderstanding."

26. "Keizai Kyōryoku Hakusho: Kunibetsu Enjo Shishin o Teigen" [ODA White Paper: Proposals on Guiding Country-by-Country Assistance], *Nihon Keizai Shimbun*, June 14, 1991, p. 5. Author's translation.

27. Of the experts, 25 percent were in agriculture and 25 percent in public administration, while 28 percent of generalists were in education and 21 percent

in agriculture. "'Jinzai ODA' JICA" ["Human Resource ODA" JICA], *Nihon Keizai Shimbun*, August 4, 1991, p. 34S. It is also worth noting that three Japanese aid workers were killed in Peru in 1991, an event that formed the basis for this article.

28. "Fuan Hanenoke Iza Tōjōkoku de Hōshi Katsudō" [Rejecting Insecurity, the Movement to Serve in Developing Countries], *Nihon Keizai Shimbun*, August 18, 1991, p. 19.

29. Jun Nishikawa, "Japan's Economic Cooperation: New Visions Wanted," *Japan Quarterly*, vol. 36 (October–December 1989), p. 397. Nishikawa, a liberal, takes a dim view of these tight commercial ties. Margee Ensign, *Doing Good or Doing Well: Japan's Foreign Aid Program* (Columbia University Press, 1992), pp. 37–42, notes that the prime consultant or contractor for the feasibility studies must be Japanese, although foreign nationals may participate in the study team and up to one-half of the subcontractors may be foreign. She also notes that much of the initial project identification (which theoretically comes from host-country governments) is done by local JICA personnel.

30. Ernest H. Preeg, "Comment," in Islam, ed., *Yen for Development*, pp. 115–16.

31. Ensign, *Doing Good or Doing Well*, pp. 52–63.

32. Ernani T. Torres, "Brazil-Japan Relations: From Fever to Chill," in Barbara Stallings and Gabriel Székely, eds., *Japan, the United States, and Latin America* (Macmillan, 1993), pp. 135–36; Ellen Hosmer, "Aid, Incorporated: The Real Beneficiaries of Japanese Foreign Assistance," *Multinational Monitor*, November 1988, p. 16; and Kubota Akira, "Foreign Aid: Giving with One Hand?" *Japan Quarterly*, vol. 32 (April–June 1985), pp. 140–44.

33. Terutomo Ozawa, *Recycling Japan's Surpluses for Developing Countries* (Paris: Organization for Economic Cooperation and Development, 1989), pp. 99–110.

34. "Indonesia: Nihon Kigyō Tōshi Rasshu Sainen" [Indonesia: Rekindling the Investment Rush by Japanese Firms], *Nihon Keizai Shimbun*, April 5, 1991, p. 13.

35. World Bank, *Thailand: Managing Public Resources for Structural Adjustment* (Washington, 1984), pp. 192–99.

36. "Deep-sea Ports—Indispensable for Thailand's Development," *Bangkok Bank Monthly Review* (April 1987), pp. 136–43.

37. "Laem Chabang Commercial Port—Buoying Thailand's International Trade," *Thailand Foreign Affairs Newsletter*, December 1990, pp. 14–15; and "Marubeni Wins Thai Container Berth Lease," *Japan Economic Journal*, March 2, 1991, p. 20. Technically, these two firms are involved through a joint venture with Thai interest in which they each have a 20 percent stake, but the headline of the newspaper article captures the Japanese attitude about who is in control.

38. Two of the five participating lenders—the Industrial Bank of Japan and the Bank of Tokyo—have been traditionally more closely tied to Japanese government interests than other commercial banks. The other lenders were general trading companies that would facilitate location of Japanese firms in the new industrial park: C. Itoh and Company, Mitsubishi Corporation, and Marubeni

Corporation. "Renewed China Loans Revive Private Ventures," *Asahi Shimbun Japan Access*, November 12, 1990, p. 6.

39. "Seifu Shusshishi Gōben; Chūgoku no Dairen Kōgyō Danchi Kaihatsu" [Joint Venture with Government Investment; Development of Industrial Park in China's Dalian], *Nihon Keizai Shimbun*, September 26, 1991, p. 1; "Dairen Kōgyō Danchi ni 51-Oku En o Shutsuyūshi" [Investing ¥5.1 billion in Dalian Industrial Park], *Nihon Keizai Shimbun*, April 18, 1992, p. 5; and "'Kita no Honkon' e Dairen no Chōsen" [Dalian's Challenge to Become a "Northern Hong Kong"], *Nihon Keizai Shimbun*, June 20, 1991, p. 9.

40. *Japan Times Weekly Overseas Edition*, April 15, 1989, p. 10.

41. Japan International Development Organization, *JAIDO* (Tokyo, 1993), app.; and "Hi ni Gōben Gaisha Painappuru Ikkan Seisan Chakushu" [Starting Off with Integrated Production of Pineapples in a Joint Venture], *Nihon Keizai Shimbun*, September 3 1990, p. 11.

42. One of the software investments in China funded by JAIDO involved $3 million, of which JAIDO supplied $2 million—an unusually high level of support compared to the average. "Nitchu ga Gōben de Sofutouea-sha" [A Sino-Japanese Combined Software Company], *Nihon Keizai Shimbun*, July 17, 1991, p. 9.

43. Robert M. Orr, Jr., "Japanese Foreign Aid in a New Global Era," *SAIS Review: A Journal of International Affairs*, vol. 11 (Summer–Fall 1991), p. 144.

44. Yoshikuni Inoue, "Keizai Kyōshitsu: ODA, Jinzai Ikusei ni Jūten o" [Economic Classroom: Placing Heavy Emphasis on Human Resource Training in ODA], *Nihon Keizai Shimbun*, April 17, 1991, p. 31.

45. Ensign, *Doing Good or Doing Well*, p. 13.

46. Nishikawa, "Japan's Economic Cooperation," p. 402; and calculated from data in Ministry of Foreign Affairs, *Japan's Official Development Assistance, ODA 1988 Annual Report*, p. 103; *1989 Report*, p. 123; and *1990 Report*, p. 144.

47. John Creighton Campbell, *Contemporary Japanese Budget Politics* (University of California Press, 1977).

48. "Enjo no Puro Ikusei, Tsūsan mo" [Professional Education on Assistance; MITI Also], *Asahi Shimbun*, August 12, 1989, p. 9.

49. Untitled material from the Ministry of International Trade and Industry outlining the Institute of Developing Economies Advanced School, July 1990.

50. Untitled material from MITI.

51. "Mayaku Bokumetsu e ODA Katsuyō" [Utilizing ODA for Eradication of Narcotics], *Nihon Keizai Shimbun*, May 5, 1990, p. 3.

52. International Monetary Fund, *Directory: Members, Quotas, Governors, Voting Power, Executive Board, Officers* (Washington, November 2, 1990), p. 9; and *IMF Survey, Supplement on the Fund*, vol. 19 (August 1990), pp. 1–4.

53. In 1992 Japan's voting rights were 7.22 percent, placing it in second place behind the United States (17.37 percent). *World Bank Annual Report 1992*, pp. 208–09. In 1982 Japan was at 6.58 percent and in third place after West Germany. *World Bank Annual Report 1983*, pp. 164–66. Its share during the decade varied from a low of 5.90 percent in 1985 (*World Bank Annual Report 1986*, p. 175), to a high of 9.43 percent in 1988 (*World Bank Annual Report 1989*, p. 195).

54. Toshiro Horiuchi, "Japan as No. 2 in the IMF," *JCER Report*, vol. 2 (June 1990), p. 2.

55. *Asian Development Bank Annual Report 1990*, p. 128.

56. *Asian Development Bank Annual Report 1990*, p. 181; and *Asian Development Bank Annual Report 1985*, p. 132. Of course, these data measure the national location of procurement, not the nationality of the firms involved. Procurement in Indonesia from a local subsidiary of a Japanese firm would count as Indonesian procurement, and this may account for some of the decline in the Japanese share in the second half of the 1980s.

57. James Clad, "Unhappy Returns: The Asian Development Bank Rumbles with Discontent," *Far Eastern Economic Review*, November 27, 1986, p. 62. Some staff believed that the share continued to be as high as 50 percent, although this was denied by Masao Fujioka, the head of the bank.

58. Ministry of Finance, *Okurashō Kokusai Kin'yūkyoku Nempō* (1991), p. 497. Total new loans directly from the Asian Development Bank as of 1990 were $2.5 billion, compared with $1.5 for the Asian Development Fund.

59. *Asian Development Bank Annual Report 1990*, pp. 111, 140, 147. Japanese dominance of the Asian Development Fund has had a long history; in 1980 Japan was the source of 47.5 percent of the total ($1.3 billion out of $2.7 billion), compared with only $492 million—or 18 percent—from the United States. *Asian Development Bank Annual Report, 1980*, p. 140.

60. These bonds were valued at $231 million, compared with $300 million issued in various markets in U.S. dollars, out of total bond issues of $848.6 million. *Asian Development Bank Annual Report 1990*, p. 197.

61. Yanagihara and Emig, "Overview of Japan's Foreign Aid," pp. 64–65.

62. "Kyōryoku Kikin o Sōsetsu: Tō'ō Shi'en" [Cooperation Fund Established: Supporting Eastern Europe], *Nihon Keizai Shimbun*, April 16, 1991, p. 1.

63. *World Bank Annual Report 1992*, p. 75. For fiscal 1992, 52 percent of all World Bank–assisted projects received some cofinancing. In 1986 the share was "almost one half" (*World Bank Annual Report 1986*, p. 27).

64. *World Bank Annual Report 1992*, p. 75; and *World Bank Annual Report 1991*, pp. 78–79.

65. Bill Clifford, "Japan Presses World Bank on Lending," *Nikkei Weekly*, March 21, 1992, p. 3.

66. Ryokichi Hirono, "Japan's Leadership Role in the Multilateral Development Institutions," in Islam, ed., *Yen for Development*, p. 176.

67. "Japan Brief No. 113: 1990 Public Opinion Survey on Japan's Foreign Relations," R03506 (Tokyo: Office of the Prime Minister, January 16, 1991), p. 2.

68. Hirono, "Japan's Leadership Role," p. 175.

69. "Kokusai Kanryōshugi" [International Bureaucratization], *Nihon Keizai Shimbun*, July 12, 1992, p. 9; Tadashi Saito, "Japan's Role in Multilateral Financial Organizations," *JEI Report*, no. 7A, February 22, 1991; and International Monetary Fund, *Directory: Members, Quotas, Governors, Voting Power, Executive Board, Officers*, November 2, 1990, p. 13.

70. *Asian Development Bank Annual Report 1990*, pp. 208–11. Ninety positions are listed in the report, but two were vacant. This particular avenue for Japanese participation goes back some time; in 1980 Japanese citizens occupied eight of sixty-three principal officer positions. *Asian Development Bank Annual Report*, pp. 152–54. Sixty-nine positions are listed in the report, but six were vacant.

71. These calculations are for professionals. According to the article, Japan had eighty-eight professionals at the UN secretariat, fewer than the number in 1985 and not much higher than in 1980. "Kokuren to Nihon: 'Hito' no Koken Mada Mada" [The United Nations and Japan: People and Contribution—Not Yet], *Nihon Keizai Shimbun*, October 21, 1991, p. 37S. Makoto Taniguchi, "Kokusai Kikō e no Nihonjin no Ishiki o Toinaosu" [Correcting Japanese Consciousness of International Organizations], *Gaikō Fōramu*, no. 46 (July 1992), p. 62, confirms this, stating that the desired level for Japanese nationals at the UN was 150–200, compared with an actual number of roughly 90 at the time.

72. "Motomu! Nihonjin: 'Segin ni Chishiki to Keiken o'" [Wanted! Japanese: Providing Experience and Knowledge to the World Bank], *Nihon Keizai Shimbun*, November 5, 1990, p. 3; and Ernest Stern, "Comment," in Islam, ed., *Yen for Development*, p. 182. He notes that Europeans are also underrepresented (p. 185).

73. "Kokuren ni Jinji no Kisetsu" [Personnel Season at the United Nations], *Nihon Keizai Shimbun*, July 7, 1991, p. 52S, notes that at the United Nations there is a problem of posted job openings not being truly open since desired candidates are already in hand. But it does go on to acknowledge a general lack of interest on the part of Japanese in seeking jobs.

74. Hirono, "Japan's Leadership Role," p. 179.

75. Susan Pharr notes that women in Japan are becoming more active politically, moving into nontraditional political activities other than just voting. Susan J. Pharr, *Political Women in Japan: The Search for a Place in Political Life* (University of California Press, 1981), p. 183. Participation in international multilateral institutions could be an extension of similar trends.

76. "NGO de Hataraku Ikigai" [A Worthwhile Life Working for NGOs], *Nihon Keizai Shimbun*, November 10, 1991, p. 21. This may be partly a result of the part-time nature of employment at small organizations of this sort.

77. "U.N. Taps Ogata as Refugee Commissioner," *Japan Times International Edition*, December 31, 1990–January 6, 1991, p. 2; and "Chikyūjin: Ogata Sadako; Kokuren Nanmin Kōtō Benmukan" [World Person: Sadako Ogata; UN High Commissioner for Refugees], *Nihon Keizai Shimbun*, February 5, 1991, p. 35.

78. Sadako Ogata and Nagayo Homma, "'Keizai Taikoku' Kara 'Jindō Taikoku' e" [From an "Economic Superpower" to a "Humanitarian Superpower"], *Gaikō Fōramu*, no. 31 (April 1991), pp. 75, 78.

79. Lawrence K. Altman, "Head of U.N. Health Agency Is Embroiled in Battle," *New York Times*, August 10, 1992, p. A3; and Altman, "U.S. Set Back in Vote on W.H.O. Chief," *New York Times*, January 21, 1993, p. A8.

80. "Hito: Nihonjin Toshite Hajimete OECD Jimujichō ni Natta Taniguchi Makotosan" [Personality: Mr. Makoto Taniguchi, the First Japanese to Become Deputy Secretary General at the OECD], *Asahi Shimbun*, February 2, 1990, p. 3.

81. Clifford, "Japan Presses World Bank on Lending."

82. Sadako Ogata, "The United Nations and Japanese Diplomacy," *Japan Review of International Affairs*, vol. 4 (Fall–Winter 1990), pp. 147–48.

83. Refugee Policy Group, *The Bellagio Statement on Humanitarian Action in the Post Cold War Era* (Bellagio, Italy, May 1992). Participants came from the United States, Senegal, the United Nations, Italy, Denmark, Switzerland, Honduras, Jordan, Canada, United Kingdom, Brazil, the Netherlands, and Australia.

84. "Ajia Shokoku ni Sangyō Ritchi Shidō" [Local Guidance for Industrial Location in Asian Countries], *Nihon Keizai Shimbun*, September 20, 1990, p. 5.

85. "Kaigai Taizaigata Rejyā Fukyū e Zaidan Setsuritsu" [Establishment of a Foundation for the Spread Of Overseas Resort-type Leisure], *Nihon Keizai Shimbun*, December 20, 1990, p. 7.

86. "MITI Urges Electronics Firms to Produce Abroad," *Nikkei Weekly*, June 13, 1992, p. 1. The article identifies Fujitsu, Hitachi, Matsushita, Sony, and Toshiba as probable participants in the study group.

87. "Tojōkoku ni Tekuno Pāku: Tsusanshō ga Kensetsu Kōsō" [Technopolis in Developing Countries: MITI Proposes a Construction Plan], *Asahi Shimbun*, November 3, 1990, p. 9.

88. "Tojōkoku no Kankyō Hozen Suishin" [Promotion of Environmental Protection in Developing Countries], *Nihon Keizai Shimbun*, June 18, 1991, p. 1.

89. "Kanmin de Ajia Ryūgakusei Shien: Nihon Kigyō Shūshoku o-Makase" [Supporting Asian Foreign Students by Public-Private Cooperation: Entrusting to Employment at Japanese Firms], *Nihon Keizai Shimbun*, April 15, 1992, p. 4.

90. "NGO De Hataraku Ikigai"; and Ministry of Foreign Affairs, *Japan's Official Development Assistance: ODA 1989 Annual Report*, p. 116. The share was 48 percent in 1984, 53 percent in 1986, and 55 percent in 1987.

91. MITI, for example, used its English-language public relations publication to portray Japan as already very active in this field. One such article provided a review of all the policies of the government, including a plan to reduce domestic carbon dioxide emissions to 1990 levels by 2000; MITI's New Earth 21 plan (introduced at the Houston G-7 summit) on the global environment; use of ODA for environmental projects; agreement on eliminating freon gas; and experiments on rain forest rejuvenation in Sarawak. "Special Report: Environmental Action in Japan," *JETRO Monitor*, vol. 6 (September 1991).

92. Alan S. Miller and Curtis Moore, *Japan and the Global Environment* (University of Maryland, Center for Global Change, 1991).

93. "Display: Air Pollutant Emissions," *Economic Eye*, vol. 12 (Winter 1991), p. 22.

94. Miller and Moore, *Japan and the Global Environment*, pp. 11–12.

95. Environmental Agency, *Kankyō Hakusho* [Environmental White Paper], 1990 ed., pp. 46–47.

96. "Whaling Research Trial Declared Successful," *Japan Times Weekly*, August 27, 1988, p. 2; and "IWC Pullout Urged Amid Whale-Ban Call," *Japan Times*, June 13, 1992, p. 3. Minister Masami Tanabu called the French proposal "outrageous."

97. Kiyohiko Arafune, "Japan as an Environmental Pariah," *Economic Eye*, vol. 12 (Winter 1991), pp. 13–17, especially p. 17. The original article was published in *Gaikō Fōramu*.

98. At the same time, the government finally caved in to foreign pressure to ban the import of ivory. "Japan to Limit Ships with Huge Nets," *New York Times International*, September 20, 1989, p. A3.

99. In 1990 Mitsubishi and Company agreed to supply money for a research institute (at Yokohama National University) to experiment with rejuvenation of the rain forest. "Nettairin Saisei Mezasu" [Aiming at Renewal of Rain Forests], *Nihon Keizai Shimbun*, July 16, 1991, p. 34; and Nobuyuki Oishi, "Japan Is Working to Preserve Amazon's Forests," *Japan Economic Journal*, September 8, 1990, p. 21.

100. Kazuo Matsushita, "Japan Offers Negative-Positive Ecological Model," *Japan Economic Journal*, July 16, 1988, p. 23.

101. Katsuro Kitamatsu, "'Save the Earth' Initiative Launched; Takeshita Promoting 'Environmental Diplomacy,'" *Japan Economic Journal*, April 29, 1989, pp. 1, 6; and "Chikyū Kankyō no Hozen Kokkyō Koete Rentai" [A Communique Going beyond National Boundaries on Preserving the Global Environment], *Asahi Shimbun*, October 11, 1989, p. 1.

102. "Kaigai Kyōryoku Kikin: Tōyushi ni Kankyō Jyōkō" [The Overseas Cooperation Fund: Environmental Conditions for Investing], *Asahi Shimbun*, November 3, 1989, p. 1.

103. Edmund Klamann, "Aid Machine Struggles with Ecology Issues," *Japan Economic Journal*, June 30, 1990, pp. 1, 5. Mexico was to receive $850 million as part of this commitment, financed through the Exim Bank to help clean air through efforts to remove sulfur from heavy fuel oil, production of lead-free gasoline, and refurbishing of railroad locomotives. "Japan to Help Clean Mexican Air," *New York Times*, June 19, 1990, p. A3.

104. "Kankyō Gijutsu Kyōryoku: Tō'ō ni 5-Nen de 2500-man Doru" [Environmental Technical Assistance: $25 Million to Eastern Europe over 5 Years], *Nihon Keizai Shimbun*, July 2, 1990, p. 17. This small amount was to be spread over a five-year period starting from fiscal 1991.

105. "Kankyō ODA: 5-nenkan de 5-bai ni Kakudai" [Environmental ODA: Expanding Fivefold in Five Years], *Nihon Keizai Shimbun*, March 1, 1992, p. 3.

106. "Tojōkoku no Kankyō Hozen Suishin" [Promotion of Environmental Protection in Developing Countries], *Nihon Keizai Shimbun*, June 18, 1991, p. 1.

107. "Industry Uneasy over Save the Earth Calls," *Japan Economic Journal*, September 16, 1989, pp. 1, 5.

108. MITI was warning in advance of the 1990 meeting that carbon dioxide controls would reduce economic growth. "MITI Warns of GNP Drop If CO_2 Limits Remain," *Japan Economic Journal*, April 28, 1990, p. 5.

109. Miller and Moore, *Japan and the Global Environment*, pp. 34–37.

110. "100-Nen Kake Chikyū Saisei; CO_2 21-Seki Hajime Genshō e" [Rejuvenation of the Environment in One Hundred Years; First Reduction of CO_2 in the Twenty-First Century], *Nihon Keizai Shimbun*, April 16, 1990, p. 1.

111. "Matta Nashi CO_2 Taisaku" [A Counterplan on CO_2 without Waiting], *Nihon Keizai Shimbun*, October 19, 1990, p. 5; and "Kankyō to Kigyō: Dai-Ichi Bu, Bijinesu to no Renkei Mosaku, 2" [The Environment and Industry: Part 1, Groping toward Cooperation with Business, 2], *Nihon Keizai Shimbun*, November 14, 1990, p. 13.

112. "Industry Uneasy over Save the Earth Calls."

113. "Kankyō Zaidan Setsuritsu e" [Toward Forming an Environmental Fund], *Nihon Keizai Shimbun*, December 27, 1990, p. 13.

114. "Chikyū to Kankyō' Saguru; Nihon Iinkai, Kyō Hassoku" [Exploring The Earth and Environment; Japan Committee Starts Today], *Nihon Keizai Shimbun*, May 21, 1991, p. 34.

115. For example, Alex Steffen, "Hypocrisy Alleged: Japan's Green Record Challenged," *Japan Times*, June 13, 1992, p. 3; or David Lascelles, "The Earth Summit: Critics Suspicious of Japanese Motives," *Financial Times*, June 12, 1992, p. 6.

116. "Kankyōcho: 'Kankyōzei' de Kenkyūkai" [Environmental Agency: "Environmental Tax" Study Group], *Nihon Keizai Shimbun*, November 18. 1991, p. 3.

117. "Jōyaku Zukuri e Kankyō Gaikō Kappatsuka" [Activating Environmental Diplomacy toward Establishing a Treaty], *Nihon Keizai Shimbun*, July 20, 1991, p. 13. This article portrayed the government as worrying about the intransigence of the United States on atmospheric warming.

118. "Ajia Zen'iki de Ondanka Taisaku; Kankyōchō 10-nen Keikaku" [A Counterplan for Warming in All of Asia; The Environmental Agency's Ten-year Plan], *Nihon Keizai Shimbun*, July 4, 1991, p. 5; and "Ajia Shokoku no Kankyō Hozen Shien" [Supporting Preservation of the Environment in Various Asian Countries], *Nihon Keizai Shimbun*, July 29, 1991, p. 21.

119. Grant aid for sulfur control equipment was to be combined with aid for development of Chinese coal fields. "Kankyō Gijutsu o Mushō Kyōyo" [Providing Environmental Technology for Free], *Nihon Keizai Shimbun*, July 22, 1991, p. 1; "Datsuryū Sōchi Nado Ajia ni Kyōyo" [Offering Suphur Scrubbers, etc., to Asia], *Nihon Keizai Shimbun*, August 15, 1991, p. 1; and "Jōyaku Zukuri e Kankyō Gaikō Kappatsuka."

Chapter Five

1. For the purposes of this chapter the Asia-Pacific region extends from China and the Korean peninsula in the north through Thailand and Burma in the southeast, plus Australia and New Zealand. South Asia is largely excluded from the discussion here (because the Japanese generally view it separately and have not upgraded their economic ties as much there). The statistical data also exclude North Korea and the Indochina countries because of lack of data.

2. E. B. Schumpeter, ed., *The Industrialization of Japan and Manchukuo 1930-1940* (Macmillan, 1940), p. 833. The share of exports destined to Asia would be even higher if Taiwan and Korea were included, but since these were direct colonial possessions, they are not included in prewar foreign trade figures. Manchuria, on the other hand, was always officially an independent country and is included as part of international trade.

3. Donald C. Hellmann, *Japan and East Asia: The New International Order* (Praeger, 1972), p. 8. Hellmann speaks of an emergent Asian regionalism led by Japan, but did so somewhat prematurely. Much of what is said in his book could be transposed to the 1990s without alteration.

4. Ministry of Finance, *Okurashō Kokusai Kin'yūkyoku Nempō* [Annual Report of the International Finance Bureau] (Tokyo: Kin'yū Zaisei Jigyō Kenkyūkai [Financial and Fiscal Research Group], 1982), pp. 351-55. For cumulative direct investment, Asia's share in the total rose from 22 percent in 1969 to 23 percent by 1973.

5. Ministry of Finance, *Okurashō Kokusai Kin'yūkyoku Nempō*, 1982, pp. 356-57. Although textiles represented a sizable portion of Japanese investment in the region at that point, ferrous and nonferrous metals (located for reasons of raw material availability) were a larger 26 percent of cumulative Japanese manufacturing investment in the region.

6. "Jakaruto: Shushō, Mata Demo no Demukae" [Jakarta: Prime Minister Again Meets Demonstrations], *Mainichi Shimbun*, January 15, 1974, pp. 1-3.

7. Robert M. Orr, Jr., "Balancing Act: Japanese Foreign Aid Policy in the Middle East," in Edward J. Lincoln, ed., *Japan and the Middle East* (Washington: Middle East Institute, 1990), pp. 34-35.

8. Ernani T. Torres, "Brazil-Japan Relations: From Fever to Chill," in Barbara Stallings and Gabriel Székeley, eds., *Japan, the United States, and Latin America* (Macmillan, 1993), pp. 125-48.

9. Bank of Japan, *Balance of Payments Monthly*, no. 261 (April 1988), p. 21.

10. Ministry of Finance, *Okurashō Kokusai Kin'yūkyoku Nempō*, 1990, pp. 444-47.

11. The lack of Japanese interest in the ASEAN countries is expressed in Bruce Roscoe, "Japan Picks Winners to Hurdle the Fences," *Far Eastern Economic Review*, September 4, 1986, p. 60.

12. A poll conducted in May 1989 showed that 48.8 percent viewed Japan as a Western nation and 26.9 percent as an Asian nation. Chikayoshi Sanada, Genji Okura, and Yasuhiro Wada, *90-Nendai no Nihon wa Dō Ugoku ka: Saishin Seron Chōsa·Ankeeto Deeta kara Yomu* [How Will Japan Move in the 1990s: Reading from the Latest Surveys and Opinion Polls] (Tokyo: Jiyū Kokumin Sha, 1990), p. 129.

13. See "Ajia no Seiki: Nihon no Yakuwari" [The Asian Century: Japan's Role], *Toyo Keizai*, November 15, 1986; Yukiko Fukagawa, "Ajia no Dainamizumu o Torikomu Nihon: Nihon·ASEAN·NICs no Shinsangyō Chizu" [Japan Grasping Asian Dynamism: The New Industrial Map of Japan·ASEAN·NICs], *Ekonomisuto*, July 4, 1988; Economic Planning Agency, *Ajia Taiheiyō Chiiki:*

Han'ei no Tetsugaku [The Asia-Pacific Region: The Philosophy of Prosperity] (Tokyo: Ministry of Finance Printing Office, 1989); "Ajia Nihon Kyōei o Mosaku" [Asia-Japan Groping for Mutual Prosperity], *Nihon Keizai Shimbun*, April 14, 1992, p. 24 (with related articles on pp. 25–26); and "Tokushū: Kagayaku Higashi Ajiaken 1: Higashi Ajia ga Sekai no Enjin ni Naru!!" [Special Feature— The Sparkling East Asian Bloc, pt. 1: East Asia Becomes the World's Engine!!], *Toyo Keizai*, November 16, 1991, pp. 8–13.

14. Exemplified by "Tokushū: Kagayaku Higashi Ajiaken 2: Enjo ga Higashi Ajia Hatten o Kasoku" [Special Feature—The Sparkling East Asia Bloc, pt. 2: Foreign Aid Accelerates Asian Development], *Toyo Keizai*, November 16, 1991, pp. 14–21.

15. "Yu'nyū Daikōzui II: Kaihatsu Yu'nyū ga Kasoku Suru Hyakketen, Sūpā no Ajia Ryūtsūken" [The Big Flood of Imports II: The Acceleration of Development Imports from the Asian Sphere by Department Stores and Superstores], *Toyo Keizai*, July 4, 1987, p. 14; "Ajia ni Kouri Rengō: Sēzon Gurūpu Chūshin ni" [Retailing Association in Asia: The Saison Group at the Center], *Nihon Keizai Shimbun*, November 25, 1990, p. 1; and "Takashimaya: Ajia·Gōshu de Jigyō Kakudai" [Takashimaya: Expanding Businesses in Asia Australia], *Nihon Keizai Shimbun*, September 3, 1990, p. 13.

16. "Nihon no Kourigyō Tatenka ni Hakusha: Ajia Shōhi mo Kyūkakudai" [Impetus to Japanese Retailers' Increase in Stores: Asian Consumption Expanding Quickly], *Nihon Keizai Shimbun*, April 15, 1992, p. 29. Of these, sixteen stores are part of the Kokusai Ryūtsū Gurūpu Yaohan [International Marketing Group Yaohan], a medium-sized Japanese retailer that made an unusual effort to establish itself widely through Asia. The other retail chains with Asian stores are Daimaru, Isetan, Jusco, Matsuzakaya, Mitsukoshi, Seibu Hyakkaten, Sogō, Takashimaya, and Tokyū Hyakkaten.

17. "Hōgin: Bei Kogaisha Tsūji Ajia ni Kyoten" [Japanese Banks: Establishing A Strong Point in Asia through Their U.S. Subsidiaries], *Nihon Keizai Shimbun*, May 31, 1990, p. 7; and "Sanwa Ginkō: Kaigai Keiretsugaisha no Jōjō Isogu" [Sanwa Bank: Quickly Entering the Stock Market with Foreign Subsidiaries], *Nihon Keizai Shimbun*, August 15, 1990, p. 4.

18. Nine banks, the six largest brokerage houses, and at least six property and casualty insurance firms had moved into Indonesia by 1991. Toshihisa Komaki, "Banks Flocking to Relaxed Jakarta," *Nikkei Weekly*, July 6, 1991, p. 15.

19. "Brokerages to Open Units in Singapore," *Japan Times*, June 13, 1992, p. 7.

20. Iwao Kubo, "Symbiotic Growth: Japanese Firms in Asia," *Tokyo Business Today*, vol. 60 (June 1992), pp. 30–31. The definition of Asia in the figure for Matsushita local subsidiaries includes India but excludes Australia.

21. Ministry of International Trade and Industry, *Wagakuni Kigyō no Kaigai Jigyō Katsudō* [Foreign Business Activities of Our Nation's Corporations], no. 18-19 (Tokyo: Ministry of Finance Printing Office, 1990), p. 18; and no. 21 (1992), pp. 18–19. Since 1986, however, the trend in the share of Asian sales has been erratic, fluctuating between 9.7 and 12.8 percent. Since these numbers result from a survey with no assurance of continuity in how many or which firms respond

each year, their accuracy is unknown and small annual changes could be artifacts of a shifting sample.

22. Kiyoshi Hasegawa, "Sekai no Chōryū: Ryūdōka Suru Ajia 'Tairitsu no Kōzu' " [World Trends: The Fluidization of the "Structure of Confrontation" in Asia], *Nihon Keizai Shimbun*, October 9, 1990, p. 9.

23. Yoshihide Ishiyama, "Regional Routes to a New World Order," *Japan Echo*, vol. 19 (Spring 1992), pp. 16–22; originally published in Japanese as "Shin Sekai Chitsujo-zukuri wa Hajimatte iru," *Chuo Koron*, November 1991, pp. 226–35. In 1991 Ishiyama was director of economic research at IBM Japan.

24. Charles Smith, "Free Trade: Protectionist Fear over Trade Blocs," *Far Eastern Economic Review*, June 8, 1989, p. 68.

25. Yukio Suzuki, "An Economist's View: Houston Summit Challenges Nation," *Japan Times Weekly*, July 30–August 5, 1990; and Michihiko Kunihiro, "Ajia·Taiheiyō Kyōryoku no Keizaiteki Sokumen" [Economic Dimensions of Asia-Pacific Cooperation], *Gaikō Fōramu*, no. 24 (September 1990), pp. 20–27.

26. Waichi Sekiguchi, "New Decade Brings New World Role for Japan," *Japan Economic Journal*, December 30, 1989–January 6, 1990, p. 6, quotes a University of Tokyo professor saying that "Japan should organize a similar [to the EC and U.S.-Canada FTA] economic sphere in the Asia-Pacific region by using its economic clout." See also Akihiro Tamiya, "Japan Set for Political Role in Asia," *Japan Economic Journal*, October 13, 1990, p. 3. An editorial in *Asahi Shimbun*, January 4, 1989, p. 5, stated "An Asian economic bloc—including Japan—is coming about naturally. What is necessary is for Japan not to give the impression to the countries into which it is advancing that it has occupied them."

27. Economic Planning Agency, *Ajia Taiheiyō Chi'iki—Han'ei no Tetsugaku: Sōgō Kokuryoku no Kanten Kara Mita Nihon no Yakuwari* [The Asia-Pacific Region—The Philosophy of Prosperity: Japan's Role Seen from the Viewpoint of Overall National Power] (Tokyo: Ministry of Finance Printing Office, 1991), p. 17. The advisory committee producing this report was the Sōgō Kokuryoku no Kanten Kara Mita Nihon no Yakuwari Kenkyūkai [the Research Committee on Japan's Role Seen from the Viewpoint of Overall National Power].

28. For example, see Seiichirō Saitō, "The Pitfalls of the New Asianism," *Japan Echo*, vol. 19, special issue (Spring 1992), pp. 14–19; originally published as "Shin Ajia Shugi no Kansei," in *Voice*, November 1991, pp. 206–19.

29. " 'Nihon wa Shidōryoku o' Nana-Wari" [70 Percent "Want Japanese Leadership"], *Nihon Keizai Shimbun*, April 20, 1992, p. 1; and "Tokushū:Kagayaku Higashi Ajiaken 1: Higashi Ajia ga Sekai no Enjin ni Naru!!," pp. 12–13.

30. *Ajia Keizai Kenkyūjo no Katsudō* [Activities of the Asian Economic Research Institute] (Tokyo: Ajia Keizai Kenkyūjo, 1985), pp. 3, 18–19. Of a cumulative total of 153 foreign visiting researchers from 1960 to 1984 from developing countries, 75 percent were from Asia and the Pacific and 25 percent from all other regions.

31. James Sterngold, "Japan Builds East Asia Links, Gaining Labor and Markets," *New York Times*, May 8, 1990, pp. A1, D18.

32. "Center Targets Japan-Asia Ties," *Japan Economic Journal*, September 2, 1989, p. 10.

33. *Gekkan NIRA* (NIRA Monthly), vol. 8 (September 1986), pp. 4–45; and *NIRA Nyūsu* [NIRA News], no. 6 (June 1989), p. 4. At the fourth NIRA China conference, the focus was on Asian cooperation in struggling against rising protectionism in the United States and Europe.

34. Tokyo Club Foundation for Global Studies, *Asia Club Papers No. 1* (Tokyo: The Foundation, June 1990). The foundation sponsored an Asian research institute conference with participants from leading institutes from Japan, Hong Kong, Indonesia, South Korea, Malaysia, the Philippines, Singapore, Taiwan, and Thailand.

35. Edward J. Lincoln, *Japan's Unequal Trade* (Brookings, 1990), p. 131.

36. MITI, *Wagakuni Kigyō no Kaigai Jigyō Katsudō*, no. 18-19 (1990), pp. 18–19, 74–75; and no. 21 (1992), pp. 18, 80–81. Total regional trade in 1989, according to the data used for figure 5-1, was $123 billion, so the sales of Japanese companies in the region generated 3.25 percent of total trade. Even if these Japanese sales are assumed to have been zero in 1975 (because of the low level of Japanese investment at that point), then only 3.25 percentage points of the large 12.7 percentage point increase in the share of total Asian trade that remained within the region was due to the presence of Japanese direct investment.

37. Robert Z. Lawrence, "An Analysis of Japanese Trade with Developing Countries," Brookings Discussion Papers in International Economics, no. 87 (April 1991), makes the point that the increase in imports from Asia was not disproportionately large in the late 1980s. Aspects of changing attitudes on the part of government, business, and consumers are detailed in Lincoln, *Japan's Unequal Trade*, pp. 95–134.

38. A statement of enthusiasm for regional intra-industry trade comes through in Economic Planning Agency, *Keizai Hakusho* [Economic White Paper] (Tokyo: Ministry of Finance Printing Office, 1988), pp. 88–127.

39. Data are from Ministry of Finance, *Okurashō Kokusai Kin'yūkyoku Nempō*, 1991, pp. 462–75, and 1986, pp. 458–59. Before 1990, this source did not provide detail by country and by type of investment. The Asia total is quite broad (including South Asia), as is Europe (including the Soviet Union).

40. Economic Planning Agency, *Ajia Taiheiyō Chi'iki*, p. 96.

41. Japanese retail stores generated 40 percent of all retail sales in Hong Kong, and there were more financial institutions from Japan (ninety) than from any other country. Paul Mooney, "Japan in Asia–Hong Kong; Japanese Money: A Welcome 'Invasion,' " *Japan Economic Journal Special Supplement: The Rising Tide: Japan in Asia* (Winter 1990), p. 27. Also, in 1989 Japan was the largest source of FDI in Hong Kong at $2 billion, which placed it ahead of the United States. "Japan Boosts HK Investments," *Hong Kong Digest: A Monthly Roundup of News and Events in Hong Kong*, August–September 1990, pp. 6–7.

42. Ministry of Finance, *Okurashō Kokusai Kin'yūkyoku Nempō*, 1990, p. 444; and 1992, p. 481.

43. Japan's share of total cumulative inward investment, according to these data, is 18 percent, followed by Hong Kong at 10.1 percent. The United States has only a 5.9 percent share. *Indonesia Facts: Investment*, September 1990, p. 1. This 18 percent share differs considerably from the 34 percent share shown in 1989 EPA data.

44. "Mitsui Bussan: Indonesia·Batamutō Kaihatsu" [Mitsui and Company: Indonesia/Batam Island Development], *Nihon Keizai Shimbun*, August 30, 1990, p. 13. Mitsui has a 5-percent equity stake and one member on the board of directors. "Growth Triangle Has Strong Investment Pull: Firms Cut Costs, Find Cheaper Labor on Batam Island," *Japan Times Weekly International Edition*, November 12-18, 1990, p. 17. At that time, nine Japanese firms had announced plans to build, compared with four American firms. "Kanden ni Kensetsu Sanka Yōsei; Indoneshia no Batamu Karyoku" [Requesting Kansai Electric to Participate in Construction; Steam Generator in Indonesia's Batam], *Nihon Keizai Shimbun*, March 4, 1991, p. 9; and "Japanese Flock to Batam Industrial Park in Indonesia," *Asahi Evening News*, September 12, 1991, p. 7.

45. Cumulative Japanese foreign direct investment in South Korea totaled only $5 million in 1968; the flow of new investment then accelerated from $10 million in 1969 to $211 million by 1973, after which it fluctuated in a range of $100 million to $200 million a year for most of the rest of the decade. Ministry of Finance, *Okurashō Kokusai Kin'yūkyoku Nempō*, 1982, p. 352.

46. Nanshi F. Matsuura, "Management Conflict and Foreign Direct Investment: The Case of Japanese Investment in South Korea," *Columbia Journal of World Business*, vol. 24 (Summer 1989), pp. 61–67. Matsuura notes that a substantial portion of Japanese firms considering investment in South Korea never carry through on their plans.

47. "Matsuda·Kia Jidōsha, Pi de Jōyōsha Seisan" [Mazda and Kia Motors to Produce Passenger Vehicles in the Philippines], *Nihon Keizai Shimbun*, October 13, 1990, p. 1.

48. This share represents the number of agreements, not their value. Only 13 percent were with U.S. firms and 11 percent with West German ones. Matsuura, "Management Conflict and Foreign Direct Investment," p. 63.

49. Republic of China, Council for Economic Planning and Development, *Taiwan Statistical Data Book, 1992*, p. 246.

50. Ian Castles, *Foreign Investment Australia, 1989–90* (Sydney: Australian Bureau of Statistics, 1991) pp. 21, 31. Relatively little of Japanese direct investment is in mining (only $2.9 billion). The largest amount is in finance, property, and business services ($20.2 billion), which includes trading companies and real estate investment. As of 1987, production at Japanese manufacturing subsidiaries in Australia amounted to only 2.0 percent of total value added in the sector, compared with 10.2 percent from U.S. subsidiaries and 10.5 percent from U.K. subsidiaries. W. McLennan, *Foreign Ownership and Control of the Manufacturing Industry Australia, 1986–87* (Sydney: Australian Bureau of Statistics, 1990), p. 4.

51. "Nihon Kigyō—Shiren no Kaigai Shinshutsu" [Japanese Corporations—Trial Overseas Advance], *Nihon Keizai Shimbun*, April 14, 1992, p. 1; and Naoki Tanaka, "Asian Relationship Dynamic," *Japan Times*, April 19, 1991, p. 22.

52. Organization for Economic Cooperation and Development, *Geographical Distribution of Financial Flows to Developing Countries 1984/1987* (Paris: OECD, 1989).

53. OECD, *Geographical Distribution of Financial Flows to Developing Countries 1988/1991* (Paris: OECD, 1993).

54. Margo Grimm, "Japan's Foreign Aid Policy: 1990 Update," *JEI Report*, no. 47A, December 14, 1990, p. 7; and Ministry of Foreign Affairs, *Japan's ODA 1992* (Tokyo: Association for Promotion of International Cooperation, 1993), p. 24.

55. Douglas Ostrom, "Japan's Emerging Role in International Financial Markets," *JEI Report*, no. 38A, October 5, 1990, p. 11. These percentages have risen over time, but the export side has stagnated at the 35 percent level, and the import side remains unusually low (compared with the pattern of currency choice by other major industrial nations) despite the increase.

56. Jeffrey A. Frankel and Shang-Jin Wei, "Yen Bloc or Dollar Bloc: Exchange Rate Policies of the East Asian Economies," paper prepared for the Third Annual East Asian Seminar on Economics, June 17–19, 1992, pp. 3–11.

57. Ralph C. Bryant, "The Evolution of the International Monetary System: Where Next?" Brookings Discussion Papers, no. 76 (July 1989), p. 40, refers to expressions of concern about loss of sovereignty by Japanese economists.

58. By the late 1980s, 30 percent of Malaysia's external debt was estimated to be denominated in yen, along with 40 percent for Thailand and 30 percent for Indonesia. The relative absence of yen-denominated export earnings, however, proved to be a problem for Indonesia in the earlier 1980s and led to negotiations with the Japan Exim Bank to redenominate loans in dollars. David D. Hale, "New Currency Zones and Strategies for the U.S. and Japan, or Will the Yen Displace the Dollar as the Pacific Rim's Reserve Currency?" Kemper Financial Services, Chicago, November 1988, pp. 12–18.

59. Robert M. Orr, Jr., *The Emergence of Japan's Foreign Aid Power* (Columbia University Press, 1990), p. 73.

60. This view of a divergence differs considerably from that of Orr, *Emergence of Japan's Foreign Aid Power*, p. 74, who argues that Japan's post-Tiananmen policies were largely consistent with those of the West.

61. The discussion, for example, rarely refers to the events in Tiananmen Square themselves, and then only as *daisanji*—a big disaster or big accident. " 'Tenanmon Jiken' Igo no Chūgoku to Nihon" [China and Japan after the "Tiananmen Incident"], *Gaikō Fōramu*, no. 12 (September 1989), p. 18. When former Finance Minister (and later Prime Minister) Kiichi Miyazawa visited China in July 1990, he referred to the Tiananmen massacre only as the *rokugatsu fukō*, the June misfortune, rather mild language. "Chūgoku ni Minshuka Doryoku Unagasu" [Requesting China to Do Its Best to Democratize], *Nihon Keizai Shimbun*, July 25, 1990, p. 2.

62. For a review of events from June 1989 to early 1990, see the excellent article by K. V. Kesavan, "Japan and the Tiananmen Square Incident: Aspects of the Bilateral Relationship," *Asian Survey*, vol. 30 (July 1990), pp. 669–81. He agrees that business relations were restored rather quickly and that Japan purposefully took a low-key diplomatic approach.

63. Sumio Kido, "Japan Moving to Normalize China Ties," *Japan Economic Journal*, August 26, 1989, pp. 1, 4. The government warning on travel to China was lifted in mid-August.

64. OECD, *Geographical Distribution of Financial Flows to Developing Countries 1986/1989* (Paris: OECD, 1991), p. 86. The net flow from Japan in 1989 was

$832 million, up from $674 million. Receipts from all other sources were $1,315 million in 1988 and $1,325 million in 1989.

65. "Japanese Development Work in China Could Resume Soon," *Japan Times Weekly Overseas Edition*, August 19, 1989, p. 11, cites a government source giving informal details on August 3 that were practically identical with what the Japanese government announced on August 17 regarding technical personnel and travel restrictions.

66. Kesavan, "Japan and the Tiananmen Square Incident." The September trip by Ito and the other LDP politicians was intended to send a signal to the Chinese government of movement in a favorable direction. See "Jinmin no Fuman, Kumitai: Tainichi Shūfuku o Motomeru" [Wanting to Reassemble, Dissatisfaction of the People: Asking for Restoration with Japan], *Asahi Shimbun*, September 18, 1990, p. 1.

67. "Taichū Keizai Shūfuku o Mosaku" [Groping to Restore Economic Ties with China], *Asahi Shimbun*, September 17, 1989, p. 1; and "Tōshi Sokushin Kikō Setsuritsu Isogu" [Hurriedly Establishing an Investment Promotion Organization], *Asahi Shimbun*, January 11, 1990, p. 9. The organization, Nitchū Tōshi Sokushin Kikō (Japan-China Investment Promotion Organization), is to act as a go-between to facilitate investment by Japanese firms in China.

68. "Japan: Harassment of Chinese Dissidents," *News from Asia Watch*, October 4, 1990. Chinese claiming to be dissidents were forcibly repatriated; requests for asylum were obstructed; and access of Chinese to legal counsel and information on asylum or refugee regulations was impeded.

69. "Chūgoku wa Kaihō Gutaisaku o" [The Government Forms Plan to Reform China], *Nihon Keizai Shimbun*, August 18, 1989, p. 2. This article indicates explicit pressure from the Japanese government, pointing out that if China did not take steps in the desired direction the upcoming aid package would be delayed, but at no subsequent point was resumption of aid at all in doubt.

70. "Taichū Enshakkan, Saikai e" [Toward Resumption of Yen Loans to China], *Asahi Shimbun*, January 9. 1990, p. 1; Robert Thomson, "Japanese Eager to Resume Aid to China," *Financial Times*, July, 13, 1990, p. A4; and "Minkan Ginkō: 3-Gatsu ni Hochūdan" [Commercial Banks: Mission to China in March], *Asahi Shimbun*, January 10, 1990, p. 9. The All Japan Bankers Association held a meeting in China in early March to discuss new loans, specifically citing the Scowcroft visit as the triggering event.

71. "Raigetsu, Minseimuke Saikai" [Next Month, Reopening (Loans) for Citizens' Life], *Nihon Keizai Shimbun*, July 7, 1990, p. 1. The actual language used by the president in his discussions with Prime Minister Kaifu was quite ambiguous: he said that Japan can "make up its own mind on a lot of questions." "Japan's China Aid Plan Gets Bush's Tacit Support," *Japan Times*, July 9, 1990.

72. Harry Harding, *A Fragile Relationship: The United States and China since 1972* (Brookings, 1992), especially pp. 247–96.

73. "Taichū En Shakkan no Saikai: Samitto de mo Rikai o Motomeru" [Reopening Yen Loans to China: Requesting Understanding at the Summit], *Nihon Keizai Shimbun*, July 9, 1990, p. 3. This article is an interview with MITI Minister Kabun Muto, expressing eagerness to resume loans on the grounds that China

was moving back toward democracy and that the forces in favor of democracy in China were eager to get the loans.

74. James Sterngold, "Tokyo Said to Tell China It Will Go Ahead on Loans," *New York Times*, July 19, 1990, p. A12; "China Loans Set to Resume This October," *Japan Economic Journal*, August 4, 1990, p. 6; and "Taichū Enshakkan Tōketsu o Kaijo" [Canceling the Freeze on Yen Loans to China], *Asahi Shimbun*, November 3, 1990, p. 1. The official papers for the new loan were signed on November 2 in Beijing, and the official release of the first installment was announced.

75. Among Japanese visitors just in the first two weeks of June 1990 were Yasusada Kitahara, science and technology advisor to Prime Minister Kaifu, who was in China with a delegation of seventeen Japanese companies (taking part in an international postal and telecommunications conference) and was quoted as making favorable comments on transfer of advanced technology to China; Kisaburo Ikeura, president of the Japan-China Investment Promotion Organization, who met with General Secretary Jiang Zemin; and Ryoichi Sasakawa, in his capacity as chairman of the Japan Firemen's Association (and enormously wealthy, conservative, backroom political fixer), who met with Premier Li Peng. Xu Yuanchao, "Japan May Transfer High-tech," *China Daily*, June 10, 1990, p. 3; "Jiang Meets Japanese Visitors," *China Daily*, June 9, 1990, p. 1; and "Li Meets Japanese," *China Daily*, June 11, 1990, p. 3.

76. "Taichū Enshakkan Tōketsu o Kaijo"; and "365-Okuen Kyōyo de Chōin: Taichū Enshakkan Dai-ichidan" [Signing to Provide ¥36.5 Billion: The First Round of the Loans to China], *Nihon Keizai Shimbun*, November 3, 1990, p. 1.

77. "Saikai Aitsugu Kakkoku" [Every Country Reopening One after Another], *Nihon Keizai Shimbun*, November 3, 1990, p. 9.

78. The government had suspended medium- and long-term trade insurance (with periods of two years or more), but had only imposed some restrictions on short-term trade insurance. What is called trade insurance is in reality export insurance against the failure of Chinese recipients to pay for goods delivered. "Taichū Bōeki Hoken mo Saikai" [Even Trade Insurance toward China Resumed], *Asahi Shimbun*, July 13, 1990, p. 8.

79. See, for example: "Sōgaku 8200-Mandoru de Gōi: Hōgin 11-ko Fukumu Taichū Kyōchō Yūshi" [Agreement on a Total Amount of $82 Million: Syndicated Loan for China Including 11 Japanese Banks], *Nihon Keizai Shimbun*, September 27, 1990, p. 7; "Fujigin ga Taichū Yūshi, Kōkūki Yu'nyūhi ni Yaku 1-Okudoru" [Fuji Bank Supplies Loan to China, Roughly $100 Million to Import Planes], *Nihon Keizai Shimbun*, October 29, 1990, p. 3; "Suzuki, Chūgoku de Keijō-yōsha" [Suzuki, Light Automobiles in China], *Nihon Keizai Shimbun*, November 5, 1990, p. 1; "Chūgoku ni 2000-Mandoru Yūshi: Hōgin 4-kō Kyō Chōin" [$20 Million in Financing for China: Four Japanese Banks to Sign Today], *Nihon Keizai Shimbun*, November, 14, 1990, p. 5; and "Hikiuke Shidan ga Katamaru: 8-Okudoru no Taichū Kyōchō Yūshi" [Underwriting Syndicate Solidified: Cooperative Financing for China of $800 Million], *Nihon Keizai Shimbun*, November 18, 1990, p. 3 (Japanese institutions provided about $400 million out of the total in this international syndicate).

80. Thomson, "Japanese Eager to Resume Aid to China."

81. "Chūgoku no Kisai Saikai Mitomeru" [Permission for China to Float Bonds], *Nihon Keizai Shimbun*, January 6, 1991, p. 1. The bonds were issued in June 1991. "Chūgoku Ginkō no Nihon de no Kisai" [Bank of China to Issue Bonds in Japan], *Nihon Keizai Shimbun*, June 21, 1991, p. 1.

82. There had been two previous loans, which together had totaled ¥1 trillion. "Kotoshichū ni 6000-Oku En Zengo; Dai-3-ji Taichū Shigen Kaihatsu Rōn Kyōyo" [In This Year About ¥600 Billion; Providing the Third Loan to China for Resource Development], *Nihon Keizai Shimbun*, January 7, 1991, p. 3. This ¥600 billion loan package was to be used largely for development of potential oil and gas fields in the Taklimakan Desert in western China, which the Japanese government hoped would become a source of oil for Japan as well as a user of Japanese machinery and pipeline construction firms. "Japanese Firms Revitalizing Trade with China," *Japan Economic Journal*, March 23, 1991, p. 14.

83. See "Nitchū Kankei shūfuku o Kakunin; En Shakkan 1,296 Okuen Kyōyo" [Japan and China Confirm Restoration of Their Relationship; Japan Loans ¥129.6 Billion to China], *Nihon Keizai Shimbun*, August 11, 1991, p. 1; and "Kaifu Leaves for Tour of China, Mongolia," Kyodo News Service, August 10, 1991, in FBIS-EAS-91-155, August 12, 1991. In spring 1991 the Chinese government had requested funding for fourteen new projects (¥55.4 billion) in addition to continuation of funding for twelve projects (¥90.5 billion), for a total of ¥146 billion. Included on these lists was funding for the Beijing subway system, telephone systems for nine provincial and city governments, port facilities, highway construction, government telephone facilities in Hainan, and an air traffic control system. "Chūgoku Enshakkan 1459-Oku Motomeru" [China Requests ¥145.9 Billion in Yen Loans], *Nihon Keizai Shimbun*, May 22, 1991, p. 5.

84. "Taichū Bōeki Kakudai e" [Toward An Expansion of Japan-China Trade], *Nihon Keizai Shimbun*, August 11, 1991, p. 3.

85. Bank of Japan, *Balance of Payments Monthly*, no. 318 (January 1993), pp. 22, 26.

86. Donald C. Hellmann, "Japanese Politics and Foreign Policy: Elitist Democracy within an American Greenhouse," in Takashi Inoguchi and Daniel I. Okimoto, eds., *The Political Economy of Japan*, vol. 2: *The Changing International Context* (Stanford University Press, 1988), p. 372.

87. "Betonamu Mokuzai Yunyū—Meiwa Sangyō, Mazu Maruta 3000 Rippō Heihō Meetoru" [Imports of Vietnam Timber—Meiwa Sangyo to Begin with 3000 Square Meters of Logs], *Nihon Keizai Shimbun*, October 29, 1990, p. 9.

88. The amount of the defaulted loans was over ¥10 billion (a rather small $74 million at 1991 exchange rates). "Keizai Kyōryoku Saikai Michi wa Kewashiku" [The Road to Reopening Foreign Aid Is Steep], *Nihon Keizai Shimbun*, October, 21, 1990, p. 3.

89. "Yen Credits End Freeze on Vietnam Aid," *Nikkei Weekly*, November 23, 1992, p. 3.

90. Akihiro Tamiya, "Japan Is Ready to Test Waters in Vietnam," *Japan Economic Journal*, September 2, 1989, p. 2. A Japanese journalist (Bunyo Ishikawa, a photographer who covered the Vietnam War) visiting Vietnam in 1990 stated

that "in both Hanoi and Ho Chi Min City, the hotels are full of Japanese trading company men." Eiichi Tanizawa, *Nihon o Utsu* [Striking Japan] (Tokyo: Kodansha, 1990), p. 91.

91. As examples of the emerging business ties, see "Rainen Kōhan ni mo Gaigin Shiten Ninka" [By the Second Half of Next Year, Approval for Branches of Foreign Banks], *Nihon Keizai Shimbun*, August 17, 1990, p. 9; "Betonamu Hokengaisha to Yasuda Kasai ga Gyōmu Teikei" [Business Cooperation between Vietnamese Insurance Firm and Yasuda Fire and Casualty], *Nihon Keizai Shimbun*, December 14, 1990, p. 7; "Tai-Betonamu Bōeki ga Kyūkakudai" [Trade with Vietnam Expanding Rapidly], *Nihon Keizai Shimbun*, November 6, 1990, p. 11; and "Betonamu de Honkaku Gōben" [Real Merger in Vietnam], *Nihon Keizai Shimbun*, November 8, 1990, p. 1 (announcing the first real joint venture in Vietnam for a Japanese firm, with Tomen entering to manufacture ingredients for shampoo). By late 1990 four large trading companies had opened offices in Vietnam.

92. This statement was made in a newspaper article about Mitsubishi Corporation setting up offices in Hanoi and Ho Chi Min City (making it the second trading company, after Nissho Iwai, with offices in Vietnam), in expectation of rapidly rising business in trade and joint ventures. The announcement by Baker that he would be willing to resume meetings with the Vietnamese government was cited specifically as the signal for Mitsubishi's move. "Tai Betonamu Bōeki ga Kyūkakudai" [Trade with Vietnam Expands Dramatically], *Nihon Keizai Shimbun*, November 6, 1990, p. 11.

93. Neil Weinberg, "Firms Get Ready for Vietnam Doors to Widen: Japanese Companies Expect Washington to Flash Green Light," *Japan Economic Journal*, May 18, 1991, p. 14; and "Nemureru Shijō Betonamu Kyakkō" [Spotlight on the Sleeping Vietnamese Market], *Nihon Keizai Shimbun*, May 20, 1991, p. 9.

94. The occasion was a visit by Deputy Premier and Foreign Minister Nguyen Co Thach to Japan in fall 1990. "Vietnam Urged to Speed Development for Investors," *Japan Times Weekly International Edition*, November 5–11, 1990, p. 17.

95. "Keidanren Backs Vietnam Trade Mission," *Japan Economic Journal*, April 20, 1991, p. 4.

96. The joint venture would also provide training for Air Vietnam staff. "JAL in Joint Venture with Vietnam Airline," *Japan Economic Journal*, May 4, 1991, p. 20.

97. "Tai Betonamu Tōshi Kyūkakudai no Mitōshi" [Investment in Vietnam Forecast to Expand Quickly], *Nihon Keizai Shimbun*, December 13, 1992, p. 34.

98. Mitsui and Company, Sumitomo Corporation, and Tomen (with some World Bank financing) were the companies involved. "3-Shōsha ga Keikakuan; Betonamu no Seiyujo Kensetsu" [Proposed Plan by Three Trading Companies; Building an Oil Refinery in Vietnam], *Nihon Keizai Shimbun*, July 14, 1991, p. 5.

99. Yanmar Diesel, for example, signed a contract to provide technical assistance to a diesel engine factory it had established in South Vietnam in 1970, including a supply of knockdown kits from Japan. "Betonamu Kōjō Shien; Yanmā Gijutsu Shidō ya Setsubi Kōshin" [Supporting a Factory in Vietnam;

Yanmar Technological Guidance and Renewal of Facilities], *Nihon Keizai Shimbun*, August 2, 1991, p. 9.

100. "Betonamu: Nihon no Tōshi ni Atsui Me" [Vietnam: Looking at Japanese Investment with Hot Eyes], *Nihon Keizai Shimbun*, April 19, 1990, p. 11.

101. "After Gulf, Japan Focuses Diplomacy on Cambodia," *Japan Economic Journal*, March 23, 1991, p. 1.

102. Konosuke Kuwabara, "North Korea Extends Hand toward Japan," *Japan Economic Journal*, October 6, 1990, p. 1; "Nitchō Honkōshō 1-Gatsu Gejun ni Kaishi" [Japan–North Korean Formal Negotiations, Opening in the Last Ten Days of January], *Asahi Shimbun*, November 2, 1990; and "Kita Chōsen, Sōki Kokkō ni Iyoku" [North Korea Eager for Early Diplomatic Recognition], *Asahi Shimbun*, November 4, 1990, p. 1.

103. "Ministry 'Increasingly Concerned' by Burma Events," Kyodo News Service, October 26, 1990, in FBIS-EAS-90-208, October 26, 1990.

104. Orr, *The Emergence of Japan's Foreign Aid Power*, pp. 85–86.

105. James S. Clad, "Don't Miss the New Japan," *Christian Science Monitor*, December 6, 1991.

106. "Kan Nihonkai Keizaiken: Jijitai Shudō de Shidō" [A Pan-Japan Sea Economic Region: Starting under the Leadership of Autonomous Groups], *Nihon Keizai Shimbun*, May 15, 1990, p. 3. This concept was becoming accepted enough in Japan that discussion was floated in the English-language MITI glossy magazine in the spring of 1991. Kazuo Ogawa, "Japan Sea Rim: Catalyst for Growth," *Journal of Japanese Trade and Industry*, vol. 10 (May–June 1991), pp. 15–17; and Tadao Kiyonari and Kazuo Koike, eds., *Ajia no Chōsen* [The Asian Challenge] (Tokyo: Toyo Keizai Shimpōsha, 1990), p. 17.

107. Lincoln Kaye, "Hinterland of Hope: Regional Powers Have Ambitious Plans for Tumen Delta," and Mark Clifford, Louise do Rosario, and Lincoln Kaye, "Trade and Trade-Offs: Potential Partners Weigh Benefits of Cooperation," *Far Eastern Economic Review*, January 16, 1992, pp. 16–17, 18–19.

108. "Tōnan Ajia Kyoten ni" [Establishing Bases in Southeast Asia], *Asahi Shimbun*, March 16, 1990, p. 11.

109. The agreement included new routes (Niigata-Irkutstk and a Nagoya-Moscow freight line), improvement of Japanese regional airports along the Japan Sea coast to further facilitate flights to the Soviet Union, and an increase in the number of Niigata-Khabarovsk flights. "Nisso Kōkūro Ōhaba Kakujū e" [Toward A Major Expansion in Japan-Soviet Transportation Routes], *Nihon Keizai Shimbun*, April 17, 1991, p. 5.

110. These included an aluminum joint venture (also involving DuPont from the United States); revival of the Fourth Siberian Forest Products Development Project, involving Komatsu (Japan's largest heavy equipment manufacturer), a consortium of general trading companies, and other equipment manufacturers; and a gift of 300 used railway cars from JR East to the Soviet Union and plans for tourist development at Lake Baikal. "Soren Arumi Kōjō to Gōben" [Joint Venture for Soviet Aluminum Factory], *Nihon Keizai Shimbun*, April 12, 1991, p. 1; "Dai-4-ji Shiberia Shinrin Shigen Kaihatsu: Go Daitoryō Hōnichiji ni Chōin" [The Fourth Siberian Forest Resources Development: Signing during

President Gorbachev's Visit to Japan], *Nihon Keizai Shimbun*, March 29, 1991, p. 12; and "Soren no Tetsudō Jigyō Shien" [Assisting Soviet Railroad Business], *Nihon Keizai Shimbun*, April 3, 1991, p. 1.

111. "Tai So Shien ni 25-Oku Doru" [$2.5 Billion in Support for the Soviet Union], *Nihon Keizai Shimbun*, October 9, 1991, p. 1.

112. "Japanese Aid to Eastern Europe Announced," *JETRO Monitor*, vol. 5 (June 1990), p. 1.

Chapter Six

1. Donald C. Hellmann, "Japanese Politics and Foreign Policy: Elitist Democracy within an American Greenhouse," in Takashi Inoguchi and Daniel I. Okimoto, eds., *The Political Economy of Japan*, vol. 2: *The Changing International Context* (Stanford University Press, 1988), pp. 345–78.

2. Karel von Wolferen, "The Japan Problem Revisited," *Foreign Affairs*, vol. 69 (Fall 1990), p. 48, emphasizes that the Japanese continue to believe that they are victims of a cold and heartless world (*higaisha ishiki*). His view seems quite accurate.

3. The NHK executive making this claim was Yoshiki Hidaka. He described Richard Perle as the agent of Israel in the Pentagon. These views are presented in the form of an extended interview in Eiichi Tanizawa, *Nihon o Utsu* [Striking Japan] (Tokyo: Kodansha, 1990), pp. 18–20.

4. Steven R. Weisman, "In a Tide of Japanese Books on Jews, An Anti-Semitic Current," *New York Times*, February 19, 1991, p. A11.

5. A proposed textbook submitted for approval by the Ministry of Education put the toll at 20 million. "Editorial: Textbook Screening," *Mainichi Daily News*, July 4, 1990.

6. David E. Sanger, "Skulls Found: Japan Doesn't Want To Know Whose," *New York Times*, August 13, 1990, pp. A1, A5.

7. The estimated number of women forced into prostitution varies widely— from 60,000 to as high as 200,000. David E. Sanger, "Japan Admits Army Forced Koreans to Work in Brothels," *New York Times*, January 14, 1992, p. A8. Sale of daughters into prostitution was not uncommon for poor families in Japan and Korea into the twentieth century, but what made this case so explosive was the combination of alleged coercive force used by the Japanese government in recruitment, the very large numbers involved, and the use of women from subjugated colonies rather than Japanese women. The implication of the government was the result of a Japanese history professor's provision of historical documents to *Asahi Shimbun*. David E. Sanger, "Wako Journal; History Scholar in Japan Exposes a Brutal Chapter," *New York Times*, January 27, 1992, p. A4.

8. Steven R. Weisman, "Akihito Visiting Asian Neighbors," *New York Times*, October 1, 1991, p. A3.

9. Paul Blustein, "Japan Issues Apology for War Actions," *Washington Post*, May 3, 1991, p. A18.

10. T. R. Reid, "Openly Apologetic, Japan Recalls War's End," *Washington Post*, August 16, 1993, p. A12.

11. These dynamics are explored in Kent E. Calder, *Crisis and Compensation: Public Policy and Political Stability in Japan, 1949–1986* (Princeton University Press, 1988).

12. Robert C. Angel, "Japanese Terrorists and Japanese Countermeasures," in Barry Rubin, ed., *The Politics of Counterterrorism: The Ordeal of Democratic States* (Washington: Johns Hopkins University Foreign Policy Institute, 1990), pp. 31–60.

13. Robert C. Angel, "Prime Ministerial Leadership in Japan: Recent Changes in Personal Style and Administrative Organization," *Pacific Affairs*, vol. 61 (Winter 1988–89), pp. 583–602.

14. Angel, "Prime Ministerial Leadership," pp. 599–600.

15. Konosuke Kuwabara, "Critic Calls for Permanent Crisis Agency: Former Security Office Chief Says Stronger Leadership Needed," *Japan Economic Journal*, September 8, 1990, p. 3.

16. Based on interview with Foreign Ministry officials, May 29, 1992.

17. "Keizai Kyōshitsu: Iraku Funsō—Kiki Kanri Taisei no Kakuritsu Kyūmu" [Economics Classroom: The Iraq Dispute—Urgent Need for Establishment of a Crisis Management System], *Nihon Keizai Shimbun*, September 13, 1990, p. 21.

18. The committee had also been expected to call for abolition of the foreign service exam and greater use of noncareer ambassadors. "Taigai Seisaku Tantō-shō o Shinsetsu" [Establishment of a Foreign Policy Minister], *Nihon Keizai Shimbun*, June 1, 1991, p. 1.

19. Hiroaki Fujii, "90-Nendai no Kokusai Keizai to Nihon no Yakuwari" [The International Economy of the 1990s and Japan's Role], *Gaikō Fōramu*, no. 28 (January 1991), p. 51.

20. Kanji Nishio, *Nihon no Fuan: Sekaishi no Tenki ni Kangaeru Koto* [Anxious Japan: Thinking about the Turning Point in World History] (Tokyo: PHP Kenkyūjo, 1990), p. 18. Nishio teaches at the University of the Air in Tokyo and is the author of eighteen books (and coauthor of three more), mostly quick, journalistic treatments dealing with Japan and Europe.

21. Nomura Research Institute, *Kokusai Shakai no Naka no Nihon Keizai* [The Japanese Economy in the Context of International Society] (Tokyo: National Institute for Research Advancement, 1988), pp. 248–55.

22. Masao Kanazashi, "Commentary: Japan Should Contribute as Best It Knows How," *Japan Economic Journal*, September 22, 1990, p. 9.

23. Keizai Shingikai, Kōzō Chōsei Bukai [Industrial Structure Council, Structural Adjustment Subcommittee], *Kōzō Chōsei Bukai Hokoku—Saranaru Kōzō Chosei o Mezashite* [Structural Adjustment Subcommittee Report—Aiming for a New Structural Adjustment], April 26, 1990, pp. 12–13.

24. R. Taggart Murphy, "Power without Purpose: The Crisis of Japan's Global Financial Dominance," *Harvard Business Review*, no. 2 (March–April 1989), p. 74.

25. Bill Emmott, *The Sun Also Sets: Why Japan Will Not Be Number One* (Simon and Schuster, 1989), p. 18.

26. Daniel Burstein, *Yen! Japan's New Financial Empire and Its Threat to America* (Fawcett, 1990).

306 NOTES TO PAGES 215–24

27. Murphy, "Power without Purpose," p. 79.

28. Nomura Research Institute, *Nomura Investment Review*, vol. 9-90 (September 1990), p. 6, forecasted a 5.2 percent real GNP growth for 1990 (even higher than the 4.9 percent in 1989), and then a lower 3.9 percent for 1991, but with the decline due to problems of capacity constraints in some capital goods industries and increased interest rates. Even the higher interest rates in their forecast were only partially related to the crisis. In addition, Barclays de Zoete Wedd, *BZW Japan* (September–October 1990), pp. 2–3, predicted Japanese growth under several possible scenarios involving differing levels of oil prices and exchange rates. GNP growth for 1990 was anticipated at 4.2 to 4.3 percent, and for 1991, 3.0 to 3.5 percent. The net oil and (oil-price caused) exchange rate effect was only -0.1 to -0.3 percentage points of GNP, and higher interest rates accounted for -0.0 to -0.3 percentage points.

29. "Shijō Jūshi no Kakaku e Ippo" [One Step Toward Valuing Markets More], *Nihon Keizai Shimbun*, September 8, 1990, p. 5. Dubbed a move to allow markets to operate, this highly controlled price change came in a joint MITI and Energy Agency statement issued after consultation with the twelve oil firms.

30. Harufumi Nakanishi, "Ill-Defined National Agenda Leaves Japan Shackled," *Japan Economic Journal*, September 29, 1990, p. 9.

31. As put by Shigeki Oyama, head of the Institute of Middle Eastern Economies in Tokyo, Japan's hands "are not dirty at all." He also had misgivings about the U.S. military presence, arguing that use of military force might bring short-run gain and long-run disaster and eventually lead to reduction of U.S. influence. "Keizai Kyōshitsu: Iraku Funsō—Nihon, Dokuji no Chūtō Gaikō o" [Economics Classroom: Iraq Conflict; An Independent Mideast Foreign Policy for Japan], *Nihon Keizai Shimbun*, September 24, 1990, p. 21, available in translation in *Japan Economic Journal*, October 6, 1990, p. 9.

32. James Risen, "Japan Envoy Blames Gulf Crisis on U.S.," *Los Angeles Times*, March 20, 1991, p. 4.

33. Makoto Watanabe, "Gekidō Suru Chūtō Jōsei to Nihon no Taiō" [Violently Stirred Up Middle East and Japan's Response], *Gaikō Fōramu*, no. 25 (October 1990), pp. 13–17.

34. "Japan Joins International Economic Sanctions Re Iraqi Invasion," *Asahi Evening News*, August 7, 1990.

35. Embassy of Japan, "Tai Iraku Keizai Seisai ni Tsuite" [Concerning Economic Sanctions Against Iraq], August 14, 1990, unnumbered pages.

36. Kaifu finally made his trip in October, visiting five countries but accomplishing little. "Wangan Kiki Irai Nihon no Ashidori" [Japan's Steps since the Gulf Crisis], *Asahi Shimbun*, March 1, 1991, p. 8.

37. Masanori Tabata, "Aborted Kaifu Trip Shows Japan's Weakness in a Crisis," *Japan Times*, August 16, 1990.

38. "News Spotlight: Japan Reacts Abroad and at Home in Gulf Crisis," *Report from Japan*, August 16, 1990.

39. "Japan Earmarks $1 Billion for Mideast Aid," *Japan Economic Journal*, September 8, 1990, p. 3.

40. "Nichibei no Tairitsu ga Senmei ni: Iraku Shūhenkoku Enjo" [A Clear Conflict between Japan and the United States: Aid to Countries Near Iraq], *Asahi Shimbun*, September 7, 1990, p. 9.

41. "Chūtō Shūhenkoku Shien Sōki ni" [Assistance Quickly for Mideast Area Countries], *Nihon Keizai Shimbun*, September 8, 1990, p. 1. Masaru Tamamoto, "Trial of an Ideal: Japan's Debate over the Gulf Crisis," *World Policy Journal*, vol. 8 (Winter 1990–91), pp. 89–106, claims that Brady pressed for Self Defense Forces soldiers to be sent to the Gulf, but nothing to this effect was admitted in public.

42. "Keizai Sonshitsu 113-Oku Doru Kosu: Wangan Kiki de Iraku Shūhen 3-kakoku" [Economic Losses Exceed $11.3 Billion: The Three Countries in the Gulf Crisis Close to Iraq], *Asahi Shimbun*, September 12, 1990, p. 1.

43. The Diet has a regular session from late January to late spring (usually May or early June), followed by an "extraordinary" session in the fall. The opening date for the fall session is variable from early September to early October, but on some occasions has been advanced to as early as the end of July when important domestic economic legislation (such as the supplementary government budget in 1987) is involved. In 1990 the Diet did not convene until early October.

44. "News Spotlight: The Gulf Crisis: Brady in Japan," *Report from Japan*, September 10, 1990, p. 2.

45. "News Spotlight: The Gulf Crisis," *Report from Japan*, September 13, 1990, p. 2.

46. R. W. Apple, Jr., "Germany and Japan Draw Harsh Attacks on Gulf Crisis Costs," *New York Times*, September 13, 1990, p. A1. The amendment was submitted by Representative David Bonior, Democrat of Michigan, who estimated the cost of his proposal to be about $4.5 billion a year.

47. "Hi ni 6-Oku Doru Enjo: Wangan Sensō de Ichibu Mae Taoshi" [$600 Million Assistance to the Philippines: Partial Advanced Disbursement before the Gulf War], *Nihon Keizai Shimbun*, January 24, 1991, p. 5.

48. Steven R. Weisman, "Japan Defends Aid to U.S. in Mideast; Says It Will Soon Announce $3 Billion More for Gulf," *New York Times*, September 14, 1990, p. A1; and Watanabe, "Gekidō Suru Chūto Jōsei to Nihon no Taiō."

49. "Sekiyu Seihin Yunyū 30% Yokusei" [Restricting Refined Petroleum Products by 30 Percent], *Nihon Keizai Shimbun*, October 11, 1990, p. 1.

50. "Highlights of Japan's Gulf Contributions (as of 02/07/91)," material from the Embassy of Japan, Washington; and "Japanese Moved by Plight of Kurds," *Financial Times*, April 30, 1991, p. 5.

51. "UNHCR ni Kikin; 'Wangan' Hinanmin Taisaku de" [A Fund in UNHCR; As Policy for "Gulf" Refugees], *Nihon Keizai Shimbun*, March 1, 1991, p. 4.

52. "Fushōsha Nado Kyūen ni 5-senman En o Enjo" [¥50 million in Assistance to Aid the Wounded, etc.], *Nihon Keizai Shimbun*, January 18, 1991, p. 34.

53. "Iryōhan 9-nin Haken" [Dispatch of a 9-Person Medical Unit], *Nihon Keizai Shimbun*, January 17, 1991, p. 34.

54. "Iryōhan 9-nin Haken."

55. Untitled material from the Japanese Red Cross, p. 11. Page 1 has the heading "Saikin no Omo na Ugoki (Heisei 3-nen-4-gatsu, Tsuitachi Genzai)" [General Recent Movements (as of April 1, 1991)].

56. "Kurudo Nanmin Kyūen no Nihon Iryōhan" [Japanese Doctors' Unit's Emergency Aid for Kurdish Refugees], *Asahi Shimbun*, May 10, 1991, p. 3.

57. Larry A. Niksch and Robert G. Sutter, *CRS Report for Congress: Japan's Response to the Persian Gulf Crisis: Implications for U.S.-Japan Relations*, no. 91-444F, Congressional Research Service, May 23, 1991.

58. Katsura Kuno, "Japan's Global Contributions," *Economic Eye*, vol. 12 (Summer 1991), p. 3.

59. Tamamoto, "Trial of an Ideal," claims that Kaifu agreed to the concept of including the SDF in his proposed group after talking with President Bush in New York at the annual UN General Assembly meeting in September.

60. Hisahiko Okazaki and Seizaburo Sato, "Nihon wa Kokusai Sekinin o Dō Hatasu no ka" [How Will Japan Take On International Responsibilities?], *Gaikō Fōramu*, no. 25 (October 1990), pp. 4–12.

61. "Kokuren Kyōryoku Hō no Jieikan Haken" [Dispatch of Self Defense Soldiers in the UN Cooperation Law], *Nihon Keizai Shimbun*, September 20, 1990, p. 1.

62. " 'Jieitai to Betsu no Kyōryokutai' " ["A Cooperation Force Separate from the Self Defense Force"], *Asahi Shimbun*, November 5, 1990, p. 4.

63. "Kyōryoku Hōan: Sekkyoku Sansei, Jimin de Hansū Waru" [Cooperation Bill: LDP Divided in Half over Positive Support], *Asahi Shimbun*, November 1, 1990, p. 1.

64. "Jieitai Haken 78% ga Hantai: Hōan Hantai mo 58%" [78 Percent Opposed to Dispatching SDF: 58 Percent Also Opposed to the Bill], *Asahi Shimbun*, November 6, 1990, p. 1.

65. "Kokuren Kyōryoku Hōan no Haian Kakutai: Arata ni Jieitai Nuki Jōsetsutai" [Decision to Withdraw UN Cooperation Bill; Establish New Permanent Force without the Self Defense Forces], *Asahi Shimbun*, November 9, 1990, p. 1.

66. Shigeru Wada, "LDP's Bill on SDF Faces Opposition Fight," *Japan Economic Journal*, October 20, 1990, p. 3; and "Chūgoku ga Tsuyoi Kenen" [China Very Anxious], *Asahi Shimbun*, October 21, 1990, p. 13.

67. "Iraku, Hōjin 77-nin Kaihō; Asu Tokubetsuki de Kikoku" [Iraq Releases 77 Japanese Nationals; Return Tomorrow on Chartered Flight], *Nihon Keizai Shimbun*, November 7, 1990, p. 1. John F. Burns, "Baghdad Says It Will Free 78 of 305 Japanese Held," *New York Times*, November 7, 1990, p. A18, put the number at seventy-eight.

68. "Wangan Kiki Irai no Nihon no Ashidori."

69. "Tai Iraku Settoku Nao Tsuzuku" [Intensified Persuasion of Iraq Continues], *Asahi Shimbun*, January 11, 1991, p. 3.

70. "ASEAN Hōmon Shushō ga Saishū Kentō" [The Final Discussion on Prime Minister's Trip to ASEAN], *Asahi Shimbun*, January 11, 1991, p. 3.

71. "Takokusekigun Shien, 90-Oku Doru Kettei e" [Toward A Decision on $9 Billion Support for the Multinational Military Force], *Nihon Keizai Shimbun*, January 23, 1991, p. 1; and "Tsuika Shien Kyō Kettei" [Additional Support To Be Decided Today], *Nihon Keizai Shimbun*, January 24, 1991, p. 1.

72. Information Section, Embassy of Japan, Washington, January 24, 1991.

73. "Tokurei Seimei de Haken: Jieitaiki, Seifu, Kyō Kakugi Kettei" [Dispatch by Special Order: Self-Defense Force Planes, Government to Decide Today at a Cabinet Meeting], *Nihon Keizai Shimbun*, January 25, 1991, p. 1.

74. "Hittorikko·Chōnan Jogai" [Excluding Only Children and Eldest Sons], *Nihon Keizai Shimbun*, February 2, 1991, p. 35.

75. The same poll also found only 34 percent fully supporting U.S. policies, and only 35 percent felt that $9 billion was appropriate (with those opposed divided between "too much" and "should not provide any at all"). " 'Wangan' Danjo de Sanpi Wakareru" [On the "Gulf," Approval/Disapproval Divided by Sex], *Nihon Keizai Shimbun*, February 2, 1991, pp. 1, 10.

76. "Yorudan Seifu Nanshoku; Jieitaiki Ukeire" [Jordan Government Disapproves; Receiving SDF Planes], *Asahi Shimbun*, January 29, 1991, p. 1.

77. As of February 1, the Japanese government had arranged for the transportation of about 1,000 refugees on flights of four Japanese civilian aircraft from Cairo to their home countries, and earlier about 800 had been transported in September and October from Amman, Jordan, on three flights provided by Japanese commercial airlines (Japan Airlines and All Nippon Airways). "Highlights of Japan's Gulf Contributions," pp. 3–4.

78. "Hinanmin Dai-2-jin Betonamu e" [The Number 2 Set of Refugees to Vietnam], *Nihon Keizai Shimbun*, February 1, 1991, p. 35.

79. These groups included a consortium of the Catholic and Protestant churches (then joined by Buddhist organizations), which created a Committee for Relief of Gulf Refugees; the Takako Doi Fund (with money mostly from housewives); and the labor federations Rengo and Nikkyōso. Rather than making arrangements directly, these groups mainly funneled money through international relief organizations in Geneva. "Gienkin de Hinanmin Yusō" [Refugee Transport through Financial Contributions], *Nihon Keizai Shimbun*, February 7, 1991, p. 35; and "Bokin Undō, Zenkoku ni; Rōso ya Shimin Dantai ni Kakudai" [Fundraising Movement throughout the Country; Spreading to Labor Unions and Civic Groups], *Nihon Keizai Shimbun*, February 17, 1991, p. 35.

80. Barbara Wanner, "Japan Caught on the Horns of Postwar Reconstruction Dilemma," *JEI Report*, no. 9B, March 8, 1991, p. 3. The funding bill (and a tax increase to supply the revenues) passed the lower house of the Diet on February 28 and the upper house on March 6.

81. "Seifu, Sōkaitei Haken o Kettei; Jieitai Hajimete Kaigai e" [Government Decides to Dispatch Minesweepers; First Time Overseas for Self Defense Force], *Nihon Keizai Shimbun*, April 25, 1991, p. 1. The liberal *Asahi Shimbun*, however, did manage to find an objection. In 1987, during the Iran-Iraq war, the Nakasone cabinet had tried to generate support for sending minesweepers to the gulf—an effort that failed. It said then that minesweepers would not violate existing law

in Japan if mines were picked up exclusively in shipping lanes used by Japanese vessels. But, worried the newspaper, the four minesweepers sent in spring 1991 might actually pick up mines outside of areas used by Japanese vessels and thereby violate the law. "Political Spectrum: Gulf Mission as Point of Honor," *Asahi Evening News*, April 16, 1991.

82. Barbara Wanner, "U.N. Peacekeeping Support Bill Becomes Law," *JEI Report*, no. 23B, June 19, 1992, p. 5.

83. "Takokusekigun Tsuika Shien: Dō Suru 90-Oku Doru" [Additional Support for the Multinational Military Force: What about the $9 Billion], *Nihon Keizai Shimbun*, January 31, 1991, p. 5.

84. "Wangan Shiensaku; No. 5, Soto Kara Osare Ketsudan" [Gulf Support Policy; No. 5; Decisions Pushed from the Outside], *Asahi Shimbun*, January 28, 1991, p. 1; and "Towareru Kokka Tetsugaku—Wangan Sensō to Nihon" [The Philosophy of the Nation Is Questioned—The Gulf War and Japan], *Nihon Keizai Shimbun*, February 9, 1991, p. 1.

Chapter Seven

1. Edward J. Lincoln, *Japan's Unequal Trade* (Brookings, 1990). p. 66.

2. This point is emphasized by Robert Gilpin, "Where Does Japan Fit In?" *Millennium: Journal of International Studies*, vol. 18, no. 3 (1989), pp. 329–42.

3. Teruhiko Mano, "Hadome Naki 'Koken' no Doronuma: Nihonjin wa Doru o Kakaeta Sekai no Dorei de Yoi no Ka" [The Quagmire of Unbraked "Contributions": Is It Good for Dollar-Holding Japanese to be Slaves of the World], *Bungei Shunju*, September 1992, p. 117. Mano is an official at the Bank of Tokyo.

4. Exemplified by Lester Thurow, *Head to Head: The Coming Economic Battle among Japan, Europe, and America* (Morrow, 1992).

5. "Enterprise for the Americas—A New Partnership for Trade, Investment, and Growth," White House press release, Office of the Press Secretary, June 27, 1990, p. 2.

6. One particularly harsh view of a regionalized world, characterized by mercantilism, blocs, and even possible participation of the then-Soviet Union in a Japan-dominated Asian bloc, was predicted by Rudiger Dornbusch, "The World's New Order: A Moscow-Tokyo Bloc?" *Washington Post*, July 16, 1989, pp. B1–B2.

7. Another 20.4 percent responded that Japan should act on its own, and 17 percent expressed no opinion. " 'Kokuren Jūshi' ga 62%" [62 Percent Emphasize United Nations], *Nihon Keizai Shimbun*, January 20, 1991, p. 2.

8. Such views were voiced, for example, in an editorial—"Bonn and Tokyo as Global Police," *New York Times*, October 22, 1990, p. A18—which endorsed dispatch of combat troops by both Japan and Germany as part of collective (not necessarily UN) security and peacekeeping operations.

9. A. M. Rosenthal, "On My Mind: MacArthur Was Right," *New York Times*, October 19, 1990, p. A35, expresses rather exaggerated fears of a revival of militarism in opposing dispatch of Japanese troops to the Gulf.

10. This figure has risen steadily from only fifteen in 1985. "Ninkan Kyohi, Saikō 90-nindai" [Rejecting Appointments, at the Highest Level of Ninety People], *Nihon Keizai Shimbun*, March 23, 1991, p. 34.

11. This distinction was made rather aptly by William Safire, "Pacifism in the Pacific," *New York Times*, September 27, 1990, p. A23.

12. For example, " 'Hongoku e no Kikan' Zemen ni" [An All-out (Effort) to Return (Refugees) to Their Home Countries], *Nihon Keizai Shimbun*, October 21, 1991, p. S41; Sadako Ogata, "Hōkatsuteki na Nanmin, Imin Seisaku o" [A Comprehensive Policy on Refugees and Emmigrants], *Gaikō Fōramu*, no. 35 (August 1991), pp. 13–15; and Yasuo Kuwahara, Toshio Tsunozaki, and Hiroshi Homma, "Zadankai: Nanmin Mondai no Muzukashisa–Atarashisa" [Roundtable Discussion: The Difficulty and Newness of the Refugee Problem], *Gaikō Fōramu*, no. 35 (August 1991), pp. 16–29.

13. The proposal was advanced by the Urban Safety Research Institute. Akira Kojima, "Relief Ship Would Be Way for Japan to Better the World," *Nikkei Weekly*, June 22, 1991, p. 6.

14. By 1985 this fund had 4.8 million Swiss francs (amounting to approximately $3 million). Japanese Red Cross Society, *Review of Activities, 1987–1989*, pp. 3–4.

15. Japanese Red Cross, *Review*, p. 6.

16. Japanese Red Cross, *Review*, pp. 28–29. In 1987 NHK campaign funds were a much larger 38 percent of the total contributions received. International contributions vary widely from year to year. In 1984 they were only ¥878 million, and in 1985 they jumped to ¥3.0 billion. In 1988 the international disaster contribution came to ¥2.1 billion (approximately $16 million at 1988 exchange rates).

17. Japanese Red Cross, *Review*, pp. 5–6. The hospitals accounted for 36,980 of the paid employees in 1989. The American Red Cross had 1,001,906 adult volunteers and a paid staff of 25,394 as of June 30, 1989. *American Red Cross Annual Report 1989: Thank You for Being There* (Washington, 1989).

18. Japanese Red Cross, *Review*, p. 33. With other revenues (from sources such as blood service processing) of $807 million, the total public support and revenues of the American Red Cross came to a total of $1.1 billion in 1989. *American Red Cross Annual Report 1989*, p. 24. Overall revenues for the Japanese Red Cross are more difficult to calculate because operations are divided into five quasi-autonomous segments for which financial data are not complete (ordinary budget of the national chapter, ordinary budget of local chapters, a special account for social welfare, a special account for hospitals, and a special budget for the blood bank).

19. Japanese Red Cross, *Review*, p. 14.

20. "Chikyūjin: Honda Kenji, Kokusai Kyūkyū Iryō Chīmu Un'ei Iinchō" [World Person: Kenji Honda; Chairman of the Board of the Japan Emergency Medical Team for Disaster Relief], *Nihon Keizai Shimbun*, July 16, 1991, p. 35.

21. "Poll Cites Human Aid as Top Goal; Peaceful SDF Role Wins Backing in U.N. Mideast Effort," *Japan Economic Journal*, December 1, 1990, p. 3. The Japanese-language original of this article was in *Nihon Keizai Shimbun*, November 21, 1990, p. 1.

22. However, the Foreign Ministry says there is some flexibility in budgeting, depending on unforeseen emergencies. Figures supplied by Katsuhiko Uko, Embassy of Japan, Washington. Six teams were sent abroad in 1990, as were shipments of supplies in the wake of the Philippine volcanic eruption. "Kokusai Kinkyū Enjo Taisei o Kyōka" [Strengthening Arrangements for International Emergency Assistance], *Asahi Shimbun*, August 18, 1991, p. 2.

23. "Poll Cites Human Aid as Top Goal"; and "46% ga Jietai no PKO Sanka Sansei; Kaigai Saigai Haken Kahansū ga Kōtei" [Forty-Six Percent Support SDF Participation in Peace Keeping Operations; More Than Half Affirm Dispatch For Overseas Disasters], *Nihon Keizai Shimbun*, June 10, 1991, p. 34.

24. "Jieitai no Kaigai Saigai Haken" [Dispatch of Self Defense Forces for International Disasters], *Asahi Shimbun*, September 4, 1991, p. 2. General statements of this sort also appeared in the 1991 Defense White Paper, in which the SDF describes itself as the *kokumin no zaisan* [the people's asset], to be used in operations such as international disaster relief. "Jieitai no Kokusai Kōken Kyōchō" [Stressing the Self Defense Forces' International Contribution], *Nihon Keizai Shimbun*, July 27, 1991, p. 9; and Japan Defense Agency, *Boei Hakusho* [White Paper on Self Defense] (Tokyo: Ministry of Finance Printing Office, 1991), pp. 75–77.

25. The group is dominated by Keidanren, the influential organization that acts as the voice of big business. "Kokusai Enjotai ni Ji'eitai o Katsuyō" [Utilizing the SDF in An International Assistance Force], *Nihon Keizai Shimbun*, June 7, 1991, p. 1.

Index

313